The Theory of Difference

SUNY Series in Contemporary Continental Philosophy
Dennis J. Schmidt, editor

The Theory of Difference

Readings in Contemporary Continental Thought

edited by
Douglas L. Donkel

STATE UNIVERSITY OF NEW YORK PRESS

Published by
State University of New York Press, Albany

Printed in the United States of America

For information, address State University of New York Press,
90 State Street, Suite 700, Albany, N.Y. 12207

Production by Michael Haggett
Marketing by Fran Keneston

Library of Congress Cataloging-in-Publication Data

The theory of difference : readings in contemporary continental thought / edited by Douglas L. Donkel.
p. cm. — (SUNY series in contemporary continental philosophy)
Includes bibliographical references and index.
ISBN 0–7914–4927–0 (alk. paper) — ISBN 0–7914–4928–9 (pbk. : alk. paper)
1. Difference (Philosophy) 2. Philosophy, European—20th century.
I. Donkel, Douglas L. (Douglas Lee), 1959– II. Series.
B809.9 T54 2001
190'.9'04—dc21 00-049236

10 9 8 7 6 5 4 3 2 1

Contents

Part Three: Gilles Deleuze

Part Four: Jacques Derrida

Part Five: Luce Irigaray

Acknowledgments

I would like to thank the many people who have supported, advised, and assisted in the preparation of this work, including Daniel Athearn, Clay Glad, John Hammond, Eric Nordling, G. Palmer Pardington III, John J. Stuhr, Peter Wolf, Kirke Wolfe, my colleagues and students at The University of Portland, and especially Dennis J. Schmidt and Jane Bunker, without whose vision, persistence, and friendship, this work would not be in hand. Let me also note with gratitude the work of Viola Donkel, who took on a number of tasks essential to such a project, not the least of which is the tedious job of proofreading the manuscript. Finally, a very special thanks goes to my family, whose unconditional love and commitment not only made this work possible, but continues to constitute and sustain the fabric of my life.

The editor and publisher gratefully acknowledge permission to reprint copyrighted material from the following:

"The Principle of Identity" & "The Onto-theo-logical Constitution of Metaphysics" from *Identity and Difference* by Martin Heidegger, translated by Joan Stambaugh, pp. 21–41; 42–76. Copyright © 1969 by Harper & Row, Publishers, Inc. Reprinted by permission of HarperCollins Publishers, Inc. Special thanks to Dennis J. Schmidt for translating four lines that were omitted from the *Onto-theo-logical Constitution of Metaphysics.*

"Language" from *Poetry, Language, Thought* by Martin Heidegger, translated by Albert Hofstadter, pp. 189–210. Copyright © 1971 by Martin Heidegger. Reprinted by permission of HarperCollins Publishers, Inc.

"Time and Being" from *On Time and Being* by Martin Heidegger, translated by Joan Stambaugh, pp. 1–24; 83–84. English language translation copyright © 1972 by Harper & Row, Publishers, Inc. Reprinted by permission of HarperCollins Publishers, Inc.

"The 'Sensation' as a Unit of Experience" from the *Phenomenology of Perception* by Maurice Merleau-Ponty, translated by Colin Smith, pp. 3–12. Copyright © 1962 by Routledge and Kegan Paul. Reprinted by permission of Routledge Publishing, Inc.

"Eye and Mind," by Maurice Merleau-Ponty, first appeared in English in *The Primacy of Perception,* translated by Carleton Dallery, edited and with an introduction by James Edie. Copyright © 1964 by Northwestern University Press. This version is from *The Merleau-Ponty Aesthetics Reader: Philosophy and Painting,* translation editor Michael B. Smith, edited and with an introduction by Galen Johnson, pp. 121–149; 388–391. Copyright © 1993 by Northwestern University Press. Reprinted by permission of Northwestern University Press.

"The Intertwining—The Chiasm" and "Working Notes" from *The Visible and the Invisible* by Maurice Merleau-Ponty, translated by Alphonso Lingis, pp. 130–155; 163; 190–197; 204–206; 210–212; 214–220; 248–251; 263–265; 269–270. Copyright © 1968 by Northwestern University Press. Reprinted by permission of Northwestern University Press.

"Elan Vital as Movement of Differentiation" from *Bergsonism* by Gilles Deleuze, translated by Hugh Tomlinson, pp. 91–113; 127–131. Copyright © 1988 by Urzone, Inc. Zone Books. Reprinted by permission of Urzone, Inc. Zone Books.

"Numerical and Real Distinction" from *Expressionism in Philosophy: Spinoza* by Gilles Deleuze, translated by Martin Joughin, pp. 27–39; 345–355; 405–407. Copyright © 1990 by Urzone, Inc. Zone Books. Reprinted by permission of Urzone, Inc. Zone Books.

"Difference in Itself" from *Difference and Repetition* by Gilles Deleuze, translated by Paul Patton, pp. 28–60; 308–313. Copyright © 1994 by Columbia University Press. Reprinted by permission of Columbia University Press.

"Signs and the Blink of an Eye" from *Speech and Phenomena: And Other Essays on Husserl's Theory of Signs* by Jacques Derrida, translated by David B. Allison, pp. 60–69. Copyright © 1973 by Northwestern University Press. Reprinted by permission of Northwestern University Press.

"The Outside X the Inside" and "The Hinge [La Brisure]" from *Of Grammatology* by Jacques Derrida, translated by Gayatri Chakravorty Spivak, pp. 44–65; 65–73; 326–329. Copyright © 1976 by The Johns Hopkins University Press. Reprinted by permission of The Johns Hopkins University Press.

"Différance" from *Margins of Philosophy* by Jacques Derrida, translated by Alan Bass, pp. 1–27. Copyright © 1982 by The University of Chicago Press. Reprinted by permission of The University of Chicago Press.

"When Our Lips Speak Together" from *This Sex Which Is Not One* by Luce Irigaray, translated by Catherine Porter and Carolyn Burke, pp. 205–218. Copyright © 1985 by Cornell University Press. Reprinted by permission of Cornell University Press.

Chapters Four & Five from *The Forgetting of Air in Martin Heidegger* by Luce Irigaray, translated by Mary Beth Mader, pp. 66–77; 79–94; 186–187. Copyright © 1999 by the University of Texas Press. Reprinted by permission of the University of Texas Press.

"Sexual Difference" from *An Ethics of Sexual Difference* by Luce Irigaray, translated by Carolyn Burke and Gillian C. Rose, pp. 5–19. Copyright © 1993 by Cornell University Press. Reprinted by permission of Cornell University Press.

The Theory of Difference

Introduction

Over the last century the story of Continental thought has, to a remarkable extent, been characterized by the attempt to think about difference and its relationship to identity.[1] The present collection brings together the work of five thinkers—Martin Heidegger, Maurice Merleau-Ponty, Gilles Deleuze, Jacques Derrida, and Luce Irigaray—who have made significant contributions to this effort. Of course, this issue is in no sense native to recent Continental thought. Reflections on difference and identity comprise a significant, if often fragmented and marginalized, subtext of the principal issues and concerns which have motivated Western thought for over twenty five hundred years, and, arguably, select traditions in Eastern thought as well.[2]

It is often noted that the roots of the contemporary discussion can be traced to the mythical-poetic account of origin gleaned from Hesiod's *Theogony*, where the separation or differentiation of earth and sky from a primordial unity sets in motion the development of the cosmogony which follows. In fact, the motif of creation through differentiation predates the *Theogony*, and all Greek thought, inasmuch as it is found in various Near Eastern creation myths, including the Babylonian *Enuma elish* and the familiar Semitic account in *Genesis* 1:2–8, where God is said to have created heaven and earth by dividing "the waters which were under the firmament from the waters which were above."[3]

Nonetheless, the Presocratic thinkers who follow Hesiod continue the concern with origins and the theme of separation, although clearly in a genre that indicates a move away from mythical-poetic discourse toward a quasi-naturalistic form of inquiry and expression, which we identify as the root of Western philosophical thought.

Specifically, Anaximander posits the *apeiron*, the "indefinite," as the "source" from which the opposites, that is, the hot, the cold, the dry, and the moist, and so on, are separated out, thus forming the world-order through a process of scission. Likewise, for Heraclitus, things are brought into being through opposition, a situation that is understood to suggest the establishment and preservation of balance and measure, characterized in terms of the unity of the *Logos.* Even Parmenides, who was to employ pure reason as a foil against the tension between the many and the one, or difference and identity, proposed by Heraclitus, relied on a subtle understanding of determination through difference to argue for the impossibility of thinking non-being, and hence, for the univocity of being.[4]

In Plato the issue of difference and identity surfaces in various dialogues, but especially in his later works, the *Parmenides* and the *Sophist.* In the latter, in an attempt to make room for truth and its other against the Parmenidean unity and totality of being, we find the Eleatic stranger concluding that speaking of "that which is not" is not a statement of non-being, but merely an affirmation of difference or otherness.[5]

Less explicit, but no less significant for the understanding of difference and identity that will come to inform the tradition, are Aristotle's arguments for an identity exclusive of difference, which he deploys in book Four of the *Metaphysics* under the rubric of the "laws of thought."[6] In moving to quiet the Heraclitean "flux," with its unity of opposites, Aristotle sets out to erect an impenetrable barrier between a thing and its other in the form of the principle of contradiction, whereby it is argued that A is not not-A. This attempt to keep A and its "other" apart fixes identity, irrespective of difference or essential relation, and sets the stage for the subsequent development of the problem in Medieval thought, where, among various concerns, the theological doctrine of the Trinity motivated thinkers to return again to the issue; this time under the heading of what came to be called "the problem of relations."[7]

It has been said that, for the Medievals, the problem of relations concerned their "ontological status," that is, "the type of being to be accorded relations";[7] a formulation which sealed their fate as something potentially distinct—if not ontologically discrete—from the things being related. An account, therefore, which suggests that "relation" as a species of difference, is to be treated as something to which identity is, at best, free to be periodically receptive.

Variations on this reading of the problem continued to inform the tradition, and after a lengthy history, ostensibly of marginal interest to the major figures of early modern philosophy,[8] a new version of the problem later appeared in the debate over so-called "internal and external relations." This issue came into focus in the early decades of the century with Russell and Moore's arguments against the absolute idealism of Bradley and his colleagues.[9] British idealism, grounded in what was arguably an idiosyncratic appropriation of Hegel's dialectical logic,[10] involved several versions of the claim that all relations are "internal" to their terms. Russell and Moore were critical of such claims, not only because of certain perceived logical difficulties, but due to the fact that the doctrine of internal relations brought with it an epistemological holism that made knowledge of particulars partial and incomplete, unless grasped within the context of the "absolute."[11] It has been suggested, however, that the debate over internal relations missed the mark, inasmuch as proponents and detractors alike—contrary to what is suggested by the term "internal" —continued to treat all relations as essentially "external," hence, as "particulars dissected out of a presumed aggregate,"[12] thus continuing the reification and exclusion of difference from identity formalized by Aristotle.

A further variation on this theme informs the work of Whitehead and Hartshorne, collected under the banner of "process" metaphysics. On Hartshorne's account, one of the distinguishing marks of this approach is its understanding of relations in terms of "asymmetry," whereby, for example, present events are said to depend upon precise predecessors, but not on specific successors.[13] Hence, the relation between the present and the past is characterized as internal, whereas the relation between the present and the future is thought to be external. It is instructive to read this asymmetrical account as motivated in part by the desire to overcome Hume's influential analysis of experience as a fortuitous conjunction of impressions from which no causal influence or necessary relational effect can be deduced, without falling victim to the aforementioned concerns associated with the normative theory of internal relations.

At any rate, an alternative account was developing, outside of the concerns that would come to dominate Anglophone thought, which was to set the stage for the contemporary Continental discussion of difference and identity.

Although humble in origin, Hegel's appropriation of Spinoza's "*Omnis determinatio est negatio*," had the effect of initiating, if not exactly a return of difference to identity, at least a reinscription of the possibility of such a move.[14] With the advent of Hegel's discussions regarding the role of difference and negation in the determination of identity,[15] a genre is established that will itself significantly determine the shape of contemporary philosophical, theological, and literary thought on the Continent and abroad. But as much as anything, this determination will come forth precisely as a rejection of Hegel, or, more specifically, as a rejection of the totalizing tendencies attributed to the dialectic of absolute knowledge. The task left for thinking after Hegel would therefore involve attempts to breach the dialectic by isolating some unthought dimension or element on which it was dependent, but of which it was naive.

In this regard, Nietzsche's affirmation of life as a festival of difference, irreducible to the measure of identity and order sought in idealism, or to the myth of equality given in Christianity, serves as an important catalyst to the contemporary discussion; a discussion which often collects its otherwise diverse aspects under the umbrella term "postmodern."

By one account,[16] the mark of the postmodern is its lack of any unifying narrative or "story" that would tie together the multiple aspects of meaning and value present in experience. Hence, the postmodern is characterized by a certain irreducible multiplicity; a certain privileged respect for difference and differences, be they gender, ethnic, political, religious, or philosophical. Of course, the term postmodern did not simply fall from theory to praxis in search of instantiation; rather, it is grounded in a unique existential experience, characteristic of our age, which seeks authentication by positing an openly ironic, if not paradoxical, theoretical sanction. In this way, the current interest in the theory of difference can be understood as an attempt to come to terms with a range of experience that seems at odds with the representatives of identity, and the representation of difference, which the enlightenment passed on to modernity.

However, the project of liberating difference from the strictures of identity has also been motivated by considerations on language. In recent Continental thought, the linguistic turn can be traced less to the influence of Wittgenstein than to the work of the Swiss linguist Saussure. Saussure's emphasis on the differential character of language, and the arbitrary nature of the sign, had a significant generative influence on the structuralist and poststructuralist thought that followed. Specifically, Saussure's claim that "in language there are only differences without positive terms,"[17] served as an important instrument of displacement to the privilege of identity. Moreover, his characterization of the subject as a function of the linguistic system called into question the received account of language as the product of a speaking subject, reversing the terms of the philosophy of subjectivity handed down from Descartes.

But beyond these immediate genealogical influences, and there are notable others as a glance at the texts contained herein will quickly reveal, it is again important to keep in mind that reflections on difference and identity, although unique in source and form of their contemporary expression, take place within the context of perennial reflection on the same that has characterized Western thought. The volume in hand is comprised of select works from five thinkers who are heirs to this tradition, as well as some of its key contemporary constituents. These works constitute a sustained reflection on the meaning of difference; reflections that, for all their currency, show a remarkable continuity with the concerns of the ancients noted above.

Heidegger's retrieval of the question of the meaning of Being begins with the recollection of an ontological difference between Being and beings; a difference that eventually comes to be understood as the unthought but constitutive aspect of metaphysics and the root of identity as the possibility of the presencing of presence. As such, Heidegger's work brings difference into the fray of sustained ontological reflection and sets up an essential passage that further reflection cannot transgress without due attention. Among many influences, Heidegger's reflections on Being and difference have come to feed a specifically post-Neitzschean tradition in theology, which has variously appropriated insights regarding presencing and difference to run the gamut from near orthodoxy to a/theology.[18]

Merleau-Ponty brought phenomenology to bear on perception as a prereflective milieu grounded in the primacy of lived bodily experience. From his early work on Gestalt theory, through his musings on the "line" in painting, to his last cryptic notes on "flesh" as "chiasmic intertwining," a consistent, if not always explicit, thread has been the figure of difference as the fabric of perception that we are. Significantly, Merleau-Ponty's work not only aimed to make good on Husserl's promise of a phenomenology of the life-world, but in so doing, set the stage for a renewed interest in the place of the body in philosophical thought.[19]

In his readings of Bergson, Nietzsche, and Spinoza, as well as his subsequent independent and collaborative work with psychoanalyst and political activist Felix Guattari, Deleuze has consistently aimed to articulate the inarticulable; a sense of difference irreducible to representation and the philosophy of identity. For Deleuze, this amounts to teasing out of the tradition a pure "internal" difference, prior to the logic of determination that drives Hegel's dialectic, and ripe for harvest through a radically "horizontal" form of thought that emphasizes the penultimacy of barriers and the permeability of boundaries. Such thought, while widely influential, has been especially adept at encouraging a praxis of creative affirmation in the social-political sphere, where the conception of immanent forces in the constitution of social organization has been said to sanction a form of radical democratic theory.[20]

Derrida's method of deconstruction has become an influential—if controversial—approach to reading the texts of the Western canon. A deconstructive reading proceeds by fixing on specific hinge points, or "undecidables," within texts, which, due to the function of difference as their condition of possibility and impossibility, are shown to be sites of contamination, where the aspirations of identity toward presence and the self-same are perpetually deferred. Derrida's *oeuvre* involves the investigation of the effects of difference, or *differance* as it is neologistically termed, in a wide range of texts and issues. Of specific interest was the early—and continuing—reception of Derrida's work among American literary critics, who find in the deconstructive critique of certain key distinctions an invitation to transcend the secondary role of reader and interpreter and assert the creative inspiration that finds their work as primary and original in its own right.

Irigaray, who must be counted as one of the most influencial French feminists, has dedicated her work to the recovery and articulation of sexual difference; a difference that, she argues, has been concealed by a tradition that lives off the reduction of the feminine "other" to the order of the masculine "same." This phallocentric privileging of unity, oneness, and identity comes forth through a discourse where the very possibility of an "outside" —the heterogeneous voice of the feminine—is closed off. Hence, Irigaray's work explores a conception of difference as multiple through a discourse that aims to steer between the twin peaks characteristic of the philosophy of identity; the assimilation of the other by the same, and the reification of the other in opposition to the same; moves that reduce the other by turning it into the same through consumption, or by positing it as an identity—that is of the same order as the same—by way of dichotomy. Both moves attempt to secure and isolate identity at the ostensible expense of its own ground in difference—the multiple—the feminine. Significantly, among many points of influence, Irigaray's writing has fueled extensive discussion regarding the question of essentialism and the scope and implications of postmodern/poststructuralist theory for feminist thought.[21]

But while these thinkers have been variously inspired, and diversely appropriated, their thought, nonetheless, unfolds along a number of common lines. First, each has a unique stake in a reading of the tradition that suggests that difference has not been allowed to flourish to the extent mandated by an adequate analysis of its function. Hence, within their own areas of concern, each reads the story of Western thought as a misplaced attempt to posit, secure, and valorize identity at the expense of difference.

Second, insofar as the thought of difference aims to displace the metaphysics of identity, it is understood to engender a problematic relationship with the order of the sensible and the intelligible. Hence, these thinkers are called into what is often an ironic, if not paradoxical, relationship with language, in that they must articulate difference in the very terms that difference would set forth—if not call into question. That is, they must speak without re-presenting identity. This situation accounts for much of the difficulty often experienced in coming to terms with their texts, which understandably show little regard for certain traditional conventions; the distinction between form and content being one of particular note.

Third, and probably most important, they are specifically committed to an understanding of difference as *constitutive* of whatever area of experience or realm of being they are concerned to explore. Indeed, for these thinkers the constitutive function of difference suggests that it is fundamental, or *ontologically basic*.

Finally, while difference is fundamentally constitutive, for Deleuze, Derrida, and Irigaray, this characterization involves an important qualification. For these thinkers, and arguably, to a lesser extent, Heidegger and Merleau-Ponty, difference is understood to reside in the very heart of identity, thereby calling into question the order and unity of the self-same on which the notion of constitution is thought to depend.[22] Hence, it is suggested by their work that a persuasive account of the constitutive function of difference supports an understanding of identity whereby it is not merely constituted *by* difference, but is, in fact, *difference itself.*

However, this leaves open the question of what a milieu of generalized difference—if it can be so named—implies; and, more significantly, whether an account that leads to such claims can be substantiated. Indeed, one of the principal aims of this collection is to reinvest in this still open question by bringing together in a focused setting some key texts in which this argument is played out. It is my concern that too often we exhibit a propensity to engage in consideration of the broader implications and praxical possibilities of such accounts without due attention to their philosophical persuasiveness. The fruits of this tendency, although at times useful, are ultimately misguided if our understanding of the dynamics of the argument, specifically, the argument for difference, remains tenuous and underdeveloped.

Given these concerns, it is important to note that the thinkers and selections which comprise the current volume are, for the most part, dedicated to the ontological import of difference. Nonetheless, it is certainly the case, both in its historical constituency and contemporary deployment, that the theory of difference is expressed through multiple concerns by multiple voices. In addition to those already named, an extended genealogy might include Kant, Kierkegaard, and Freud; whereas a catalog of contemporary representatives would be amiss if it did not include Bataille, Gadamer, Adorno, Levinas, Blanchot, Lyotard, Foucault, Badiou, Kristeva, and Nancy among its pages. Hence, the selection of these five thinkers, as well as the consonant privileging of the ontological motif, already suggests a decisive narrowing of the field.

Like any collection, this work is a function of notable interpretive license, both in terms of reflecting the proximal interests and concerns of the editor, and, more significantly, in expressing how those interests and concerns are framed in the context of the tradition in question. With this acknowledged, it is nonetheless arguable that these five thinkers have produced some of the most compelling and influential accounts of difference within the Continental tradition, and hence, from a geneological point of view, are some of the most significant representatives—as close to canonical as we dare suggest—of a tradition of discourse on difference which has literally exploded with multiple issues and concerns. Hence, in no way is this collection intended to be definitive with respect to the litany of thinkers and issues that might otherwise be compiled under the banner of difference; rather, more modestly, it aims to collect some of the key texts from five major thinkers around a theme that has both historical and contemporary importance in grounding further discussion of this perennial issue.

In regard for these considerations, from Heidegger, I have specifically chosen instances of his later work, including "The Principle of Identity" and "The Onto-theo-logical Constitution of Metaphysics" from *Identity and Difference*, a work that is genetically pivotal to the contemporary discussion; the essay "Language" from *Poetry, Language, Thought*, where difference is articulated through a reading of Trakl's poem "A Winter Evening"; and "Time and Being" from *On Time and Being*, an essay that advances difference by way of the concept of *Ereignis*. However, this is not to suggest that the motif of difference is absent from his earlier thought; it is arguable that this motif—although latent—is at work prior to *Being and Time*.[23] But it is also clear that there is a developmental aspect to Heidegger's account, and that in terms of clarity and focus it appears most explicitly in his later work.

The situation with Merleau-Ponty is somewhat different, inasmuch as the theme of difference motivates his early interest and reflections on Gestalt theory; remains near in his discussions of painting; and becomes all the more explicit in his later ontology of perception. Hence, I have included a short selection from the *Phenomenology of Perception,* which displays his appropriation of, and distance from, Gestalt theory; the classic "Eye and Mind," of which Sartre wrote "says all provided one knows how to decipher it,"[24] and which contains suggestive passages on the formative power of the "line" in painting; and a key chapter—plus selections from his "Working Notes"—from the posthumously published *The Visible and the Invisible,* where, by way of terms such as dehiscence, *écart,* flesh, and reversibility, difference explicitly takes center stage.

Deleuze presents a different challenge, in that it may be argued that his theory of difference is developed with a certain thematic intensity in his early "historical" work and then elaborated through a range of issues and styles that we have come to recognize in his later independent and collaborative work with Guattari. On this premise, I have chosen to include predominantly early writings, including the final chapter from *Bergsonism,* where he punctuates his reading of Bergson as a thinker of difference; an important section from the opening pages of *Expressionism in Philosophy: Spinoza,* where, with reference to Descartes, he explores Spinoza's development of non-numerical distinction; and "Difference in Itself" from *Difference and Repetition,* where these themes come together in a work that Deleuze characterized as the first in which he tried to "do philosophy."[25] These selections specifically highlight the conceptual moves involved in the development of the notion of "internal difference"; the fruits of which become especially significant in his subsequent work.

The logic of selection for Derrida mirrors Deleuze. Again, it is arguable that the theory of *differance* is developed through a range of arguments characteristic of his early work, whereas his more recent reflections display the nuanced development of those arguments through multiple concerns. Hence, I have again opted to focus on the early works, including a key chapter from *Speech and Phenomena,* where, by way of a reading of Husserl's *Phenomenology of Internal Time-Consciousness,*[26] difference is shown to inhabit the ostensible purity of the "now"; two sections from *Of Grammatology,* which are dedicated to the further explication of *differance,* especially with respect to the figure of linguistic or semiotic "form"; and the now classic essay "Differance" from *Margins of Philosophy,* which stands as a watermark for Derrida's subsequent work, as well as the tradition of difference that follows.

From Irigaray, I have sought to include selections that specifically highlight the ontological dimensions of her work. They include "When Our Lips Speak Together" from *This Sex Which Is Not One,* an essay that renders the symbolic figure of the "lips" as representative of a non-reductive understanding of the "other"; two sections from *The Forgetting of Air in Martin Heidegger,* which find Irigaray locating a certain reserve in Heidegger's ostensibly iconoclastic disavowal of the "proper" within the discourse of the "four-fold"; and "Sexual Difference" from *An Ethics of Sexual Difference,* where the neglect of sexual difference is understood as a symptom of the philosophical hegemony of the "same." Each of these works variously show Irigaray involved in the articulation of the feminine as a site of difference irreducible to the simple identity indigenous to the masculine *Logos*.

Throughout, given the constitutive constraints of space, availability, and preference, I have, by way of inclusion, privileged selections that I believe display an exceptionally rich thematic focus with respect to the theory of difference. But these same constraints insure that what is included here is only a limited instance. Nonetheless, I trust it is an instance adequate to the aims of this collection.

But this work has also been guided by a more general concern, especially insofar as it aims to be a representative collection of otherwise disparate—and often hard to aquire—works in contemporary Continental thought, suitable not only as a concise resource for specialists in this and related fields, but for students and instructors faced with the prospect of courses in the same, as well as metaphysics, religious studies, contemporary theology, literary theory, and postmodernism. Hence, unlike other recent and otherwise useful anthologies in Continental thought, this work is guided by a pedagogical disposition that favors the focus of a specific issue as the most effective way to nurture interest and substantive understanding of the tradition in question. In my experience, students are often more captivated, and in general better served, by the minutia of detail and depth of analysis in the context of a specific issue well covered than with a smorgasbord of thinkers, or survey of Humean "snapshots," none of which is sufficient in detail to show the essential connections and historical significance that makes an issue, thinker, or tradition meaningful. Indeed, such an approach would seem especially ironic, given the historical understanding of philosophy characteristic of the Continental tradition.

Interest in Continental thought is currently flourishing, whereby the question of difference has come to have a certain ubiquity. May the present collection serve as a useful resource for the clarification of its logic and the extension of its reach.

Notes

1. For further accounts of this story, see Vincent Descombes, *Modern French Philosophy*, trans. L. Scott-Fox and J. M. Harding (Cambridge: Cambridge University Press, 1980); Luc Ferry and Alain Renaut, *French Philosophy of the Sixties: An Essay on Antihumanism*, trans. Mary H. S. Cattani (Amherst: University of Massachusetts Press, 1990); and Gianni Vattimo, *The Adventure of Difference: Philosophy after Nietzsche and Heidegger*, trans. Cyprian Blamires and Thomas Harrison (Baltimore: The Johns Hopkins University Press, 1993).

2. It is clear, at least in the diverse tradition of Buddhism, that one of the prefiguring issues has been the hermeneutic question of how to understand the difference embodied

in *pratitya-samutpada*, or "dependent co-arising." See for example Garma C. C. Chang, *The Buddhist Teaching of Totality: The Philosophy of Hwa Yen Buddhism* (University Park: The Pennsylvania State University Press, 1971); Jay Garfield, *The Fundamental Wisdom of the Middle Way: Nagarjuna's Mulamadhyamakakarika* (Oxford: Oxford University Press, 1995); David J. Kalupahana, *Nagarjuna: The Philosophy of the Middle Way* (Albany: The State University of New York Press, 1986); T. R. V. Murti, *The Central Philosophy of Buddhism* (London: Allen and Unwin, 1955); and Mervyn Sprung, ed., *The Problem of Two Truths in Buddhism and Vendanta* (Dordrecht: D. Reidel Publishing, 1973).

3. See G. S. Kirk, J. E. Raven and M. Schofield, *The Presocratic Philosophers: A Critical History with a Selection of Texts*, 2nd. ed. (Cambridge; New York: Cambridge University Press, 1983); and Barbara Sproul, *Primal Myths: Creating the World* (San Francisco: Harper and Row, 1979).

4. Note Brian J. Martine's discussion of this point in *Indeterminacy and Intelligibility* (Albany: The State University of New York Press, 1992), 61 ff.

5. Plato, *Sophist, 257b*, in Edith Hamilton and Huntington Cairns, eds., *Plato: The Collected Dialogues* (Princeton: Princeton University Press, 1987).

6. Aristotle, *Metaphysics*, 4.4.1006b10–30, in Richard McKeon, ed., *The Basic Works of Aristotle* (New York: Random House, 1941).

7. For this account I am indebted to Mark G. Henninger's *Relations: Medieval Theories 1250–1325* (Oxford: Clarendon Press, 1989).

8. See Kenneth Barber and Jorge J. E. Gracia, eds., *Individuation and Identity in Early Modern Philosophy: Descartes to Kant* (Albany: The State University of New York Press, 1994). However, this apparent disinterest does not suggest that the work of the early moderns is devoid of significant resources. Witness Deleuze's creative reading of Spinoza in *Expressionism in Philosophy: Spinoza*, trans. Martin Joughin (New York: Zone Books, 1990); and Leibniz in *The Fold: Leibniz and the Baroque*, trans. Tom Conley (Minneapolis: The University of Minnesota Press, 1993).

9. F. H. Bradley, *Appearance and Reality* (London: Oxford University Press, 1930); J. E. M. McTaggart, *Studies in the Hegelian Dialectic* (Cambridge: Cambridge University Press, 1922); H. H. Joachim, *The Nature of Truth: An Essay* (Oxford: Clarendon Press, 1906). Also see the general account of this issue by Richard Rorty in Paul Edwards, ed., *The Encyclopedia of Philosophy*, vol. 7 (New York: Macmillan/Free Press, 1967), under the heading "Relations, External and Internal."

10. See the thoughtful exposition of this point in Harold Kincaid's "Hegel on External Relations and Partial Understanding," *Idealistic Studies*, 21, no. 1 (January 1991): 29–47.

11. See for example G. E. Moore, *Philosophical Studies* (London: Routledge and Kegan Paul, Ltd., 1922), especially "External and Internal Relations," 276–309.

12. Errol Harris, *Formal, Transcendental, and Dialectical Thinking* (Albany: The State University of New York Press, 1987), 133–134.

13. Charles Hartshorne, *Insights and Oversights of Great Thinkers* (Albany: The State University of New York Press, 1983), chap. 14, "The Neglect of Relative Predicates in Modern Philosophy," 151–169.

14. For an account of the complexities of this "appropriation," see Pierre Macherey, *Hegel ou Spinoza* (Paris: Maspero, 1979), 141 ff. One should also note that it is, in part, precisely the distance between Hegel's "negation" and Spinoza's affirmative "expression" that animates Deleuze's *oeuvre*.

15. G. W. F. Hegel, *The Logic of Hegel: Being Part One of the "Encyclopaedia of the Philosophical Sciences"* (1830), 2nd ed., trans. William Wallace (London: Oxford/Clarendon Press, 1892), 171–174.

16. Jean-Francois Lyotard, *The Postmodern Condition: A Report on Knowledge*, trans. Geoffrey Bennington and Brian Massumi (Minneapolis: The University of Minnesota Press, 1984).

17. Ferdinand De Saussure, *Course in General Linguistics*, trans. Wade Baskin (New York: Philosophical Library, 1959), 120.

18. As representative instances, see John Macquarrie, *Principles of Christian Theology* (New York: Scribner, 1977); and Mark C. Taylor, *Erring: A Postmodern A/theology* (Chicago: The University of Chicago, 1984).

19. For example, see Mary Rose Barral, *Body in Interpersonal Relations: Merleau-Ponty* (Lanham: University Press of America, 1984).

20. This has been suggested specifically by Michael Hardt in *Gilles Deleuze: An Apprenticeship in Philosophy* (Minneapolis: The University of Minnesota Press, 1993), 119–122.

21. On the question of essentialism, see Tina Chanter, *Ethics of Eros: Irigaray's Rewriting of the Philosophers* (London: Routledge, 1995).

22. The extent to which Heidegger and Merleau-Ponty may still be implicated in a subtle version of the philosophy of identity is open to question. For recent discussions that broach this issue, see John Caputo, *Radical Hermeneutics: Repetition, Deconstruction, and the Hermeneutic Project* (Bloomington: Indiana University Press, 1987); Douglas L. Donkel, *The Understanding of Difference in Heidegger and Derrida* (New York: Peter Lang Publishing Inc., 1992); Rodolphe Gasche, *The Tain of the Mirror: Derrida and the Philosophy of Reflection* (Cambridge, Mass.: Harvard University Press, 1986); Reiner Schurmann, *Heidegger on Being and Acting: From Principles to Anarchy*, trans. Christine-Marie Gros (Bloomington: Indiana University Press, 1987); M. C. Dillon, *Merleau-Ponty's Ontology*, 2nd rev. ed. (Evanston, Ill.: Northwestern University Press, 1997); M. C. Dillon, ed. *Ecart & Difference: Merleau-Ponty and Derrida on Seeing and Writing* (Atlantic Highlands, N.J.: Humanities Press, 1997); and Gary Madison, *The Phenomenology of Merleau-Ponty: A Search for the Limits of Consciousness* (Athens: Ohio University Press, 1981).

23. Martin Heidegger, *Being and Time*, trans. John Macquarrie and Edward Robinson (New York: Harper and Row, 1962).

24. Jean-Paul Sartre, *Les Temps Modernes* 372 (Oct. 1961): 184–185.

25. Gilles Deleuze, *Difference and Repetition* (New York: Columbia University Press, 1994), xv. But the distinction between "writing history of philosophy" and "writing philosophy" is not strict. See the translators' introduction to Gilles Deleuze, *Bergsonism*, trans. Hugh Tomlinson and Barbara Habberjam (New York: Zone Books, 1988), 7–8.

26. Edmund Husserl, *The Phenomenology of Internal Time-Consciousness*, trans. James S. Churchill (Bloomington: Indiana University Press, 1964).

PART ONE

Martin Heidegger

Preface

The *Principle of Identity* is the unchanged text of a lecture given on the occasion of the 500th anniversary of the University of Freiburg im Breisgau, for the faculty day on June 27, 1957.

The Onto-theo-logical Constitution of Metaphysics is the explication that concluded a seminar during the winter semester 1956–57 on Hegel's *Science of Logic*. It has in part been revised. The lecture took place on February 24, 1957 in Todtnauberg.

The Principle of Identity glances ahead and backward, too; ahead into the realm from which stems the subject matter of the lecture *The Thing* (see notes); back to the realm where the essence of metaphysics has its source; the constitution of metaphysics is defined by *difference*.

The close relation of *identity and difference* will be shown in this publication to be that which gives us thought.

The reader is to discover for himself in what way difference stems from the essence of identity, by listening to the harmony presiding over *the event of appropriation* and *perdurance*.

In this realm one cannot prove anything, but one can point out a great deal.

Todtnauberg
September 9, 1957

References

Concerning the attempt to think the thing, cf. *Das Ding*, to be published by Harper & Row. The lecture "The Thing" was first given in the context of a series of lectures entitled "Insight into that which is" in Bremen in December, 1949, and in Bühlerhöhe, Spring, 1950.

Concerning the interpretation of Parmenides, cf. *Moira*.

Concerning the essence of modern technology and modern science, cf. *Die Frage nach der Technik*.

Concerning the determination of Being as ground, cf. *Logs* and *Der Satz vom Grund*.

Concerning the explanation of the difference, cf. *What Is Called Thinking?* published by Harper & Row, 1968, and *Zur Seinsfrage*.

Concerning the interpretation of Hegel's metaphysics, cf. my *Hegel's Concept of Experience*, in preparation for publication by Harper & Row.

The *Letter on Humanism*, which speaks everywhere only by implication, can become a possible stimulus to an explication of the matter of thinking only in retrospect from this publication and those cited here.

The Principle of Identity

The usual formulation of the principle of identity reads: A = A. The principle of identity is considered the highest principle of thought. We shall try to think about this principle for a while. For we should like to find out through this principle what identity is.

When thinking attempts to pursue something that has claimed its attention, it may happen that on the way it undergoes a change. It is advisable, therefore, in what follows to pay attention to the path of thought rather than to its content. To dwell properly upon the content would simply block the progress of the lecture.

What does the formula A = A state which is customarily used to represent the principle of identity? The formula expresses the equality of A and A. An equation requires at least two elements. One A is equal to another. Is this what the principle of identity is supposed to mean? Obviously not. That which is identical, in Latin "idem," is in Greek τὸ αὐτό. Translated, τὸ αὐτό means "the same." If someone constantly repeats himself, for example: "the plant is a plant," he speaks in a tautology. For something to be the same, one is always enough. Two are not needed, as they are in the case of equality.

The formula A = A speaks of equality. It doesn't define A as the same. The common formulation of the principle of identity thus conceals precisely what the principle is trying to say: A is A, that is, every A is itself the same.

While we are circumscribing in this fashion what is identical, we are reminded of an old word by which Plato makes the identical perceptible, a word that points back to a still older word. In the dialogue *The Sophist*, 254d, Plato speaks of στάσις and κίνησις, rest and motion. Plato has the stranger say at this point: οὐκοῦν αὐτῶν ἕκαστον τοιν μὲν δυοιν ἕτερόν ἐστιν, αὐτὸ δ'ἑαυτῷταὐτόν.

"Each one of them is different from the (other) two, but itself the same for itself." Plato doesn't just say: ἕκαστον αὐτο ταὐτόν, "each itself the same," but says ἕκαστον ἑαυτῷταὐτόν, "each itself the same for itself."

The dative ἑαυτῷ means: each thing itself is returned to itself, each itself is the same for itself with itself. Our language, like the Greek, offers the advantage of making clear with one and the same word what is identical and again clarifying that word in the unity of all its various forms.

The more fitting formulation of the principle of identity "A = A" would accordingly mean not only that every A is itself the same; but rather that every A is itself the same with itself. Sameness implies the relation of "with," that is, a mediation, a connection, a synthesis: the unification into a unity. This is why throughout the history of Western thought identity appears as unity. But that unity is by no means the stale emptiness of that which, in itself without relation, persists in monotony. However, to get to the point where the relationship of the same with itself—which prevails in that identity which was already implicitly present very early—emerges as this mediation in a decisive and characteristic way, and where an abode is found for this radiant emergence, of mediation within identity, Western thought required more than two thousand years. For it is only the philosophy of speculative Idealism, prepared by Leibniz and Kant, that through Fichte, Schelling, and Hegel established an abode for the essence, in itself synthetic, of identity. This abode cannot be demonstrated here. Just one thing we must keep in mind: since the era of speculative Idealism, it is no longer possible for thinking to represent the unity of identity as mere sameness, and to disregard the mediation that prevails in unity. Wherever this is done, identity is represented only in an abstract manner.

Even in the improved formula "A is A," abstract identity alone appears. Does it get that far? Does the principle of identity really say anything about the nature of identity? No, at least not directly. Rather, the principle already presupposes what identity means and where it belongs. How do we get any information about this presupposition? The principle of identity itself gives it to us, if we listen carefully to its key note, if we think about that key note instead of just thoughtlessly mouthing the formula "A *is* A." For the proposition really says: "A is A." What do we hear? With this "is," the principle tells us how every being is, namely: it itself is the same with itself. The principle of identity speaks of the Being of beings. As a law of thought, the principle is valid only insofar as it is a principle of Being that reads: To every being as such there belongs identity, the unity with itself.

What the principle of identity, heard in its fundamental key, states is exactly what the whole of Western European thinking has in mind—and that is: the unity of identity forms a basic characteristic in the Being of beings. Everywhere, wherever and however we are related to beings of every kind, we find identity making its claim on us. If this claim were not made, beings could never appear in their Being. Accordingly, there would then also not be any science. For if science could not be sure in advance of the identity of its object in each case, it could not be what it is. By this assurance, research makes certain that its work is possible. Still, the leading idea of the identity of the object is never of any palpable use to the sciences. Thus, what is successful and fruitful about scientific knowledge is everywhere based on something useless. The claim of the identity of the object *speaks*, whether the sciences hear it or not, whether they throw to the winds what they have heard or let themselves be strongly affected by it.

The claim of identity speaks from the Being of beings. However, where the Being of beings appears, most early and most authentically in Western thought—with Parmenides—there speaks τὸ αὐτό, that which is identical, in a way that is almost too powerful. One of Parmenides' fragments reads: τὸ γὰρ αὐτὸ νοεῖν ἐστίν τε καὶ εἶναι.

"For the same perceiving (thinking) as well as being."

Different things, thinking and Being, are here thought of as the Same. What does this say? It says something wholly different from what we know otherwise as the doctrine of metaphysics, which states that identity belongs to Being. Parmenides says: Being belongs to an identity. What does identity mean here? What does the word τὸ αὐτό, the Same, say in Parmenides' fragment? Parmenides gives us no answer. He places us before an enigma which we may not sidestep. We must acknowledge the fact that in the earliest period of thinking, long before thinking had arrived at a principle of identity, identity itself speaks out in a pronouncement which rules as follows: thinking and Being belong together in the Same and by virtue of this Same.

Unintentionally we have here already interpreted τὸ αὐτό, the Same. We interpret Sameness to mean a belonging together. The obvious thing to do would be to represent this belonging together in the sense of identity as it was thought and generally understood later on. What could prevent us? None other than the principle itself which we read in Parmenides. For it says something else—it says that Being, together with thinking, belongs in the Same. Being is determined by an identity as a characteristic of that identity. Later on, however, identity as it is thought of in metaphysics is represented as a characteristic of Being. Thus we must not try to determine the identity that Parmenides speaks of in terms of this metaphysically represented identity.

The Sameness of thinking and Being that speaks in Parmenides' fragment stems from further back than the kind of identity defined by metaphysics in terms of Being as a characteristic of Being.

The key word in Parmenides' fragment, τὸ αὐτό, the Same, remains obscure. We shall leave it obscure. But we shall at the same time take a hint from the sentence that begins with this key word.

But meanwhile we have already fixed the Sameness of thinking and Being as the belonging together of the two. That was rash, perhaps of necessity. We must repair that rashness. And we can do so, since we do not consider the belonging together of which we have spoken as the ultimate or even the only authoritative interpretation of the Sameness of thinking and Being.

If we think of belonging *together* in the customary way, the meaning of belonging is determined by the word together, that is, by its unity. In that case, "to belong" means as much as: to be assigned and placed into the order of a "together," established in the unity of a manifold, combined into the unity of a system, mediated by the unifying center of an authoritative synthesis. Philosophy represents this belonging together as *nexus* and *connexio*, the necessary connection of the one with the other.

However, belonging together can also be thought of as *belonging* together. This means: the "together" is now determined by the belonging. Of course, we must still ask here what "belong" means in that case, and how its peculiar "together" is determined only in its terms. The answer to these questions is closer to us than we imagine, but it is not obvious. Enough for now that this reference makes us note the possibility of no longer representing belonging in terms of the unity of the together, but rather of experiencing this together in terms of belonging. However, does not the reference to this possibility amount to no more than an empty play on words, an artifice without support in verfiable facts?

That is how things look—until we take a closer look and let the matter speak for itself.

The idea of belonging together in the sense of a *belonging* together arises in respect of a situation which has already been mentioned. That situation is of course difficult to keep in mind, because it is so simple. But it comes closer to us just as soon as we pay heed to the following: In the interpretation of belonging together as *belonging* together we, taking Parmenides' hint, already had in mind thinking as well as Being, and thus what belongs to each other in the Same.

When we understand thinking to be the distinctive characteristic of man, we remind ourselves of a *belonging* together that concerns man and Being. Immediately we find ourselves grappling with the questions: What does Being mean? Who, or what, is man? Everybody can see easily that without a sufficient answer to these questions we lack the foundation for determining anything reliable about the *belonging* together of man and Being. But as long as we ask our questions in this way, we are confined within the attempt to represent the "together" of man and Being as a coordination, and to establish and explain this coordination either in terms of man or in terms of Being. In this procedure, the traditional concepts of man and Being constitute the toe-hold for the coordination of the two.

How would it be if, instead of tenaciously representing merely a coordination of the two in order to produce their unity, we were for once to note whether and how a belonging to one another first of all is at stake in this "together"? There is even the possibility that we might catch sight of the belonging together of man and Being, though only from afar, already in the traditional definitions of their essence. How so?

Man obviously is a being. As such he belongs to the totality of Being—just like the stone, the tree, or the eagle. To "belong" here still means to be in the order of Being. But man's distinctive feature lies in this, that he, as the being who thinks, is open to Being, face to face with Being; thus man remains referred to Being and so answers to it. Man *is* essentially this relationship of responding to Being, and he is only this. This "only" does not mean a limitation, but rather an excess. A belonging to Being prevails within man, a belonging which listens to Being because it is appropriated to Being. And Being? Let us think of Being according to its original meaning, as presence. Being is present to man neither incidentally nor only on rare occasions. Being is present and abides only as it concerns man through the claim it makes on him. For it is man, open toward Being, who alone lets Being arrive as presence. Such becoming present needs the openness of a clearing, and by this need remains appropriated to human being. This does not at all mean that Being is posited first and only by man. On the contrary, the following becomes clear:

Man and Being are appropriated to each other. They belong to each other. From this belonging to each other, which has not been thought out more closely, man and Being have first received those determinations of essence by which man and Being are grasped metaphysically in philosophy.

We stubbornly misunderstand this prevailing *belonging* together of man and Being as long as we represent everything only in categories and mediations, be it with or without dialectic. Then we always find only connections that are established either in terms of Being or in terms of man, and that present the belonging together of man and Being as an intertwining.

We do not as yet enter the domain of the *belonging* together. How can such an entry come about? By our moving away from the attitude of representational thinking. This move is a leap in the sense of a spring. The spring leaps away, away from the habitual idea of man as the rational animal who in modern times has become a subject for his objects. Simultaneously, the spring also leaps away from Being. But Being, since the beginning of Western thought, has been interpreted as the ground in which every being as such is grounded.

Where does the spring go that springs away from the ground? Into an abyss? Yes, as long as we only represent the spring in the horizon of metaphysical thinking. No, insofar as we spring and let go. Where to? To where we already have access: the belonging to Being. Being itself, however, belongs to us; for only with us can Being be present as Being, that is, become present.

Thus a spring is needed in order to experience authentically the *belonging* together of man and Being. This spring is the abruptness of the unbridged entry into that belonging which alone can grant a toward-each-other of man and Being, and thus the constellation of the two. The spring is the abrupt entry into the realm from which man and Being have already reached each other in their active nature,[1] since both are mutually appropriated, extended as a gift, one to the other. Only the entry into the realm of this mutual appropriation determines and defines the experience of thinking.

What a curious leap, presumably yielding us the insight that we do not reside sufficiently as yet where in reality we already are. Where are we? In what constellation of Being and man?

Today we no longer need complicated directives, as we did some years ago, to catch sight of the constellation by virtue of which man and Being concern each other. Or so it seems. It is enough, one would think, to say the words "atomic age" in order to let us experience how Being becomes present to us today in the world of technology. But may we simply equate the world of technology with Being? Obviously not, not even if we imagine this world as the totality in which atomic energy, the calculating plans of man, and automation are conjoined. Why does such a directive concerning the world of technology, even if it were the most circumstantial description, never let us catch sight of the constellation of Being and man? Because every analysis of the situation falls in its thinking short of the mark, in that the above-mentioned totality of the world of technology is interpreted in advance in terms of man, as being of man's making. Technology, conceived in the broadest sense and in its manifold manifestations, is taken for the plan which man projects, the plan which finally compels man to decide whether he will become the servant of his plan or will remain its master.

By this conception of the totality of the technological world, we reduce everything down to man, and at best come to the point of calling for an ethics of the technological world. Caught up in this conception, we confirm our own opinion that technology is of man's making alone. We fail to hear the claim of Being which speaks in the essence of technology.

Let us at long last stop conceiving technology as something purely technical, that is, in terms of man and his machines. Let us listen to the claim placed in our age not only upon man, but also upon all beings, nature and history, with regard to their Being.

What claim do we have in mind? Our whole human existence everywhere sees itself challenged—now playfully and now urgently, now breathlessly and now ponderously—to devote itself to the planning and calculating of everything. What speaks in this challenge? Does it stem merely from man's spontaneous whim? Or are we here already concerned with beings themselves, in such a way that they make a claim on us with respect to their aptness to be planned and calculated? Is it that Being itself is faced with the challenge of letting beings appear within the horizon of what is calculable? Indeed. And not only this. To the same degree that Being is challenged, man, too, is challenged, that is, forced to secure all beings that are his concern as the substance for his planning and calculating; and to carry this manipulation on past all bounds.

The name for the gathering of this challenge which places man and Being face to face in such a way that they challenge each other by turns is "the framework."

That in which and from which man and Being are of concern to each other in the technological world claims us in the manner of the framework. In the mutual confrontation of man and Being we discern the claim that determines the constellation of our age. The framework concerns us everywhere, immediately. The frame, if we may still speak in this manner, is more real than all of atomic energy and the whole world of machinery, more real than the driving power of organization, communications, and automation. Because we no longer encounter what is called the frame within the purview of representation which lets us think the Being of beings as presence—the frame no longer concerns us as something that is present—therefore the frame seems at first strange. It remains strange above all because it is not an ultimate, but rather first gives us That which prevails throughout the constellation of Being and Man.

The *belonging* together of man and Being in the manner of mutual challenge drives home to us with startling force that and how man is delivered over to the ownership of Being and Being is appropriate to the essence of man. Within the framework there prevails a strange ownership and a strange appropriation. We must experience simply this owning in which man and Being are delivered over to each other, that is, we must enter into what we call *the event of appropriation*. The words event of appropriation, thought of in terms of the matter indicated, should now speak as a key term in the service of thinking. As such a key term, it can no more be translated than the Greek λόγος or the Chinese Tao. The term event of appropriation here no longer means what we would otherwise call a happening, an occurrence. It now is used as a *singulare tantum*. What it indicates happens only in the singular, no, not in any number, but uniquely. What we experience in the frame as the constellation of Being and man through the modern world of technology is a prelude to what is called the event of appropriation. This event, however, does not necessarily persist in its prelude. For in the event of appropriation the possibility arises that it may overcome the mere dominance of the frame to turn it into a more original appropriating. Such a transformation of the frame into the event of appropriation, by virtue of that event, would bring the appropriate recovery—appropriate, hence never to be produced by man alone—of the world of technology from its dominance back to servitude in the realm by which man reaches more truly into the event of appropriation.

Where are we now? At the entry of our thinking into that simplicity which we call in the strict sense of the term the event of appropriation. It seems as if we were now in danger of directing our thinking, all too carelessly, toward something that is remote and general; while in fact what the term event of appropriation wishes to indicate really speaks to us directly from the very nearness of that neighborhood in which we already reside. For what could be closer to us than what brings us nearer to where we belong, to where we are belongers, to the event of appropriation?

The event of appropriation is that realm, vibrating within itself, through which man and Being reach each other in their nature, achieve their active nature by losing those qualities with which metaphysics has endowed them.

To think of appropriating as the event of appropriation means to contribute to this self-vibrating realm. Thinking receives the tools for this self-suspended structure from language. For language is the most delicate and thus[2] the most susceptible vibration holding everything within the suspended structure of the appropriation. We dwell in the appropriation inasmuch as our active nature is given over to language.

We have now reached a point on our path where we must ask the crude but inevitable question: What does appropriation have to do with identity? Answer: Nothing. Identity, on the other hand, has much, perhaps everything, to do with appropriation. How so? We can answer this question by retracing our path in a few steps.

The appropriation appropriates man and Being to their essential togetherness. In the frame, we glimpse a first, oppressing flash of the appropriation. The frame constitutes the active nature of the modern world of technology. In the frame we witness a *belonging* together of man and Being in which the letting belong first determines the manner of the "together" and its unity. We let Parmenides' fragment "For the Same are thinking as well as Being" introduce us to the question of a belonging together in which belonging has precedence over "together." The question of the meaning of this Same is the question of the active nature of identity. The doctrine of metaphysics represents identity as a fundamental characteristic of Being. Now it becomes clear that Being belongs with thinking to an identity whose active essence stems from that letting belong together which we call the appropriation. The essence of identity is a property of the event of appropriation.

If the attempt to guide our thinking to the abode of the essential origin of identity is to some extent tenable, what would have become of the title of our lecture? The meaning of the title "The principle of identity" would have undergone a transformation.

The law appears at first in the form of a fundamental principle which presupposes identity as a characteristic of Being, that is, of the ground of beings. This principle in the sense of a statement has in the meantime become a principle bearing the characteristics of a spring that departs from Being as the ground of beings, and thus springs into the abyss. But this abyss is neither empty nothingness nor murky confusion, but rather: the event of appropriation. In the event of appropriation vibrates the active nature of what speaks as language, which at one time was called the house of Being. "Principle of identity" means now: a spring demanded by the essence of identity because it needs that spring if the *belonging* together of man and Being is to attain the essential light of the appropriation.

On its way from the principle as a statement about identity to the principle as a spring into the essential origin of identity, thinking has undergone a transformation. Thus looking toward the present, beyond the situation of man, thinking sees the constellation of Being and man in terms of that which joins the two—by virtue of the event of appropriation.

Assuming we could look forward to the possibility that the frame—the mutual challenge of man and Being to enter the calculation of what is calculable—were to address itself to us as the event of appropriation which first surrenders man and Being to their own being; then a path would be open for man to experience beings in a more originary way—the totality of the modern technological world, nature and history, and above all their Being.

As long as reflection on the world of the atomic age, however earnestly and responsibly, strives for no more than the peaceful use of atomic energy, and also will not be content with any other goal, thinking stops halfway. Such halfwayness only secures the technological world all the more in its metaphysical predominance.

But what authority has decided that nature as such must forever *remain* the nature of modern physics, and that history must forever appear only as subject matter for historians? We cannot, of course, reject today's technological world as devil's work, nor may we destroy it—assuming it does not destroy itself.

Still less may we cling to the view that the world of technology is such that it will absolutely prevent a spring out of it. For this view is obsessed by the latest news, and regards them as the only thing that is real. This view is indeed fantastical; but the same is not true of a thinking ahead, looking toward that which approaches us as the call of the active nature of identity between man and Being.

Thinking has needed more than two thousand years really to understand such a simple relation as that of the mediation within identity. Do *we* then have a right to the opinion that the thinking entry into the essential source of identity could be achieved in a day? Precisely because this entry requires a spring, it must take its time, the time of thinking which is different from the time of calculation that pulls our thinking in all directions. Today, the computer calculates thousands of relationships in one second. Despite their technical uses, they are inessential.

Whatever and however we may try to think, we think within the sphere of tradition. Tradition prevails when it frees us from thinking back to a thinking forward, which is no longer a planning.

Only when we turn thoughtfully toward what has already been thought, will we be turned to use for what must still be thought.

Notes

1. Heidegger's term is "Wesen." It is used in the verbal meaning of φύσις rather than the more static meaning of nature or essence. —Tr.

2. In conversation with the translator, Professor Heidegger here amended the published text of this essay, substituting the words "*und daher*" for the original "*aber auch*." The German text retains the original published version. —Tr.

The Onto-theo-logical Constitution of Metaphysics

This seminar made an attempt to begin a conversation with *Hegel*. A conversation with a thinker can be concerned only with the matter of thinking. According to the usual definition "matter" refers to the point of contention ["Streit"], to that which is contested, that which alone is *the* case for thinking, that which concerns thinking. The struggle ["Streit"] of this contested matter is in no way first set forth as a point of contention ["Streit"] by means of thinking. The matter of thinking is that which is the contested in itself of this issue [das in sich Strittige eines Streites"]. Our word "contention" ["Streit"] (Old High German, "Strit") does not primarily mean discord, but rather distress. The matter of thinking presses upon thinking in such a way that only thus does it bring thinking to the heart of the matter and from there to thinking itself.

For Hegel, the matter of thinking is: Thinking as such. In order not to misinterpret this definition of the matter—thinking as such—in psychological or epistemological terms, we must add by way of explanation: thinking as such—in the developed fullness in which what has been thought, has been and now is thought. What this means here we can understand only from Kant's viewpoint, from the essence of the transcendental which Hegel, however, thinks absolutely, and that for him means speculatively. This is Hegel's aim when he says of the thinking of thinking as such that it is developed "purely in the element of thinking" (*Encyclopedia*, Introduction, 14). To give it a short title, which yet is very difficult to think through rigorously, this means: the matter of thinking is for Hegel "the idea" (*der Gedanke*). "The idea," developed to its highest essential freedom, becomes "the absolute

Idea" (*Idee*). Near the end of the *Science of Logic* (Lasson edition, Vol. II, 484), Hegel says of the absolute Idea: "Only the absolute Idea is *Being*, imperishable *Life, self-knowing Truth,* and it is *all Truth*." Thus Hegel himself explicitly gives to the matter of his thinking that name which is inscribed over the whole matter of Western thinking, the name: *Being*.

(In our seminar, the manifold yet unified use of the word "Being" was discussed. For Hegel, Being means first, but *never exclusively,* "indeterminate immediacy." Being is seen here from the viewpoint of determining mediation, that is, from the viewpoint of the absolute concept, and thus with reference to the absolute concept. "The truth of Being is essence," that is, absolute reflection. The truth of essence is the concept in the sense of in-finite self-knowledge. Being is the absolute self-thinking of thinking. Absolute thinking alone is the truth of Being, "is" Being. Truth here means always that the knowable as such is known with a knowledge absolutely certain of itself.)

At the same time, Hegel rigorously thinks about the matter of his thinking in the context of a conversation with the previous history of thinking. Hegel is the first thinker who can and must think in this way. Hegel's relation to the history of philosophy is the speculative, and only as such a historical, relation. The character of the movement of history is an occurrence in the sense of the dialectical process. Hegel writes: "The same development of thinking which is portrayed in the history of philosophy is portrayed in philosophy itself, but freed from that element of historical externality, *purely in the element of thinking*" (*Encyclopedia,* 14).

We stop, baffled. According to Hegel's own words, philosophy itself and the history of philosophy are supposed to be related to each other externally. But the externality of which Hegel thinks is by no means external in the crude sense of being something merely superficial and indifferent. Externality here means that outside dimension in which all history and every real course of events have their place in comparison to the movement of the absolute Idea. The externality of history as explained here, in relation to the Idea, emerges as the result of the Idea's self-externalization. Externality is itself a dialectical determination. We thus fall far short of Hegel's real thought if we state that Hegel has brought historical representation and systematic thinking into a unity in philosophy. For Hegel is concerned neither with historiography, nor with the system in the sense of a doctrinal structure.

What is the purpose of these remarks about philosophy and its relation to history? They mean to suggest that, for Hegel, the matter of thinking is in itself historical—but historical in the sense of occurrence. The process-character of thinking is determined by the dialectic of Being. For Hegel, the matter of thinking is: Being, as thinking thinking itself; and thinking comes to itself only in the process of its speculative development, thus running through stages of the variously developed, and hence of necessity previously undeveloped, forms.

Only from the matter of thinking thus experienced does a peculiar principle arise for Hegel—the criterion for the manner in which he speaks with those thinkers that preceded him.

Therefore, when we attempt a thinking conversation with Hegel, we must speak with him not just about the same matter, but about the same matter in the same way. But the same is not the merely identical. In the merely identical, the difference disappears. In the same the difference appears, and appears all the more pressingly, the more resolutely thinking is concerned with the same matter in the same way. Hegel thinks of the Being of beings speculative-historically. But inasmuch as Hegel's thinking belongs to a period of history (this does not mean at all that it belongs to the past), we are attempting to think of Being, as Hegel thought of it, in the same manner, that is, to think of it historically.

Thinking can stay with its matter only if it becomes ever more rigorous in its constancy, only if the same matter becomes for it ever more sharply contested. In this way the matter requires thinking to stay with it in its own manner of being, to remain steadfast toward that manner of being, answering to it by sustaining the matter to its completion. If its matter is Being, the thinking which stays with its matter must involve itself in the perdurance of Being. Accordingly, in a conversation with Hegel we are expected to clarify in advance the sameness of the same matter for the sake of that conversation. According to what has been said, we are required in our conversation with the history of philosophy to elucidate the otherness of the historical at the same time as we elucidate the otherness of the matter of thinking. Such a clarification must of necessity turn out to be short and sketchy.

In order to clarify the diversity that prevails between Hegel's thinking and our own attempt at thinking, we shall note three things.

We shall ask,

1. What is the matter of thinking for Hegel, and what is it for us?
2. What is the criterion for the conversation with the history of thinking for Hegel, and what is it for us?
3. What is the character of this conversation for Hegel, and what is it for us?

To the first question:

For Hegel, the matter of thinking is: Being with respect to beings having been thought in absolute thinking, and as absolute thinking. For us, the matter of thinking is the Same, and thus is Being—but Being with respect to its difference from beings. Put more precisely: for Hegel, the matter of thinking is the idea as the absolute concept. For us, formulated in a preliminary fashion, the matter of thinking is the difference *as* difference.

To the second question:

For Hegel, the criterion for the conversation with the history of philosophy is: to enter into the force and sphere of what has been thought by earlier thinkers. It is not by chance that Hegel advances his principle in the context of a conversation with Spinoza and before a conversation with Kant (*Science of Logic*, book III, Lasson edition, vol. II, p. 216 ff.). In Spinoza, Hegel finds the fully developed "standpoint of substance" which cannot, however, be the highest standpoint because Being is not yet thought equally fundamentally and resolutely as thinking thinking itself. Being, as substance and substantiality, has not yet developed into the subject in its absolute subjectivity. Still, Spinoza appeals always afresh to the whole thinking of German Idealism, and at the same time provokes its contradiction, because he lets thinking begin with the absolute. Kant's path, in contrast, is different, and is even more decisive than Spinoza's system for the thinking of absolute idealism and for philosophy generally. Hegel sees in Kant's idea of the original synthesis of apperception "one of the most profound principles for speculative development" (Ibid.). For Hegel, the force of each thinker lies in what each has thought, in that their thought can be incorporated into absolute thinking as one of its stages. Absolute thinking is absolute only by moving within its dialectical speculative process, and thus requiring stages.

For us, the criterion for the conversation with historical tradition is the same, insofar as it is a question of entering into the force of earlier thinking. We, however, do not seek that force in what has already been thought: we seek it in something that has not been thought, and from which what has been thought receives its essential space. But only what has already been thought prepares what has not yet been thought, which enters ever anew into its abundance. The criterion of what has not been thought does not lead to the inclusion of previous thought into a still higher development and systematization that surpass it. Rather, the criterion demands that traditional thinking be set free into its essential past which is still preserved. This essential past prevails throughout the tradition in an originary way, is always in being in advance of it, and yet is never expressly thought in its own right and as the Originary.

To the third question:

For Hegel, the conversation with the earlier history of philosophy has the character of *Aufhebung*,[1] that is, of the mediating concept in the sense of an absolute foundation.

For us, the character of the conversation with the history of thinking is no longer *Aufhebung* (elevation), but the step back.

Elevation leads to the heightening and gathering area of truth posited as absolute, truth in the sense of the completely developed certainty of self-knowing knowledge.

The step back points to the realm which until now has been skipped over, and from which the essence of truth becomes first of all worthy of thought.

After this brief characterization of the difference between Hegel's thinking and ours with respect to the matter, and with respect to the criterion and character, of a conversation with the history of thinking, let us now try to proceed with the conversation begun with Hegel and clarify it a little more. This means: we venture an attempt with the step back. The term "step back" suggests various misinterpretations. "Step back" does not mean an isolated step of thought, but rather means the manner in which thinking moves, and a long path. Since the step back determines the character of our conversation with the history of Western thinking, our thinking in a way leads us away from what has been thought so far in philosophy. Thinking recedes before its matter, Being, and thus brings what is thought into a confrontation in which we behold the whole of this history—behold it with respect to what constitutes the source of this entire thinking, because it alone establishes and prepares for this thinking the area of its abode. In contrast to Hegel, this is not a traditional problem, already posed, but what has always remained unasked throughout this history of thinking. We speak of it, tentatively and unavoidably, in the language of tradition. We speak of the *difference* between Being and beings. The step back goes from what is unthought, from the difference as such, into what gives us thought.[2] That is the *oblivion* of the difference. The oblivion here to be thought is the veiling of the difference as such, thought in terms of Λήθη (concealment); this veiling has in turn withdrawn itself from the beginning. The oblivion belongs to the difference because the difference belongs to the oblivion. The oblivion does not happen to the difference only afterward, in consequence of the forgetfulness of human thinking.

The difference between beings and Being is the area within which metaphysics, Western thinking in its entire nature, can be what it is. The step back thus moves out of metaphysics into the essential nature of metaphysics. The remark about Hegel's use of the ambiguous key word "Being" shows that discourse about Being and beings can never be pinned down to *one* epoch in the history of the clearing of "Being." Nor does discourse about "Being" ever understand this name in the sense of a genus, an empty generality under which the historically represented doctrines of beings are subsumed as individual cases. "Being" ever and always speaks as destiny, and thus permeated by tradition.

But the step back out of metaphysics into its essential nature requires a duration and an endurance whose dimensions we do not know. Only one thing is clear: the step back calls for a preparation which must be ventured here and now; but it must be ventured in the face of being as such and as a whole, as they *are* now and are visibly beginning to show themselves ever more unequivocally. What now *is*, is marked by the dominance of the active nature of modern technology. This dominance is already presenting itself in all areas of life, by various identifiable traits such as functionalization, systematic improvement, automation, bureaucratization, communications. Just as we call the idea of living things biology, just so the presentation and full articulation of all beings, dominated as they now are everywhere by the nature of the technical, may be called technology. The expression may serve as a term for the metaphysics of the atomic age. Viewed from the present and drawn from our insight into the present, the step back out of metaphysics into the essential nature of metaphysics is the step out of technology and technological description and interpretation of the age, into the *essence* of modern technology which is still to be thought.

This remark ought to prevent the other obvious misinterpretation of the term "step back": the view that the step back consists in a historical return to the earliest thinkers of Western philosophy. The "whither" to which the step back directs us, develops and shows itself only in the execution of the step.

In order to gain perspective in the seminar on the whole of Hegelian metaphysics, we chose as a temporary expedient an interpretation of the section which opens the first book of the *Science of Logic*, "The doctrine of Being." The section title alone gives us in each of its words enough to think about. It reads: "*With what must the beginning of science be made?*" Hegel's answer to this question consists in the demonstration that the beginning is "of a speculative nature." This means: the beginning is neither something immediate nor something mediated. We tried to express this nature of the beginning in a speculative sentence: "The beginning is the result." In accordance with the dialectical plurality of meanings of the "is," this means several things. It means for one thing: the beginning—taking *resultare* in its literal meaning[3]—is the rebound of thinking thinking itself out of the completion of the dialectical movement. The completion of this movement, the absolute Idea, is the totality developed within itself, the fullness of Being. The rebound from this fullness results in the emptiness of Being. In science (the absolute, self-knowing knowledge) the beginning must be made with this emptiness. The beginning and the end of the movement, and before them the movement itself, always remains Being. It has its being as the movement, revolving within itself, from fullness into the most extreme self-externalization and again from there into self-completing fullness. The matter of thinking thus is for Hegel thinking thinking itself as Being revolving within itself. In an inversion which is not only legitimate but necessary, the speculative sentence concerning the beginning runs: "The result is the beginning." The beginning must really be made with the result, since the beginning results from that result.

This says the same as the remark which Hegel adds in an aside and in parentheses, near the end of the section about the beginning: "(and *God* would have the uncontested right to have the beginning made with him)" (Lasson edition, vol. I, 63). According to the question that is the title of the section, we are now dealing with the "beginning of science." If science must begin with God, then it is the science of God: theology. This name is taken here in its later meaning of theo-logy as statements of representational thinking about

God. θεόλογος, θεόλογία mean at this point the mythopoetic utterance about the gods, with no reference to any creed or ecclesiastical doctrine.

Why is "science"—which since Fichte is the name for metaphysics—why is science theology? Answer: because science is the systematic development of knowledge, the Being of beings knows itself as this knowledge, and thus it is in truth. The schoolmen's name which during the transition from the medieval to the modern period emerges for the science of Being, that is, for the science of beings as such in general, is ontosophy or ontology. Western metaphysics, however, since its beginning with the Greeks has eminently been both ontology and theology, still without being tied to these rubrics. For this reason my inaugural lecture *What Is Metaphysics?* (1929) defines metaphysics as the question about beings as such *and* as a whole. The wholeness of this whole is the unity of all beings that unifies as the generative ground. To those who can read, this means: metaphysics is onto-theo-logy. Someone who has experienced theology in his own roots, both the theology of the Christian faith and that of philosophy, would today rather remain silent about God when he is speaking in the realm of thinking. For the onto-theological character of metaphysics has become questionable for thinking, not because of any kind of atheism, but from the experience of a thinking which has discerned in onto-theo-logy the still *unthought* unity of the essential nature of metaphysics. This nature of metaphysics, however, still remains what is most worth of thought for thinking, as long as thinking does not break off the conversation with its tradition, permeated by destiny, in an arbitrary manner thus unrelated to destiny.

In the fifth (1949) edition of *What Is Metaphysics?*, a new introduction explicitly refers to the onto-theological nature of metaphysics. But it would be rash to assert that metaphysics is theology because it is ontology. One would say first: Metaphysics is theology, a statement about God, because the deity enters into philosophy. Thus the question about the onto-theological character of metaphysics is sharpened to the question: How does the deity enter into philosophy, not just modern philosophy, but philosophy as such? This question can be answered only after it has first been sufficiently developed as a question.

We can properly think through the question, How does the deity enter into philosophy?, only when that *to which* the deity is to come has become sufficiently clear: that is, philosophy itself. As long as we search through the history of philosophy merely historically, we shall find everywhere that the deity has entered into it. But assuming that philosophy, as thinking, is the free and spontaneous self-involvement with being as such, then the deity can come into philosophy only insofar as philosophy, of its own accord and by its own nature, requires and determines that and how the deity enters into it. The question, How does the deity enter into philosophy?, leads back to the question, What is the origin of the onto-theological essential constitution of metaphysics? To accept this kind of question means to accomplish the step back.

In this step, we turn our thought to the essential origin of the onto-theological structure of all metaphysics. We ask: How does the deity, and therewith accordingly theology, and with theology the onto-theological character, enter into metaphysics? We raise this question in the context of a conversation with the whole of the history of philosophy. But we are questioning at the same time with a particular regard to Hegel. Here we are prompted to give thought first to a curious fact.

Hegel thinks of Being in its most empty emptiness, that is, in its most general aspect. At the same time, he thinks of Being in its fully completed fullness. Still, he does not call speculative philosophy, that is, philosophy proper, onto-theo-logy but rather "Science of Logic." By giving it this name, Hegel brings to light something decisive. It would be easy, of course, to explain the designation of metaphysics as "logic" by pointing out that for Hegel the matter of thinking is "the idea," understanding that word as a *singulare tantum*. The idea, thinking, is obviously and by ancient custom the theme of logic. Certainly. But it is just as incontestable that Hegel, faithful to tradition, sees the matter of thinking in beings as such and as a whole, in the movement of Being from its emptiness to its developed fullness.

But how can "Being" ever come to present itself as "thought"? How else than by the fact that Being is previously marked as ground, while thinking—since it belongs together with Being—gathers itself toward Being as its ground, in the manner of giving ground and accounting for the ground.[4] Being manifests itself as thought. This means: the Being of beings reveals itself as the ground that gives itself ground and accounts for itself. The ground, the *ratio* by their essential origin are the Λόγος, in the sense of the gathering of beings and letting them be. They are the Ἓν Πάντα. Thus "science," that is, metaphysics, is in truth "logic" for Hegel not because the theme of science is thinking, but because *Being* remains the matter of thinking; while Being, ever since the early days when it became unconcealed in the character of Λόγος, the ground that grounds, claims thinking—the accounting of the ground—for itself.

Metaphysics thinks of beings as such, that is, in general. Metaphysics thinks of beings as such, as a whole. Metaphysics thinks of the Being of beings both in the ground-giving unity of what is most general, what is indifferently valid everywhere, and also in the unity of the all that accounts for the ground, that is, of the All-Highest. The Being of beings is thus thought of in advance as the grounding ground. Therefore all metaphysics is at bottom, and from the ground up, what grounds, what gives account of the ground, what is called to account by the ground, and finally what calls the ground to account.

Why do we mention this? So that we may experience the shop-worn terms ontology, theology, onto-theology in their true gravity. At first and commonly, the terms ontology and theology do, of course, look like other familiar terms: psychology, biology, cosmology, archeology. The last syllable, -logy, means broadly and usually that we are dealing with the science of the soul, of living things, of the cosmos, of ancient things. But -logy hides more than just the logical in the sense of what is consistent and generally in the nature of a statement, what structures, moves, secures, and communicates all scientific knowledge. In each case, the -Logia is the totality of a nexus of grounds accounted for, within which nexus the objects of the sciences are represented in respect of their ground, that is, are conceived. Ontology, however, and theology are "Logies" inasmuch as they provide the ground of beings as such and account for them within the whole. They account for Being as the ground of beings. They account to the Λόγος, and are in an essential sense in accord with the Λόγος-, that is they are the logic of the Λόγος. Thus they are more precisely called onto-logic and theo-logic. More rigorously and clearly thought out, metaphysics is: onto-theo-logic.

We now understand the name "logic" in the essential sense which includes also the title used by Hegel, and only thus explains it: as the name for that kind of thinking which everywhere provides and accounts for the ground of beings as such within the whole in terms of Being as the ground (Λόγος). The fundamental character of metaphysics is onto-theo-logic. We should now be in a position to explain how the deity enters into philosophy.

To what extent is an explanation successful? To the extent that we take heed of the following: the matter of thinking is beings as such, that is, Being. Being shows itself in the nature of the ground. Accordingly, the matter of thinking, Being as the ground, is thought out fully only when the ground is represented as the first ground, πρώτη ἀρχή. The original matter of thinking presents itself as the first cause, the *causa prima* that corresponds to the reason-giving path back to the *ultima ratio*, the final accounting. The Being of beings is represented fundamentally, in the sense of the ground, only as *causa sui*. This is the metaphysical concept of God. Metaphysics must think in the direction of the deity because the matter of thinking is Being; but Being is in being as ground in diverse ways: as Λόγος, as ὑποκείμενον, as substance, as subject.

This explanation, though it supposedly touches upon something that is correct, is quite inadequate for the interpretation of the essential nature of metaphysics, because metaphysics is not only theo-logic but also onto-logic. Metaphysics, first of all, is neither only the one nor the other *also*. Rather, metaphysics is theo-logic because it is onto-logic. It is onto-logic because it is theo-logic. The onto-theological essential constitution of metaphysics cannot be explained in terms of either theologic or ontologic, even if an explanation could ever do justice here to what remains to be thought out.

For it still remains unthought by what unity ontologic and theologic belong together, what the origin of this unity is, and what the difference of the differentiated which this unity unifies. All of this still remains unthought. The problem here is obviously not a union of two independent disciplines of metaphysics, but the unity of *what* is in question, and in thought, in ontologic and theologic: beings as such in the universal and primal *at one with* beings as such in the highest and ultimate. The unity of this One is of such a kind that the ultimate in its own way accounts for the primal, and the primal in its own way accounts for the ultimate. The difference between the two ways of accounting belongs to the still-unthought difference we mentioned.

The essential constitution of metaphysics is based on the unity of being as such in the universal and that which is highest.

Our task here is to deal with the question about the onto-theo-logical nature of metaphysics first of all simply as a question. Only the matter itself can direct us to the point with which the question about the onto-theological constitution of metaphysics deals. It can do so in this way, that we attempt to think of the matter of thinking in a more rigorous manner. The matter of thinking has been handed down to Western thinking under the name "Being." If we think of this matter just a bit more rigorously, if we take more heed of what is in contest in the matter, we see that *Being* means always and everywhere: the Being of *beings*. The genitive in this phrase is to be taken as a *genitivus objectivus*. *Beings* means always and everywhere the beings of *Being;* here the genitive is to be taken as a *genitivus subjectivus*. It is, however, with certain reservations that we speak of a genitive in respect to object and subject, because these terms, subject and object, in their turn stem from a particular character of Being. Only this much is clear, that when we deal with the Being of beings and with the beings of Being, we deal in each case with a difference.

Thus we think of Being rigorously only when we think of it in its difference with beings, and of beings in their difference with Being. The difference thus comes specifically into view. If we try to form a representational idea of it, we will at once be misled into conceiving of difference as a relation which our representing has added to Being and to beings. Thus the difference is reduced to a distinction, something made up by our understanding *(Verstand)*.

But if we assume that the difference is a contribution made by our representational thinking, the question arises: a contribution to what? One answers: to beings. Good. But what does that mean: "beings"? What else could it mean than: something that *is*? Thus we give to the supposed contribution, the representational idea of difference, a place within Being. But "Being" itself says: Being which is *beings*. Whenever we come to the place to which we were supposedly first bringing difference along as an alleged contribution, we always find that Being and beings in their difference are already there. It is as in Grimm's fairytale *The Hedgehog and the Hare:* "I'm here already." Now it would be possible to deal with this strange state of affairs—that Being and beings are always found to be already there by virtue of and within the difference—in a crude manner and explain it as follows: our representational thinking just happens to be so structured and constituted that it will always, so to speak over its own head and out of its own head, insert the difference ahead of time between beings and Being. Much might be said, and much more might be asked, about this seemingly convincing but also rashly given explanation—

and first of all, we might ask: where does the "between" come from, into which the difference is, so to speak, to be inserted?

We shall discard all views and explanations, and instead note the following: this thing that is called difference, we encounter it everywhere and always in the matter of thinking, in beings as such—encounter it so unquestioningly that we do not even notice this encounter itself. Nor does anything compel us to notice it. Our thinking is free either to pass over the difference without a thought or to think of it specifically as such. But this freedom does not apply in every case. Unexpectedly it may happen that thinking finds itself called upon to ask: what does it say, this Being that is mentioned so often? If Being here shows itself concurrently as the Being of . . . , thus in the genitive of the difference, then the preceding question is more properly: what do you make of the difference if Being as well as beings appear *by virtue of the difference*, each in its own way? To do justice to this question, we must first assume a proper position face to face with the difference. Such a confrontation becomes manifest to us once we accomplish the step back. Only as this step gains for us greater distance does what is near give itself as such, does nearness achieve its first radiance. By the step back, we set the matter of thinking, Being as difference, free to enter a position face to face, which may well remain wholly without an object.

While we are facing the difference, though by the step back we are already releasing it into that which gives thought, we can say: the Being of beings means Being which is beings. The "is" here speaks transitively, in transition. Being here becomes present in the manner of a transition to beings. But Being does not leave its own place and go over to beings, as though beings were first without Being and could be approached by Being subsequently. Being transits (that), comes unconcealingly over (that) which arrives as something of itself unconcealed only by that coming-over.[5] Arrival means: to keep concealed in unconcealedness—to abide present in this keeping—to be a being.

Being shows itself as the unconcealing overwhelming. Beings as such appear in the manner of the arrival that keeps itself concealed in unconcealedness.

Being in the sense of unconcealing overwhelming, and beings as such in the sense of arrival that keeps itself concealed, are present, and thus differentiated, by virtue of the Same, the differentiation. That differentiation alone grants and holds apart the "between," in which the overwhelming and the arrival are held toward one another, are borne away from and toward each other. The difference of Being and beings, as the differentiation of overwhelming and arrival, is the perdurance (Austrag) of the two in *unconcealing keeping in concealment*. Within this perdurance there pervails a clearing of what veils and closes itself off—and this its prevalence bestows the being apart, and the being toward each other, of overwhelming and arrival.

In our attempt to think of the difference as such, we do not make it disappear; rather, we follow it to its essential origin. On our way there we think of the perdurance of overwhelming and arrival. This is the matter of thinking, thought closer to rigorous thinking—closer by the distance of one step back: Being thought in terms of the difference.

We here need to insert a remark, however, concerning what we said about the matter of thinking—a remark that again and again calls for our attention. When we say "Being," we use the word in its widest and least define general meaning. But even when we speak merely of a general meaning, we have thought of Being in an inappropriate way. We represent Being in a way in which It, Being, never gives itself. The manner in which the matter of thinking—Being—comports itself, remains a unique state of affairs. Initially, our customary ways of thinking are never able to clarify it more than inadequately. This we shall try to show by an example, bearing in mind from the start that nowhere in beings is there an example for the active nature of Being, because the nature of Being is itself the unprecedented exemplar.

Hegel at one point mentions the following case to characterize the generality of what is general: Someone wants to buy fruit in a store. He asks for fruit. He is offered apples and pears, he is offered peaches, cherries, grapes. But he rejects all that is offered. He absolutely wants to have fruit. What was offered to him in every instance *is* fruit and yet, it turns out, fruit cannot be bought.

It is still infinitely more impossible to represent "Being" as the general characteristic of particular beings. There is Being only in this or that particular historic character: Φύσις, Λόγος, Ἕν, Ἰδέα, Ενέργεια. Substantiality, Objectivity, Subjectivity, the Will, the Will to Power, the Will to Will. But these historic forms cannot be found in rows, like apples, pears, peaches, lined up on the counter of historical representational thinking.

And yet, did we not hear of Being in the historical order and sequence of the dialectical process that is in Hegel's thought? Certainly. But here, too, Being gives itself only in the light that cleared itself for Hegel's thinking. That is to say: the manner in which it, Being, gives itself, is itself determined by the way in which it clears itself. This way, however, is a historic, always epochal character which has being for us as such only when we release it into its own native past. We attain to the nearness of the historic only in that sudden moment of a recall in thinking. The same also holds true for the experience of the given character of that difference of Being and beings to which corresponds a given interpretation of beings as such. What has been said holds true above all also for our attempt in the step back out of the oblivion of the difference as such, to think this difference as the perdurance of unconcealing overcoming and of self-keeping arrival. If we listen more closely, we shall realize, of course, that in this discussion about perdurance we have already allowed the essential past to speak inasmuch as we are thinking of unconcealing and keeping concealed, of transition (transcendence), and of arrival (presence). In fact, it may be that this discussion, which assigns the difference of Being and beings to perdurance as the approach to their essence, even brings to light something all-pervading which pervades Being's destiny from its beginning to its completion. Yet it remains difficult to say how this all-pervasiveness is to be thought, if it is neither something universal, valid in all cases, nor a law guaranteeing the necessity of a process in the sense of the dialectical.

The only thing that now matters for our task is an insight into a possibility of thinking of the difference as a perdurance so as to clarify to what extent the onto-theological constitution of metaphysics has its essential origin in the perdurance that begins the history of metaphysics, governs all of its epochs, and yet remains everywhere concealed as perdurance, and thus forgotten in an oblivion which even escapes itself.

In order to facilitate that insight, let us think of Being, and in Being of the difference, and in the difference of perdurance in terms of that character of Being through which Being has cleared itself as Λόγος, as the ground. Being shows itself in the unconcealing overwhelming as that which allows whatever arrives to lie before us, as the grounding in the manifold ways in which beings are brought about before us. Beings as such, the arrival that keeps itself concealed in unconcealedness, is what is grounded; so grounded and so generated, it in turn grounds in its own way, that is, it effects, it causes. The perdurance of that which grounds and that which is grounded, as such, not only holds the two apart, it holds them facing each other. What is held apart is held in the tension of perdurance in such a way that not only does Being ground beings as their ground, but beings in their turn ground, cause Being in their way. Beings can do so only insofar as they "are" the fullness of Being: they are what *is* most of all.

Here our reflections reach an exciting juncture. Being becomes present as Λόγος in the sense of ground, of allowing to let lie before us. The same Λόγος, as the gathering of what unifies, is the Ἕν. This Ἕν, however, is twofold. For one thing, it is the unifying One in the sense of what is everywhere primal and thus most universal; and at the same time it is the unifying One in the sense of the All-Highest (Zeus). The Λόγος grounds and gathers everything into the universal, and accounts for and gathers everything in terms of the unique. It may be noted in passing that the same Λόγος also contains within itself the essential origin of the character of all language, and thus determines the way of utterance as a logical way in the broader sense.

Inasmuch as Being becomes present as the Being of beings, as the difference, as perduration, the separateness and mutual relatedness of grounding and of accounting for endures, Being grounds beings, and beings, as what *is* most of all, account for Being. One comes over the other, one arrives in the other. Overwhelming and arrival appear in each other in reciprocal reflection. Speaking in terms of the difference, this means: perdurance is a circling, the circling of Being and beings around each other. Grounding itself appears within the clearing of perdurance as something that *is*, thus itself as a being that requires the corresponding accounting for through a being, that is, causation, and indeed causation by the highest cause.

One of the classic examples in the history of metaphysics of this situation is found in a generally neglected text of Leibniz, which we shall call for short "The 24 Theses of Metaphysics" (Gerh. Phil. VII, 289 ff.; cf. M. Heidegger, *Der Satz vom Grund*, 1957, 51 ff.).

Metaphysics responds to Being as Λόγος, and is accordingly in its basic characteristics everywhere logic, but a logic that thinks of Being of beings, and thus the logic which is determined by what differs in the difference: onto-theo-logic.

Since metaphysics thinks of beings as such as a whole, it represents beings in respect of what differs in the difference, and without heeding the difference as difference.

What differs shows itself as the Being of beings in general, and as the Being of beings in the Highest.

Because Being appears as ground, beings are what is grounded; the highest being, however, is what accounts in the sense of giving the first cause. When metaphysics thinks of beings with respect to the ground that is common to all beings as such, then it is logic as onto-logic. When metaphysics thinks of beings as such as a whole, that is, with respect to the highest being which accounts for everything, then it is logic as theo-logic.

Because the thinking of metaphysics remains involved in the difference which as such is unthought, metaphysics is both ontology and theology in a unified way, by virtue of the unifying unity of perdurance.

The onto-theological constitution of metaphysics stems from the prevalence of that difference which keeps Being as the ground, and beings as what is grounded and what gives account, apart from and related to each other; and by this keeping, perdurance is achieved.

That which bears such a name directs our thinking to the realm which the key words of metaphysics—Being and beings, the ground and what is grounded—are no longer adequate to utter. For what these words name, what the manner of thinking that is guided by them represents, originates as that which differs by virtue of the difference. The origin of the difference can no longer be thought of within the scope of metaphysics.

The insight into the onto-theological constitution of metaphysics shows a possible way to answer the question, "How does the deity enter into philosophy?," in terms of the essence of metaphysics.

The deity enters into philosophy through the perdurance of which we think at first as the approach to the active nature of the difference between Being and beings. The difference constitutes the ground plan in the structure of the essence of metaphysics. The perdurance results in and gives Being as the generative ground. This ground itself needs to be properly accounted for by that for which it accounts, that is, by the causation through the supremely original matter—and that is the cause as *causa sui*. This is the right name for the god of philosophy. Man can neither pray nor sacrifice to this god. Before the *causa sui*, man can neither fall to his knees in awe nor can he play music and dance before this god.

The god-less thinking which must abandon the god of philosophy, god as *causa sui*, is thus perhaps closer to the divine God. Here this means only: god-less thinking is more open to Him than onto-theo-logic would like to admit.

This remark may throw a little light on the path to which thinking is on its way, that thinking which accomplishes the step back, back out of metaphysics into the active essence of metaphysics, back out of the oblivion of the difference as such into the destiny of the withdrawing concealment of perdurance.

No one can know whether and when and where and how this step of thinking will develop into a proper (needed in appropriation) path and way and road-building. Instead, the rule of metaphysics may rather entrench itself, in the shape of modern technology with its developments rushing along boundlessly. Or, everything that results by way of the step back may merely be exploited and absorbed by metaphysics in its own way, as the result of representational thinking.

Thus the step back would itself remain unaccomplished, and the path which it opens and points out would remain untrod.

Such reflections impose themselves easily, but they carry no weight compared with an entirely different difficulty through which the step back must pass.

That difficulty lies in language. Our Western languages are languages of metaphysical thinking, each in its own way. It must remain an open question whether the nature of Western languages is in itself marked with the exclusive brand of metaphysics, and thus marked permanently by onto-theo-logic, or whether these languages offer other possibilities of utterance—and that means at the same time of a telling silence. The difficulty to which thoughtful utterance is subject has appeared often enough in the course of this seminar. The little word "is," which speaks everywhere in our language, and tells of Being even where It does not appear expressly, contains the whole destiny of Being—from the ἔστιν γὰρ εἶναι of Parmenides to the "is" of Hegel's speculative sentence, and to the dissolution of the "is" in the positing of the Will to Power with Nietzsche.

Our facing this difficulty that stems from language should keep us from hastily recasting the language of the thinking here attempted into the coin of a terminology, and from speaking right away about perdurance, instead of devoting all our efforts to thinking through what has been said. For what was said, was said in a seminar. A seminar, as the word implies, is a place and an opportunity to sow a seed here and there, a seed of thinking which some time or other may bloom in its own way and bring forth fruit.

Notes

1. Aufhebung. This *terminus technicus* of Hegel's philosophy has the triple meaning of negating something in its mere individuality as a partial reality *(negare)*, of preserving it in its essential being *(conservare)*, and of elevating it into the higher sphere of the whole of reality *(elevare)*. —Tr.

2. *Das zu-Denkende* is that which gives thinking to us and it is that which is to be thought. —Tr.

3. *resultare*—to leap back, to rebound.

4. There are three closely related terms in the German text: "*begründen*" (to account for), "*ergründen*" (to give the ground), and "*gründen*" (to ground). In a consultation Heidegger clarified the relation of these terms as follows: "*Begründen*" has to do with beings and is ontic. "*Ergründen*" belongs to Being and is ontological. "*Gründen*" is the relationship of "*begründen*" and "*ergründen*" and encompasses both. —Tr.

5. *Überkommnis*, coming-over, overwhelming. —Tr.

Language

Man speaks. We speak when we are awake and we speak in our dreams. We are always speaking, even when we do not utter a single word aloud, but merely listen or read, and even when we are not particularly listening or speaking but are attending to some work or taking a rest. We are continually speaking in one way or another. We speak because speaking is natural to us. It does not first arise out of some special volition. Man is said to have language by nature. It is held that man, in distinction from plant and animal, is the living being capable of speech. This statement does not mean only that, along with other faculties, man also possesses the faculty of speech. It means to say that only speech enables man to be the living being he is as man. It is as one who speaks that man is—man. These are Wilhelm von Humboldt's words. Yet it remains to consider what it is to be called—man.

In any case, language belongs to the closest neighborhood of man's being. We encounter language everywhere. Hence it cannot surprise us that as soon as man looks thoughtfully about himself at what is, he quickly hits upon language too, so as to define it by a standard reference to its overt aspects. Reflection tries to obtain an idea of what language is universally. The universal that holds for each thing is called its essence or nature. To represent universally what holds universally is, according to prevalent views, the basic feature of thought. To deal with language thoughtfully would thus mean to give an idea of the nature of language and to distinguish this idea properly from other ideas. This lecture, too, seems to attempt something of that kind. However, the title of the lecture is not "On the Nature of Language." It is only "Language." "Only," we say, and yet we are clearly placing a far more presumptuous title at the head of our project than if we were to rest content with just making a few remarks about language. Still, to talk about language is presumably even worse than to write about silence. We do not wish to assault language in order to force it into the grip of ideas already fixed beforehand. We do not wish to reduce the nature of language to a concept, so that this concept may provide a generally useful view of language that will lay to rest all further notions about it.

To discuss language, to place it, means to bring to its place of being not so much language as ourselves: our own gathering into the appropriation.

We would reflect on language itself, and on language only. Language itself is—language and nothing else besides. Language itself is language. The understanding that is schooled in logic, thinking of everything in terms of calculation and hence usually overbearing, calls this proposition an empty tautology. Merely to say the identical thing twice—language is language—how is that supposed to get us anywhere? But we do not want to get anywhere. We would like only, for once, to get to just where we are already.

This is why we ponder the question, "What about language itself?" This is why we ask, "In what way does language occur as language?" We answer: *Language speaks.* Is this, seriously, an answer? Presumably—that is, when it becomes clear what speaking is.

To reflect on language thus demands that we enter into the speaking of language in order to take up our stay with language, i.e., within *its* speaking, not within our own. Only in that way do we arrive at the region within which it may happen—or also fail to happen—that language will call to us from there and grant us its nature. We leave the speaking to language. We do not wish to ground language in something else that is not language itself, nor do we wish to explain other things by means of language.

On the tenth of August, 1784 Hamann wrote to Herder *(Hamanns Schriften,* ed. Roth, VII, pp. 151 f.)[1]:

> If I were as eloquent as Demosthenes I would yet have to do nothing more than repeat a single word three times: reason is language, *logos*. I gnaw at this marrow-bone and will gnaw myself to death over it. There still remains a darkness, always, over this depth for me; I am still waiting for an apocalyptic angel with a key to this abyss.

For Hamann, this abyss consists in the fact that reason is language. Hamann returns to language in his attempt to say what reason is. His glance, aimed at reason, falls into the depths of an abyss. Does this abyss consist only in the fact that reason resides in language, or is language itself the abyss? We speak of an abyss where the ground falls away and a ground is lacking to us, where we seek the ground and set out to arrive at a ground, to get to the bottom of something. But we do not ask now what reason may be; here we reflect immediately on language and take as our main clue the curious statement, "Language is language." This statement does not lead us to something else in which language is grounded. Nor does it say anything about whether language itself may be a ground for something else. The sentence, "Language is language," leaves us to hover over an abyss as long as we endure what it says.

Language is—language, speech. Language speaks. If we let ourselves fall into the abyss denoted by this sentence, we do not go tumbling into emptiness. We fall upward, to a height. Its loftiness opens up a depth. The two span a realm in which we would like to become at home, so as to find a residence, a dwelling place for the life of man.

To reflect on language means—to reach the speaking of language in such a way that this speaking takes place as that which grants an abode for the being of mortals.

What does it mean to speak? The current view declares that speech is the activation of the organs for sounding and hearing. Speech is the audible expression and communication of human feelings. These feelings are accompanied by thoughts. In such a characterization of language three points are taken for granted:

First and foremost, speaking is expression. The idea of speech as an utterance is the most common. It already presupposes the idea of something internal that utters or externalizes itself. If we take language to be utterance, we give an external, surface notion of it at the very moment when we explain it by recourse to something internal.

Secondly, speech is regarded as an activity of man. Accordingly we have to say that man speaks, and that he always speaks some language. Hence we cannot say, "Language speaks." For this would be to say: "It is language that first brings man about, brings him into existence." Understood in this way, man would be bespoken by language.

Finally, human expression is always a presentation and representation of the real and the unreal.

It has long been known that the characteristics we have advanced do not suffice to circumscribe the nature of language. But when we understand the nature of language in terms of expression, we give it a more comprehensive definition by incorporating expression, as one among many activities, into the total economy of those achievements by which man makes himself.

As against the identification of speech as a merely human performance, others stress that the word of language is of divine origin. According to the opening of the Prologue of the Gospel of St. John, in the beginning the Word was with God. The attempt is made not only to free the question of origin from the fetters of a rational-logical explanation, but also to set aside the limits of a merely logical description of language. In opposition to the exclusive characterization of word-meanings as concepts, the figurative and symbolical character of language is pushed into the foreground. Biology and philosophical anthropology, sociology and psychopathology, theology and poetics are all then called upon to describe and explain linguistic phenomena more comprehensively.

In the meantime, all statements are referred in advance to the traditionaly standard way in which language appears. The already fixed view of the whole nature of language is thus consolidated. This is how the idea of language in grammar and logic, philosophy of language and linguistics, has remained the same for two and a half millennia, although knowledge about language has progressively increased and changed. This fact could even be adduced as evidence for the unshakable correctness of the leading ideas about language. No one would dare to declare incorrect, let alone reject as useless, the identification of language as audible utterance of inner emotions, as human activity, as a representation by image and by concept. The view of language thus put forth is correct, for it conforms to what an investigation of linguistic phenomena can make out in them at any time. And all *questions* associated with the description and explanation of linguistic phenomena also move within the precincts of this correctness.

We still give too little consideration, however, to the singular role of these correct ideas about language. They hold sway, as if unshakable, over the whole field of the varied scientific perspectives on language. They have their roots in an ancient tradition. Yet they ignore completely the oldest natural cast of language. Thus, despite their antiquity and despite their comprehensibility, they never bring us to language as language.

Language speaks. What about its speaking? Where do we encounter such speaking? Most likely, to be sure, in what is spoken. For here speech has come to completion in what is spoken. The speaking does not cease in what is spoken. Speaking is kept safe in what is spoken. In what is spoken, speaking gathers the ways in which it persists as well as that which persists by it—its persistence, its presencing. But most often, and too often, we encounter what is spoken only as the residue of a speaking long past.

If we must, therefore, seek the speaking of language in what is spoken, we shall do well to find something that is spoken purely rather than to pick just any spoken material at random. What is spoken purely is that in which the completion of the speaking that is proper to what is spoken is, in its turn, an original. What is spoken purely is the poem. For the moment, we must let this statement stand as a bare assertion. We may do so, if we succeed in hearing in a poem something that is spoken purely. But what poem shall speak to us? Here we have only one choice, but one that is secured against mere caprice. By what? By what is already told us as the presencing element in language, if we follow in thought the speaking of *language*. Because of this bond between what we think and what we are told by language we choose, as something spoken purely, a poem which more readily than others can help us in our first steps to discover what is binding in that bond. We listen to what is spoken. The poem bears the title:

A Winter Evening

Window with falling snow is arrayed,
Long tolls the vesper bell,
The house is provided well,
The table is for many laid.

Wandering ones, more than a few,
Come to the door on darksome courses.
Golden blooms the tree of graces
Drawing up the earth's cool dew.

Wanderer quietly steps within;
Pain has turned the threshold to stone.
There lie, in limpid brightness shown,
Upon the table bread and wine.

The two last verses of the second stanza and the third stanza read in the first version (Letter to Karl Kraus, December 13, 1913):

Love's tender power, full of graces,
Binds up his wound's anew.

O! man's naked hurt condign.
Wrestler with angels mutely held,
Craves, by holy pain compelled,
Silently God's bread and wine.

(Cf. the new Swiss edition of the poems of G. Trakl edited by Kurt Horwitz, 1946.)[2]

The poem was written by Georg Trakl. Who the author is remains unimportant here, as with every other masterful poem. The mastery consists precisely in this, that the poem can deny the poet's person and name.

The poem is made up of three stanzas. Their meter and rhyme pattern can be defined accurately according to the schemes of metrics and poetics. The poem's content is comprehensible. There is not a single word which, taken by itself, would be unfamiliar or unclear. To be sure, a few of the verses sound strange, like the third and fourth in the second stanza:

Golden blooms the tree of graces
Drawing up the earth's cool dew.

Similarly, the second verse of the third stanza is startling:

Pain has turned the threshold to stone.

But the verses here singled out also manifest a particular beauty of imagery. This beauty heightens the charm of the poem and strengthens its aesthetic perfection as an artistic structure.

The poem describes a winter evening. The first stanza describes what is happening outside: snowfall, and the ringing of the vesper bell. The things outside touch the things inside the human homestead. The snow falls on the window. The ringing of the bell enters into every house. Within, everything is well provided and the table set.

The second stanza raises a contrast. While many are at home within the house and at the table, not a few wander homeless on darksome paths. And yet such—possibly evil—roads sometimes lead to the door of the sheltering house. To be sure, this fact is not presented expressly. Instead, the poem names the tree of graces.

The third stanza bids the wanderer enter from the dark outdoors into the brightness within. The houses of the many and the tables of their daily meals have become house of God and altar.

The content of the poem might be dissected even more distinctly, its form outlined even more precisely, but in such operations we would still remain confined by the notion of language that has prevailed for thousands of years. According to this idea language is the expression, produced by men, of their feelings and the world view that guides them. Can the spell this idea has cast over language be broken? Why should it be broken? In its essence, language is neither expression nor an activity of man. Language speaks. We are now seeking the speaking of language in the poem. Accordingly, what we seek lies in the poetry of the spoken word.

The poem's title is "A Winter Evening." We expect from it the description of a winter evening as it actually is. But the poem does not picture a winter evening occurring somewhere, sometime. It neither merely describes a winter evening that is already there, nor does it attempt to produce the semblance, leave the impression, of a winter evening's presence where there is no such winter evening. Naturally not, it will be replied. Everyone knows that a poem is an invention. It is imaginative even where it seems to be descriptive. In his fictive act the poet pictures to himself something that could be present in its presence. The poem, as composed, images what is thus fashioned for our own act of imaging. In the poem's speaking the poetic imagination gives itself utterance. What is spoken in the poem is what the poet enunciates out of himself. What is thus spoken out, speaks by enunciating its content. The language of the poem is a manifold enunciating. Language proves incontestably to be expression. But this conclusion is in conflict with the proposition "Language speaks," assuming that speaking, in its essential nature, is not an expressing.

Even when we understand what is spoken in the poem in terms of poetic composition, it seems to us, as if under some compulsion, always and only to be an expressed utterance. Language is expression. Why do we not reconcile ourselves to this fact? Because the correctness and currency of this view of language are insufficient to serve as a basis for an account of the nature of language. How shall we gauge this inadequacy? Must we not be bound by a different standard before we can gauge anything in that manner? Of course. That standard reveals itself in the proposition "Language speaks." Up to this point this guiding proposition has had merely the function of warding off the ingrained habit of disposing of speech by throwing it at once among the phenomena of expression instead of thinking it in its own terms. The poem cited has been chosen because, in a way not further explicable, it demonstrates a peculiar fitness to provide some fruitful hints for our attempt to discuss language.

Language *speaks*. This means at the same time and before all else: *language* speaks. Language? And not man? What our guiding proposition demands of us now—is it not even worse than before? Are we, in addition to everything else, also going to deny now that man is the being who speaks? Not at all. We deny this no more than we deny the possibility of classifying linguistic phenomena under the heading of "expression." But we ask, "How does man speak?" We ask, "What is it to speak?"

> Window with falling snow is arrayed
> Long tolls the vesper bell.

This speaking names the snow that soundlessly strikes the window late in the waning day, while the vesper bell rings. In such a snowfall, everything lasting lasts longer. Therefore the vesper bell, which daily rings for a strictly fixed time, tolls long. The speaking names the winter evening time. What is this naming? Does it merely deck out the imaginable familiar objects and events—snow, bell, window, falling, ringing—with words of a language? No. This naming does not hand out titles, it does not apply terms, but it calls into the word. The naming calls. Calling brings closer what it calls. However this bringing closer does not fetch what is called only in order to set it down in closest proximity to what is present, to find a place for it there. The call does indeed call. Thus it brings the presence of what was previously uncalled into a nearness. But the call, in calling it here, has already called out to what it calls. Where to? Into the distance in which what is called remains, still absent.

The calling here calls into a nearness. But even so the call does not wrest what it calls away from the remoteness, in which it is kept by the calling there. The calling calls into itself and therefore always here and there—here into presence, there into absence. Snowfall and tolling of vesper bell are spoken to us here and now in the poem. They are present in the call. Yet they in no way fall among the things present here and now in this lecture hall. Which presence is higher, that of these present things or the presence of what is called?

The house is provided well,
The table is for many laid

The two verses speak like plain statements, as though they were noting something present. The emphatic "is" sounds that way. Nevertheless it speaks in the mode of calling. The verses bring the well-provided house and the ready table into that presence that is turned toward something absent.

What does the first stanza call? It calls things, bids them come. Where? Not to be present among things present; it does not bid the table named in the poem to be present here among the rows of seats where you are sitting. The place of arrival which is also called in the calling is a presence sheltered in absence. The naming call bids things to come into such an arrival. Bidding is inviting. It invites things in, so that they may bear upon men as things. The snowfall brings men under the sky that is darkening into night. The tolling of the evening bell brings them, as mortals, before the divine. House and table join mortals to the earth. The things that were named, thus called, gather to themselves sky and earth, mortals and divinities. The four are united primally in being toward one another, a fourfold. The things let the fourfold of the four stay with them. This gathering, assembling, letting-stay is the thinging of things. The unitary fourfold of sky and earth, mortals and divinities, which is stayed in the thinging of things, we call—the world. In the naming, the things named are called into their thinging. Thinging, they unfold world, in which things abide and so are the abiding ones. By thinging, things carry out world. Our old language calls such carrying *bern, bären—Old* High German *beran—to bear;* hence the words *gebaren,* to carry, gestate, give birth, and *Gebärde,* bearing, gesture. Thinging, things are things. Thinging, they gesture—gestate—world.

The first stanza calls things into their thinging, bids them come. The bidding that calls things calls them here, invites them, and at the same time calls out to the things, commending them to the world out of which they appear. Hence the first stanza names not only things. It simultaneously names world. It calls the "many" who belong as mortals to the world's fourfold. Things be-thing—i.e., condition—mortals. This now means: things, each in its time, literally visit mortals with a world. The first stanza speaks by bidding the things to come.

The second stanza speaks in a different way. To be sure, it too bids to come. But its calling begins as it calls and names mortals:

Wandering ones, more than a few . . .

Not all mortals are called, not the many of the first stanza, but only "more than a few"—those who wander on dark courses. These mortals are capable of dying as the wandering toward death. In death the supreme concealedness of

Being crystallizes. Death has already overtaken every dying. Those "wayfarers" must first wander their way to house and table through the darkness of their courses; they must do so not only and not even primarily for themselves, but for the many, because the many think that if they only install themselves in houses and sit at tables, they are already bethinged, conditioned, by things and have arrived at dwelling.

The second stanza begins by calling more than a few of the mortals. Although mortals belong to the world's fourfold along with the divinities, with earth and sky, the first two verses of the second stanza do not expressly call the world. Rather, very much like the first stanza but in a different sequence, they at the same time name things—the door, the dark paths. It is the two remaining verses that expressly name the world. Suddenly they name something wholly different:

> Golden blooms the tree of graces
> Drawing up the earth's cool dew.

The tree roots soundly in the earth. Thus it is sound and flourishes into a blooming that opens itself to heaven's blessing. The tree's towering has been called. It spans both the ecstasy of flowering and the soberness of the nourishing sap. The earth's abated growth and the sky's open bounty belong together. The poem names the tree of graces. Its sound blossoming harbors the fruit that falls to us unearned—holy, saving, loving toward mortals. In the golden-blossoming tree there prevail earth and sky, divinities and mortals. Their unitary fourfold is the world. The word "world" is now no longer used in the metaphysical sense. It designates neither the universe of nature and history in its secular representation nor the theologically conceived creation *(mundus)*, nor does it mean simply the whole of entities present *(kosmos)*.

The third and fourth lines of the second stanza call the tree of graces. They expressly bid the world to come. They call the world–fourfold here, and thus call world to the things.

The two lines start with the word "golden." So that we may hear more clearly this word and what it calls, let us recollect a poem of Pindar's: *Isthmians V*. At the beginning of this ode the poet calls gold *periosion panton*, that which above all shines through everything, *panta*, shines through each thing present all around. The splendor of gold keeps and holds everything present in the unconcealedness of its appearing.

As the calling that names things calls here and there, so the saying that names the world calls into itself, calling here and there. It entrusts world to the things and simultaneously keeps the things in the splendor of world. The world grants to things their presence. Things bear world. World grants things.

The speaking of the first two stanzas speaks by bidding things to come to world, and world to things. The two modes of bidding are different but not separated. But neither are they merely coupled together. For world and things do not subsist alongside one another. They penetrate each other. Thus the two traverse a middle. In it, they are at one. Thus at one they are intimate. The middle of the two is intimacy—in Latin, *inter.* The corresponding German word is *unter*, the English *inter-*. The intimacy of world and thing is not a fusion. Intimacy obtains only where the intimate—world and thing—divides itself cleanly and remains separated. In the midst of the two, in the between of world and thing, in their *inter*, division prevails: a *dif-ference.*

The intimacy of world and thing is present in the separation of the between; it is present in the dif-ference. The word difference is now removed from its usual and customary usage. What it now names is not a generic concept for various kinds of differences. It exists only as this single difference. It is unique. Of itself, it holds apart the middle in and through which world and things are at one with each other. The intimacy of the difference is the unifying element of the *diaphora*, the carrying out that carries through. The dif-ference carries out world in its worlding, carries out things in their thinging. Thus carrying them out, it carries them toward one another. The dif-ference does not mediate after the fact by connecting world and things through a middle added on to them. Being the middle, it first determines world and things in their presence, i.e., in their being toward one another, whose unity it carries out.

The word consequently no longer means a distinction established between objects only by our representations. Nor is it merely a relation obtaining between world and thing, so that a representation coming upon it can establish it. The dif-ference is not abstracted from world and thing as their relationship after the fact. The dif-ference for world and thing *disclosingly appropriates* things into bearing a world; it *disclosingly appropriates* world into the granting of things.

The dif-ference is neither distinction nor relation. The difference is, at most, dimension for world and thing. But in this case "dimension" also no longer means a precinct already present independently in which this or that comes to settle. The dif-ference is *the* dimension, insofar as it measures out, apportions, world and thing, each to its own. Its allotment of them first opens up the separateness and towardness of world and thing. Such an opening up is the way in which the dif-ference here spans the two. The dif-ference, as the middle for world and things, metes out the measure of their presence. In the bidding that calls thing and world, what is really called is: the dif-ference.

The first stanza of the poem bids the things to come which, thinging, bear world. The second stanza bids that world to come which, worlding, grants things. The third stanza bids the middle for world and things to come: the carrying out of the intimacy. On this account the third stanza begins with an emphatic calling:

Wanderer quietly steps within.

Where to? The verse does not say. Instead, it calls the entering wanderer into the stillness. This stillness ministers over the doorway. Suddenly and strangely the call sounds:

Pain has turned the threshold to stone.

This verse speaks all by itself in what is spoken in the whole poem. It names pain. What pain? The verse says merely "pain." Whence and in what way is pain called?

Pain has turned the threshold to stone.

"Turned . . . to stone"—these are the only words in the poem that speak in the past tense. Even so, they do not name something gone by, something no longer present. They name something that persists and that has already persisted. It is only in turning to stone that the threshold presences at all.

The threshold is the ground-beam that bears the doorway as a whole. It sustains the middle in which the two, the outside and the inside, penetrate each other. The threshold bears the between. What goes out and goes in, in the between, is joined in the between's dependability. The dependability of the middle must never yield either way. The settling of the between needs something that can endure, and is in this sense hard. The threshold, as the settlement of the between, is hard because pain has petrified it. But the pain that became appropriated to stone did not harden into the threshold in order to congeal there. The pain presences unflagging in the threshold, as pain.

But what is pain? Pain rends. It is the rift. But it does not tear apart into dispersive fragments. Pain indeed tears asunder, it separates, yet so that at the same time it draws everything to itself, gathers it to itself. Its rending, as a separating that gathers, is at the same time that drawing which, like the pen-drawing of a plan or sketch, draws and joins together what is held apart in separation. Pain is the joining agent in the rending that divides and gathers. Pain is the joining of the rift. The joining is the threshold. It settles the between, the middle of the two that are separated in it. Pain joins the rift of the difference. Pain is the dif-ference itself.

Pain has turned the threshold to stone.

The verse calls the dif-ference, but it neither thinks it specifically nor does it call its nature by this name. The verse calls the separation of the between, the gathering middle, in whose intimacy the bearing of things and the granting of world pervade one another.

Then would the intimacy of the dif-ference for world and thing be pain? Certainly. But we should not imagine pain anthropologically as a sensation that makes us feel afflicted. We should not think of the intimacy psychologically as the sort in which sentimentality makes a nest for itself.

> Pain has turned the threshold to stone.

Pain has already fitted the threshold into its bearing. The difference presences already as the collected presence, from which the carrying out of world and thing appropriatingly takes place. How so?

> There lie, in limpid brightness shown,
> Upon the table bread and wine.

Where does the pure brightness shine? On the threshold, in the settling of the pain. The rift of the dif-ference makes the limpid brightness shine. Its luminous joining decides the brightening of the world into its own. The rift of the difference expropriates the world into its worlding, which grants things. By the brightening of the world in their golden gleam, bread and wine at the same time attain to their own gleaming. The nobly named things are lustrous in the simplicity of their thinging. Bread and wine are the fruits of heaven and earth, gifts from the divinities to mortals. Bread and wine gather these four to themselves from the simple unity of their fourfoldness. The things that are called bread and wine are simple things because their bearing of world is fulfilled, without intermediary, by the favor of the world. Such things have their sufficiency in letting the world's fourfold stay with them. The pure limpid brightness of world and the simple gleaming of things go through their between, the dif-ference.

The third stanza calls world and things into the middle of their intimacy. The seam that binds their being toward one another is pain.

Only the third stanza gathers the bidding of things and the bidding of world. For the third stanza calls primally out of the simplicity of the intimate bidding which calls the dif-ference by leaving it unspoken. The primal calling, which bids the intimacy of world and thing to come, is the authentic bidding. This bidding is the nature of speaking. Speaking occurs in what is spoken in the poem. It is the speaking of language. Language speaks. It speaks by bidding the bidden, thing-world and world-thing, to come to the between of the dif-ference. What is so bidden is commanded to arrive from out of the dif-ference into the dif-ference. Here we are thinking of the old sense of command, which we recognize still in the phrase, "Commit thy way unto the Lord." The bidding of language commits the bidden thus to the bidding of the dif-ference. The dif-ference lets the thinging of the thing rest in the worlding of the world. The dif-ference expropriates the thing into the repose of the fourfold. Such expropriation does not diminish the thing. Only so is the thing exalted into its own, so that it stays world. To keep in repose is to still. The dif-ference stills the thing, as thing, into the world.

Such stilling, however, takes place only in such a way that at the same time the world's fourfold fulfills the bearing of the thing, in that the stilling grants to the thing the sufficiency of staying world. The dif-ference stills in a twofold manner. It stills by letting things rest in the world's favor. It stills by letting the world suffice itself in the thing. In the double stilling of the dif-ference there takes place: stillness.

What is stillness? It is in no way merely the soundless. In soundlessness there persists merely a lack of the motion of entoning, sounding. But the motionless is neither limited to sounding by being its suspension, nor is it itself already something genuinely tranquil. The motionless always remains, as it were, merely the other side of that which rests. The motionless itself still rests on rest. But rest has its being in the fact that it stills. As the stilling of stillness, rest, conceived strictly, is always more in motion than all motion and always more restlessly active than any agitation.

The dif-ference stills particularly in two ways: it stills the things in thinging and the world in worlding. Thus stilled, thing and world never escape from the dif-ference. Rather, they rescue it in the stilling, where the dif-ference is itself the stillness.

In stilling things and world into their own, the dif-ference calls world and thing into the middle of their intimacy. The dif-ference is the bidder. The dif-ference gathers the two out of itself as it calls them into the rift that is the dif-ference itself. This gathering calling is the pealing. In it there occurs something different from a mere excitation and spreading of sound.

When the dif-ference gathers world and things into the simple onefold of the pain of intimacy, it bids the two to come into their very nature. The dif-ference is the command out of which every bidding itself is first called, so that each may follow the command. The command of the dif-ference has ever already gathered all bidding within itself. The calling, gathered together with itself, which gathers to itself in the calling, is the pealing as the peal.

The calling of the dif-ference is the double stilling. The gathered bidding, the command, in the form of which the difference calls world and things, is the peal of stillness. Language speaks in that the command of the dif-ference calls world and things into the simple onefold of their intimacy.

Language speaks as the peal of stillness. Stillness stills by the carrying out, the bearing and enduring, of world and things in their presence. The carrying out of world and thing in the manner of stilling is the appropriative taking place of the difference. Language, the peal of stillness, is, inasmuch as the difference takes place. Language goes on as the taking place or occurring of the dif-ference for world and things.

The peal of stillness is not anything human. But on the contrary, the human is indeed in its nature given to speech—it is linguistic. The word "linguistic" as it is here used means: having taken place out of the speaking of language. What has thus taken place, human being, has been brought into its own by language, so that it remains given over or appropriated to the nature of language, the peal of stillness. Such an appropriating takes place in that the very *nature,* the *presencing,* of language *needs and uses* the speaking of mortals in order to sound as the peal of stillness for the hearing of mortals. Only as men belong within the peal of stillness are mortals able to speak in *their own* way in sounds.

Mortal speech is a calling that names, a bidding which, out of the simple onefold of the difference, bids thing and world to come. What is purely bidden in mortal speech is what is spoken in the poem. Poetry proper is never merely a higher mode *(melos)* of everyday language. It is rather the reverse: everyday language is a forgotten and therefore used-up poem, from which there hardly resounds a call any longer.

The opposite of what is purely spoken, the opposite of the poem, is not prose. Pure prose is never "prosaic." It is as poetic and hence as rare as poetry.

If attention is fastened exclusively on human speech, if human speech is taken simply to be the voicing of the inner man, if speech so conceived is regarded as language itself, then the nature of language can never appear as anything but an expression and an activity of man. But human speech, as the speech of mortals, is not self-subsistent. The speech of mortals rests in its relation to the speaking of language.

At the proper time it becomes unavoidable to think of how mortal speech and its utterance take place in the speaking of language as the peal of the stillness of the dif-ference. Any uttering, whether in speech or writing, breaks the stillness. On what does the peal of stillness break? How does the broken stillness come to sound in words? How does the broken stillness shape the mortal speech that sounds in verses and sentences?

Assuming that thinking will succeed one day in answering these questions, it must be careful not to regard utterance, let alone expression, as the decisive element of human speech.

The structure of human speech can only be the manner (*melos*) in which the speaking of language, the peal of the stillness of the dif-ference, appropriates mortals by the command of the dif-ference.

The way in which mortals, called out of the dif-ference into the dif-ference, speak on their own part, is: by responding. Mortal speech must first of all have listened to the command, in the form of which the stillness of the dif-ference calls world and things into the rift of its onefold simplicity. Every word of mortal speech speaks out of such a listening, and as such a listening.

Mortals speak insofar as they listen. They heed the bidding call of the stillness of the dif-ference even when they do not know that call. Their listening draws from the command of the dif-ference what it brings out as sounding word. This speaking that listens and accepts is responding.

Nevertheless by receiving what it says from the command of the dif-ference, mortal speech has already, in its own way, followed the call. Response, as receptive listening, is at the same time a recognition that makes due acknowledgment. Mortals speak by responding to language in a twofold way, receiving and replying. The mortal word speaks by cor-responding in a multiple sense.

Every authentic hearing holds back with its own saying. For hearing keeps to itself in the listening by which it remains appropriated to the peal of stillness. All responding is attuned to this restraint that reserves itself. For this reason such reserve must be concerned to be ready, in the mode of listening, for the command of the dif-ference. But the reserve must take care not just to hear the peal of stillness afterward, but to hear it even beforehand, and thus as it were to anticipate its command.

This anticipating while holding back determines the manner in which mortals respond to the dif-ference. In this way mortals live in the speaking of language.

Language speaks. Its speaking bids the dif-ference to come which expropriates world and things into the simple onefold of their intimacy.

Language speaks.

Man speaks in that he responds to language. This responding is a hearing. It hears because it listens to the command of stillness.

It is not a matter here of stating a new view of language. What is important is learning to live in the speaking of language. To do so, we need to examine constantly whether and to what extent we are capable of what genuinely belongs to responding: anticipation in reserve. For:

Man speaks only as he responds to language.

Language speaks.

Its speaking speaks for us in what has been spoken:

A Winter Evening

Window with falling snow is arrayed,
Long tolls the vesper bell,
The house is provided well,
The table is for many laid.

Wandering ones, more than a few,
Come to the door on darksome courses.
Golden blooms the tree of graces
Drawing up the earth's cool dew.

Wanderer quietly steps within;
Pain has turned the threshold to stone.
There lie, in limpid brightness shown,
Upon the table bread and wine.

Notes

1. [Johann Georg Hamann. *Schriften.* Edited by F. Roth and G. A. Wiener. Berlin: G. Reimer, 1821. 8 Parts, the last in 2 subdivisions, VIIIa and VIIIb.—Tr.]

2. [Georg Trakl, *Die Dichtungen. Gesamtausgabe mit einem Anhang: Zeugnisse und Erinnerungen,* edited by Kurt Horwitz. Zürich: Arche Verlag, 1946. This poem, "Ein Winterabend," may also be found in *Die Dichtungen,* 11th edition. Salzburg: Otto Müller, 1938, p. 124. The letter to Karl Kraus may be found in *Erinnerung an Georg Trakl: Zeugnisse und Briefe,* Salzburg: Otto Müller, 1959, pp. 172–173.—Tr.]

References

"Die Sprache," in *Unterwegs zur Sprache* (Pfullingen: Neske, 1959). In this volume's references Heidegger writes: "The lecture was given on October 7, 1950, at Bühlerhöhe in memory of Max Kommerell and was repeated on February 14, 1951 at the Württembergische Bibliotheksgesellschaft in Stuttgart. The lecture, hitherto unpublished, has become known in the form of many transcripts and notes."

Time and Being

The following lecture calls for a few words of introduction. If we were to be shown right now two pictures by Paul Klee, in the original, which he painted in the year of his death—the watercolor "Saints from a Window," and "Death and Fire," tempera on burlap—we should want to stand before them for a long while—and should abandon any claim that they be immediately intelligible.

If it were possible right now to have Georg Trakl's poem "Septet of Death" recited to us, perhaps even by the poet himself, we should want to hear it often, and should abandon any claim that it be immediately intelligible.

If Werner Heisenberg right now were to present some of his thoughts in theoretical physics, moving in the direction of the cosmic formula for which he is searching, two or three people in the audience, at most, would be able to follow him, while the rest of us would, without protest, abandon any claim that he be immediately intelligible.

Not so with the thinking that is called philosophy. That thinking is supposed to offer "worldly wisdom" and perhaps even be a "Way to the Blessed Life." But it might be that this kind of thinking is today placed in a position which demands of it reflections that are far removed from any useful, practical wisdom. It might be that a kind of thinking has become necessary which must give thought to matters from which even the painting and the poetry which we have mentioned and the theory of mathematical physics receive their determination. Here, too, we should then have to abandon any claim to immediate intelligibility. However, we should still have to listen, because we must think what is inevitable, but preliminary.

Therefore, we must be neither surprised nor amazed if the majority of the audience objects to the lecture. Whether a few will, now or later, be prompted by the lecture to think further on such matters, cannot be foreseen. We want to say something about the attempt to think Being without regard to its being grounded in terms of beings. The attempt to think Being without beings becomes necessary because otherwise, it seems to me, there is no longer any possibility of explicitly bringing into view the Being of what *is* today all over the earth, let alone of adequately determining the relation of man to what has been called "Being" up to now.

Let me give a little hint on how to listen. The point is not to listen to a series of propositions, but rather to follow the movement of showing.

What prompts us to name time and Being together? From the dawn of Western-European thinking until today, Being means the same as presencing. Presencing, presence speaks of the present. According to current representations, the present, together with past and future, forms the character of time. Being is determined as presence by time. That this is so could in itself be sufficient to introduce a relentless disquiet into thinking. This disquiet increases as soon as we set out to think through in what respect there is such a determination of Being by time.

In what respect? Why, in what manner and from what source does something like time have a voice in Being? Every attempt to think adequately the relation of Being and time with the help of the current and imprecise representations of time and Being immediately becomes ensnared in a hopeless tangle of relations that have hardly been thought out.

We name time when we say: every thing has its time. This means: everything which actually is, every being comes and goes at the right time and remains for a time during the time allotted to it. Every thing has its time.

But is Being a thing? Is Being like an actual being in time? *Is* Being at all? If it were, then we would incontestably have to recognize it as something which is and consequently discover it as such among other beings. This lecture hall *is*. The lecture hall *is* illuminated. We recognize the illuminated lecture hall at once and with no reservations as something that is. But where in the whole lecture hall do we find the "is"? Nowhere among things do we find Being. Every thing has its time. But Being is not a thing, is not in time. Yet Being as presencing remains determined as presence by time, by what is temporal.

What is in time and is thus determined by time, we call the temporal. When a man dies and is removed from what is here, from beings here and there, we say that his time has come. Time and the temporal mean what is perishable, what passes away in the course of time. Our language says with still greater precision: what passes away with time. For time itself passes away. But by passing away constantly, time remains as time. To remain means: not to disappear, thus, to presence. Thus time is determined by a kind of Being. How, then, is

Being supposed to be determined by time? Being speaks out of the constancy of time's passing away. Nevertheless, nowhere do we find time as something that is like a thing.

Being is not a thing, thus nothing temporal, and yet it is determined by time as presence.

Time is not a thing, thus nothing which is, and yet it remains constant in its passing away without being something temporal like the beings in time.

Being and time determine each other reciprocally, but in such a manner that neither can the former—Being—be addressed as something temporal nor can the latter—time—be addressed as a being. As we give thought to all this, we find ourselves adrift in contradictory statements.

(Philosophy knows a way out of such situations. One allows the contradictions to stand, even sharpens them and tries to bring together in comprehensive unity what contradicts itself and thus falls apart. This procedure is called dialectic. Supposing the contradictory statements about Being and about time could be reconciled by an encompassing unity, this indeed would be a way out—it would be a way out which evades the matters and the issues in question; for it allows itself to become involved neither with Being as such nor with time as such nor with the relation of the two. The question is totally excluded here of whether the relation of Being and time is a connection which can then be brought about by combining the two, or whether Being *and* time name a matter at stake from which both Being and time first result.)

But how can we become properly involved with this matter at stake named by the titles "Being and time," "time and Being"?

Answer: by cautiously thinking over the matters named here. Cautiously means at first: not hastily invading the matters with unexamined notions, but rather reflecting on them carefully.

But may we take Being, may we take time, as matters? They are not matters if "matter" means: something which is. The word "matter," "a matter," should mean for us now what is decisively at stake in that something inevitable is concealed within it. Being—a matter, presumably *the* matter of thinking.

Time—a matter, presumably *the* matter of thinking, if indeed something like time speaks in Being as presence. Being *and* time, time *and* Being, name the relation of both issues, the matter at stake which *holds* both issues toward each other and endures their relation. To reflect upon this situation is the task of thinking, assuming that thinking remains intent on persisting in its matter.

Being—a matter, but not a being.

Time—a matter, but nothing temporal.

We say of beings; they are. With regard to the matter "Being" and with regard to the matter "time," we remain cautious. We do not say: Being is, time is, but rather: there is Being and there is time.[1] For the moment we have only changed the idiom with this expression. Instead of saying "it is," we say "there is," "It gives."

In order to get beyond the idiom and back to the matter, we must show how this "there is" can be experienced and seen. The appropriate way to get there is to explain what is given in the "It gives," what "Being" means, which—It gives; what "time" means, which—It gives. Accordingly, we try to look ahead to the It which—gives Being and time. Thus looking ahead, we become foresighted in still another sense. We try to bring the It and its giving into view, and capitalize the "It. "

First, we shall think Being in order to think It itself into its own element.

Then, we shall think time in order to think it itself into its own element.

In this way, the manner must become clear how there is, It gives Being and how there is, It gives time. In this giving, it becomes apparent how that giving is to be determined which, as a relation, first holds the two toward each other and brings them into being.

Being, by which all beings as such are marked, Being means presencing. Thought with regard to what presences, presencing shows itself as letting-presence. But now we must try to think this letting-presence explicitly insofar as presencing is admitted. Letting shows its character in bringing into unconcealment. To let presence means: to unconceal, to bring to openness. In unconcealing prevails a giving, the giving that gives presencing, that is, Being, in letting-presence.

(To think the matter "Being" explicitly requires our reflection to follow the direction which shows itself in letting-presence. But from unconcealing speaks a giving, an It gives.)

However, the giving named above remains just as obscure for us as the It named here which gives.

To think Being itself explicitly requires disregarding Being to the extent that it is only grounded and interpreted in terms of beings and for beings as their ground, as in all metaphysics. To think Being explicitly requires us to relinquish Being as the ground of beings in favor of the giving which prevails concealed in unconcealment, that is, in favor of the It gives. As the gift of this It gives, Being belongs to giving. As a gift, Being is not expelled from giving. Being, presencing is transmuted. As allowing-to-presence, it belongs to unconcealing; as the gift of unconcealing it is retained in the giving. Being *is* not. There is, It gives Being as the unconcealing; as the gift of unconcealing it is retained in the giving. Being *is* not. There is, It gives Being as the unconcealing of presencing.

This "It gives, there is Being" might emerge somewhat more clearly once we think out more decisively the giving we have in mind here. We can succeed by paying heed to the wealth of the transformation of what, indeterminately enough, is called Being, and at the same time is misunderstood in its core as long as it is taken for the emptiest of all empty concepts. Nor is this representation of Being as the *abstractum* par excellence given up in principle, but only confirmed, when Being as the *abstractum* par excellence is absorbed and elevated into the concreteness par excellence of the reality of the absolute Spirit—as was accomplished in the most powerful thinking of modern times, in Hegel's speculative dialectic, and is presented in his *Science of Logic*.

An attempt to think upon the abundance of Being's transformations secures its first foothold—which also shows the way—when we think Being in the sense of presencing.

(I mean think, not just parrot the words and act as if the interpretation of Being as presencing were a matter of course.)

But what gives us the right to characterize Being as presencing? This question comes too late. For this character of Being has long since been decided without our contribution, let alone our merit. Thus we are bound to the characterization of Being as presencing. It derives its binding force from the beginning of the unconcealment of Being as something that can be said, that is, can be thought. Ever since the beginning of Western thinking with the Greeks, all saying of "Being" and "Is" is held in remembrance of the determination of Being as presencing which is binding for thinking. This also holds true of the thinking that directs the most modern technology and industry, though by now only in a certain sense. Now that modern technology has arranged its expansion and rule over the whole earth, it is not just the sputniks and their by-products that are circling around our planet; it is rather Being as presencing in a sense of calculable material that claims all the inhabitants of the earth in a uniform manner without the inhabitants of the non-European continents explicitly knowing this or even being able or wanting to know of the origin of this determination of Being. (Evidently those who desire such a knowledge least of all are those busy developers who today are urging the so-called underdeveloped countries into the realm of hearing of that claim of Being which speaks from the innermost core of modern technology.)

But we do not by any means perceive Being as presencing exclusively, primarily in the remembrance of the early presentation of the unconcealment of Being accomplished by the Greeks. We perceive presencing in every simple, sufficiently unprejudiced reflection on things of nature (*Vorhandenheit*) and artifacts (*Zuhandenheit*). Things of nature and artifacts are both modes of presencing. The vast reach of presencing shows itself most oppressively when we consider that absence, too, indeed absence most particularly, remains determined by a presencing which at times reaches uncanny proportions.

However, we can also note historically the abundance of transformations of presencing by pointing out that presencing shows itself as the *hen*, the unifying unique One, as the *logos*, the gathering that preserves the All, as *idea*, *ousia*, *energeia*, *substantia*, *actualitas*, *perceptio*, *monad*, as objectivity, as the being posited on self-positing in the sense of the will of reason, of love, of the spirit, of power, as the will to will in the eternal recurrence of the same. Whatever can be noted historically can be found within history. The development of the abundance of transformations of Being looks at first like a history of Being. But

Being does not have a history in the way in which a city or a people have their history. What is history-like in the history of Being is obviously determined by the way in which Being takes place and by this alone. After what has just been explained, this means the way in which It gives Being.

At the beginning of Being's unconcealment, Being, *einai, eon* is thought, but not the "It gives," "there is." Instead, Parmenides says *esti gar einai,* "For Being is."

Years ago, in 1947, in the *Letter on Humanism* (*Wegmarken,* p. 165), I noted with reference to this saying of Parmenides: "The *esti gar einai* of Parmenides is still unthought today." This note would like to point out for once that we must not rashly give to the saying "For Being is" a ready interpretation which makes what is thought in it inaccessible. Anything of which we say "it is" is thereby represented as a being. But Being is not a being. Thus the *esti* that is emphasized in Parmenides' saying cannot represent the Being which it names as some kind of a being. Translated literally, the *esti* thus emphasized does mean "it is." But the emphasis discerns in the *esti* what the Greeks thought even then in the *esti* thus emphasized and which we can paraphrase by: "It is capable." However, the meaning of this capability remained just as unthought, then and afterward, as the "It" which is capable of Being. To be capable of Being means: to yield and give Being. In the *esti* there is concealed the It gives.

In the beginning of Western thinking, Being is thought, but not the "It gives" as such. The latter withdraws in favor of the gift which It gives. That gift is thought and conceptualized from then on exclusively as Being with regard to beings.

A giving which gives only its gift, but in the giving holds itself back and withdraws, such a giving we call sending. According to the meaning of giving which is to be thought in this way, Being—that which It gives—is what is sent. Each of its transformations remains destined in this manner. What is historical in the history of Being is determined by what is sent forth in destining, not by an indeterminately thought up occurrence.

The history of Being means destiny of Being in whose sendings both the sending and the It which sends forth hold back with their self-manifestation. To hold back is, in Greek, *epoche*. Hence we speak of the epochs of the destiny of Being. Epoch does not mean here a span of time in occurrence, but rather the fundamental characteristic of sending, the actual holding-back of itself in favor of the discernibility of the gift, that is, of Being with regard to the grounding of beings. The sequence of epochs in the destiny of Being is not accidental, nor can it be calculated as necessary. Still, what is appropriate shows itself in the destiny, what is appropriate shows itself in the belonging together of the epochs. The epochs overlap each other in their sequence so that the original sending of Being as presence is more and more obscured in different ways.

Only the gradual removal of these obscuring covers—that is what is meant by "dismantling"—procures for thinking a preliminary insight into what then reveals itself as the destiny of Being. Because one everywhere represents the destiny of Being only as history, and history only as a kind of occurrence, one tries in vain to interpret this occurrence in terms of what was said in *Being and Time* about the historicity of man (*Dasein*) (not of Being). By contrast, the only possible way to anticipate the latter thought on the destiny of Being from the perspective of *Being and Time* is to think through what was presented in *Being and Time* about the dismantling of the ontological doctrine of the Being of beings.

When Plato represents Being as *idea* and as the *koinonia* of the Ideas, when Aristotle represents it as *energeia*, Kant as position, Hegel as the absolute concept, Nietzsche as the will to power, these are not doctrines advanced by chance, but rather words of Being as answers to a claim which speaks in the sending concealing itself, in the "there is, It gives, Being." Always retained in the withdrawing sending, Being is unconcealed for thinking with its epochal abundance of transmutations. Thinking remains bound to the tradition of the epochs of the destiny of Being, even when and especially when it recalls in what way and from what source Being itself receives its appropriate determination, from the "there is, It gives Being." The giving showed itself as sending.

But how is the "It" which gives Being to be thought? The opening remark about the combination of "Time and Being" pointed out that Being as presence, as the present in a still undetermined sense, is characterized by a time-character and thus by time. This gives rise to the supposition that the It which gives Being, which determines Being as presencing and allowing-to-presence, might be found in what is called "time" in the title *Time and Being*.

We shall pursue this supposition and think about time. "Time" is familiar to us by way of current representations in the same way as "Being." But it is also unknown in the same way once we propose to explain what is peculiar to time. While we were just now thinking about Being, we found: what is peculiar to Being, that to which Being belongs and in which it remains retained, shows itself in the It gives and its giving as sending. What is peculiar to Being is not anything having the character of Being. When we explicitly think about Being, the matter itself leads us in a certain sense away from Being, and we think the destiny that gives Being as a gift. By noting this fact we are prepared to find that what is peculiar to time also can no longer be determined with the aid of the current characteristics of time as commonly represented. But the combination of time and Being contains the directive to explain time in its peculiarity in the light of what was said of Being. Being means: presencing, letting-be-present: presence. Thus we might read somewhere the notice: "The celebration took place in the presence of many guests." The sentence could be formulated just as well: "with many guests being present."

The present—as soon as we have named it by itself, we are already thinking of the past and the future, the earlier and the later as distinct from the now. But the present understood in terms of the now is not at all identical with the present in the sense in which the guests are present. We never say and we cannot say: "The celebration took place in the now of many guests."

But if we are to characterize time in terms of the present, we understand the present as the now as distinct from the no-longer-now of the past and the not-yet-now of the future. But the present speaks at the same time of presence. However, we are not accustomed to defining the peculiar character of time with regard to the present in the sense of presence. Rather, we represent time—the unity of present, past and future—in terms of the now. Even Aristotle says that that of time which *is*, that is, presence, is the actual now. Past and future are a *me on ti:* something which is not, though not an absolute nullity, but rather something present which lacks something. This lack is named with the "no longer now" and the "not yet now." Viewed in this way, time appears as the succession of nows, each of which, barely named, already disappears into the "ago" and is already being pursued by the "soon." Kant says of time thus represented: "It has only one dimension" (*Critique of Pure Reason,* A31 B47). Time familiar to us as the succession in the sequence of nows is what we mean when measuring and calculating time. It seems that we have calculated time immediately and palpably before us when we pick up a watch or chronometer, look at the hands, and say: "Now it is eight-fifty (o'clock)." We say "now" and mean time. But time cannot be found anywhere in the watch that indicates time, neither on the dial nor in the mechanism, nor can it be found in modern technological chronometers. The assertion forces itself upon us: the more technological—the more exact and informative—the chronometer, the less occasion to give thought first of all to time's peculiar character.

But where is time? *Is* time at all and does it have a place? Obviously, time is not nothing. Accordingly, we maintain caution and say: there is time. We become still more cautious, and look carefully at that which shows itself to us as time, by looking ahead to Being in the sense of presence, the present. However, the present in the sense of presence differs so vastly from the present in the sense of the now that the present as presence can in no way be determined in terms of the present as the now. The reverse would rather seem possible. (Cf. *Being and Time,* section 81.) If such were the case, the present as presence and everything which belongs to such a present would have to be called real time, even though there is nothing immediately about it of time as time is usually represented in the sense of a succession of a calculable sequence of nows.

But we have so far omitted showing more clearly what the present in the sense of presence means. Presence determines Being in a unified way as presencing and allowing-to-presence, that is, as unconcealing. What matter are we thinking when we say presencing?

To presence means to last. But we are too quickly content to conceive lasting as mere duration, and to conceive duration in terms of the customary representation of time as a span of time from one now to a subsequent now. To talk of presencing, however, requires that we perceive biding and abiding in lasting as lasting in present being. What is present concerns us, the present, that is: what, lasting, comes toward us, us human beings.

Who are we? We remain cautious in our answer. For it might be that that which distinguishes man as man is determined precisely by what we must think about here: man, who is concerned with and approached by presence, who, through being thus approached, is himself present in his own way for all present and absent beings.

Man: standing within the approach of presence, but in such a way that he receives as a gift the presencing that It gives by perceiving what appears in letting-presence. If man were not the constant receiver of the gift given by the "It gives presence," if that which is extended in the gift did not reach man, then not only would Being remain concealed in the absence of this gift, not only closed off, but man would remain excluded from the scope of: It gives Being. Man would not be man.

Now it looks as if the reference to man had led us astray from the way upon which we would like to think about what is peculiar to time. In a way this is so. Yet we are closer than we believe to the matter which is called time and which is to show itself explicitly in the light of the present as presence.

Presence means: the constant abiding that approaches man, reaches him, is extended to him. But what is the source of this extending reach to which the present belongs as presencing, insofar as there is presence? True, man always remains approached by the presencing of something actually present without explicitly heeding presencing itself. But we have to do with absence just as often, that is, constantly. For one thing, there is much that is no longer present in the way we know presencing in the sense of the present. And yet, even that which is no longer present presences immediately in its absence—in the manner of what has been, and still concerns us. What has been does not just vanish from the previous now as does that which is merely past. Rather, what has been presences, but in its own way. In what has been, presencing is extended.

But absence also concerns us in the sense of what is not yet present in the manner of presencing in the sense of coming toward us. To talk of what is coming toward us has meanwhile become a cliché. Thus we hear: "the future has already begun," which is not so, because the future never just begins since absence, as the presencing of what is not yet present, always in some way already concerns us, is present no less immediately than what has been. In the future, in what comes toward us, presencing is offered.

If we heed still more carefully what has been said, we shall find in absence—be it what has been or what is to come—a manner of presencing and approaching which by no means coincides with presencing in the sense of the immediate present. Accordingly, we must note: Not every presencing is necessarily the present. A curious matter. But we find such presencing, the approaching that reaches us, in the present, too. In the present, too, presencing is given.

How are we to determine this giving of presencing that prevails in the present, in the past, in the future? Does this giving lie in this, that it reaches us, or does it reach us because it is in itself a reaching? The latter. Approaching, being not yet present, at the same time gives and brings about what is no longer present, the past, and conversely what has been offers future to itself. The reciprocal relation of both at the same time gives and brings about the present. We say "at the same time," and thus ascribe a time character to the mutual giving to one another of future, past and present, that is, to their own unity.

This procedure is obviously not in keeping with the matter, assuming that we must give the name "time" to the unity of reaching out and giving which we have now shown, to this unity alone. For time itself is nothing temporal, no more than it is something that is. It is thus inadmissible to say that future, past and present are before us "at the same time." Yet they belong together in the way they offer themselves to one another. Their unifying unity can be determined only by what is their own; that they offer themselves to one another. But what do they offer to one another?

Nothing other than themselves—which means: the presencing that is given in them. With this presencing, there opens up what we call time-space. But with the word "time" we no longer mean the succession of a sequence of nows. Accordingly, time-space no longer means merely the distance between two now-points of calculated time, such as we have in mind when we note, for instance: this or that occurred within a time-span of fifty years. Time-space now is the name for the openness which opens up in the mutual self-extending of futural approach, past and present. This openness exclusively and primarily provides the space in which space as we usually know it can unfold. The self-extending, the opening up, of future, past and present is itself prespatial; only thus can it make room, that is, provide space.

Time-space as commonly understood, in the sense of the distance measured between two time-points, is the result of time calculation. In this calculation, time represented as a line and parameter and thus one-dimensional is measured out in terms of numbers. The dimensionality of time, thought as the succession of the sequence of nows, is borrowed from the representation of three-dimensional space.

But prior to all calculation of time and independent of such calculation, what is germane to the time-space of true time consists in the mutual reaching out and opening up of future, past and present. Accordingly, what we call dimension and dimensionality in a way easily misconstrued, belongs to true time and to it alone. Dimensionality consists in a reaching out that opens up, in which futural approaching brings about what has been, what has been brings about futural approaching, and the reciprocal relation of both brings about the opening up of openness. Thought in terms of this threefold giving, true time proves to be three-dimensional. Dimension, we repeat, is here thought not only as the area of possible measurement, but rather as reaching throughout, as giving and opening up. Only the latter enables us to represent and delimit an area of measurement.

But from what source is the unity of the three dimensions of true time determined, the unity, that is, of its three interplaying ways of giving, each in virtue of its own presencing? We already heard: In the approaching of what is no longer present and even in the present itself, there always plays a kind of approach and bringing about, that is, a kind of presencing. We cannot attribute the presencing to be thus thought to one of the three dimensions of time, to the present, which would seem obvious. Rather, the unity of time's three dimensions consists in the interplay of each toward each. This interplay proves to be the true extending, playing in the very heart of time, the fourth dimension, so to speak—not only so to speak, but in the nature of the matter.

True time is four-dimensional.

But the dimension which we call the fourth in our count is, in the nature of the matter, the first, that is, the giving that determines all. In future, in past, in the present, that giving brings about to each its own presencing, holds them apart thus opened and so holds them toward one another in the nearness by which the three dimensions remain near one another. For this reason we call the first, original, literally incipient extending in which the unity of true time consists "nearing nearness," "nearhood" (*Nahheit*), an early word still used by Kant. But it brings future, past and present near to one another by distancing them. For it keeps what has been open by denying its advent as present. This nearing of nearness keeps open the approach coming from the future by withholding the present in the approach. Nearing nearness has the character of denial and withholding. It unifies in advance the ways in which what has-been, what is about to be, and the present reach out toward each other.

Time *is* not. There is, It gives time. The giving that gives time is determined by denying and withholding nearness. It grants the openness of time-space and preserves what remains denied in what has-been, what is withheld in approach. We call the giving which gives true time an extending which opens and conceals. As extending is itself a giving, the giving of a giving is concealed in true time.

But where *is* there time and time-space, where are they given? As urgent as this question may be at first sight, we may no longer ask in this manner for a where, for the place for time. For true time itself, the realm of its threefold extending determined by nearing nearness, is the prespatial region which first gives any possible "where."

True, from its beginning, whenever it thought about time, philosophy also asked where time belongs. What philosophy primarily had in view was time calculated as a sequence of the succession of consecutive nows. It was explained that there could be no numerically measured time with which we calculate without the *psyche*, without the *animus*, without the soul, without consciousness, without spirit. There is no time without man. But what does this "not without" mean? Is man the giver or the receiver of time? Is man first of all man, and then after that occasionally—that is, at some time or other—receives time and relates himself to it? True time is the nearness of presencing out of present, past and future—the nearness that unifies time's threefold opening extending. It has already reached man as such so that he can be man only by standing within the threefold extending, perduring the denying, and withholding nearness which determines that extending. Time is not the product of man, man is not the product of time. There is no production here. There is only giving in the sense of extending which opens up time-space.

But granted that the manner of giving in which time is given requires our characterization of time, we are still faced with the enigmatic It which we named in the expression: It gives time; It gives Being. There is a growing danger that when we speak of "It," we arbitrarily posit an indeterminate power which is supposed to bring about all giving of Being and of time. However, we shall escape indeterminancy and avoid arbitrariness as long as we hold fast to the determinations of giving which we attempted to show, if only we look ahead toward Being as presence and toward time as the realm where, by virtue of offering, a manifold presencing takes place and opens up. The giving in "It gives Being" proved to be a sending and a destiny of presence in its epochal transmutations.

The giving in "It gives time" proved to be an extending, opening up the four-dimensional realm.

Insofar as there is manifest in Being as presence such a thing as time, the supposition mentioned earlier grows stronger that true time, the fourfold extending of the open, could be discovered as the "It" that gives Being, i.e., gives presence. The supposition appears to be fully confirmed when we note that absence, too, manifests itself as a mode of presence. What has-been which, by refusing the present, lets that become present which is no longer present; and the coming toward us of what is to come which, by withholding the present, lets that be present which is not yet present—both made manifest the manner of an extending opening up which gives all presencing into the open.

Thus true time appears as the "It" of which we speak when we say: It gives Being. The destiny in which It gives Being lies in the extending of time. Does this reference show time to be the "It" that gives Being? By no means. For time itself remains the gift of an "It gives" whose giving preserves the realm in which presence is extended. Thus the "It" continues to be undetermined, and we ourselves continue to be puzzled. In such cases it is advisable to determine the It which gives in terms of the giving that we have already described. This giving proved to be the sending of Being, as time in the sense of an opening up which extends.

(Or are we puzzled now only because we have allowed ourselves to be led astray by language or, more precisely, by the grammatical interpretation of language; staring at an It that is supposed to give, but that itself is precisely not there. When we say "It gives Being," "It gives time," we are speaking sentences. Grammatically, a sentence consists of a subject and a predicate. The subject of a sentence is not necessarily a subject in the sense of an ego or a person. Grammar and logic, accordingly, construe it-sentences as impersonal, subject-less sentences. In other Indo-Germanic languages, in Greek and Latin, the It is lacking, at least as a separate word and phonetic form; but that does not mean that what is meant by the It is not also in their thought: in Latin, *pluit,* it is raining; in Greek, *chre,* it is needful.

But what does this "It" mean? Philologists and philosophers of language have given the matter much thought without arriving at any valid clarification. The area of meaning meant by the It extends from the irrelevant to the demonic. The "It" of which we speak when we say "It gives Being," "It gives time," presumably indicates something distinctive which we shall not discuss here. We shall be content, therefore, with a fundamental consideration.

Interpreted by the rules of grammar and logic, that about which a statement is made appears as the subject: *hypokeimenon*—that which already lies before us, which is present in some way. What is then predicated of the subject appears as what is already present along with the present subject, the *symbebekos, accidens:* "The auditorium is illuminated." In the "It" of "It gives" speaks a presence of something that is present, that is, there speaks, in a way, a Being. If we substitute Being for It in our sentence "It gives Being," it says as much as "Being gives Being." And here we are back in the same difficulty that we mentioned at the beginning of the lecture: Being is. But Being "is" just as little as time "is." We shall therefore now abandon the attempt to determine "It" by itself, in isolation, so to speak. But this we must keep in mind: The It, at least in the interpretation available to us for the moment, names a presence of absence.

When we say "It gives Being," "It gives time," we are not making statements about beings. However, the syntax of sentences as we have it from the Greek and Roman grammarians has such statements exclusively in view. In view of this fact we must also consider the possibility that, contrary to all appearances, in saying "It gives Being." "It gives time," we are not dealing with statements that are always fixed in the sentence structure of the subject-predicate relation. And yet, how else are we to bring the "It" into view which we say when we say "It gives Being," "It gives time"? Simply by thinking the "It" in the light of the kind of giving that belongs to it: giving as destiny, giving as an opening up which reaches out. Both belong together, inasmuch as the former, destiny, lies in the latter, extending opening up.

In the sending of the destiny of Being, in the extending of time, there becomes manifest a dedication, a delivering over into what is their own, namely of Being as presence and of time as the realm of the open. What determines both, time and Being, in their own, that is, in their belonging together, we shall call: *Ereignis,* the event of Appropriation. *Ereignis* will be translated as Appropriation or event of Appropriation. One should bear in mind, however, that "event" is not simply an occurrence, but that which makes any occurrence possible. What this word names can be thought now only in the light of what becomes manifest in our looking ahead toward Being and toward time as destiny and as extending, to which time and Being belong. We have called both—Being and time—"matters." The "and" between them left their relation to each other indeterminate.

We now see: What lets the two matters belong together, what brings the two into their own and, even more, maintains and holds them in their belonging together—the way the two matters stand, the matter at stake—is Appropriation. The matter at stake is not a relation retroactively superimposed on Being and time. The matter at stake first appropriates Being and time into their own in virtue of their relation, and does so by the appropriating that is concealed in destiny and in the gift of opening out. Accordingly, the It that gives in "It gives Being," "It gives time," proves to be Appropriation. The statement is correct and yet also untrue: it conceals the matter at stake from us; for, unawares, we have represented it as some present being, whereas in fact we are trying to think presence as such. But could it not be that we might suddenly be relieved of all the difficulties, all these complicated and seemingly fruitless discussions, by raising and answering this simple and long-overdue question: What is the event of appropriation?

At this point we must be permitted an interim question: What is meant here by "answering," by "answer"? Answer means the Saying that co-responds to the matter at stake which we must think here, to Appropriation. But if the matter at stake prohibits our speaking of it by way of a statement, then we must give up the declaratory sentence that is anticipated by the question we have raised. But to do so means to admit our inability to think fittingly what has to be thought here. Or would it be more advisable to give up not just the answer, but even the question? How about this convincingly justified and candidly posed question: What is Appropriation? The question asks for whatness, for the essence, it asks how Appropriation becomes present, how it presences.

Our seemingly innocent question, What is Appropriation? demands information about the Being of Appropriation. But if Being itself proves to be such that it belongs to Appropriation and from there receives its determination as presence, then the question we have advanced takes us back to what first of all demands its own determination: Being in terms of time. This determination showed itself as we looked ahead to the "It" that gives, looked through the interjoined modes of giving: sending and extending. Sending of Being lies in the extending, opening and concealing of manifold presence into the open realm of time-space. Extending, however, lies in one and the same with sending, in Appropriating. This, that is, the peculiar property of Appropriation, determines also the sense of what is here called "lying."

What we have said now allows and in a way even compels us to say how Appropriation must *not* be thought. What the name "event of Appropriation" names can no longer be represented by means of the current meaning of the word; for in that meaning "event of Appropriation" is understood in the sense of occurrence and happening—not in terms of Appropriating as the extending and sending which opens and preserves.

Thus, we heard it proclaimed recently that the agreement reached within the European economic community was a European event of world-historic significance. Now, if the word "event" is heard in the context of a discussion of Being, and if we take the word only in its current meaning, it becomes almost inevitable to speak of the event of Being. For without Being, no being is capable of being as such. Accordingly, Being can be proffered as the highest, most significant event of all.

However, the sole purpose of this lecture was to bring before our eyes Being itself as the event of Appropriation. But what the word "Appropriation" denotes says something altogether different. The inconspicuous word "as," always treacherous because of its several meanings, must also be thought accordingly. Even assuming that in our discussion of Being and time we abandon the common meaning of the word "event" and instead adopt the sense that suggests itself in the sending of presence and the extending of time-space which opens out—even then our talk about "Being as Appropriation" remains indeterminate.

"Being as the event of Appropriation": Formerly, philosophy thought Being in terms of beings as *idea, energeia, actualitas,* will—and now, one might think, as Appropriation. Understood in this way, "Appropriation" means a transformed interpretation of Being which, if it is correct, represents a continuation of metaphysics. In this case, the "as" signifies: Appropriation as a species of Being, subordinated to Being which represents the leading concept that is retained. But if we do what was attempted, and think Being in the sense of the presencing and allowing-to-presence that are there in destiny—which in turn lies in the extending of true time which opens and conceals—then Being belongs into Appropriating. Giving and its gift receive their determination from Appropriating. In that case, Being would be a species of Appropriation, and not the other way around.

To take refuge in such an inversion would be too cheap. Such thinking misses the matter at stake. Appropriation is not the encompassing general concept under which Being and time could be subsumed. Logical classifications mean nothing here. For as we think Being itself and follow what is its own, Being proves to be destiny's gift of presence, the gift granted by the giving of time. The gift of presence is the property of Appropriating. Being vanishes in Appropriation. In the phrase "Being as Appropriation," the word "as" now means: Being, letting-presence sent in Appropriating, time extended in Appropriating. Time and Being appropriated in Appropriation. And Appropriation itself? Can we say anything more about it?

Along the way, we have already thought more about it, although it was not explicitly said: namely, that to giving as sending there belongs keeping back—

such that the denial of the present and the withholding of the present, play within the giving of what has been and what will be. What we have mentioned just now—keeping back, denial, withholding—shows something like a self-withdrawing, something we might call for short: withdrawal. But inasmuch as the modes of giving that are determined by withdrawal—sending and extending—lie in Appropriation, withdrawal must belong to what is peculiar to the Appropriation. This, however, no longer belongs to the matter of this lecture.

(Briefly, and inadequately as is the way of a lecture, we would here point out what is peculiar to Appropriation.

(The sending in the destiny of Being has been characterized as a giving in which the sending source keeps itself back and, thus, withdraws from unconcealment.

(In true time and its time-space, the giving of what has-been, that is, of what is no longer present, the denial of the present manifested itself. In the giving of future, that is, of what is not yet present, the withholding of the present manifested itself. Denial and withholding exhibit the same trait as self-withholding in sending: namely, self-withdrawal.

(Insofar as the destiny of Being lies in the extending of time, and time, together with Being, lies in Appropriation, Appropriating makes manifest its peculiar property, that Appropriation withdraws what is most fully its own from boundless unconcealment. Thought in terms of Appropriating, this means: in that sense it expropriates itself of itself. Expropriation belongs to Appropriation as such. By this expropriation, Appropriation does not abandon itself—rather, it preserves what is its own.

(We catch sight of the other peculiar property in Appropriation as soon as we think clearly enough what has already been said. In Being as presence, there is manifest the concern which concerns us humans in such a way that in perceiving and receiving it we have attained the distinction of human being. Accepting the concern of presence, however, lies in standing within the realm of giving. In this way, four-dimensional true time has reached us.

(Because Being and time are there only in Appropriating, Appropriating has the peculiar property of bringing man into his own as the being who perceives Being by standing within true time. Thus Appropriated, man belongs to Appropriation.

(This belonging lies in the assimilation that distinguishes Appropriation. By virtue of this assimilation, man is admitted to the Appropriation. This is why we can never place Appropriation in front of us, neither as something opposite us nor as something all-encompassing. This is why thinking which represents and gives account corresponds to Appropriation as little as does the saying that merely states.)

Since time as well as Being can only be thought from Appropriation as the gifts of Appropriation, the relation of space to Appropriation must also be considered in an analogous way. We can admittedly succeed in this only when we have previously gained insight into the origin of space in the properties peculiar to site and have thought them adequately. (Cf. "Building Dwelling Thinking" in *Poetry, Language, Thought,* translated by Albert Hofstadter, Harper & Row 1971.) The attempt in *Being and Time,* section 70, to derive human spatiality from temporality is untenable.

True, as we look through Being itself, through time itself, and look into the destiny of Being and the extending of time-space, we have glimpsed what "Appropriation" means. But do we by this road arrive at anything else than a mere thought-construct? Behind this suspicion there lurks the view that appropriation must after all "be" something. However: Appropriation neither *is,* nor *is* Appropriation *there.* To say the one or to say the other is equally a distortion of the matter, just as if we wanted to derive the source from the river.

What remains to be said? Only this: Appropriation appropriates. Saying this, we say the Same in terms of the Same about the Same. To all appearances, all this says nothing. It does indeed say nothing so long as we hear a mere sentence in what was said, and expose that sentence to the cross-examination of logic. But what if we take what was said and adopt it unceasingly as the guide for our thinking, and consider that this Same is not even anything new, but the oldest of the old in Western thought: that ancient something which conceals itself in *a-letheia?* That which is said before all else by this first source of all the *leitmotifs* of thinking gives voice to a bond that binds all thinking, providing that thinking submits to the call of what must be thought.

The task or our thinking has been to trace Being to its own from Appropriation—by way of looking through true time without regard to the relation of Being to beings.

To think Being without beings means: to think Being without regard to metaphysics. Yet a regard for metaphysics still prevails even in the intention to overcome metaphysics. Therefore, our task is to cease all overcoming, and leave metaphysics to itself.

If overcoming remains necessary, it concerns that thinking that explicitly enters Appropriation in order to say It in terms of It about It.

Our task is unceasingly to overcome the obstacles that tend to render such saying inadequate.

The saying of Appropriation in the form of a lecture remains itself an obstacle of this kind. The lecture has spoken merely in propositional statements.

Notes

1. "There is" is used here to translate the German idiom "*es gibt,*" literally "it gives," but with the idiomatic meaning "there is" as in the French "*il y a.*" In his *Letter on Humanism,* commenting on the use of the idiom "there is," and in *Being and*

Time, Heidegger writes: "The 'it' which here 'gives' is Being itself. The 'gives,' however, indicates the giving nature of Being granting its truth." —Tr.

References

The lecture "Time and Being" was given on January 31, 1962 at the Studium Generale, University of Freiburg im Br, directed by Eugen Fink. In the structure of the treatise *Being and Time* (1927), the title "Time and Being" characterizes the third section of the first part of the treatise. The author was at the time not capable of a sufficient development of the theme designated in the title "Time and Being." The publication of *Being and Time* was interrupted at that point.

What this text contains, written three and a half decades later, can no longer be a continuation of the text of *Being and Time*. The leading question has indeed remained the same, but this simply means: the question has become still more questionable and still more alien to the spirit of the times. (The sections in parentheses in the text were written at the same time as the text of the lecture, but were not read.)

The first printing of the German text, together with a French translation by François Fedier, appeared in the *Festschrift* for Jean Beaufret which was issued under the title *L'Endurance de la Pensée* (Endurance of Thinking) 1968 by the publisher Plon, Paris.

PART TWO

Maurice Merleau-Ponty

The 'Sensation' as a Unit of Experience

At the outset of the study of perception, we find in language the notion of sensation, which seems immediate and obvious: I have a sensation of redness, of blueness, of hot or cold. It will, however, be seen that nothing could in fact be more confused, and that because they accepted it readily, traditional analyses missed the phenomenon of perception.

I might in the first place understand by sensation the way in which I am affected and the experiencing of a state of myself. The greyness which, when I close my eyes, surrounds me, leaving no distance between me and it, the sounds that encroach on my drowsiness and hum 'in my head' perhaps give some indication of what pure sensation might be. I might be said to have sense-experience (*sentir*) precisely to the extent that I coincide with the sensed, that the latter ceases to have any place in the objective world, and that it signifies nothing for me. This entails recognizing that sensation should be sought on the hither side of any qualified content, since red and blue, in order to be distinguishable as two colours, must already form some picture before me, even though no precise place be assigned to them, and thus cease to be part of myself. Pure sensation will be the experience of an undifferentiated, instantaneous, dotlike impact. It is unnecessary to show, since authors are agreed on it, that this notion corresponds to nothing in our experience, and that the most rudimentary *factual perceptions* that we are acquainted with, in creatures such as the ape or the hen, have a bearing on relationships and not on any absolute terms.[1] But this does not dispose of the question as to why we feel justified *in theory* in distinguishing within experience a layer of 'impressions'. Let us imagine a white patch on a homogeneous background. All the points in the patch have a certain 'function' in common, that of forming themselves into a 'shape'. The colour of the shape is more intense, and as it were more resistant than that of the background; the edges of the white patch 'belong' to it, and are not part of the background although they adjoin it: the patch appears to be placed on the background and does not break it up. Each part arouses the expectation of more than it contains, and this elementary perception is therefore already charged with a *meaning*. But if the shape and the background, as a whole, are not sensed, they must be sensed, one may object, in each of their points. To say this is to forget that each point in its turn can be perceived only as a figure on a background. When Gestalt theory informs us that a figure on a background is the simplest sense-given available to us, we reply that this is not a contingent characteristic of factual perception, which leaves us free, in an ideal analysis, to bring in the notion of impressions. It is the very definition of the phenomenon of perception, that without which a phenomenon cannot be said to be perception at all. The perceptual 'something' is always in the middle of something else, it always forms part of a 'field'. A really homogeneous area offering *nothing to be* cannot be given to *any perception*. The structure of actual perception alone can teach us what perception is. The pure impression is, therefore, not only undiscoverable, but also imperceptible and so inconceivable as an instant of perception. If it is introduced, it is because instead of attending to the experience of perception, we overlook it in favour of the object perceived. A visual field is not made up of limited views. But an object seen is made up of bits of matter, and spatial points are external to each other. An isolated datum of perception is inconceivable, at least if we do the mental experiment of attempting to perceive such a thing. But in the world there are either isolated objects or a physical void.

I shall therefore give up any attempt to define sensation as pure impression. Rather, to see is to have colours or lights, to hear is to have sounds, to sense (*sentir*) is to have qualities. To know what sense-experience is, then, is it not enough to have seen a red or to have heard an A? But red and green are not sensations, they are the sensed (*sensibles*), and quality is not an element of consciousness, but a property of the object. Instead of providing a simple means of delimiting sensations, if we consider it in the experience itself which evinces it, the quality is as rich and mysterious as the object, or indeed the whole spectacle, perceived. This red patch which I see on the carpet is red only in virtue of a shadow which lies across it, its quality is apparent only in relation to the play of light upon it, and hence as an element in a spatial configuration. Moreover the colour can be said to be there only if it occupies an area of a certain size, too small an area not being describable in these terms. Finally this red would literally not be the same if it were not the 'woolly red' of a carpet.[2] Analysis, then, discovers in each quality meanings which reside in it. It may be objected that this is true only of the qualities which form part of our actual experience, which are overlaid with a body of knowledge, and that we are still justified in conceiving a 'pure quality' which would set limits to a pure sensation. But as we have just seen, this pure sensation would amount to no sensation, and thus to not feeling at all. The alleged self-evidence of sensation is not based on any testimony of consciousness, but on widely held prejudice. We think we know perfectly well what 'seeing', 'hearing', 'sensing' are, because perception has long provided us with objects which are coloured or which emit sounds. When we try to analyse it, we transpose these objects into consciousness. We commit what psychologists call 'the experience error', which means that what we know to be in things themselves we immediately take as being in our consciousness of them. We make perception out of things perceived. And since perceived things themselves are obviously accessible only through perception, we end by understanding neither. We are caught up in the world and we do not succeed in extricating ourselves from it in order to achieve consciousness of the world. If we did we should see that the quality is never experienced immediately, and that all consciousness is consciousness of something. Nor is this 'something' necessarily an identifiable object. There are two ways of being mistaken about quality: one is to make it into an element of consciousness, when in fact it is an object *for* consciousness, to treat it as an incommunicable impression, whereas it always has a meaning; the other is to think that this meaning and this object, at the level of quality, are fully developed and determinate. The second error, like the first, springs from our prejudice about the world. Suppose we construct, by the use of optics and geometry, that bit of the world which can at any moment throw its image on our retina. Everything outside its perimeter, since it does not reflect upon any sensitive area, no more affects our vision than does light falling on our closed eyes. We ought, then, to perceive a segment of the world precisely delimited, surrounded by a zone of blackness, packed full of qualities with no interval between them, held together by definite relationships of size similar to those lying on the retina. The fact is that experience offers nothing like this, and we shall never, using the world as our starting-point, understand what a *field of vision* is. Even if it is possible to trace out a perimeter of vision by gradually approaching the centre of the lateral stimuli, the results of such measurement vary from one moment to another, and one never manages to determine the instant when a stimulus once seen is seen no longer. The region surrounding the visual field is not easy to describe, but what is certain is that it is neither black nor grey. There occurs here an *indeterminate vision, a vision of something or other,* and, to take the extreme case, what is behind my back is not without some element of visual presence. The two straight lines in Müller-Lyer's optical illusion (Fig. 1) are neither of equal nor unequal length; it is only in the objective world that this question arises.[3] The visual field is that strange zone in which contradictory notions jostle each other because the objects—the straight lines of Müller-Lyer—are not, in that field, assigned to the realm of being, in which a comparison would be possible, but each is taken in its private context as if it did not belong to the same universe as the other. Psychologists have for a long time taken great care to overlook these phenomena. In the world taken in itself everything is determined. There are many unclear sights, as for example a landscape on a misty day, but then we always say that no real landscape is in itself unclear. It is so only for us. The object, psychologists would assert, is never ambiguous, but becomes so only through our inattention. The bounds of the visual field are not themselves variable, and there is a moment when the approaching object begins absolutely to be seen, but we do not 'notice' it. But the notion of attention, as we shall show more fully, is supported by no evidence provided by consciousness. It is no more than an auxiliary hypothesis, evolved to save the prejudice in favour of an objective world. We must recognize the indeterminate as a positive phenomenon. It is in this atmosphere that quality arises. Its meaning is an equivocal meaning; we are concerned with an expressive value rather than with logical signification. The determinate quality by which empiricism tried to define sensation is an object, not an element, of consciousness, indeed it is the very lately developed object of scientific consciousness. For these two reasons, it conceals rather that reveals subjectivity.

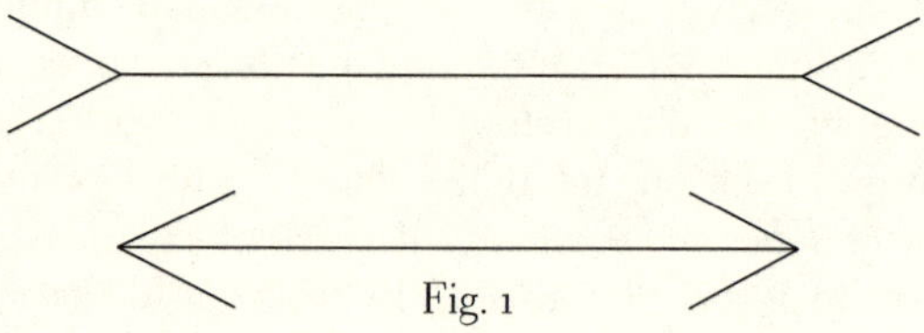

Fig. 1

The two definitions of sensation which we have just tried out were only apparently direct. We have seen that they were based on the object perceived. In this they were in agreement with common sense, which also identifies the sensible by the objective conditions which govern it. The visible is what is seized upon *with* the eyes, the sensible is what is seized on *by* the senses. Let us follow up the idea of sensation on this basis,[4] and see what becomes of this 'by' and this 'with', and the notion of sense-organ, in the first-order thinking constituted by science. Having shown that there is no experience of sensation, do we at least find, in its causes and objective origins, any reason for retaining it as an explanatory concept? Physiology, to which the psychologist turns as to a higher court of appeal, is in the same predicament as psychology. It too first situates its object in the world and treats it as a bit of extension. *Behaviour* is thus hidden by the reflex, the elaboration and patterning of stimuli, by a longitudinal theory of nervous functioning, which establishes a theoretical correspondence between each element of the situation and an element of the reaction.[5] As in the case of the reflex arc theory, physiology of perception begins by recognizing an anatomical path leading from a *receiver* through a definite *transmitter* to a recording station,[6] equally specialized. The objective world being given, it is assumed that it passes on to the sense-organs messages which must be registered, then deciphered in such a way as to reproduce in us the original text. Hence we have in principle a point-by-point correspondence and constant connection between the stimulus and the elementary perception. But this 'constancy hypothesis'[7] conflicts with the data of consciousness, and the very psychologists who accept it recognize its purely theoretical character.[8] For example, the intensity of a sound under certain circumstances lowers its pitch; the addition of auxiliary lines makes two figures unequal which are objectively equal;[9] a coloured area appears to be the same colour over the whole of its surface, whereas the chromatic thresholds of the different parts of the retina ought to make it red in one place, orange somewhere else, and in certain cases colourless.[10] Should these cases in which the phenomenon does not correspond to the stimulus be retained within the framework of the law of constancy, and explained by additional factors—attention and judgement—or must the law itself be jettisoned? When red and green, presented together, give the result grey, it is conceded that the central combination of stimuli can immediately give rise to a different sensation from what the objective stimuli would lead us to expect. When the apparent size of an object varies with its apparent distance, or its apparent colour with our recollections of the object, it is recognized that 'the sensory processes are not immune to central influences'.[11] In this case, therefore, the 'sensible' cannot be defined as the immediate effect of an external stimulus. Cannot the same conclusion be drawn from the first three examples we have mentioned? If attention, more precise instructions, rest or prolonged practice finally bring perception into line with the law of constancy, this does not prove the law's universal validity, for, in the examples quoted, the first appearance possessed a sensory character just as incontestable as the final results obtained. So the question is whether attentive perception, the subject's concentration on one point of the visual field—for example, the 'analytic perception' of the two main lines in Müller-Lyer's optical illusion—do not, instead of revealing the 'normal sensation', substitute a special set-up for the original phenomenon.[12] The law of constancy cannot avail itself, against the testimony of consciousness, of any crucial experiment in which it is not already implied, and wherever we believe that we are establishing it, it is already presupposed.[13] If we turn back to the phenomena, they show us that the apprehension of a quality, just as that of size, is bound up with a whole perceptual context, and that the stimuli no longer furnish us with the indirect means we were seeking of isolating a layer of immediate impressions. But when we look for an 'objective' definition of sensation, it is not only the physical stimulus which slips through our fingers. The sensory apparatus, as conceived by modern physiology, is no longer fitted for the rôle of 'transmitter' cast for it by traditional science. Non-cortical lesions of the apparatus of touch no doubt lessen the concentration of points sensitive to heat and cold, or pressure, and diminish the sensitivity of those that remain. But if, to the injured system, a sufficiently extensive stimulus be applied, the specific sensations reappear. The raising of the thresholds is compensated by a more vigorous movement of the hand.[14]

One can discern, at the rudimentary stage of sensibility, a working together on the part of partial stimuli and a collaboration of the sensory with the motor system which, in a variable physiological constellation, keeps sensation constant, and rules out any definition of the nervous process as the simple transmission of a given message. The destruction of sight, wherever the injuries be sustained, follows the same law: all colours are affected in the first place,[15] and lose their saturation. Then the spectrum is simplified, being reduced to four and soon to two colours; finally a grey monochrome stage is reached, although the pathological colour is never identifiable with any normal one. Thus in central as in peripheral lesions 'the loss of nervous substance results not only in a deficiency of certain qualities, but in the change to a less differentiated and more primitive structure'.[16] Conversely, normal functioning must be understood as a process of integration in which the text of the external world is not so much copied, as composed. And if we try to seize 'sensation' within the perspective of the bodily phenomena which pave the way to it, we find not a psychic individual, a function of certain known variables, but a formation already bound up with a larger whole, already endowed with a meaning, distinguishable only in degree from the more complex perceptions, and which therefore gets us no further in our attempt to delimit pure sensation. There is no physiological definition of sensation, and more generally there is no physiological psychology which is autonomous, because the physiological event itself obeys biological and psychological laws. For a long time it was thought that peripheral conditioning was the surest method of identifying 'elementary' psychic functions, and of distinguishing them from 'superior' functions less strictly bound up with the bodily substructure. A closer analysis, however, reveals that the two kinds of function overlap. The elementary is no longer that which by addition will cumulatively constitute the whole, nor is it a mere occasion for the whole to constitute itself. The elementary event is already invested with meaning, and the higher function will bring into being only a more integrated mode of existence or a more valid adaptation, by using and sublimating the subordinate operations. Conversely, 'sense-experience is a vital process, no less than procreation, breathing or growth'.[17] Psychology and physiology are no longer, then, two parallel sciences, but two accounts of behaviour, the first concrete, the second abstract.[18] We said that when the psychologist asks the physiologist for a definition of sensation 'in causal terms', he encounters once more on this new ground his familiar difficulties, and now we can see why. The physiologist for his part has to rid himself of the realistic prejudice which all the sciences borrow from common sense, and which hampers them in their development. The changed meaning of the terms 'elementary' and 'more advanced' in modern physiology proclaims a changed philosophy.[19] The scientist too must learn to criticize the idea of an external world in itself, since the facts themselves prompt him to abandon that of the body as a transmitter of messages. The sensible is what is apprehended *with* the senses, but now we know that this 'with' is not merely instrumental, that the sensory apparatus is not a conductor, that even on the periphery the physiological impression is involved in relations formerly considered central.

Once more, reflection—even the second-order reflection of science—obscures what we thought was clear. We believed we knew what feeling, seeing and hearing were, and now these words raise problems. We are invited to go back to the experiences to which they refer in order to redefine them. The traditional notion of sensation was not a concept born of reflection, but a late product of thought directed towards objects, the last element in the representation of the world, the furthest removed from its original source, and therefore the most unclear. Inevitably science, in its general effort towards objectification, evolved a picture of the human organism as a physical system undergoing stimuli which were themselves identified by their physico-chemical properties, and tried to reconstitute actual perception[20] on this basis, and to close the circle of scientific knowledge by discovering the laws governing the production of knowledge itself, by establishing an objective science of subjectivity.[21] But it is also inevitable that this attempt should fail. If we return to the objective investigations themselves, we first of all discover that the conditions external to the sensory field do not govern it part for part, and that they exert an effect only to the extent of making possible a basic pattern—which is what Gestalt theory makes clear. Then we see that within the organism the structure depends on variables such as the biological meaning of the situation, which are no longer physical variables, with the result that the whole eludes the well-known instruments of physico-mathematical analysis, and opens the way to another type of intelligibility.[22] If we now turn back, as is done here, towards perceptual experience, we notice that science succeeds in constructing only a semblance of subjectivity: it introduces sensations which are things, just where experience shows that there are meaningful patterns; it forces the phenomenal universe into categories which make sense only in the universe of science. It requires that two perceived lines, like two real lines, should be equal or unequal, that a perceived crystal should have a definite number of sides,[23] without realizing that the perceived, by its nature, admits of the ambiguous, the shifting, and is shaped by its context. In Müller-Lyer's illusion, one of the lines ceases to be equal to the other without becoming 'unequal': it becomes 'different'. That is to say, an isolated, objective line, and the same line taken in a figure, cease to be, for perception, 'the same'. It is identifiable in these two functions only by analytic perception, which is not natural. In the same way the perceived contains gaps which are not mere 'failures to perceive'. I may, through sight or touch, recognize a crystal as having a 'regular' shape without having, even tacitly, counted its sides. I may be familiar with a face without ever having perceived the colour of the eyes in themselves. The theory of sensation, which builds up all knowledge out of determinate qualities, offers us objects purged of all ambiguity, pure and absolute, the ideal rather than the real themes of knowledge: in short, it is compatible only with the lately developed superstructure of consciousness. That is where 'the idea of sensation is approximately realized'.[24]

The images which instinct projects before it, those which tradition recreates in each generation, or simply dreams, are in the first place presented on an equal footing with genuine perceptions, and gradually, by critical labour, the true, present and explicit perception is distinguished from phantasms. The word perception indicates a *direction* rather than a primitive function.[25] It is known that the uniformity of apparent size of objects at different distances, or of their colour in different lights, is more perfect in children than in adults.[26] It follows that perception is more strictly bound up with the local stimulus in its developed than in its undeveloped state, and more in conformity with the theory of sensation in the adult than in the child. It is like a net with its knots showing up more and more clearly.[27] 'Primitive thought' has been pictured in a way which can be understood only if the responses of primitive people, their pronouncements and the sociologists' interpretations are related to the fund of perceptual experience which they are all trying to translate.[28] It is sometimes the adherence of the perceived object to its context, and, as it were, its viscosity, sometimes the presence in it of a positive indeterminate which prevents the spatial, temporal and numerical wholes from becoming articulated into manageable, distinct and identifiable terms. And it is this pre-objective realm that we have to explore in ourselves if we wish to understand sense experience.

Notes

1. See *La Structure du Comportement*, pp. 142 and ff.
2. J. P. Sartre, *L'Imaginaire*, p. 241.
3. Koffka, *Psychologie*, p. 530.
4. There is no justification for dodging the issue, as does Jaspers, for example *(Zur Analyse der Trugwahrnehmungen)* by setting up in opposition, on the one hand a descriptive psychology which 'understands' phenomena, and on the other an explanatory psychology, which concerns itself with their origin. The psychologist always sees consciousness as placed in the body in the midst of the world, and for him the series stimulus—impression—perception is a sequence of events at the end of which perception begins. Each consciousness is born in the world and each perception is a new birth of consciousness. In this perspective the 'immediate' data of perception can always be challenged as mere appearances and as complex products of an origin. The descriptive method can acquire a genuine claim only from the transcendental point of view. But, even from this point of view, the problem remains as to how consciousness perceives it-

self or appears to itself as inserted in a nature. For the philosopher, as for the psychologist, there is therefore always a problem of origins, and the only method possible is to follow, in its scientific development, the causal explanation in order to make its meaning quite clear, and assign to it its proper place in the body of truth. That is why there will be found no *refutation*, but only an effort to understand the difficulties peculiar to causal thinking.

5. See *La Structure du Comportement*, Chap. I.

6. We are translating roughly the series 'Empfänger-Übermittler-Empfinder spoken of by J. Stein, *Über die Veränderung der Sinnesleistungen und die Entstehung von Trugwahrnehmungen*, p. 351.

7. Koehler, *Über unbemerkte Empfindungen und Urteilstäuschungen.*

8. Stumpf does so explicitly. Cf. Koehler, ibid., p. 54.

9. Koehler, ibid., pp. 57–58, cf. pp. 58–66.

10. R. Déjean, *Les Conditions objectives de la Perception visuelle*, pp. 60 and 83.

11. Stumpf, quoted by Koehler, ibid., p. 58.

12. Koehler, ibid., pp. 58–63.

13. It is only fair to add that this is true of all theories, and that nowhere is there a crucial experiment. For the same reason the constancy hypothesis cannot be completely refuted on the basis of induction. It is discredited because it overlooks phenomena and does not permit any understanding of them. To discern them and to pass judgement on the hypothesis, indeed, one must 'suspend' it.

14. Stein, op. cit., pp. 357–59.

15. Even daltonism does not prove that certain systems are, and are alone in being, entrusted with 'seeing' red and green, since a colour-blind person manages to distinguish red if a large area in that colour is put before him, or if the presentation of the colour is made to last a long time. Id. ibid., p. 365.

16. Weizsäcker, quoted by Stein, ibid., p. 364.

17. Weizsäcker, quoted by Stein, ibid., p. 354.

18. On all these points see *La Structure du Comportement*, in particular pp. 52 and ff., 65 and ff.

19. Gelb, *Die Farbenkonstanz der Sehdinge*, p. 595.

20. 'The sensations are certainly artificial products, but not arbitrary ones, they are the last component wholes into which the natural structures can be decomposed by the "analytical attitude". Seen from this point of view, they contribute to the knowledge of structures, and consequently the results of the study of sensations, correctly interpreted, are an important element in the psychology of perception.' Koffka, *Psychologie*, p. 548.

21. Cf. Guillaume, *L'Objectivité en Psychologie.*

22. Cf. *La Structure du Comportement*, Chap. III.

23. Koffka, *Psychologie*, pp. 530 and 549.

24. M. Scheler, *Die Wissenformen und die Gesellschaft*, p. 412.

25. M. Scheler, *Die Wissenformen und die Gesellschaft*, p. 397. 'Man approaches, ideal and exact images better than the animal, the adult better than the child, men better than women, the individual better than the member of a group, the man who thinks historically and systematically better than the man impelled by tradition, "imprisoned"

in it and incapable of objectivizing, by building up recollection, the environment in which he is involved, of localizing it in time and possessing it by setting it away from himself in a past context.'

26. Hering, Jaensch.

27. Scheler, *Die Wissenformen und die Gesellschaft*, p. 412.

28. Cf. Wertheimer, *Über das Denken der Naturvölker*, in *Drei Abhandlungen zur Gestalttheorie*.

Eye and Mind

> What I am trying to convey to you is more mysterious; it is entwined in the very roots of being, in the impalpable source of sensations.
>
> —J. Gasquet, *Cézanne*

I

Science manipulates things and gives up living in them.[1] Operating within its own realm, it makes its constructs of things; operating upon these indices or variables to effect whatever transformations are permitted by their definition, it comes face to face with the real world only at rare intervals. It is, and always has been, that admirably active, ingenious, and bold way of thinking whose fundamental bias is to treat everything as though it were an object-in-general—as though it meant nothing to us and yet was predestined for our ingenious schemes.

But classical science clung to a feeling for the opaqueness of the world, and it expected through its constructions to get back into the world. For this reason it felt obliged to seek a transcendent or transcendental foundation for its operations. Today we find—not in science but in a widely prevalent philosophy of the sciences—an entirely new approach. Constructive scientific activities see themselves and represent themselves to be autonomous, and their thinking deliberately reduces itself to a set of data-collecting techniques which it has invented. To think is thus to test out, to operate, to transform—the only restriction being that this activity is regulated by an experimental control that admits only the most "worked-up" phenomena, more likely produced by the apparatus than recorded by it.

Whence all sorts of vagabond endeavors. Today more than ever, science is sensitive to intellectual fads and fashions. When a model has succeeded in one order of problems, it is tried out everywhere else. At the present time, for example, our embryology and biology are full of "gradients." Just how these differ from what classical tradition called "order" or "totality" is not at all clear. This question, however, is not raised; it is not even allowed. The gradient is a net we throw out to sea, without knowing what we will haul back in it. It is the slender twig upon which unforeseeable crystalizations will form. No doubt this freedom of operation will serve well to overcome many a pointless dilemma—provided only that from time to time we take stock, and ask ourselves why the apparatus works in one place and fails in others. For all its flexibility, science must understand itself; it must see itself as a construction based on a brute, existent world and not claim for its blind operations the constitutive value that "concepts of nature" were granted in a certain idealist philosophy. To say that the world is, by nominal definition, the object *x* of our operations is to treat the scientist's knowledge as if it were absolute, as if everything that is and has been was meant only to enter the laboratory. Thinking "operationally" has become a sort of absolute artificialism, such as we see in the ideology of cybernetics, where human creations are derived from a natural information process, itself conceived on the model of human machines. If this kind of thinking were to extend its dominion over humanity and history; and if, ignoring what we know of them through contact and our own situations, it were to set out to construct them on the basis of a few abstract indices (as a decadent psychoanalysis and culturalism have done in the United States)—then, since the human being truly becomes the *manipulandum* he thinks he is, we enter into a cultural regimen in which there is neither truth nor falsehood concerning humanity and history, into a sleep, or nightmare from which there is no awakening.

Scientific thinking, a thinking which looks on from above, and thinks of the object-in-general, must return to the "there is" which precedes it; to the site, the soil of the sensible and humanly modified world such as it is in our lives and for our bodies—not that possible body which we may legitimately think of as an information machine but this actual body I call mine, this sentinel standing quietly at the command of my words and my acts. Further, *associated bodies* must be revived along with my body—"others," not merely as my congeners, as the zoologist says, but others who haunt me and whom I haunt; "others" along with whom I haunt a single, present, and actual Being as no animal ever haunted those of his own species, territory, or habitat. In this primordial historicity, science's agile and improvisatory thought will learn to ground itself upon things themselves and upon itself, and will once more become philosophy. . . .

Now art, especially painting, draws upon this fabric of brute meaning which operationalism would prefer to ignore. Art and only art does so in full innocence. From the writer and the philosopher, in contrast, we want opinions and advice. We will not allow them to hold the world suspended. We want them to take a stand; they cannot waive the responsibilities of humans who speak. Music, at the other extreme, is too far on the hither side of the world and the designatable to depict anything but certain schemata of Being—its ebb and flow, its growth, its upheavals, its turbulence.

Only the painter is entitled to look at everything without being obliged to appraise what he sees. For the painter, we might say, the watchwords of knowledge and action lose their meaning and force. Political regimes which denounce "degenerate" painting rarely destroy paintings. They hide them, and one senses here an element of "one never knows" amounting almost to an acknowledgment. The reproach of escapism is seldom aimed at the painter; we do not hold it against Cézanne that he lived hidden away at L'Estaque during the Franco-Prussian War. And we recall with respect his "life is frightening," although the most insignificant student, after Nietzsche, would flatly reject philosophy if he or she were told that it did not teach us how to live life to the fullest. It is as if in the painter's calling there were some urgency above all other claims on him. Strong or frail in life, but incontestably sovereign in his rumination of the world, possessed of no other "technique" than the skill his eyes and hands discover in seeing and painting, he gives himself entirely to drawing from the world—with its din of history's glories and scandals—*canvases* which will hardly add to the angers or the hopes of humanity; and no one complains.[2] What, then, is the secret science which he has or which he seeks? That dimension which lets Van Gogh say he must go "still further"? What is this fundamental of painting, perhaps of all culture?

II

The painter "takes his body with him," says Valéry. Indeed we cannot imagine how a *mind* could paint. It is by lending his body to the world that the artist changes the world into paintings. To understand these transubstantiations we must go back to the working, actual body—not the body as a chunk of space or a bundle of functions but that body which is an intertwining of vision and movement.

I have only to see something to know how to reach it and deal with it, even if I do not know how this happens in the nervous system. My moving body makes a difference in the visible world, being a part of it; that is why I can steer it through the visible. Moreover, it is also true that vision is attached to movement. We see only what we look at. What would vision be without eye movement? And how could the movement of the eyes not blur things if movement were blind? If it were only a reflex? If it did not have its antennae, its clairvoyance? If vision were not prefigured in it?

All my changes of place figure on principle in a corner of my landscape; they are carried over onto the map of the visible. Everything I see is on principle within my reach, at least within reach of my sight, and is marked upon the map of the "I can." Each of the two maps is complete. The visible world and the world of my motor projects are both total parts of the same Being.

This extraordinary overlapping, which we never give enough thought to, forbids us to conceive of vision as an operation of thought that would set up before the mind a picture or a representation of the world, a world of immanence and of ideality. Immersed in the visible by his body, itself visible, the see-er does not appropriate what he sees; he merely approaches it by looking, he opens onto the world. Arid for its part, that world of which he is a part is not *in itself*, or matter. My movement is not a decision made by the mind, an absolute doing which would decree, from the depths of a subjective retreat, some change of place miraculously executed in extended space. It is the natural sequel to, and maturation of, vision. I say of a thing that it is moved; but my body moves itself; my movement is self-moved. It is not ignorance of self, blind to itself; it radiates from a self. . . .

The enigma derives from the fact that my body simultaneously sees and is seen. That which looks at all things can also look at itself and recognize, in what it sees, the "other side" of its power of looking. It sees itself seeing; it touches itself touching; it is visible and sensitive for itself. It is a self, not by transparency, like thought, which never thinks anything except by assimilating it, constituting it, transforming it into thought—but a self by confusion, narcissism, inherence of the see-er in the seen, the toucher in the touched, the feeler in the felt—a self, then, that is caught up in things, having a front and a back, a past and a future. . . .

This initial paradox cannot but produce others. Visible and mobile, my body is a thing among things; it is one of them. It is caught in the fabric of the world, and its cohesion is that of a thing. But because it moves itself and sees, it holds things in a circle around itself.[3] Things are an annex or prolongation of itself; they are incrusted in its flesh, they are part of its full definition; the world is made of the very stuff of the body. These reversals, these antinomies,[4] are different ways of saying that vision is caught or comes to be in things—in that place where something visible undertakes to see, becomes visible to itself and in the sight of all things, in that place where there persists, like the original solution still present within crystal, the undividedness of the sensing and the sensed.

This interiority no more precedes the material arrangement of the human body than it results from it. What if our eyes were made in such a way as to prevent our seeing any part of our body, or some diabolical contraption were to let us move our hands over things, while preventing us from touching our own body? Or what if, like certain animals, we had lateral eyes with no cross-blending of visual fields? Such a body would not reflect itself; it would be an almost adamantine body, not really flesh, not really the body of a human being. There would be no humanity.

But humanity is not produced as the effect of our articulations or by the way our eyes are implanted in us (still less by the existence of mirrors, though they alone can make our entire bodies visible to us). These contingencies and others like them, without which mankind would not exist, do not by simple summation bring it about that there *is* a single man. The body's animation is not the assemblage or juxtaposition of its parts. Nor is it a question of a mind or spirit coming down from somewhere else into an automation—which would still imply that the body itself is without an inside and without a "self." A human body is present when, between the see-er and the visible, between touching and touched, between one eye and the other, between hand and hand a kind of crossover occurs, when the spark of the sensing/sensible is lit, when the fire starts to burn that will not cease until some accident befalls the body, undoing what no accident would have sufficed to do. . . .

Once this strange system of exchanges is given, we find before us all the problems of painting. These problems illustrate the enigma of the body, which enigma in turn legitimates them. Since things and my body are made of the same stuff, vision must somehow come about in them; or yet again, their manifest visibility must be repeated in the body by a secret visibility. "Nature is on the inside," says Cézanne. Quality, light, color, depth, which are there before us, are there only because they awaken an echo in our bodies and because the body welcomes them.

Things have an internal equivalent in me; they arouse in me a carnal formula of their presence. Why shouldn't these correspondences in turn give rise to some tracing rendered visible again, in which the eyes of others could find an underlying motif to sustain their inspection of the world?[5] Thus there appears a "visible" to the second power, a carnal essence or icon of the first. It is not a faded copy, a *trompe l'oeil,* or another *thing.* The animals painted on the walls of Lascaux are not there in the same way as are the fissures and limestone formations. Nor are they *elsewhere.* Pushed forward here, held back there, supported by the wall's mass they use so adroitly, they radiate about the wall without ever breaking their elusive moorings. I would be hard pressed to say *where* the painting is I am looking at. For I do not look at it as one looks at a thing, fixing it in its place. My gaze wanders within it as in the halos of Being. Rather than seeing it, I see according to, or with it.

The word "image" is in bad repute because we have thoughtlessly believed that a drawing was a tracing, a copy, a second thing, and that the mental image was such a drawing, belonging among our private bric-a-brac. But if in fact it is nothing of the kind, then neither the drawing nor the painting belongs to the in-itself any more than the image does. They are the inside of the outside and the outside of the inside, which the duplicity of feeling [*le sentir*] makes possible and without which we would never understand the quasi presence and imminent visibility which make up the whole problem of the imaginary. The picture, the actor's mimicry—these are not devices borrowed from the real world in order to refer to prosaic things which are absent. For the imaginary is much nearer to, and much farther away from, the actual—nearer because it is in my body as a diagram of the life of the actual, with all its pulp and carnal obverse exposed to view for the first time. In this sense, Giacometti says energetically, "What interests me in all paintings is likeness—that is, what likeness is for me: something that makes me uncover the external world a little."[6] And the imaginary is much farther away from the actual because the painting is an analogue or likeness only according to the body; because it does not offer the mind an occasion to rethink the constitutive relations of things, but rather it offers the *gaze* traces of vision, from the inside, in order that it may espouse them; it gives vision that which clothes it within, the imaginary texture of the real.[7]

Shall we say, then, that there is an inner gaze, that there is a third eye which sees the paintings and even the mental images, as we used to speak of a third ear which grasps messages from the outside through the noises they caused inside us? But how would this help us when the whole point is to understand that our fleshly eyes are already much more than receptors for light rays, colors, and lines? They are computers of the world, which have the gift of the visible, as we say of the inspired man that he has the gift of tongues. Of course this gift is earned by exercise; it is not in a few months, or in solitude, that a painter comes into full possession of his vision. But that is not the question; precocious or belated, spontaneous or cultivated in museums, his vision in any event learns only by seeing and learns only from itself. The eye sees the world, and what it would need to be a painting, sees what keeps a painting from being itself, sees—on the palette—the colors awaited by the painting, and sees, once it is done, the painting that answers to all these inadequacies just as it sees the paintings of others as other answers to other inadequacies.

It is no more possible to make a restrictive inventory of the visible than it is to catalog the possible expressions of a language or even its vocabulary and turns of phrase. The eye is an instrument that moves itself, a means which invents its own ends; it is *that which* has been moved by some impact of the world, which it then restores to the visible through the traces of a hand.

In whatever civilization it is born, from whatever beliefs, motives, or thoughts, no matter what ceremonies surround it—and even when it appears devoted to something else—from Lascaux to our time, pure or impure, figurative or not, painting celebrates no other enigma but that of visibility.

What we have just said amounts to a truism. The painter's world is a visible world, nothing but visible: a world almost mad, because it is complete though only partial. Painting awakens and carries to its highest pitch a delirium which is vision itself, for to see is *to have at a distance*; painting extends this strange possession to all aspects of Being, which must somehow become visible in order to enter into the work of art. When, apropos of Italian painting, the young

Berenson spoke of an evocation of tactile values, he could hardly have been more mistaken; painting evokes nothing, least of all the tactile. What it does is entirely different, almost the inverse. It gives visible existence to what profane vision believes to be invisible; thanks to it we do not need a "muscular sense" in order to possess the voluminosity of the world. This voracious vision, reaching beyond the "visual givens," opens upon a texture of Being of which the discrete sensorial messages are only the punctuations or the caesurae. The eye lives in this texture as a man in his house.

Let us remain within the visible in the narrow and prosaic sense. The painter, any painter, *while he is painting*, practices a magical theory of vision. He is obliged to admit that objects before him pass into him or else that, according to Malebranche's sarcastic dilemma, the mind goes out through the eyes to wander among objects; for he never ceases adjusting his clairvoyance to them. (It makes no difference if he does not paint from "nature"; he paints, in any case, because he has seen, because the world has at least once emblazoned in him the ciphers of the visible.) He must affirm, as one philosopher has said, that vision is a mirror or concentration of the universe or that, in another's words, the *idios kosmos* opens by virtue of vision upon a *koinos kosmos*; in short, that the same thing is both out there in the world and here at the heart of vision—the same or, if you will, a *similar* thing, but according to an efficient similarity which is the parent, the genesis, the metamorphosis of being into its vision. It is the mountain itself which from out there makes itself seen by the painter; it is the mountain that he interrogates with his gaze.

What exactly does he ask of it? To unveil the means, visible and not otherwise, by which it makes itself mountain before our eyes. Light, lighting, shadows, reflections, color, all these objects of his quest are not altogether real objects; like ghosts, they have only visual existence. In fact they exist only at the threshold of profane vision; they are not ordinarily seen. The painter's gaze asks them what they do to suddenly cause something to be and to be *this* thing, what they do to compose this talisman of a world, to make us see the visible. The hand pointing toward us in *The Nightwatch* is truly there only when we see that its shadow on the captain's body presents it simultaneously in profile. The spatiality of the captain lies at the intersection of the two perspectives which are incompossible and yet together. Everyone with eyes has at some time or other witnessed this play of shadows, or something like it, and has been made by it to see things and a space. But it worked in them without them; it hid to make the object visible. To see the object, it was necessary *not* to see the play of shadows and light around it. The visible in the profane sense forgets its premises; it rests upon a total visibility which is to be recreated and which liberates the phantoms captive in it. The moderns, as we know, have liberated many others; they have added many a muted tone to the official gamut of our means of seeing. But the interrogation of painting in any case looks toward this secret and feverish genesis of things in our body.

And so it is not a question asked of someone who doesn't know by someone who does—the schoolmaster's question. The question comes from one who does not know, and it is addressed to a vision, a seeing, which knows everything and which we do not make, for it makes itself in us. Max Ernst (with the surrealists) says rightly, "Just as the role of the poet since [Rimbaud's] famous *Lettre du voyant* consists in writing under the dictation of what is being thought, of what articulates itself in him, the painter's role is to circumscribe and project what is making itself seen within himself."[8] The painter lives in fascination. The actions most proper to him—those gestures, those tracings of which he alone is capable and which will be revelations to others because they do not lack what he lacks—to him they seem to emanate from the things themselves, like figures emanating from the constellations.

Inevitably the roles between the painter and the visible switch. That is why so many painters have said that things look at them. As André Marchand says, after Klee: "In a forest, I have felt many times over that it was not I who looked at the forest. Some days I felt that the trees were looking at me, were speaking to me. . . . I was there, listening. . . . I think that the painter must be penetrated by the universe and not want to penetrate it. . . . I expect to be inwardly submerged, buried. Perhaps I paint to break out."[9]

We speak of "inspiration," and the word should be taken literally. There really is inspiration and expiration of Being, respiration in Being, action and passion so slightly discernible that it becomes impossible to distinguish between who sees and who is seen, who paints and what is painted. We say that a human being is born the moment when something that was only virtually visible within the mother's body becomes at once visible for us and for itself. The painter's vision is an ongoing birth.

In paintings themselves we could seek a figured philosophy[10] of vision—its iconography, perhaps. It is no accident, for example, that frequently in Dutch paintings (as in many others) an interior in which no one is present is "digested" by the "round eye of the mirror."[11] This prehuman way of seeing things is emblematic of the painter's way. More completely than lights, shadows, and reflections, the mirror image anticipates, within things, the labor of vision. Like all other technical objects, such as tools and signs, the mirror has sprung up along the open circuit *between* the seeing and the visible body. Every technique is a "technique of the body," illustrating and amplifying the metaphysical structure of our flesh. The mirror emerges because I am a visible see-er, because there is a reflexivity of the sensible; the mirror translates and reproduces that reflexivity. In it, my externality becomes complete. Everything that is most secret about me passes into that face, that flat, closed being of which I was already dimly aware, from having seen my reflection mirrored in water. Schilder observes that, smoking a pipe before a mirror, I feel the sleek, burning surface of the wood not only where my fingers are but also in those otherworldly fingers, those merely visible ones inside the mirror.[12] The mirror's phantom draws my flesh into the outer world, and at the same time the invisible of my body can invest its psychic energy in the other bodies I see.[13] Hence my body can include elements drawn from the body of another, just as my substance passes into them; man is a mirror for man. Mirrors are instruments of a universal magic that converts things into spectacle, spectacle into things, myself into another, and another into myself. Artists have often mused upon mirrors because beneath this "mechanical trick," they recognized, as they did in the case of the "trick" of perspective,[14] the metamorphosis of seeing and seen that defines both our flesh and the painter's vocation. This explains why they have so often chosen to draw themselves in the act of painting (they still do—witness Matisse's drawings), adding to what *they* could see of things at that moment, what *things* could see of them—as if to attest to there being a total or absolute vision, leaving nothing outside, including themselves. Where in the realm of the understanding can we place these occult operations, together with the potions and idols they concoct? What can we call them? Consider, as Sartre did in *Nausea*, the smile of a long-dead monarch which keeps producing and reproducing itself on the surface of a canvas. It is too little to say that it is there as an image or essence; it is there as itself, as that which was always most alive about it, the moment I look at the painting. The "world's instant" that Cézanne wanted to paint, an instant long since passed away, is still hurled toward us by his paintings.[15] His *Mont. Sainte-Victoire* is made and remade from one end of the world to the other in a way different from but no less energetic than in the hard rock above Aix. Essence and existence, imaginary and real, visible and invisible—painting scrambles all our categories, spreading out before us its oneiric universe of carnal essences, actualized resemblances, mute meanings.

III

How crystal clear everything would be in our philosophy if only we would exorcise these specters, make illusions or objectless perceptions out of them, brush them to one side of an unequivocal world!

Descartes's *Dioptrics* is an attempt to do just that. It is the breviary of a thought that wants no longer to abide in the visible and so decides to reconstruct it according to a model-in-thought. It is worthwhile to remember this attempt and its failure.

Here there is no concern to cling to vision. The problem is to know "how it happens," but only enough to invent, whenever the need arises, certain "artificial organs" which correct it.[16] We are to reason not so much upon the light we see as upon the light which, from outside, enters our eyes and regulates our vision. And for that we are to rely upon "two or three comparisons which help us to conceive it [light]" in such a way as to explain its known properties and to deduce others.[17] The question being so formulated, it is best to think of light as an action by contact—not unlike the action of things upon the blind man's cane. The blind, says Descartes, "see with their hands."[18] The Cartesian model of vision is modeled after the sense of touch.

At one swoop, then, Descartes eliminates action at a distance and relieves us of that ubiquity which is the whole problem of vision (as well as its peculiar virtue). Why should we henceforth puzzle over reflections and mirrors? These unreal duplications are a class of things; they are real effects like a ball bouncing back. If the reflection resembles the thing itself, it is because this reflection acts upon the eyes more or less as a thing would. It deceives the eye by engendering a perception which has no object, yet this perception does not affect our conception of the world. In the world there is the thing itself, and outside this thing itself there is that other thing which is only reflected light rays and which happens to have an ordered correspondence with the real thing; there are two individuals, then, bound together externally by causality. As far as the thing and its mirror image are concerned, their resemblance is only an external denomination; the resemblance belongs to thought. The dubious relationship of likeness is—among things—an unequivocal relationship of projection.

The Cartesian does not see *himself* in the mirror; he sees a puppet, an "outside," which, he has every reason to believe, other people see in the very same way, but which is no more for himself than for others a body in the flesh. His "image" in the mirror is an effect of the mechanics of things. If he recognizes himself in it, if he thinks it "looks like him," it is his thought that weaves this connection. The mirror image is in no sense *a part of* him. For him, icons lose their powers.[19] However vividly an etching may "represent" forests, towns, men, battles, storms, it does not resemble them. It is only a bit of ink put down here and there on the paper. A figure flattened down onto a plane surface scarcely retains the forms of things; it is a deformed figure that *must* be deformed—the square becomes a lozenge, the circle an oval—*in order to* represent the object. It is an image only as long as it does not resemble its object. If not through resemblance, how, then, does it work? It "excites our thought" to "conceive," as do signs and words "which in no way resemble the things they signify."[20] The etching gives us sufficient indices, unequivocal "means" for forming an idea of the thing that does not come from the icon itself; rather, it arises in us, as "occasioned" by the icon. The magic of intentional species—the old idea of effective resemblance so strongly suggested to us by mirrors and paintings—loses its final argument if the entire potential of a painting is that of a text to be read, a text totally free of promiscuity between the seeing and the seen. We need no longer try to understand how a painting of things in the body could make them felt in the soul—an impossible task, since the very resemblance between this painting and those things would have to be seen in turn, since we would "have to have other eyes in our minds with which to apperceive it,"[21] and since the problem of vision remains intact even after we have introduced these simulacra, wandering between things and us. What the light casts upon our eyes, and thence upon our brain, does not resemble the visible world any more than etchings do. Nothing goes from things to the eyes, and from the eyes to vision, no more than from things to a blind man's hands, and from his hands to his thoughts.

Vision is not the metamorphosis of things themselves into the sight of them; it is not a matter of things' belonging simultaneously to the world at large and a little private world. It is a thinking that unequivocally decodes signs given within the body. Resemblance is the result of perception, not its basis. Thus, the mental image, the visualization which renders present to us what is absent, is a fortiori nothing like a breakthrough to the heart of Being. It too is a thought relying upon bodily indices—this time insufficient ones—which are made to say more than they mean. Nothing is left of the oneiric world of analogy. . . .

What interests us in these famous analyses is that they make us aware of the fact that every theory of painting is a metaphysics. Descartes does not say much about painting, and one might think it unfair on our part to make so much of a few pages on engravings. And yet the very fact that he speaks of painting only in passing is itself significant. Painting for him is not a central operation contributing to the definition of our access to Being; it is a mode or a variant of thinking, where thinking is canonically defined as intellectual possession and self-evidence. His very brevity is the indication of a choice; a closer study of painting would lead to a different philosophy. It is significant, too, that when he speaks of "pictures" [*tableaux*] he takes line drawings as typical. We shall see that the whole of painting is present in each of its modes of expression; there is a kind of drawing, even a single line, that can embrace all of painting's bold potential.

But what Descartes likes most about engravings is that they preserve the form of objects, or at least give us sufficient signs of their forms. They present the object by its outside, or its envelope. If he had examined that other, deeper opening upon things given us by the secondary qualities, especially color, then—since there is no rule-governed or projective relationship between them and the true properties of things, and we understand their message all the same—he would have found himself faced with the problem of a conceptless universality and opening upon things. He would have been obliged to find out how the uncertain murmur of colors can present us with things, forests, storms—in short the world. He would have been obliged, perhaps, to integrate perspective, as a particular case, into a broader ontological power. But for him it goes without saying that color is an ornament, mere coloring, and that the real power of painting lies in drawing, whose power in turn rests upon the ordered relationship between it and objective space established by perspectival projection. Pascal's famous saying that painting is frivolous because it attaches us to images whose originals would not move us is a Cartesian saying. For Descartes it is self-evident that one can paint only existing things, that their existence consists in being extended, and line drawing alone makes painting possible by making possible the representation of extension. Thus painting is only an artifice that puts before our eyes a projection similar to the one things themselves would (and do, according to the commonsense view) inscribe in them. Painting causes us to see, without real objects, just as we see things in everyday life; and in particular it makes us see empty space where there is none.[22]

The picture is a flat thing contriving to give us what we would see in the presence of "diversely positioned" things, by offering sufficient diacritical signs, through height and width, of the missing dimension.[23] Depth is a *third dimension* derived from the other two.

It will be worth our while to dwell for a moment upon this third dimension. There is, at first glance, something paradoxical about it. I see objects that hide each other and that consequently I do not see; each one stands behind the other. I see depth and yet it is not visible, since it is reckoned from our bodies to things, and we are [as Cartesians] confined to our bodies. There is no real mystery here. I do not really see depth or, if I do, it is only another *size.* On the line from my eyes to the horizon, the foreground forever hides all the other planes, and if on either side I think I see things staggered at intervals, it is because they do not completely hide each other. Thus I see each thing outside the others, according to a width measured differently.[24] We are [as Cartesians] always on the hither side of depth, or beyond it. It is never the case that things really *are* one behind the other. The encroachment and latency do not enter into their definition. They express only my incomprehensible solidarity with one of them—my body; and by their positivity they are thoughts of mine and not attributes of things. I know that at this very moment another person, situated elsewhere—or better, God, who is everywhere—could penetrate their hiding place and see them openly deployed. What I call depth is either nothing, or else it is my participation in a Being without restriction, first and foremost a participation in the being of space beyond every particular point of view. Things encroach upon one another *because they are outside one another.* The proof of this is that I can see depth in a painting which everyone agrees has none and which organizes for me an illusion of an illusion. . . . This two-dimensional being,[25] which makes me see a third, is a being that is pierced [*troué*]—as the men of the Renaissance said, a window. . . . But in the final analysis the window opens only upon *partes extra partes,* upon height and breadth merely seen from another angle—upon the absolute positivity of Being.

It is this space without hiding places which in each of its points is only what it is, neither more nor less, this identity of Being that underlies the analysis of engravings. Space is in itself; rather, it is the in-itself par excellence. Its definition is *to be* in itself. Every point of space is, and is thought as being, right where it is—one here, another there; space is the self-evidence of the "where." Orientation, polarity, envelopment are, in space, derived phenomena linked to my presence. *Space* remains absolutely in itself, everywhere equal to itself, homogeneous; its dimensions, for example, are by definition interchangeable.

Like all classical ontologies, this one elevates certain properties of beings into a structure of Being, and in so doing it is both true and false. Reversing Leibniz's remark, we might say that it is true in what it denies and false in what it affirms. Descartes's space is true, when contrasted with a thought too empirically dominated, which dares not construct. It was necessary first to idealize space, to conceive of that being—perfect of its kind, clear, manageable, and homogeneous—which an unsituated thinking glides over without a vantage point of its own: a being which thought transcribes in its entirety onto three right-angled axes—so that subsequent thinkers could one day experience the limitations of that construction and understand that space does not have precisely three dimensions (as an animal has either four or two legs), and that dimensions are taken by different systems of measurement from a single dimensionality, a polymorphous Being, which justifies all of them without being fully expressed by any. Descartes was right in liberating space: his mistake was to erect it into a positive being, beyond all points of view, all latency and depth, devoid of any real thickness.

He was also right in taking his inspiration from the perspectival techniques of the Renaissance; they encouraged painting to experiment freely with depth and the presentation of Being in general. These techniques were false only in that they presumed to bring an end to painting's quest and history, to found once and for all an exact and infallible art of painting. As Panofsky has shown concerning the men of the Renaissance, this enthusiasm was not without bad faith.[26] The theoreticians tried to forget the spherical visual field of the ancients, their angular perspective which relates the apparent size not to distance but to the angle from which we see the object. They wanted to forget what they disdainfully called *perspectiva naturalis*, or *communis*, in favor of a *perspectiva artificialis* capable in principle of founding an exact construction. To accredit this myth, they went so far as to expurgate Euclid, omitting from their translations the eighth theorem, which was inconvenient. But the painters knew from experience that no technique of perspective is an exact solution and that there is no projection of the existing world which respects it in all aspects and deserves to become the fundamental law of painting. They knew that linear perspective was far from being an ultimate breakthrough; on the contrary, it opened several pathways for painting. For example, the Italians took the way of representing the object, but the Northern painters discovered and worked out the formal technique of *Hochraum*, *Nahraum*, and *Schrägraum*. Thus plane projection does not always stimulate our thought to rediscover the true form of things, as Descartes believed. Beyond a certain degree of deformation, it refers us back, on the contrary, to our own vantage point; as for the things, they flee into a remoteness out of reach of all thought. Something about space evades our attempts to survey it from above.

The truth is that no means of expression, once mastered, resolves the problems of painting or transforms it into a technique. For no symbolic form ever functions as a stimulus. Symbolic form works and acts only in conjunction with the entire context of the *work*, and not at all by means of a *trompe-l'oeil*. The *Stilmoment* never dispenses with the *Wermoment*.[27] The language of painting is never "instituted by nature"; it must be made and remade. The perspective of the Renaissance is no infallible "gimmick." It is only one particular case, a date, a moment in a poetic information of the world which continues after it.

Yet Descartes would not have been Descartes if he had thought to *eliminate* the enigma of vision. For him, there is no vision without thought: but *it is not enough* to think in order to see. Vision is a conditioned thought; it is born "as occasioned" by what happens in the body; it is "incited" to think by the body. It does not *choose* either to be or not to be or to think this thing or that. It must carry in its heart that heaviness, that dependence which cannot come to it by some intrusion from outside. Such bodily events are "instituted by nature" in order to bring us to see this thing or that. The thinking that belongs to vision functions according to a program and a law which it has not given itself. It does not possess its own premises; it is not a thought altogether present and actual; there is in its center a mystery of passivity.

Thus the Cartesian situation is as follows. Everything we say and think of vision has to make a *thought* of it. When, for example, we wish to understand how we see the location of objects, we have no other recourse than to suppose the soul to be capable, knowing where the parts of its body are, of "transferring its attention from there" to all the points of space that lie along the prolongation of its bodily members.[28] But so far this is only a "model" of the event. For how does the soul know that space of its body which it extends toward things, that primary *here* from which all the theres will come? This space is not, like them, just another mode or specimen of extension; it is the place of the body the soul calls "mine," a place the soul inhabits. The body it animates is not, for it, an object among objects, and it does not deduce from its body all the rest of space as an implied premise. The soul thinks according to the body, not according to itself, and space, or exterior distance, is also stipulated within the natural pact that unites them. If, at a certain degree of ocular accommodation and convergence the soul becomes aware of a certain distance, the thought which draws the second relationship from the first is as if immemorially encoded in our inner workings. "Usually this comes about without our reflecting upon it—just as, when we clasp a body with our hand, we conform the hand to the size and shape of the body and thereby sense the body, without having need to think of those movements of the hand."[29] The body is both the soul's native space, and the matrix of every other existing space. Thus vision doubles. There is the vision upon which I reflect; I cannot think it except *as* thought, the mind's inspection, judgment, a reading of signs. And then there is the vision that actually occurs, an honorary or established thought, collapsed into a body—its own body, of which we can have no idea except in the exercise of it, and which introduces, between space and thought, the autonomous order of the composite of soul and body. The enigma of vision is not done away with; it is shifted from the "thought of seeing" to vision in act.

Still, this de facto vision and the "there is" which it contains do not upset Descartes's philosophy. Since it is thought united with a body, it cannot, by definition, truly be conceived. One can practice it, exercise it, and, so to speak, exist it; yet one can draw nothing from it which deserves to be called true. If, like Queen Elizabeth,[30] we want at all costs to think *something* about it, all we can do is go back to Aristotle and scholasticism, to conceive thought as a corporeal something which cannot be conceived but which is the only way to formulate, for our understanding, the union of soul and body. The truth is that it is absurd to submit to pure understanding the mixture of understanding and body. These would-be thoughts are the emblems of "the practice of everyday life," the verbal blazons of union, permissible only if not taken to be thoughts. They are indices of an order of existence—of humanity and world as existing—of which we are not held to produce a concept. For this order there is no *terra incognita* on our map of Being. It does not confine the reach of our thoughts, because it, just as much as they, is sustained by a Truth which grounds its obscurity as well as our own lights.[31]

We have to go to these lengths to find in Descartes something like a metaphysics of depth. For we are not present at the birth of this Truth; God's being is for us an abyss. An anxious trembling quickly mastered; for Descartes it is just as futile to plumb that abyss as it is to think the space of the soul and the depth of the visible. Our very position, he would say, disqualifies us from looking into such things. That is the secret of Cartesian equilibrium: a metaphysics which gives us definitive reasons to leave off doing metaphysics, which validates our self-evidence while limiting it, which opens up our thinking without rending it.

The secret has been lost, and lost for good, it seems. If we are ever again to find a balance between science and philosophy, between our models and the obscurity of the "there is," it must be of a new kind. Our science has rejected the justifications as well as the restrictions which Descartes assigned to its domain. It no longer pretends to deduce its invented models from the attributes of God. The depth of the existing world and an unfathomable God no longer stand over against the flatness of "technicized" thought. Science manages without the excursion into metaphysics that Descartes had to make at least once in his life; it begins from the point he ultimately reached. Operational thought claims for itself, in the name of psychology, that domain of contact with oneself and with the world which Descartes reserved for a blind but irreducible experience. Operational thought is fundamentally hostile to philosophy as thought-in-contact, and if it rediscovers a sense of such a philosophy, it will be through the very excess of its daring; when, having introduced all sorts of notions that Descartes would have held to arise from confused thought—quality, scalar structures, solidarity of observer and observed—it suddenly realizes that one cannot summarily speak of all these beings as *constructs*.

Meanwhile, philosophy maintains itself against such operationalist thinking, plunging itself into that dimension of the composite of soul and body, of the existent world, of the abyssal Being that Descartes opened up and so quickly closed again. Our science and our philosophy are two faithful and unfaithful offshoots of Cartesianism, two monsters born of its dismemberment.

Nothing is left for our philosophy but to set out to prospect the actual world. We *are* the compound of soul and body, and so there must be a thought of it. It is to this knowledge by position or situation that Descartes owes what he himself says of it, or what he sometimes says of the presence of the body "against the soul," or of the exterior world "at the tip" of our hands. Here the body is no longer the means of vision and touch, but their depository.

Our organs are not instruments; on the contrary, our instruments are added-on organs. Space is not what it was in the *Dioptrics*, a network of relations between objects such as would be seen by a third party, witnessing my vision, or by a geometer looking over it and reconstructing it from outside. It is, rather, a space reckoned starting from me as the null point or degree zero of spatiality. I do not see it according to its exterior envelope; I live it from the inside; I am immersed in it. After all, the world is around me, not in front of me. Light is found once more to be action at a distance. It is no longer reduced to the action of contact or, in other words, conceived as it might be by those who cannot see.[32] Vision reassumes its fundamental power of manifestation, of showing more than itself. And since we are told that a bit of ink suffices to make us see forests and storms, light must have its own power to generate the imaginary. Its transcendence is not delegated to a reading mind which deciphers the impacts of the light qua thing upon the brain and which could do this quite as well if it had never inhabited a body. No longer is it a matter of speaking about space and light, but of making space and light, which are *there*, speak to us. There is no end to this questioning, since the vision to which it is addressed is itself a question. All the inquiries we believed closed have been reopened. What is depth, what is light, τι το ὄν? What are they—not for the mind that cuts itself off from the body but for the mind Descartes says is suffused throughout the body? And what are they, finally, not only for the mind but for themselves, since they pass through us and surround us?

This philosophy, which is yet to be elaborated, is what animates the painter—not when he expresses opinions about the world but in that instant when his vision becomes gesture, when, in Cézanne's words, he "thinks in painting."[33]

IV

The entire history of painting in the modern period, with its efforts to detach itself from illusionism and acquire its own dimensions, has a metaphysical significance. There can be no question of demonstrating this here. Not because of the limits of objectivity in history and the inevitable plurality of interpretations, which would forbid linking a philosophy and an event, for the metaphysics we have in mind is not a separate body of ideas for which inductive justifications could then be sought in the experiential realm—and there are, in the flesh of contingency, a structure of the event and a virtue peculiar to the scenario that do not prevent the plurality of interpretations but in fact are the deepest reason for it. They make the event a durable theme of historical life, and have a right to philosophical status. In a sense everything that may have been said and will be said about the French Revolution has always been and will henceforth be within it, in that wave arising from a roil of discrete facts, with its froth of the past and its crest of the future. And it is always by looking more deeply into *how it came about* that we make and will go on making new representations of it. As for the history of works of art, in any case, if they are great, the sense we give to them later on has issued from them. It is the work itself that has opened the perspective from which it appears in another light. It transforms *itself* and *becomes* what follows; the interminable interpretations to which it is *legitimately* susceptible change it only into itself. And if the historian unearths beneath its manifest content a surplus and thickness of meaning, a texture which field the promise of a long history, then this active manner of being, this possibility he unveils in the work, this monogram he finds there—all are grounds for a philosophical meditation. But such a labor demands a long familiarity with history. I lack everything for its execution, both competence and space. But since the power or the fecundity of works of art exceeds every positive causal or linear relation, it is not illegitimate for a layman such as myself, speaking from his memory of a few paintings and books, to express how painting enters into his reflections, and to register his sense of a profound dissonance, a transformation in the relationship between humanity and Being, when he holds up a universe of classical thought, contrasting it en bloc with the explorations of modern painting. A sort of history by contact, that perhaps does not go beyond the limits of one person, though it owes everything to his frequentation of others. . . .

"I believe Cézanne was seeking depth all his life," says Giacometti.[34] Says Robert Delaunay, "Depth is the new inspiration."[35] Four centuries after the "solutions" of the Renaissance and three centuries after Descartes, depth is still new, and it insists on being sought, not "once in a lifetime" but all through life. It cannot be merely a question of an unmysterious interval, as seen from an airplane, between these trees nearby and those farther away. Nor is it a matter of the way things are conjured away, one by another, as we see so vividly portrayed in a perspective drawing. These two views are very explicit and raise no problems. The enigma, though, lies in their bond, in what is between them. The enigma consists in the fact that I see things, each one in its place, precisely because they eclipse one another, and that they are rivals before my sight precisely because each one is in its own place—in their exteriority, known through their envelopment, and their mutual dependence in their autonomy. Once depth is understood in this way, we can no longer call it a third dimension. In the first place, if it were a dimension, it would be the *first* one; there are forms and definite planes only if it is stipulated how far from me their different parts are. But a *first* dimension that contains all the others is no longer a dimension, at least in the ordinary sense of a *certain relationship* according to which we make measurements. Depth thus understood is, rather, the experience of the reversibility of dimensions, of a global "locality" in which everything is in the same place at the same time, a locality from which height, width, and depth are abstracted, a voluminosity we express in a word when we say that a thing is *there.* In pursuing depth, what Cézanne is seeking is this deflagration of Being, and it is all in the modes of space, and in form as well. Cézanne already knew what cubism would restate: that the external form, the envelope, is secondary and derived, that it is not what makes a thing to take form, that that shell of space must be shattered—the fruit bowl must be broken. But then what should be painted instead? Cubes, spheres, and cones—as he said once? Pure forms having the solidity of what could be defined by an internal law of construction, forms which taken together, as traces or cross-sections of the thing, let it appear between them like a face in the reeds? This would be to put Being's solidity on one side and its variety on the other. Cézanne had already made an experiment of this kind in his middle period. He went directly to the solid, to space—and came to find that inside this space—this box or container too large for them—the things began to move, color against color; they began to modulate in the instability.[36] Thus we must seek space and its content *together.* The problem becomes generalized; it is no longer solely that of distance, line, and form; it is also, and equally, the problem of color.

Color is the "place where our brain and the universe meet," he says in that admirable idiom of the artisan of Being which Klee liked to quote.[37] It is for the sake of color that we must break up the form *qua* spectacle. Thus the question is not of colors, "simulacra of the colors of nature."[38] The question, rather, concerns the dimension of color, that dimension which creates—from itself to itself—identities, differences, a texture, a materiality, a something. . . .

Yet there is clearly no one master key of the visible, and color alone is no closer to being such a key than space is. The return to color has the virtue of getting somewhat nearer to "the heart of things,"[39] but this heart is beyond the color envelope just as it is beyond the space envelope. The *Portrait of Vallier* sets white spaces between the colors which take on the function of giving shape to, and setting off, a being more general than yellow-being or green-being or blue-being. Similarly, in the water colors of Cézanne's last years, space (which had been taken to be self-evidence itself and of which it was believed that the question of *where* was not to be asked) radiates around planes that cannot be assigned to any place at all: "a superimposing of transparent surfaces," "a flowing movement of planes of color which overlap, advance and retreat."[40]

As we can see, it is not a matter of adding one more dimension to those of the flat canvas, of organizing an illusion or an objectless perception whose perfection consists in simulating an empirical vision to the maximum degree. Pictorial depth (as well as painted height and width) comes "I know not whence" to alight upon, and take root in, the sustaining support. The painter's vision is not a view upon the *outside*, a merely "physical-optical"[41] relation with the world. The world no longer stands before him through representation; rather, it is the painter to whom the things of the world give birth by a sort of concentration or coming-to-itself of the visible. Ultimately the painting relates to nothing at all among experienced things unless it is first of all "autofigurative."[42] It is a spectacle of something only by being a "spectacle of nothing,"[43] by breaking the "skin of things"[44] to show how the things become things, how the world becomes world. Apollinaire said that in a poem there are phrases which do not appear to have been *created*, which seem to have *shaped themselves*. And Henri Michaux said that sometimes Klee's colors seem to have been born slowly upon the canvas, to have emanated from some primordial ground, "exhaled at the right spot"[45] like a patina or a mold. Art is not construction, artifice, the meticulous relationship to a space and a world existing outside. It is truly the "inarticulate cry," as Hermes Trismegistus said, "which seemed to be the voice of the light." And once it is present it awakens powers dormant in ordinary vision, a secret of preexistence. When through the water's thickness I see the tiled bottom of the pool, I do not see it *despite* the water and the reflections; I see it through them and because of them. If there were no distortions, no ripples of sunlight, if it were without that flesh that I saw the geometry of the tiles, then I would cease to see it *as* it is and where it is—which is to say, beyond any identical, specific place. I cannot say that the water itself—the aqueous power, the syrupy and shimmering element—is *in* space; all this is not somewhere else either, but it is not in the pool. It inhabits it, is materialized there, yet it is not contained there; and if I lift my eyes toward the screen of cypresses where the web of reflections plays, I must recognize that the water visits it as well, or at least sends out to it its active, living essence. This inner animation, this radiation of the visible, is what the painter seeks beneath, the words *depth, space,* and *color*.

Anyone who thinks about the matter finds it astonishing that very often a good painter can also produce good drawings or good sculpture. Since neither the means of expression nor the creative gestures are comparable, this is proof that there is a system of equivalences, a Logos of lines, of lighting, of colors, of reliefs, of masses—a nonconceptual presentation of universal Being. The effort of modern painting has been directed not so much toward choosing between line and color, or even between figurative depiction and the creation of signs, as it has been toward multiplying the systems of equivalences, toward severing their adherence to the envelope of things. This effort may require the creation of new materials or new means of expression, but it may well be realized at times by the reexamination and reuse of those already at hand.

There has been, for example, a prosaic conception of the line as a positive attribute and property of the object in itself. Thus, it is the outer contour of the apple or the border between the plowed field and the meadow, considered as present in the world, such that, guided by points taken from the real world, the pencil or brush would only have to pass over them. But this line has been contested by all modern painting, and probably by all painting, as we are led to think by da Vinci's comment in his *Treatise on Painting*: "The secret of the art of drawing is to discover in each object the particular way in which a certain flexuous line, which is, so to speak, its generating axis, is directed through its whole extent."[46] Both Ravaisson and Bergson sensed something important in this, without daring to decipher the oracle all the way. Bergson scarcely looked for the "sinuous outline [*serpentement*]" outside living beings, and he rather timidly advanced the idea that the undulating line "could be no one of the visible lines of the figure," that it is "no more here than there," and yet "gives the key to the whole."[47] He was on the threshold of that gripping discovery, already familiar to the painters, that there are no lines visible in themselves, that neither the contour of the apple nor the border between field and meadow is in *this* place or that, that they are always on the near or the far side of the point we look at. They are always between or behind whatever we fix our eyes upon; they are indicated, implicated, and even very imperiously demanded by the things, but they themselves are not things. They were thought to circumscribe the apple or the meadow, but the apple and the meadow "form themselves" from themselves, and come into the visible as if they had come from a prespatial world behind the scenes.

Yet this challenging of the prosaic line is far from ruling out all lines in painting, as the impressionists may have thought. It is simply a matter of freeing the line, of revivifying its constituting power; and we are not faced with a contradiction when we see it reappear and triumph in painters like Klee or Matisse, who more than anyone believed in color. For henceforth, as Klee said, the line no longer imitates the visible; it "renders visible"; it is the blueprint of a genesis of things. Perhaps no one before Klee had "let a line muse."[48] The beginning of the line's path establishes or installs a certain level or mode of the linear, a certain manner for the line to be and to make itself a line, "to go line."[49] Relative to it, every subsequent inflection will have a diacritical value, will be another aspect of the line's relationship to itself, will form an adventure, a history, a meaning of the line—all this according as it slants more or less, more or less rapidly, more or less subtly. Making its way in space, it nevertheless corrodes prosaic space and its *partes extra partes*; it develops a way of extending itself actively into that space which sub-tends the spatiality of a thing quite as much as that of a man or an apple tree. It is just that, as Klee said, to give the generating axis of a man the painter "would have to have a network of lines so entangled that it could no longer be a question of a truly elementary representation."[50]

In view of this situation two alternatives are open, and it makes little difference which one is chosen. First, the painter may, like Klee, decide to hold rigorously to the principle of the genesis of the visible, the principle of fundamental, indirect, or—as Klee used to say—absolute painting, and then leave it up to the *title* to designate by its prosaic name the entity thus constituted, in order to leave the painting free to function more purely as a painting. Or alternatively he may undertake, with Matisse (in his drawings), to put into a single line both the prosaic, identifying characteristics of the entity and the hidden operation which combines such indolence or inertia and such force in it as are required to constitute it as *nude*, as *face*, as *flower*.

There is a painting by Klee of two holly leaves, done in the most representational manner. At first glance the leaves are thoroughly indecipherable, and they remain to the end monstrous, unbelievable, ghostly, *on account of their exactness*. And Matisse's women (let us keep in mind his contemporaries' sarcasm) were not immediately women; they became women. It is Matisse who taught us to see his shapes not in a "physical-optical" way but rather as structural filaments [*des nervures*], as the axes *of* a corporeal system of activity and passivity. Whether it be representational or nonrepresentational, the line is no longer a thing or an imitation of a thing. It is a certain disequilibrium contrived within the indifference of the white paper; it is a certain hollow opened up within the in-itself, a certain constitutive emptiness—an emptiness which, as Moore's statues show decisively, sustains the supposed positivity of things. The line is no longer the apparition of an entity upon a vacant background, as it was in classical geometry. It is, as in modern geometries, the restriction, segregation, or modulation of a pregiven spatiality.

Just as painting has created the latent line, it has made for itself a movement without displacement, a movement by vibration or radiation. And well it should, since, as they say, painting is an art of space, is carried out upon a canvas or sheet of paper and so lacks the wherewithal to devise things that actually move. But an immobile canvas could suggest a change of place, just as a shooting star's track on my retina suggests a transition, a motion not contained in it. The painting itself would then offer to my eyes almost the same thing offered them by real movements: a series of appropriately mixed, instantaneous glimpses along with, if a living thing is involved, attitudes unstably suspended between a before and an after—in short, the externals of a change of place which the spectator would read from the imprint it leaves. Here Rodin's well-known remark reveals its full weight: instantaneous glimpses, unstable attitudes petrify movement, as is shown by so many photographs in which an athlete-in-motion is forever frozen. We could not thaw him out by multiplying the glimpses. Marey's photographs, the cubists' analyses, Duchamp's *La Mariée* do not move; they give a Zenonian reverie on movement. We see a rigid body as if it were a piece of armor going through its motions; it is here and it is there, magically, but it does not *go* from here to there. Cinema portrays movement, but *how?* Is it, as we are inclined to believe, by copying more closely the changes of place? We may presume not, since slow motion shows a body being carried along, floating among objects like seaweed, but not *moving itself.*

Movement is given, says Rodin, by an image in which the arms, the legs, the trunk, and the head are each taken at a different instant, an image which therefore portrays the body in an attitude which it never at any instant really held and which imposes fictive linkages between the parts, as if this mutual confrontation of incompossibles could—and alone could—cause transition and duration to arise in bronze and on canvas.[51] The only successful instantaneous glimpses of movement are those which approach this paradoxical arrangement—when, for example, a walking man or woman is taken at the moment when both feet are touching the ground; for then we almost have the temporal ubiquity of the body which brings it about that the person *bestrides* space. The picture makes movement visible by its internal discordance. Each member's position, precisely by virtue of its incompatibility with that of the others (according to the body's logic), is dated differently or is not "in time" with the others; and since all of them remain visibly within the unity of one body, it is the body which comes to bestride duration. Its movement is something conspired between legs, trunk, arms, and head in some locus of virtuality, and it breaks forth only subsequently by actual change of place. When a horse is photographed at that instant when he is completely off the ground, with his legs almost folded under him—an instant, therefore, when he must be moving—why does he look as if he were leaping in place? And why, by contrast, do Géricault's horses really *run* on canvas, in a posture impossible for a real horse at a gallop? It is because the horses in *Epsom Derby* bring me to see the body's grip upon the ground and that, according to a logic of body and world I know well, these "grips" upon space are also ways of taking hold of duration. Rodin said profoundly, "It is the artist who is truthful, while the photograph lies; for, in reality, time never stops."[52] The photograph keeps open the instants which the onrush of time closes up forthwith; it destroys the overtaking, the overlapping, the "metamorphosis" [Rodin] of time. This is what painting, in contrast, makes visible, because the horses have in them that "leaving here, going there,"[53] because they have a foot in each instant. Painting searches not for the outside of movement but for its secret ciphers, of which there are some still more subtle than those of which Rodin spoke. All flesh, and even that of the world, radiates beyond itself. But whether or not one is, depending on the era and the "school," attached more to manifest movement or the monumental, the art of painting is never altogether outside time, because it is always within the carnal.

Now perhaps we have a better sense of how much is contained in that little word "see." Seeing is not a certain mode of thought or presence to self; it is the means given me for being absent from myself, for being present from within at the fission of Being only at the end of which do I close up into myself.

Painters have always known this. Da Vinci invoked a "pictorial science" which does not speak in words (and still less in numbers) but in works that exist in the visible just as natural things do—yet pass on that science "to all the generations of the universe."[54] A silent science, says Rilke (apropos of Rodin), that brings into the work the forms of things "whose seal has not been broken"; it comes from the eye and addresses itself to the eye.[55] We must understand the eye as the "window of the soul." "The eye . . . through which the beauty of the universe is revealed to our contemplation is of such excellence that whoever should resign himself to losing it would deprive himself of the knowledge of all the works of nature, the sight of which makes the soul live happily in its body's prison, thanks to the eyes which show him the infinite variety of creation: whoever loses them abandons his soul in a dark prison where all hope of once more seeing the sun, the light of the universe, must vanish." The eye accomplishes the prodigious work of opening the soul to what is not soul—the joyous realm of things and their god, the sun.

A Cartesian can believe that the existing world is not visible, that the only light is of the mind, and that all vision takes place in God. A painter cannot agree that our openness to the world is illusory or indirect, that what we see is not the world itself, or that the mind has to do only with its thoughts or another mind. He accepts, with all its difficulties, the myth of the windows of the soul; what is without place must be subjected to a body—or, what is even more: what is without place must be initiated *by* the body to all the others and to nature. We must take literally what vision teaches us: namely, that through it we touch the sun and the stars, that we are everywhere at once, and that even our power to imagine ourselves elsewhere—"I am in Petersburg in my bed, in Paris, my eyes see the sun"[56]—or freely to envision real beings, wherever they are, borrows from vision and employs means we owe to it. Vision alone teaches us that beings that are different, "exterior," foreign to one another, are yet absolutely *together*, are "simultaneity"; which is a mystery psychologists handle the way a child handles explosives. Robert Delaunay says succinctly, "The railroad track is the image of succession which comes closest to the parallel: the parity of the rails."[57] The rails converge and do not converge; they converge *in order to* remain equidistant farther away. The world is in accordance with my perspective *in order to* be independent of me, is for me *in order to be* without me, to be a world. The "visual quale" gives me, and is alone in doing so, the presence of what is not me, of what *is* simply and fully.[58] It does so because, as a texture, it is the concretion of a universal visibility, of one sole Space that separates and reunites, that sustains every cohesion (and even that of past and future, since there would be no such cohesion if they were not essentially parts of the same space). Every visual something, as individual as it is, functions also as a dimension, because it is given as the result of a dehiscence of Being. What this ultimately means is that the hallmark of the visible is to have a lining of invisibility in the strict sense, which it makes present as a certain absence. "In their time, our erstwhile opposites, the Impressionists, were perfectly right in electing domicile among the scrub and stubble of the daily spectacle. As for us, our heart throbs to get closer to the depths. . . . These oddities will become . . . realities . . . because instead of being limited to the diversely intense restoration of the visible, they also annex the occultly perceived portion of the invisible."[59] There is that which reaches the eye head on, the frontal properties of the visible; but there is also that which reaches it from below—the profound postural latency whereby the body raises itself to see—and that which reaches vision from above like the phenomena of flight, of swimming, of movement, where it participates no longer in the heaviness of origins but in free accomplishments.[60] Through vision, then, the painter touches both extremities. In the immemorial depth of the visible, something has moved, caught fire, which engulfs his body; everything he paints is in answer to this incitement, and his hand is "nothing but the instrument of a distant will." Vision is the meeting, as at a crossroads, of all the aspects of Being. "A certain fire wills to live; it wakes. Working its way along the hand's conductor, it reaches the canvas and invades it; then, a leaping spark, it arcs the gap in the circle it was to trace: the return to the eye, and beyond."[61] There is no break at all in this circuit; it is impossible to say that here nature ends and the human being or expression begins. It is, then, silent Being that itself comes to show forth its own meaning. Herein lies the reason why the dilemma between figurative and nonfigurative art is wrongly posed; it is at once true and uncontradictory that no grape was ever what it is in the most figurative painting and that no painting, no matter how abstract, can get away from Being, that even Caravaggio's grape is the grape itself.[62] This precession of what is upon what one sees and makes seen, of what one sees and makes seen upon what is—this is vision itself. And to give the ontological formula of painting we hardly need to force the painter's own words, Klee's words written at the age of thirty-seven and ultimately inscribed on his tomb: "I cannot be grasped in immanence."[63]

V

Because depth, color, form, line, movement, contour, physiognomy are all branches of Being and because each entwines the tufts of all the rest, there are no separated, distinct "problems" in painting, no really opposed paths, no partial "solutions," no cumulative progress, no irretrievable options. There is nothing to prevent the painter from going back to one of the emblems he has shied away from—making it, of course, speak differently. Rouault's contours are not those of Ingres. Light is the "old sultana," says Georges Limbour, "whose charms withered away at the beginning of this century."[64] Expelled at first by the painters of matter, it reappears finally in Dubuffet as a certain texture of matter. One is never immune to these avatars or to the least expected convergences; some of Rodin's fragments are statues by Germaine Richier *because they were sculptors*—that is to say, enmeshed in a single, identical network of Being.

For the same reason nothing is ever finally acquired and possessed for good. In "working over" a favorite problem, even if it is just the problem of velvet or wool, the true painter unknowingly upsets the givens of all the other problems. His quest is total even where it looks partial. Just when he has reached proficiency in some area, he finds that he has reopened another one where everything he said before must be said again in a different way. Thus what he has found he does not yet have. It remains to be sought out; the discovery itself calls forth still further quests. The idea of universal painting, of a totalization of painting, of painting's being fully and definitively accomplished is an idea bereft of sense. For painters, if any remain, the world will always be yet to be painted; even if it lasts millions of years . . . it will all end without having been completed.

Panofsky shows that the "problems" of painting that structure its history are often solved obliquely, not in the course of inquiries instigated to solve them but, on the contrary, at some point when painters, having reached an impasse, apparently forget those problems and allow themselves to be attracted by other things. Then suddenly, their attention elsewhere, they happen upon the old problems and surmount the obstacle. This hidden historicity, advancing through the labyrinth by detours, transgression, slow encroachments and sudden drives, does not imply that the painter does not know what he wants, but that what he wants is on the hither side of means and goals, commanding and overseeing all our *useful* activity.

We are so fascinated by the classical idea of intellectual adequation that painting's mute "thought" sometimes leaves us with the impression of a vain swirl of significations, a paralyzed or miscarried utterance. And if one answers that no thought ever detaches itself completely from a sustaining support; that the sole privilege of speaking thought is to have rendered its own support manageable; that the figurations of literature and philosophy are no more settled than those of painting and are no more capable of being accumulated into a stable treasure; that even science learns to recognize a zone of the "fundamental," peopled with dense, open, rent beings of which an exhaustive treatment is out of the question—like the cyberneticians' "aesthetic information" or mathematicophysical "groups of operations"; that, in the end, we are never in a position to take stock of everything objectively or to think of progress in itself; and that the whole of human history is, in a certain sense, stationary: *What,* says the understanding, like [Stendhal's] Lamiel, is *that all there is to it?* Is this the highest point of reason, to realize that the soil beneath our feet is shifting, to pompously call "interrogation" what is only a persistent state of stupor, to call "research" or "quest" what is only trudging in a circle, to call "Being" that which never fully is?

But this disappointment issues from that spurious fantasy[65] which claims for itself a positivity capable of making up for its own emptiness. It is the regret of not being everything, and a rather groundless regret at that. For if we cannot establish a hierarchy of civilizations or speak of progress—neither in painting nor even elsewhere—it is not because some fate impedes us; it is, rather, because the very first painting in some sense went to the farthest reach of the future. If no painting completes painting, if no work is itself ever absolutely completed, still, each creation changes, alters, clarifies, deepens, confirms, exalts, recreates, or creates by anticipation all the others. If creations are not permanent acquisitions, it is not just that, like all things, they pass away: it is also that they have almost their entire lives before them.

Notes

1. "L'oeil et l'esprit" was the last work Merleau-Ponty saw published. It appeared in the inaugural issue of *Art de France* 1, no. 1 (January 1961). After his death it was reprinted in *Les Temps Modernes* 184–85, along with seven articles devoted to him. It has now been published, in book form, by Gallimard (1964). Both the *Art de France* article and the book contain illustrations chosen by Merleau-Ponty. According to Professor Claude Lefort, "L'oeil et l'esprit" is a preliminary statement of ideas that were to be developed in the second part of the book Merleau-Ponty was writing at the time of his death—*Le visible et l'invisible* (part of which was published post-humously by Gallimard in February 1964). The translator wishes to acknowledge his immense debt to George Downing, who spent many long hours working over the final revisions of the translation. Also, thanks are due to Michel Beaujour, Arleen B. Dallery, and Robert Reitter for their advice and encouragement. —Tr.

2. [Il est là, fort ou faible dans la vie, mais souverain sans conteste dans sa rumination du monde, sans autre "technique" que celle que ses yeux et ses mains se donnent à force de voir, à force de peindre, acharné à tirer de ce monde où sonnent les scandales et les gloires de l'histoire des *toiles* qui n'ajouteront guère aux colères ni aux espoirs des hommes, et personne ne murmure.]

3. Cf. *Le visible et l'invisible* (Paris: Gallimard, 1964), 273, 308–11. —Tr.

4. See *Signes* (Paris: Gallimard, 1960), 210, 222–23, especialiy the footnotes, for a clarification of the "circularity" at issue here. —Tr.

5. [Cet équivalent interne, cette formule charnelle de leur presence que les choses suscitent en moi, pourquoi à leur tour ne susciteraient-ils pas un tracé visible encore, où tout autre regard retrouvera les motifs qui soutiennent son inspection do monde?]

6. G. Charbonnier, *Le monologue du peintre* (Paris, 1959), 172.

7. [Beaucoup plus loin, puisque le tableau n'est un analogue que selon le corps, qu'il n'offre pas à l'esprit une occasion de repenser les rapports constitutifs des choses, mais au regard, pour qu'il les épouse, les traces de la vision du dedans, à la vision ce qui la tapisse intérieurement, la texture imaginaire du réel.]

8. Charbonnier, *Le monologue*, 34.

9. Ibid., 143–45.

10. " . . . Line philosophie figurée." Cf. Bergson (Ravaisson), note 46 below. —Tr.

11. P. Claudel, *Introduction à la peinture hollandaise* (Paris, 1935).

12. P. Schilder, *The Image and Appearance of the Human Body* (London, 1935; New York, 1950), 223–24. ["the body-image is not confined to the borderlines of one's own body. It transgresses them in the mirror. There is a body-image outside ourselves, and it is remarkable that primitive peoples even ascribe a substantial existence to the picture in the mirror" (278). Schilder's earlier, shorter study, *Das Körperschema* (Berlin, 1923), is cited several times in *The Structure of Behavior* and in *Phenomenology of Perception*. Schilder's later work is of especial interest with regard to Merleau-Ponty's own elaborations of the meaning of the human body; it is worth examining for that reason, as well as for the chance it provides to discern some fundamental coincidences between Merleau-Ponty and certain American pragmatists.]

13. Cf. Schilder, *Image*, 281–82. —Tr.

14. Robert Delaunay, *Du cubisme à l'art abstrait* (Paris, 1957).

15. "A minute in the world's life passes! to paint it in its reality! and forget everything for that. To become that minute, be the sensitive plate, . . . give the image of what we see, forgetting everything that has appeared before our time." Cézanne, quoted in B. Dorvial, *Paul Cézanne*, trans. H. H. A. Thackthwaite (London, 1948), 101. —Tr.

16. Descartes, *La Dioptrique*, Discours VII [conclusion]. Edition Adam et Tannery, VI, 165.

17. Ibid., Discours I. Adam et Tannery, 83. [*Oeuvres et lettres de Descartes*, ed. André Bridoux, Edition Pléiade, 181. Page references from the Bridoux selections have been added in the belief that this volume is more widely accessible today than the Adam and Tannery complete edition.]

18. Ibid., Adam et Tannery, 84. [Bridoux, 182].

19. This paragraph continues the exposition of the *Dioptrics*. —Tr.

20. Ibid., Discours IV. Adam et Tannery, 112–14. [Bridoux, 203–4; in English, *Descartes: Philosophical Writings*, ed. and trans. N. Kemp Smith (Modern Library Edition), 145–47.]

21. Ibid., 130. [Bridoux, 217; Smith, 148.]

22. The system of means by which painting makes us see is a scientific matter. Why, then, do we not methodically produce perfect images of the world, arriving at a universal art purged of personal art, just as the universal language would free us of all the confused relationships that lurk in existent languages?

23. *Dioptrique*, Discours IV. [Note 20 above.]

24. Discours V of the *Dioptrique*, especially Descartes's diagrams, helps considerably to clarify this compressed passage. —Tr.

25. That is, the painting. —Tr.

26. E. Panofsky, *Die Perspektive als symbolische Form*, in *Vorträge der Bibliotek Warburg*, vol. 4 (1924–25).

27. Ibid. [The *Stilmoment*, or moment of an instituted style, does not dispense with the *Wermoment*, or moment of the individual perception. —Tr.]

28. Descartes, Discours IV, Adam et Tannery, 135. [Bridoux, 220; Smith, 154.] Here is N. Kemp Smith's translation of the passage under discussion: "Our knowledge of it (the situation of an object) does not depend on any image or action which comes to us

from the object, but solely on the situation of the small parts of the brain whence the nerves take their origin. For this situation—a situation which changes with every change however small in the points at which these nerve-fibers are located—is instituted by nature in order to secure, not only that the mind be aware of the location of each part of the body which it animates, relatively to all the others, but also that it be able to transfer its attention to all the positions contained in the straight line that can be imaged as drawn from the extremity of each of these parts, and as prolonged to infinity."]

29. Ibid., Adam et Tannery, 137. [Bridoux, 222; Smith, 155. N. Kemp Smith's translation is given here.]

30. No doubt Merleau-Ponty is speaking of Princess Elizabeth, Descartes's correspondent. Cf. *Phénoménologie de la perception*, 230–32 (C. Smith translation, 198–99), and Descartes's letter to Elizabeth of 28 June 1643 (Bridoux, 1157–60). —Tr.

31. That is the obscurity of the "existential" order is just as necessary, just as grounded in God, as is the clarity of true thoughts ("nos lumières")—Tr.

32. Cf. note 18, above. —Tr.

33. B. Dorival, *Paul Cézanne* (Paris, 1948), 103ff. [H. H. A. Thackthwaite's translation (London, 1948), 101–3.1]

34. Charbonnier, *Le monologue*, 176.

35. Delaunay, *Du cubisme*, 109.

36. F. Novotny, *Cézanne und das Ende der wissenschaftlichen Perspective* (Vienna, 1938).

37. W. Grohmann, *Paul Klee* (Paris, 1954), 141. [New York, 1956.]

38. Delaunay, *Du cubisme*, 118.

39. Klee, *Journal*. French trans. P. Klossowski (Paris, 1959).

40. George Schmidt, *Les aquarelles de Cézanne*, 21. [*The Watercolors of Cézanne* (New York, 1953).]

41. Klee. *Journal*.

42. "The spectacle is first of all a spectacle of itself before it is a spectacle of' something outside of it."—*Translator's note from Merleau-Ponty's 1961 lectures.*

43. C. P. Bru, *Esthétique de l'abstraction* (Paris, 1959), 99, 86.

44. Henri Michaux, *Aventures de lignes.*

45. Ibid.

46. Ravaisson, cited by Bergson, "La vie et l'oeuvre de Ravaisson," in *La pensée et le mouvant* (Paris, 1934), 264–65. [The passage quoted here is from M. L. Andison's translation of that work, *The Creative Mind* (New York, 1946), 229. It remains moot whether these are Ravaisson's or da Vinci's words.]

47. Bergson, ibid.

48. Michaux, *Aventures de lignes.* ["laisse rêver une ligne."]

49. Ibid. ["d'aller ligne."]

50. Grohmann, *Paul Klee*, 192.

51. Rodin, *L'art.* Interviews collected by Paul Gsell (Paris, 1911).

52. Ibid., 86. Rodin uses the word "metamorphosis," quoted below.

53. Michaux, *Aventures de lignes.*

54. Cited by Delaunay, Du *cubisme*, 175.

55. Rilke, *Auguste Rodin*, French translation by Maurice Betz (Paris, 1928), 150. [English translation by Jessie Lamont and Hans Trausil (New York, 1919; republished 1945).]

56. Delaunay, *Du cubisme*, 115, 110.

57. Ibid.

58. Ibid.

59. Klee, *Conférence d'Iena* (1924), according to Grohmann, *Paul Klee*, 365.

60. Klee, *Wege des Naturstudiums* (1923), as found in G. di San Lazzaro, *Klee.*

61. Klee, cited by Grohmann, *Paul Klee*, 99.

62. A. Berne-Joffroy, *Le dossier Caravage* (Paris, 1959), and Michel Butor, "La Corbeille de l'Ambrosienne," *Nouvelle Revue Française* (1959), 969–89.

63. Klee, *Journal*. ["Je suis insaisissable dans l'immanence."]

64. G. Limbour, *Tableau bon levain à vous de cuire la pâte: L'art brut de Jean Dubuffet* (Paris, 1953), 54–55.

65. "Mais cette déception est celle du faux imaginaire, qui . . ."

The Intertwining—The Chiasm

If it is true that as soon as philosophy declares itself to be reflection or coincidence it prejudges what it will find, then once again it must recommence everything, reject the instruments reflection and intuition had provided themselves, and install itself in a locus where they have not yet been distinguished, in experiences that have not yet been "worked over," that offer us all at once, pell-mell, both "subject" and "object," both existence and essence, and hence give philosophy resources to redefine them. Seeing, speaking, even thinking (with certain reservations, for as soon as we distinguish thought from speaking absolutely we are already in the order of reflection), are experiences of this kind, both irrecusable and enigmatic. They have a name in all languages, but a name which in all of them also conveys significations in tufts, thickets of proper meanings and figurative meanings, so that, unlike those of science, not one of these names clarifies by attributing to what is named a circumscribed signification. Rather, they are the repeated index, the insistent reminder of a mystery as familiar as it is unexplained, of a light which, illuminating the rest, remains at its source in obscurity. If we could rediscover within the exercise of seeing and speaking some of the living references that assign them such a destiny in a language, perhaps they would teach us how to form our new instruments, and first of all to understand our research, our interrogation, themselves.

The visible about us seems to rest in itself. It is as though our vision were formed in the heart of the visible, or as though there were between it and us an intimacy as close as between the sea and the strand. And yet it is not possible that we blend into it, nor that it passes into us, for then the vision would vanish at the moment of formation, by disappearance of the seer or of the visible. What there is then are not things first identical with themselves, which would then offer themselves to the seer, nor is there a seer who is first empty and who, afterward, would open himself to them—but something to which we could not be closer than by palpating it with our look, things we could not dream of seeing "all naked" because the gaze itself envelops them, clothes them with its own flesh. Whence does it happen that in so doing it leaves them in their place, that the vision we acquire of them seems to us to come from them, and that to be seen is for them but a degradation of their eminent being? What is this talisman of color, this singular virtue of the visible that makes it, held at the end of the gaze, nonetheless much more than a correlative of my vision, such that it imposes my vision upon me as a continuation of its own sovereign existence? How does it happen that my look, enveloping them, does not hide them, and, finally, that, veiling them, it unveils them?[1]

We must first understand that this red under my eyes is not, as is always said, a *quale*, a pellicle of being without thickness, a message at the same time indecipherable and evident, which one has or has not received, but of which, if one has received it, one knows all there is to know, and of which in the end there is nothing to say. It requires a focusing, however brief; it emerges from a less precise, more general redness, in which my gaze was caught, into which it sank, before—as we put it so aptly—*fixing* it. And, now that I have fixed it, if my eyes penetrate into it, into its fixed structure, or if they start to wander round about again, the *quale* resumes its atmospheric existence. Its precise form is bound up with a certain wooly, metallic, or porous [?] configuration or texture, and the *quale* itself counts for very little compared with these participations. Claudel has a phrase saying that a certain blue of the sea is so blue that only blood would be more red. The color is yet a variant in another dimension of variation, that of its relations with the surroundings: this red is what it is only by connecting up from its place with other reds about it, with which it forms a constellation, or with other colors it dominates or that dominate it, that it attracts or that attract it, that it repels or that repel it. In short, it is a certain node in the woof of the simultaneous and the successive. It is a concretion of visibility, it is not an atom. The red dress a fortiori holds with all its fibers onto the fabric of the visible, and thereby onto a fabric of invisible being. A punctuation in the field of red things, which includes the tiles of roof tops, the flags of gatekeepers and of the Revolution, certain terrains near Aix or in Madagascar, it is also a punctuation in the field of red garments, which includes, along with the dresses of women, robes of professors, bishops, and advocate generals, and also in the field of adornments and that of uniforms. And its red literally is not the same as it appears in one constellation or in the other, as the pure essence of the Revolution of 1917 precipitates in it, or that of the eternal feminine, or that of the public prosecutor, or that of the gypsies dressed like hussars who reigned twenty-five years ago over an inn on the Champs-Elysées. A certain red is also a fossil drawn up from the depths of imaginary worlds. If we took all these participations into account, we would recognize that a naked color, and in general a visible, is not a chunk of absolutely hard, indivisible being, offered all naked to a vision which could be only total or null, but is rather a sort of straits between exterior horizons and interior horizons ever gaping open, something that comes to touch lightly and makes diverse regions of the colored or visible world resound at the distances, a certain differentiation, an ephemeral modulation of this world—less a color or a thing, therefore, than a difference between things and colors, a momentary crystallization of colored being or of visibility. Between the alleged colors and visibles, we would find anew the tissue that lines them, sustains them, nourishes them, and which for its part is not a thing, but a possibility, a latency, and a *flesh* of things.

If we turn now to the seer, we will find that this is no analogy or vague comparison and must be taken literally. The look, we said, envelops, palpates, espouses the visible things. As though it were in a relation of pre-established harmony with them, as though it knew them before knowing them, it moves in its own way with its abrupt and imperious style, and yet the views taken are not desultory—I do not look at a chaos, but at things—so that finally one cannot say if it is the look or if it is the things that command. What is this prepossession of the visible, this art of interrogating it according to its own wishes, this inspired exegesis? We would perhaps find the answer in the tactile palpation where the questioner and the questioned are closer, and of which, after all, the palpation of the eye is a remarkable variant. How does it happen that I give to my hands, in particular, that degree, that rate, and that direction of movement that are capable of making me feel the textures of the sleek and the rough? Between the exploration and what it will teach me, between my movements and what I touch, there must exist some relationship by principle, some kinship, according to which they are not only, like the pseudopods of the amoeba, vague and ephemeral deformations of the corporeal space, but the initiation to and the opening upon a tactile world. This can happen only if my hand, while it is felt from within, is also accessible from without, itself tangible, for my other hand, for example, if it takes its place among the things it touches, is in a sense one of them, opens finally upon a tangible being of which it is also a part. Through this crisscrossing within it of the touching and the tangible, its own movements incorporate themselves into the universe they interrogate, are recorded on the same map as it; the two systems are applied upon one another, as the two halves of an orange. It is no different for the vision—except, it is said, that here the exploration and the information it gathers do not belong "to the same sense." But this delimitation of the senses is crude. Already in the "touch" we have just found three distinct experiences which subtend one another, three dimensions which overlap but are distinct: a touching of the sleek and of the rough, a touching of the things—a passive sentiment of the body and of its space—and finally a veritable touching of the touch, when my right hand touches my left hand while it is palpating the things, where the "touching subject" passes over to the rank of the touched, descends into the things, such that the touch is formed in the midst of the world and as it were in the things. Between the massive sentiment I have of the sack in which I am enclosed, and the control from without that my hand exercises over my hand, there is as much difference as between the movements of my eyes and the changes they produce in the visible. And as, conversely, every experience of the visible has always been given to me within the context of the movements of the look, the visible spectacle belongs to the touch neither more nor less than do the "tactile qualities." We must habituate ourselves to think that every visible is cut out in the tangible, every tactile being in some manner promised to visibility, and that there is encroachment, infringement, not only between the touched and the touching, but also between the tangible and the visible, which is encrusted in it, as, conversely, the tangible itself is not a nothingness of visibility, is not without visual existence. Since the same body sees and touches, visible and tangible belong to the same world. It is a marvel too little noticed that every movement of my eyes—even more, every displacement of my body—has its place in the same visible universe that I itemize and explore with them, as, conversely, every vision takes place somewhere in the tactile space. There is double and crossed situating of the visible in the tangible and of the tangible in the visible; the two maps are complete, and yet they do not merge into one. The two parts are total parts and yet are not superposable.

Hence, without even entering into the implications proper to the seer and the visible, we know that, since vision is a palpation with the look, it must also be inscribed in the order of being that it discloses to us; he who looks must not himself be foreign to the world that he looks at. As soon as I see, it is necessary that the vision (as is so well indicated by the double meaning of the word) be doubled with a complementary vision or with another vision: myself seen from without, such as another would see me, installed in the midst of the visible, occupied in considering it from a certain spot. For the moment we shall not examine how far this identity of the seer and the visible goes, if we have a complete experience of it, or if there is something missing, and what it is. It suffices for us for the moment to note that he who sees cannot possess the visible unless he is possessed by it, unless he *is of it*,[2] unless, by principle, according to what is required by the articulation of the look with the things, he is one of the visibles, capable, by a singular reversal, of seeing them—he who is one of them.[3]

We understand then why we see the things themselves, in their places, where they are, according to their being which is indeed more than their being-perceived—and why at the same time we are separated from them by all the thickness of the look and of the body; it is that this distance is not the contrary of this proximity, it is deeply consonant with it, it is synonymous with it. It is that the thickness of flesh between the seer and the thing is constitutive for the thing of its visibility as for the seer of his corporeity; it is not an obstacle between them, it is their means of communication. It is for the same reason that I am at the heart of the visible and that I am far from it: because it has thickness and is thereby naturally destined to be seen by a body. What is indefinable in the *quale*, in the color, is nothing else than a brief, peremptory manner of giving in one sole something, in one sole tone of being, visions past, visions to come, by whole clusters. I who see have my own depth also, being backed up by this same visible which I see and which, I know very well, closes in behind me. The thickness of the body, far from rivaling that of the world, is on the contrary the sole means I have to go unto the heart of the things, by making myself a world and by making them flesh.

The body interposed is not itself a thing, an interstitial matter, a connective tissue, but a *sensible for itself*, which means, not that absurdity: color that sees itself, surface that touches itself—but this paradox [?]: a set of colors and surfaces inhabited by a touch, a vision, hence an *exemplar sensible*, which offers to him who inhabits it and senses it the wherewithal to sense everything that resembles himself on the outside, such that, caught up in the tissue of the things, it draws it entirely to itself, incorporates it, and, with the same movement, communicates to the things upon which it closes over that identity without superposition, that difference without contradiction, that divergence between the within and the without that constitutes its natal secret.[4] The body unites us directly with the things through its own ontogenesis, by welding to one another the two outlines of which it is made, its two laps: the sensible mass it is and the mass of the sensible wherein it is born by segregation and upon which, as seer, it remains open. It is the body and it alone, because it is a two-dimensional being, that can bring us to the things themselves, which are themselves not flat beings but beings in depth, inaccessible to a subject that would survey them from above, open to him alone that, if it be possible, would coexist with them in the same world. When we speak of the flesh of the visible, we do not mean to do anthropology, to describe a world covered over with all our own projections, leaving aside what it can be under the human mask. Rather, we mean that carnal being, as a being of depths, of several leaves or several faces, a being in latency, and a presentation of a certain absence, is a prototype of Being, of which our body, the sensible sentient, is a very remarkable variant, but whose constitutive paradox already lies in every visible. For already the cube assembles within itself incompossible *visibilia*, as my body is at once phenomenal body and objective body, and if finally it is, it, like my body, is by a tour de force. What we call a visible is, we said, a quality pregnant with a texture, the surface of a depth, a cross section upon a massive being, a grain or corpuscle borne by a wave of Being. Since the total visible is always behind, or after, or between the aspects we see of it, there is access to it only through an experience which, like it, is wholly outside of itself. It is thus, and not as the bearer of a knowing subject, that our body commands the visible for us, but it does not explain it, does not clarify it, it only concentrates the mystery of its scattered visibility; and it is indeed a paradox of Being, not a paradox of man, that we are dealing with here. To be sure, one can reply that, between the two "sides" of our body, the body as sensible and the body as sentient (what in the past we called objective body and phenomenal body), rather than a spread, there is the abyss that separates the In Itself from the For Itself. It is a problem—and we will not avoid it—to determine how the sensible sentient can also be thought. But here, seeking to form our first concepts in such a way as to avoid the classical impasses, we do not have to honor the difficulties that they may present when confronted with a *cogito*, which itself has to be re-examined. Yes or no: do we have a body—that is, not a permanent object of thought, but a flesh that suffers when it is wounded, hands that touch? We know: hands do not suffice for touch—but to decide for this reason alone that our hands do not touch, and to relegate them to the world of objects or of instruments, would be, in acquiescing to the bifurcation of subject and object, to forego in advance the understanding of the sensible and to deprive ourselves of its lights. We propose on the contrary to take it literally to begin with. We say therefore that our body is a being of two leaves, from one side a thing among things and otherwise what sees them and touches them; we say, because it is evident, that it unites these two properties within itself, and its double belongingness to the order of the "object" and to the order of the "subject" reveals to us quite unexpected relations between the two orders. It cannot be by incomprehensible accident that the body has this double reference; it teaches us that each calls for the other. For if the body is a thing among things, it is so in a stronger and deeper sense than they: in the sense that, we said, it *is of them*, and this means that it detaches itself upon them, and, accordingly, detaches itself from them. It is not simply a thing *seen* in fact (I do not see my back), it is visible by right, it falls under a vision that is both ineluctable and deferred. Conversely, if it touches and sees, this is not because it would have the visibles before itself as objects: they are about it, they even enter into its enclosure, they are within it, they line its looks and its hands inside and outside. If it touches them and sees them, this is only because, being of their family, itself visible and tangible, it uses its own being as a means to participate in theirs, because each of the two beings is an archetype for the other, because the body belongs to the order of the things as the world is universal flesh. One should not even say, as we did a moment ago, that the body is made up of two leaves, of which the one, that of the "sensible," is bound up with the rest of the world. There are not in it two leaves or two layers; fundamentally it is neither thing seen only nor seer only, it is Visibility sometimes wandering and sometimes reassembled. And as such it is not in the world, it does not detain its view of the world as within a private garden: it sees the world itself, the world of everybody, and without having to leave "itself," because it is wholly—because its hands, its eyes, are nothing else than—this reference of a visible, a tangible-standard to all those whose resemblance it bears and whose evidence it gathers, by a magic that is the vision, the touch themselves. To speak of leaves or of layers is still to flatten and to juxtapose, under the reflective gaze, what coexists in the living and upright body. If one wants metaphors, it would be better to say that the body sensed and the body sentient are as the obverse and the reverse, or again, as two segments of one sole circular course which goes above from left to right and below from right to left, but which is but one sole movement in its two phases. And everything said about the sensed body pertains to the whole of the sensible of which it is a part, and to the world. If the body is one sole body in its two phases, it incorporates into itself the whole of the sensible and with the same movement incorporates itself into a "Sensible in itself." We have to reject the age-old assumptions that put the body in the world and the seer in the body, or, conversely, the world and the body in the seer as in a box. Where are we to put the limit between the body and the world, since the world is flesh? Where in the body are we to put the seer, since evidently there is in the body only "shadows stuffed with organs," that is, more of the visible? The world seen is not "in" my body, and my body is not "in" the visible world ultimately: as flesh applied to a flesh, the world neither surrounds it nor is surrounded by it. A participation in and kinship with the visible, the vision neither envelops it nor is enveloped by it definitively. The superficial pellicle of the visible is only for my vision and for my body. But the depth beneath this surface contains my body and hence contains my vision. My body as a visible thing is contained within the full spectacle. But my seeing body subtends this visible body, and all the visibles with it. There is reciprocal insertion and intertwining of one in the other. Or rather, if, as once again we must, we eschew the thinking by planes and perspectives, there are two circles, or two vortexes, or two spheres, concentric when I live naïvely, and as soon as I question myself, the one slightly decentered with respect to the other. . . .

We have to ask ourselves what exactly we have found with this strange adhesion of the seer and the visible. There is vision, touch, when a certain visible, a certain tangible, turns back upon the whole of the visible, the whole of the tangible, of which it is a part, or when suddenly it finds itself *surrounded* by them, or when between it and them, and through their commerce, is formed a Visibility, a Tangible in itself, which belong properly neither to the body qua fact nor to the world qua fact—as upon two mirrors facing one another where two indefinite series of images set in one another arise which belong really to neither of the two surfaces, since each is only the rejoinder of the other, and which therefore form a couple, a couple more real than either of them. Thus since the seer is caught up in what he sees, it is still himself he sees: there is a fundamental narcissism of all vision. And thus, for the same reason, the vision he exercises, he also undergoes from the things, such that, as many painters have said, I feel myself looked at by the things, my activity is equally passivity—which is the second and more profound sense of the narcissim: not to see in the outside, as the others see it, the contour of a body one inhabits, but especially to be seen by the outside, to exist within it, to emigrate into it, to be seduced, captivated, alienated by the phantom, so that the seer and the visible reciprocate one another and we no longer know which sees and which is seen. It is this Visibility, this generality of the Sensible in itself, this anonymity innate to Myself that we have previously called flesh, and one knows there is no name in traditional philosophy to designate it. The flesh is not matter, in the sense of corpuscles of being which would add up or continue on one another to form beings. Nor is the visible (the things as well as my own body) some "psychic" material that would be—God knows how—brought into being by the things factually existing and acting on my factual body. In general, it is not a fact or a sum of facts "material" or "spiritual." Nor is it a representation for a mind: a mind could not be captured by its own representations; it would rebel against this insertion into the visible which is essential to the seer. The flesh is not matter, is not mind, is not substance. To designate it, we should need the old term "element," in the sense it was used to speak of water, air, earth, and fire, that is, in the sense of a *general thing*, midway between the spatio-temporal individual and the idea, a sort of incarnate principle that brings a style of being wherever there is a fragment of being. The flesh is in this sense an "element" of Being. Not a fact or a sum of facts, and yet adherent to *location* and to the *now*. Much more: the inauguration of the *where* and the *when*, the possibility and exigency for the fact; in a word: facticity, what makes the fact be a fact. And, at the same time, what makes the facts have meaning, makes the fragmentary facts dispose themselves about "something." For if there is flesh, that is, if the hidden face of the cube radiates forth somewhere as well as does the face I have under my eyes, and coexists with it, and if I who see the cube also belong to the visible, I am visible from elsewhere, and if I and the cube are together caught up in one same "element" (should we say of the seer, or of the visible?), this cohesion, this visibility by principle, prevails over every momentary discordance. In advance every vision or very partial visible that would here definitively come to naught is not nullified (which would leave a gap in its place), but, what is better, it is replaced by a more exact vision and a more exact visible, according to the principle of visibility, which, as though through a sort of abhorrence of a vacuum, already invokes the true vision and the true visible, not only as substitutes for their errors, but also as their explanation, their relative justification, so that they are, as Husserl says so aptly, not erased, but "crossed out." . . . Such are the extravagant consequences to which we are led when we take seriously, when we question, vision. And it is, to be sure, possible to refrain from doing so and to move on, but we would simply find again, confused, indistinct, non-clarified, scraps of this ontology of the visible mixed up with all our theories of knowledge, and in particular with those that serve, desultorily, as vehicles of science. We are, to be sure, not finished ruminating over them. Our concern in this preliminary outline was only to catch sight of this strange domain to which interrogation, properly so-called, gives access. . . .

But this domain, one rapidly realizes, is unlimited. If we can show that the flesh is an ultimate notion, that it is not the union or compound of two substances, but thinkable by itself, if there is a relation of the visible with itself that traverses me and constitutes me as a seer, this circle which I do not form, which forms me, this coiling over of the visible upon the visible, can traverse, animate other bodies as well as my own. And if I was able to understand how this wave arises within me, how the visible which is yonder is simultaneously my landscape, I can understand a fortiori that elsewhere it also closes over upon itself and that there are other landscapes besides my own. If it lets itself be captivated by one of its fragments, the principle of captation is established, the field open for other Narcissus, for an "intercorporeity." If my left hand can touch my right hand while it palpates the tangibles, can touch it touching, can turn its palpation back upon it, why, when touching the hand of another, would I not touch in it the same power to espouse the things that I have touched in my own? It is true that "the things" in question are my own, that the whole operation takes place (as we say) "in me," within my landscape, whereas the problem is to institute another landscape. When one of my hands touches the other, the world of each opens upon that of the other because the operation is reversible at will, because they both belong (as we say) to one sole space of consciousness, because one sole man touches one sole thing through both hands. But for my two hands to open upon one sole world, it does not suffice that they be given to one sole *consciousness*—or if that were the case the difficulty before us would disappear: since other bodies would be known by me in the same way as would be my own, they and I would still be dealing with the same world. No, my two hands touch the same things because they are the hands of one same body. And yet each of them has its own tactile experience. If nonetheless they have to do with one sole tangible, it is because there exists a very peculiar relation from one to the other, across the corporeal space—like that holding between my two eyes—making of my hands one sole organ of experience, as it makes of my two eyes the channels of one sole Cyclopean vision. A difficult relation to conceive—since one eye, one hand, are capable of vision, of touch, and since what has to be comprehended is that these visions, these touches, these little subjectivities, these "consciousnesses of . . ." could be assembled like flowers into a bouquet, when each being "consciousness of," being For Itself, reduces the others into objects. We will get out of the difficulty only by renouncing the bifurcation of the "consciousness of" and the object, by admitting that my synergic body is not an object, that it assembles into a cluster the "consciousnesses" adherent to its hands, to its eyes, by an operation that is in relation to them lateral, transversal; that "my consciousness" is not the synthetic, uncreated, centrifugal unity of a multitude of "consciousnesses of . . ." which would be centrifugal like it is, that it is sustained, subtended, by the prereflective and preobjective unity of my body. This means that while each monocular vision, each touching with one sole hand has its own visible, its tactile, each is bound to every other vision, to every other touch; it is bound in such a way as to make up with them the experience of one sole body before one sole world, through a possibility for reversion, reconversion of its language into theirs, transfer, and reversal, according to which the little private world of each is not juxtaposed to the world of all the others, but surrounded by it, levied off from it, and all together are a Sentient in general before a Sensible in general. Now why would this generality, which constitutes the unity of my body, not open it to other bodies? The handshake too is reversible; I can feel myself touched as well and at the same time as touching, and surely there does not exist some huge animal whose organs our bodies would be, as, for each of our bodies, our hands, our eyes are the organs. Why would not the synergy exist among different organisms, if it is possible within each? Their landscapes interweave, their actions and their passions fit together exactly: this is possible as soon as we no longer make belongingness to one same "consciousness" the primordial definition of sensibility, and as soon as we rather understand it as the return of the visible upon itself, a carnal adherence of the sentient to the sensed and of the sensed to the sentient. For, as overlapping and fission, identity and difference, it brings to birth a ray of natural light that illuminates all flesh and not only my own. It is said that the colors, the tactile reliefs given to the other, are for me an absolute mystery, forever inaccessible. This is not completely true; for me to have not an idea, an image, nor a representation, but as it were the imminent experience of them, it suffices that I look at a landscape, that I speak of it with someone. Then, through the concordant operation of his body and my own, what I see passes into him, this individual green of the meadow under my eyes invades his vision without quitting my own, I recognize in my green his green, as the customs officer recognizes suddenly in a traveler the man whose description he had been given. There is here no problem of the *alter ego* because it is not I who sees, not *he* who sees, because an anonymous visibility inhabits both of us, a vision in general, in virtue of that primordial property that belongs to the flesh, being here and now, of radiating everywhere and forever, being an individual, of being also a dimension and a universal.

What is open to us, therefore, with the reversibility of the visible and the tangible, is—if not yet the incorporeal—at least an intercorporeal being, a presumptive domain of the visible and the tangible, which extends further than the things I touch and see at present.

There is a circle of the touched and the touching, the touched takes hold of the touching; there is a circle of the visible and the seeing, the seeing is not without visible existence;[5] there is even an inscription of the touching in the visible, of the seeing in the tangible—and the converse; there is finally a propagation of these exchanges to all the bodies of the same type and of the same style which I see and touch—and this by virtue of the fundamental fission or segregation of the sentient and the sensible which, laterally, makes the organs of my body communicate and founds transitivity from one body to another.

As soon as we see other seers, we no longer have before us only the look without a pupil, the plate glass of the things with that feeble reflection, that phantom of ourselves they evoke by designating a place among themselves whence we see them: henceforth, through other eyes we are for ourselves fully visible; that lacuna where our eyes, our back, lie is filled, filled still by the visible, of which we are not the titulars. To believe that, to bring a vision that is not our own into account, it is to be sure inevitably, it is always from the unique treasury of our own vision that we draw, and experience therefore can teach us nothing that would not be outlined in our own vision. But what is proper to the visible is, we said, to be the surface of an inexhaustible depth: this is what makes it able to be open to visions other than our own. In being realized, they therefore bring out the limits of our factual vision, they betray the solipsist illusion that consists in thinking that every going beyond is a surpassing accomplished by oneself. For the first time, the seeing that I am is for me really visible; for the first time I appear to myself completely turned inside out under my own eyes. For the first time also, my movements no longer proceed unto the things to be seen, to be touched, or unto my own body occupied in seeing and touching them, but they address themselves to the body in general and for itself (whether it be my own or that of another), because for the first time, through the other body, I see that, in its coupling with the flesh of the world, the body contributes more than it receives, adding to the world that I see the treasure necessary for what the other body sees. For the first time, the body no longer couples itself up with the world, it clasps another body, applying [itself to it][6] carefully with its whole extension, forming tirelessly with its hands the strange statue which in its turn gives everything it receives; the body is lost outside of the world and its goals, fascinated by the unique occupation of floating in Being with another life, of making itself the outside of its inside and the inside of its outside. And henceforth movement, touch, vision, applying themselves to the other and to themselves, return toward their source and, in the patient and silent labor of desire, begin the paradox of expression.

Yet this flesh that one sees and touches is not all there is to flesh, nor this massive corporeity all there is to the body. The reversibility that defines the flesh exists in other fields; it is even incomparably more agile there and capable of weaving relations between bodies that this time will not only enlarge, but will pass definitively beyond the circle of the visible. Among my movements, there are some that go nowhere—that do not even go find in the other body their resemblance or their archetype: these are the facial movements, many gestures, and especially those strange movements of the throat and mouth that form the cry and the voice. Those movements end in sounds and I hear them. Like crystal, like metal and many other substances, I am a sonorous being, but I hear my own vibration from within; as Malraux said, I hear myself with my throat. In this, as he also has said, I am incomparable; my voice is bound to the mass of my own life as is the voice of no one else. But if I am close enough to the other who speaks to hear his breath and feel his effervescence and his fatigue, I almost witness, in him as in myself, the awesome birth of vociferation. As there is a reflexivity of the touch, of sight, and of the touch-vision system, there is a reflexivity of the movements of phonation and of hearing; they have their sonorous inscription, the vociferations have in me their motor echo. This new reversibility and the emergence of the flesh as expression are the point of insertion of speaking and thinking in the world of silence.[7]

At the frontier of the mute or solipsist world where, in the presence of other seers, my visible is confirmed as an exemplar of a universal visibility, we reach a second or figurative meaning of vision, which will be the *intuitus mentis* or idea, a sublimation of the flesh, which will be mind or thought. But the factual presence of other bodies could not produce thought or the idea if its seed were not in my own body. Thought is a relationship with oneself and with the world as well as a relationship with the other; hence it is established in the three dimensions at the same tirne. And it must be brought to appear directly in the infrastructure of vision. Brought to appear, we say, and not brought to birth: for we are leaving in suspense for the moment the question whether it would not be already implicated there. Manifest as it is that feeling is dispersed in my body, that for example my hand touches, and that consequently we may not in advance ascribe feeling to a thought of which it would be but a mode—it yet would be absurd to conceive the touch as a colony of assembled tactile experiences. We are not here proposing any empiricist genesis of thought: we are asking precisely what is that central vision that joins the scattered visions, that unique touch that governs the whole tactile life of my body as a unit, that *I think* that must be able to accompany all our experiences. We are proceeding toward the center, we are seeking to comprehend how there is a center, what the unity consists of, we are not saying that it is a sum or a result; and if we make the thought appear upon an infrastructure of vision, this is only in virtue of the uncontested evidence that one must see or feel in some way in order to think, that every thought known to us occurs to a flesh.

Once again, the flesh we are speaking of is not matter. It is the coiling over of the visible upon the seeing body, of the tangible upon the touching body, which is attested in particular when the body sees itself, touches itself seeing and touching the things, such that, simultaneously, *as* tangible it descends among them, *as* touching it dominates them all and draws this relationship and even this double relationship from itself, by dehiscence or fission of its own mass. This concentration of the visibles about one of them, or this bursting forth of the mass of the body toward the things, which makes a vibration of my skin become the sleek and the rough, makes me *follow with my eyes* the movements and the contours of the things themselves, this magical relation, this pact between them and me according to which I lend them my body in order that they inscribe upon it and give me their resemblance, this fold, this central cavity of the visible which is my vision, these two mirror arrangements of the seeing and the visible, the touching and the touched, form a closebound system that I count on, define a vision in general and a constant style of visibility from which I cannot detach myself, even when a particular vision turns out to be illusory, for I remain certain in that case that in looking closer I would have had the true vision, and that in any case, whether it be this one or another, *there is a true vision.* The flesh (of the world or my own) is not contingency, chaos, but a texture that returns to itself and conforms to itself. I will never see my own retinas, but if one thing is certain for me it is that *one* would find at the bottom of my eyeballs those dull and secret membranes. And finally, I believe it—I believe that I have a man's senses, a human body—because the spectacle of the world that is my own, and which, to judge by our confrontations, does not notably differ from that of the others, with me as with them refers with evidence to typical dimensions of visibility, and finally to a virtual focus of vision, to a detector also typical, so that at the joints of the opaque body and the opaque world there is a ray of generality and of light. Conversely, when, starting from the body, I ask how it makes itself a seer, when I examine the critical region of the aesthesiological body, everything comes to pass (as we have shown in an earlier work[8]) as though the visible body remained incomplete, gaping open; as though the physiology of vision did not succeed in closing the nervous functioning in upon itself, since the movements of fixation, of convergence, are suspended upon the advent to the body of a visible world for which they were supposed to furnish the explanation; as though, therefore, the vision came suddenly to give to the material means and instruments left here and there in the working area a convergence which they were waiting for; as though, through all these channels, all these prepared but unemployed circuits, the current that will traverse them was rendered probable, in the long run inevitable: the current making of an embryo a newborn infant, of a visible a seer, and of a body a mind, or at least a flesh. In spite of all our substantialist ideas, the seer is being premeditated in counterpoint in the embryonic development; through a labor upon itself the visible body provides for the hollow whence a vision will come, inaugurates the long maturation at whose term suddenly it will see, that is, will be visible for itself, will institute the interminable gravitation, the indefatigable metamorphosis of the seeing and the visible whose principle is posed and which gets underway with the first vision. What we are calling flesh, this interiorly worked-over mass, has no name in any philosophy. As the formative medium of the object and the subject, it is not the atom of being, the hard in itself that resides in a unique place and moment: one can indeed say of my body that it is not *elsewhere*, but one cannot say that it is *here* or *now* in the sense that objects are; and yet my vision does not soar over them, it is not the being that is wholly knowing, for it has its own inertia, its ties. We must not think the flesh starting from substances, from body and spirit—for then it would be the union of contradictories—but we must think it, as we said, as an element, as the concrete emblem of a general manner of being. To begin with, we spoke summarily of a reversibility of the seeing and the visible, of the touching and the touched. It is time to emphasize that it is a reversibility always imminent and never realized in fact. My left hand is always on the verge of touching my right hand touching the things, but I never reach coincidence; the coincidence eclipses at the moment of realization, and one of two things always occurs: either my right hand really passes over to the rank of touched, but then its hold on the world is interrupted; or it retains its hold on the world, but then I do not really touch *it*—my right hand touching, I palpate with my left hand only its outer covering. Likewise, I do not hear myself as I hear the others, the sonorous existence of my voice is for me as it were poorly exhibited; I have rather an echo of its articulated existence, it vibrates through my head rather than outside. I am always on the same side of my body; it presents itself to me in one invariable perspective. But this incessant escaping, this impotency to superpose exactly upon one another the touching of the things by my right hand and the touching of this same right hand by my left hand, or to superpose, in the exploratory movements of the hand, the tactile experience of a point and that of the "same" point a moment later, or the auditory experience of my own voice and that of other voices—this is not a failure. For if these experiences never exactly overlap, if they slip away at the very moment they are about to rejoin, if there is always a "shift," a "spread," between them, this is precisely because my two hands are part of the same body, because it moves itself in the world, because I hear myself both from within and from without. I experience—and as often as I wish—the transition and the metamorphosis of the one experience into the other, and it is only as though the hinge between them, solid, unshakeable, remained irremediably hidden from me. But this hiatus between my right hand touched and my right hand touching, between my voice heard and my voice uttered, between one moment of my tactile life and the following one, is not an ontological void, a non-being: it is spanned by the total being of my body, and by that of the world; it is the zero of pressure between two solids that makes them adhere to one another. My flesh and that of the world therefore involve clear zones, clearings, about which pivot their opaque zones, and the primary visibility, that of the *quale* and of the things, does not come without a second visibility, that of the lines of force and dimensions, the massive flesh without a rarefied flesh, the momentary body without a glorified body. When Husserl spoke of the horizon of the things—of their exterior horizon, which everybody knows, and of their "interior horizon," that darkness stuffed with visibility of which their surface is but the limit—it is necessary to take the term seriously. No more than are the sky or the earth is the horizon a collection of things held together, or a class name, or a logical possibility of conception, or a system of "potentiality of consciousness": it is a new type of being, a being by porosity, pregnancy, or generality, and he before whom the horizon opens is caught up, included within it. His body and the distances participate in one same corporeity or visibility in general, which reigns between them and it, and even beyond the horizon, beneath his skin, unto the depths of being.

We touch here the most difficult point, that is, the bond between the flesh and the idea, between the visible and the interior armature which it manifests and which it conceals. No one has gone further than Proust in fixing the relations between the visible and the invisible, in describing an idea that is not the contrary of the sensible, that is its lining and its depth. For what he says of musical ideas he says of all cultural beings, such as *The Princess* of *Clèves* and *René,* and also of the essence of love which "the little phrase" not only makes present to Swann, but communicable to all who hear it, even though it is unbeknown to themselves, and even though later they do not know how to recognize it in the loves they only witness. He says it in general of many other notions which are, like music itself "without equivalents," "the notions of light, of sound, of relief, of physical voluptuousness, which are the rich possessions with which our inward domain is diversified and adorned."[9] Literature, music, the passions, but also the experience of the visible world are—no less than is the science of Lavoisier and Ampère—the exploration of an invisible and the disclosure of a universe of ideas.[10] The difference is simply that this invisible, these ideas, unlike those of that science, cannot be detached from the sensible appearances and be erected into a second positivity. The musical idea, the literary idea, the dialectic of love, and also the articulations of the light, the modes of exhibition of sound and of touch speak to us, have their logic, their coherence, their points of intersection, their concordances, and here also the appearances are the disguise of unknown "forces" and "laws." But it is as though the secrecy wherein they lie and whence the literary expression draws them were their proper mode of existence. For these truths are not only hidden like a physical reality which we have not been able to discover, invisible in fact but which we will one day be able to see facing us, which others, better situated, could already see, provided that the screen that masks it is lifted. Here, on the contrary, there is no vision without the screen: the ideas we are speaking of would not be better known to us if we had no body and no sensibility; it is then that they would be inaccessible to us. The "little phrase," the notion of the light, are not exhausted by their manifestations, any more than is an "idea of the intelligence"; they could not be given to us *as ideas* except in a carnal experience. It is not only that we would find in that carnal experience the *occasion* to think them; it is that they owe their authority, their fascinating, indestructible power, precisely to the fact that they are in transparency behind the sensible, or in its heart. Each time we want to get at it[11] immediately, or lay hands on it, or circumscribe it, or see it unveiled, we do in fact feel that the attempt is misconceived, that it retreats in the measure that we approach. The explicitation does not give us the idea itself; it is but a second version of it, a more manageable derivative. Swann can of course close in the "little phrase" between the marks of musical notation, ascribe the "withdrawn and chilly tenderness" that makes up its essence or its sense to the narrow range of the five notes that compose it and to the constant recurrence of two of them: while he is thinking of these signs and this sense, he no longer has the "little phrase" itself, he has only "bare values substituted for the mysterious entity he had perceived, for the convenience of his understanding."[12] Thus it is essential to this sort of ideas that they be "veiled with shadows," appear "under a disguise." They give us the assurance that the "great unpenetrated and discouraging night of our soul" is not empty, is not "nothingness"; but these entities, these domains, these worlds that line it, people it, and whose presence it feels like the presence of someone in the dark, have been acquired only through its commerce with the visible, to which they remain attached. As the secret blackness of milk, of which Valéry spoke, is accessible only through its whiteness, the idea of light or the musical idea doubles up the lights and sounds from beneath, is their other side or their depth. Their carnal texture presents to us what is absent from all flesh; it is a furrow that traces itself out magically under our eyes without a tracer, a certain hollow, a certain interior, a certain absence, a negativity that is not nothing, being limited very precisely to *these* five notes between which it is instituted, to that family of sensibles we call lights. We do not see, do not hear the ideas, and not even with the mind's eye or with the third ear: and yet they are there, behind the sounds or between them, behind the lights or between them, recognizable through their always special, always unique manner of entrenching themselves behind them, "perfectly distinct from one another, unequal among themselves in value and in significance."[13]

With the first vision, the first contact, the first pleasure, there is initiation, that is, not the positing of a content, but the opening of a dimension that can never again be closed, the establishment of a level in terms of which every other experience will henceforth be situated. The idea is this level, this dimension. It is therefore not a *de facto* invisible, like an object hidden behind another, and not an absolute invisible, which would have nothing to do with the visible. Rather it is the invisible *of* this world, that which inhabits this world, sustains it, and renders it visible, its own and interior possibility, the Being of this being. At the moment one says "light," at the moment that the musicians reach the "little phrase," there is no lacuna in me; what I live is as "substantial," as "explicit," as a positive thought could be—even more so: a positive thought is what it is, but, precisely, is only what it is and accordingly cannot hold us. Already the mind's volubility takes it elsewhere. We do not possess the musical or sensible ideas, precisely because they are negativity or absence circumscribed; they possess us. The performer is no longer producing or reproducing the sonata: he feels himself, and the others feel him to be at the service of the sonata; the sonata sings through him or cries out so suddenly that he must "dash on his bow" to follow it. And these open vortexes in the sonorous world finally form one sole vortex in which the ideas fit in with one another. "Never was the spoken language so inflexibly necessitated, never did it know to such an extent the pertinence of the questions, the evidence of the responses."[14] The invisible and, as it were, weak being is alone capable of having this close texture. There is a strict ideality in experiences that are experiences of the flesh: the moments of the sonata, the fragments of the luminous field, adhere to one another with a cohesion without concept, which is of the same type as the cohesion of the parts of my body, or the cohesion of my body with the world. Is my body a thing, is it an idea? It is neither, being the measurant of the things. We will therefore have to recognize an ideality that is not alien to the flesh, that gives it its axes, its depth, its dimensions.

But once we have entered into this strange domain, one does not see how there could be any question of *leaving* it. If there is an animation *of* the body; if the vision and the body are tangled up in one another; if, correlatively, the thin pellicle of the *quale*, the surface of the visible, is doubled up over its whole extension with an invisible reserve; and if finally, in our flesh as in the flesh of things, the actual, empirical, ontic visible, by a sort of folding back, invagination, or padding, exhibits a visibility, a possibility that is not the shadow of the actual but is its principle, that is not the proper contribution of a "thought" but is its condition, a style, allusive and elliptical like every style, but like every style inimitable, inalienable, an interior horizon and an exterior horizon between which the actual visible is a provisional partitioning and which, nonetheless, open indefinitely only upon other visibles—then (the immediate and dualist distinction between the visible and the invisible, between extension and thought, being impugned, not that extension be thought or thought extension, but because they are the obverse and the reverse of one another, and the one forever behind the other) there is to be sure a question as to how the "ideas of the intelligence" are initiated over and beyond, how from the ideality of the horizon one passes to the "pure" ideality, and in particular by what miracle a created generality, a culture, a knowledge come to add to and recapture and rectify the natural generality of my body and of the world. But, however we finally have to understand it, the "pure" ideality already streams forth along the articulations of the aesthesiological body, along the contours of the sensible things, and, however new it is, it slips through ways it has not traced, transfigures horizons it did not open, it derives from the fundamental mystery of those notions "without equivalent," as Proust calls them, that lead their shadowy life in the night of the mind only because they have been divined at the junctures of the visible world. It is too soon now to clarify this type of surpassing that does not leave its field of origin. Let us only say that the pure ideality is itself not without flesh nor freed from horizon structures: it lives of them, though they be another flesh and other horizons. It is as though the visibility that animates the sensible world were to emigrate, not outside of every body, but into another less heavy, more transparent body, as though it were to change flesh, abandoning the flesh of the body for that of language, and thereby would be emancipated but not freed from every condition. Why not admit—what Proust knew very well and said in another place—that language as well as music can sustain a sense by virtue of its own arrangement, catch a meaning in its own mesh, that it does so without exception each time it is conquering, active, creative language, each time something is, in the strong sense, said? Why not admit that, just as the musical notation is a *facsimile* made after the event, an abstract portrait of the musical entity, language as a system of explicit relations between signs and signified, sounds and meaning, is a result and a product of the operative language in which sense and sound are in the same relationship as the "little phrase" and the five notes found in it afterwards? This does not mean that musical notation and grammar and linguistics and the "ideas of the intelligence"—which are acquired, available, honorary ideas—are useless, or that, as Leibniz said, the donkey that goes straight to the fodder knows as much about the properties of the straight line as we do; it means that the system of objective relations, the acquired ideas, are themselves caught up in something like a second life and perception, which make the mathematician go straight to entities no one has yet seen, make the *operative* language and algorithm make use of a second visibility, and make ideas be the other side of language and calculus. When I think they animate my interior speech, they haunt it as the "little phrase" possesses the violinist, and they remain beyond the words as it remains beyond the notes—not in the sense that under the light of another sun hidden from us they would shine forth but because they are that certain divergence, that never-finished differentiation, that openness ever to be reopened between the sign and the sign, as the flesh is, we said, the dehiscence of the seeing into the visible and of the visible into the seeing. And just as my body sees only because it is a part of the visible in which it opens forth, the sense upon which the arrangement of the sounds opens reflects back upon that arrangement. For the linguist language is an ideal system, a fragment of the intelligible world. But, just as for me to see it is not enough that my look be visible for X, it is necessary that it be visible for itself, through a sort of torsion, reversal, or specular phenomenon, which is given from the sole fact that I am born; so also, if my words have a meaning, it is not *because* they present the systematic organization the linguist will disclose, it is because that organization, like the look, refers back to itself: the operative Word is the obscure region whence comes the instituted light, as the muted reflection of the body upon itself is what we call natural light. As there is a reversibility of the seeing and the visible, and as at the point where the two metamorphoses cross what we call perception is born, so also there is a reversibility of the speech and what it signifies; the signification is what comes to seal, to close, to gather up the multiplicity of the physical, physiological, linguistic means of elocution, to contract them into one sole act, as the vision comes to complete the aesthesiological body. And, as the visible takes hold of the look which has unveiled it and which forms a part of it, the signification rebounds upon its own means, it annexes to itself the speech that becomes an object of science, it antedates itself by a retrograde movement which is never completely belied—because already, in opening the horizon of the nameable and of the sayable, the speech acknowledged that it has its place in that horizon; because no locutor speaks without making himself in advance allocutary, *be it only for himself*; because with one sole gesture he closes the circuit of his relation to himself and that of his relation to the others and, with the same stroke, also sets himself up as *delocutary*, speech of which one speaks: he offers himself and offers every word to a universal Word. We shall have to follow more closely this transition from the mute world to the speaking world. For the moment we want only to suggest that one can speak neither of a destruction nor of a conservation of silence (and still less of a destruction that conserves or of a realization that destroys—which is not to solve but to pose the problem). When the silent vision falls into speech, and when the speech in turn, opening up a field of the nameable and the sayable, inscribes itself in that field, in its place, according to its truth—in short, when it metamorphoses the structures of the visible world and makes itself a gaze of the mind, *intuitus mentis*—this is always in virtue of the same fundamental phenomenon of reversibility which sustains both the mute perception and the speech and which manifests itself by an almost carnal existence of the idea, as well as by a sublimation of the flesh. In a sense, if we were to make completely explicit the architectonics of the human body, its ontological framework, and how it sees itself and hears itself, we would see that the structure of its mute world is such that all the possibilities of language are already given in it. Already our existence as seers (that is, we said, as beings who turn the world back upon itself and who pass over to the other side, and who catch sight of one another, who see one another with eyes) and especially our existence as sonorous beings for others and for ourselves contain everything required for there to be speech from the one to the other, speech about the world. And, in a sense, to understand a phrase is nothing else than to fully welcome it in its sonorous being, or, as we put it so well, to *hear what it says (l'entendre)*. The meaning is not on the phrase like the butter on the bread, like a second layer of "psychic reality" spread over the sound: it is the totality of what is said, the integral of all the differentiations of the verbal chain; it is given with the words for those who have ears to hear. And conversely the whole landscape is overrun with words as with an invasion, it is henceforth but a variant of speech before our eyes, and to speak of its "style" is in our view to form a metaphor. In a sense the whole of philosophy, as Husserl says, consists in restoring a power to signify, a birth of meaning, or a wild meaning, an expression of experience by experience, which in particular clarifies the special domain of language. And in a sense, as Valéry said, language is everything, since it is the voice of no one, since it is the very voice of the things, the waves, and the forests. And what we have to understand is that there is no dialectical reversal from one of these views to the other; we do not have to reassemble them into a synthesis: they are two aspects of the reversibility which is the ultimate truth.

Notes

1. Here in the course of the text itself, these lines are inserted: "it is that the look is itself incorporation of the seer into the visible, quest for itself, which *is* of *it,* within the visible—it is that the visible of the world is not an envelope of *quale,* but what is between the qualia, a connective tissue of exterior and interior horizons—it is as flesh offered to flesh that the visible has its aseity, and that it is mine—The flesh as *Sichtigkeit* and generality. → whence vision is question and response. . . . The openness through flesh: the two leaves of my body and the leaves of the visible world. . . . It is between these intercalated leaves that there is visibility. . . . My body model of the things and the things model of my body: the body bound to the world through all its parts, up against it → all this means: the world, the flesh not as fact or sum of facts, but as the locus of an inscription of truth: the false crossed out, not nullified."—Ed.

2. The *Uerpräsentierbarkeit* is the flesh.

3. The visible is not a tangible zero, the tangible is not a zero of visibility (relation of encroachment).

4. Here, in the course of the text itself, between brackets, these lines are inserted: "One can say that we perceive the things themselves, that we are the world that thinks itself—or that the world is at the heart of our flesh. In any case, once a body-world relationship is recognized, there is a ramification of my body and a ramification of the world and a correspondence between its inside and my outside, between my inside and its outside."—Ed.

5. Here is inserted between brackets, in the course of the text itself, the note: "what are these adhesions compared with those of the voice and the hearing?"—Ed.

6. These words, which we reintroduce into the text, had been erased apparently by error.—Ed.

7. Inserted here between brackets: "in what sense we have not yet introduced thinking: to be sure, we are not in the in itself. From the moment we said *seeing, visible,* and described the dehiscence of the sensible, we were, if one likes, in the order of thought. We were not in it in the sense that the thinking we have introduced was *there is,* and not *it appears to me that* . . . (appearing that would make up the whole of being, self-appearing). Our thesis is that this *there is* by inherence is necessary, and our problem to show that thought, in the restrictive sense (pure signification, thought of seeing and of feeling), is comprehensible only as the accomplishment by other means of the will of the *there is,* by sublimation of the *there is* and realization of an invisible that is exactly the reverse of the visible, the power of the visible. Thus between sound and meaning, speech and what it means to say, there is still the relation of reversibility, and no question of priority, since the exchange of words is exactly the differentiation of which the thought is the integral."—Ed.

8. *The Structure of Behavior* [trans. Alden L. Fisher (Boston, 1963)].

9. *Du côté de chez Swann, II* (Paris, 1926), 190. [English translation by C. K. Scott Moncrieff, *Swann's Way* (New York, 1928), p. 503.]

10. Ibid., p. 192. [Eng. trans., p. 505.]

11. It: that is, the idea.—Ed.

12. *Du côté de chez Swann, II,* 189. [Eng. trans., p. 503.]

13. Ibid.

14. Ibid., p. 192. [Eng. trans., p. 505.]

Working Notes

Husserl *Zeitbewusstsein*—

May, 1959

1. What is the "receptive" element of the absolute consciousness?—H. is right to say that it is not I who constitute time, that it constitutes itself, that it is a *Selbsterscheinung*—But the term "receptivity" is improper precisely because it evokes a Self distinct from the present and who *receives* it—It must be understood simply by opposition to spontaneous acts (thought, etc.)

2. Is it the new present, in its individuality, that pushes the preceding one into the past, and that *fills* a part of the future? In that case there would not be *time*, but times—Time must be understood as a system that embraces everything—Although it is graspable only for him who *is there*, is at a present

3. What is the impressional consciousness, the *Urerlebnis?* Like the *Selbstgegebenheit* of the exterior thing, it is in reality not a term *effectively* untraversable (temporal knob), but a transcendent, an optimum, an *etwas . . . (a Gestalt* and not an individual) —And the "to be conscious" of this *Urerlebnis* is not coincidence, fusion with . . . nor is it an act or *Auffassung* (this Husserl said), nor is it a nihilating (Sartre), it is separation *(écart)*, such as the corporeal schema, which is the foundation of space *and of time*, makes comprehensible—It is a perception-imperception, i.e. an operative and not thematized meaning (this is at bottom what Husserl means when he considers retention to be fundamental: that means that the absolute present which I am is as if it were not)—

4. All this still leaves untouched the question: what is "to know," "to be conscious," "to perceive," "to think" in the Cartesian sense—A question never

raised—One discusses around theses such as "connection" *(liaison)*, "thought of seeing and of feeling" in the sense of presumption, "meaning"—One shows that a binding *(liant)* is needed, that a "pure *denken*" is necessary, or a *Selbsterscheinung*, an auto-apparition, an apparition that is pure apparition. . . . But all this presupposes the idea of the for itself and in the end cannot explain transcendence—Look in a completely different direction: the for itself itself as an incontestable, but derived, characteristic: it is the culmination of separation *(écart)* in *differentiation*—Self-presence *is* presence to a differentiated world—The perceptual separation *(écart)* as making up the "view" such as it is implicated in the reflex, for example—and enclosing being for itself by means of language as differentiation. To be conscious = to have a figure on a ground—one cannot go back any further.

Transcendence of the thing and transcendence of the phantasm

May, 1959

The transcendence of the thing compels us to say that it is plenitude only by being inexhaustible, that is, by not being all actual under the look—but it promises this total actuality, since it *is there*. . . .

When we say that—on the contrary—the phantasm is not observable, that it is empty, non-being, the contrast with the sensible is therefore not absolute. The senses are apparatus to form concretions of the inexhaustible, to form existent significations—But the thing is not really *observable:* there is always a skipping over in every observation, one is never at the thing itself. What we call the *sensible* is only the fact that the indefinite [succession] of *Abschattungen precipitates*—But, conversely, there is a precipitation or crystallization of the imaginary, of the existentials, of the symbolic matrices—

[on the same page]

"Thought," "consciousness," and being at . . .

Retention (inasmuch as it does not posit, does not aim at the immediate past, and only *has it* behind itself), the perceptual presence (for example, the presence of what is behind my back), the presence of my whole past sedimented into existentials, my reference to what I mean in speech, and to the diacritical apparatus of the available significations, my motor reference to the spot I want to go to, the *Vorhabe* (the *Stiftung* of a field or an idea), the installation in a space by the corporeal schema, and the founding of a time in the embryology of behavior—all this turns around the problem of an existence that is not a *thought* of existing—and which Husserl finds again in the heart of the psychological reflection as an absolute retentional flux (but in Husserl there is here the idea of a time of *Empfindung* which is not good: the present in the broad sense is a symbolic matrix and not only *a* present that breaks up toward the past)—I.e. of a Self-presence that is not an *absence from oneself*, a contact with Self *through* the divergence *(écart)* with regard to Self—The figure on a ground, the simplest "*Etwas*"—the *Gestalt* contains the key to the problem of the mind

see Wertheimer's *Productive Thinking*[1] to determine in what sense the *Gestalt* contains and does not contain the significations of the highest degree

The looks that cross = *eine Art der Reflexion*

May, 1959

It is already the flesh of things that speaks to us of our own flesh, and that speaks to us of the flesh of the other—My "look" is one of those givens of the "sensible," of the brute and primordial world, that defies the analysis into being and nothingness, into existence as consciousness and existence as a thing, and requires a complete reconstruction of philosophy. The analytics of being and nothingness at the same time discloses and masks this order: it discloses it as a menace of being on nothingness and of nothingness on being, it masks it because the entity and the negentity remain in principle isolable.

the look that kills
decentering, not annihilation.
to call into question for Sartre (nothingness)
= to kill; to be in question = to cease to be

(Bergson) Transcendence—*forgetting*—time

May 20, 1959

I said: the openness to the world such as we rediscover it in ourselves and the perception we divine within life (a perception that at the same time is spontaneous being (thing) and being-self ("subject")—Bergson once explicitly said, in the text of *La Pensée et le mouvant* where he speaks of the consciousness seeking to see time and not to measure it, that there is a consciousness that is *at the same time spontaneous and reflected*[2]) intertwine, encroach upon, or cling to one another.

Make clear what that means.

That evokes, beyond the "point of view of the object" and the "point of view of the subject," a common nucleus which is the "winding" *(serpentement)*,[3] being as a winding (what I called "modulation of the being in the world"). It is necessary to make understood how that (or any *Gestalt*) is a perception "being formed in the things." This is still only an approximative expression, in the subject-object language (Wahl, Bergson) of what there is to be said. That is, that the things have us, and that it is not we who have the things. That the being that has been cannot stop having been. The "Memory of the World." That language has us and that it is not we who have language. That it is being that speaks within us and not we who speak of being.[4]

But then how understand the subjectivity? Inadequacy of the Bergsonian representation of a soul that conserves everything (this makes it impossible that the perceived-imaginary difference be a difference in nature). Insufficiency also of the Malebranche representation of a vision in god: that is the equivalent of the transcendental consciousness, it is "conservation" in the form of "signification." The solution is to be sought in vision itself: memory will be understood only by means of it. Vision has to be already a modulation or a winding in the one, a variant of a perceptual system of the world, in order that memory can be and can involve forgetting. The description of retention in Husserl (and that of subjectivity as time, of the absolute flux, of the pre-intentional retention) is a start, but leaves open the question: whence comes the "shrinking" of the temporal perspective, the passage of the remote retentions into the horizon, the forgetting?

The problem of forgetting: lies essentially in the fact that it is discontinuous. If at each phase of the *Ablaufphänomen*, a segment of the past would fall into oblivion, we would have a field of the present like a diaphragm of an objective, and forgetting would be occultation resulting from the removal of the efficacious stimuli, it would be the point where the *clear image* is no longer produced because the corporeal trace is effaced. Or again, in idealist language: forgetting would be a part of the present-past system, in exact correspondence with a new segment of present descended from the future.

But it is not so: there are retentions that are not forgotten, even very remote ones. There are fragments "perceived" just now, that disappear (have they been perceived? And what exactly is the relation between the perceived and the *imperceived*?)—And besides there is no objective segment of the present that descends from the future. Husserl's diagram is dependent on the convention that one can represent the series of nows by points on a line.[5] To be sure, Husserl at this point adds the whole recasting of the retentions and the retentions of retentions that result therefrom, and it is in this that he does not conceive of time as serial and as a succession of punctual events. But even complicated in this fashion, the representation of the phenomenon of flow is faulty. Not inasmuch as it is spatial. For in fact space does not comprise *points, lines* any more than time does. Understand that the *Gestalt* is already transcendence: it makes me understand that a line is a vector, that a point is a center of forces—There are neither absolute lines nor points nor colors in the things. The field vision and the field notion—Bergson saying that the winding perhaps reproduces no *real* line.[6] But there is no line that would be "*real*." Hence space is not to be blamed, as Bergson does. And correlatively it does not suffice to pass to time as fusion to have the solution—That is a false antithesis—We have to pass from the thing (spatial or temporal) as identity, to the thing (spatial or temporal) as difference, i.e. as transcendence, i.e. as always "behind," beyond, far-off . . . the present itself is not an absolute coincidence without transcendence; even the *Urerlebnis* involves not total coincidence, but partial coincidence, because it has horizons and would not be without them—the present, also, is ungraspable from close-up, in the forceps of attention, it is an encompassing. Study exactly the *Erfülllung* of the present: the danger of this metaphor: it makes me think that there is a *certain void* that has *its own* dimensions and that is filled by a defined quantity of the present (it is always a field defined by the objective diaphragm). When Husserl speaks of a "norm," he means precisely that one cannot presuppose such a norm as given. It is a question of a *Normierung*. I.e. (Heidegger) of the positing of a *measurant (mesurant)*. One sees then that the norm and the diaphragm, etc. *derive* from a total phenomenon which is finally the "world" (cf. Manchester lecture:[7]) (each perception is a "thought," but the whole is "*inscribed*" in the world—Every event belongs to the type of historical event that Péguy speaks of, "a rhythm of the event of the world"—again the winding—the problems of knowing what is the subject of the State, of war, etc. are exactly of the same type as the problem of knowing what is the subject of perception: one will not clear up the philosophy of history except by working out the problem of perception)

Whence the impossibility of a philosophy of *Being and Nothingness:* the future is not nothingness, the past is not the imaginary in the sense Sartre takes it—To be sure *there is* the present, but the transcendence of the present makes it precisely able to connect up with a past and a future, which conversely are not a nihilation—

In short: nothingness (or rather non being) is hollow and not *hole*. The open, in the sense of a *hole*, that is Sartre, is Bergson, is negativism or ultra positivism (Bergson)—indiscernible. There is no *nichtiges Nichts*. Bring to a focus my discussion of Bergson's ideas on nothingness: I am right in saying that Bergson proves too much, but wrong in seeming to conclude from that that Sartre is right. The negintuition of nothingness is to be rejected because nothingness also is always *elsewhere*. The true solution: *Offenheit* of the *Umwelt, Horizonhaftigkeit*.

The problem of forgetting: it comes, I said, from the fact that forgetting is discontinuous. It must be conceived not as an occultation (Bergson), not as a passage into nothingness, annihilation—and not as a positive function that envelops a knowledge of what it hides (Freud—Sartre),[8] but as a manner of being to . . . in turning away from . . .—The to-be-conscious itself is to be conceived as transcendence, as to be surpassed by . . . and hence as ignorance But still there is the perceptual [?]?—Yes, but it is not an immediation in the sense of *contact.* (And it is not a distance in the way Sartre means it: a *nothing that is me*, and that separates me from the thing) —It is true that it is not in "blending" perception and imperception that one will explain forgetting.

It is in better understanding perception (and hence imperception)—i.e.: understand perception as differentiation, forgetting as undifferentiation. The fact that one no longer sees the memory = not a destruction of a psychic *material* which would be *the* sensible, but its disarticulation which makes there be no longer a *separation (écart)*, a *relief.* This is the night of forgetting. Understand that the "to be conscious" = to have a figure on a ground, and that it disappears by disarticulation—the figure-ground distinction introduces a third term between the "subject" and the "object." It is *that separation (écart)* first of all that is the perceptual *meaning.*

Philosophy and Literature

[undated, probably June, 1959]

Philosophy, precisely as "Being speaking within us," expression of the mute experience by itself, is creation. A creation that is at the same time a reintegration of Being: for it is not a creation in the sense of one of the commonplace *Gebilde* that history fabricates: it knows itself to be a *Gebilde* and wishes to surpass itself as *pure Gebilde,* to find again its origin. It is hence a creation in a radical sense: a creation that is at the same time an adequation, the only way to obtain an adequation.

This considerably deepens Souriau's views on philosophy as supreme art:[9] for art and philosophy *together* are precisely not arbitrary fabrications in the universe of the "spiritual" (of "culture"), but contact with Being precisely as creations. Being is *what requires creation of us* for us to experience it.

Make an analysis of literature in this sense: as *inscription* of Being.

The problem of analysis

September, 1959

Do we have the right to comprehend the time, the space of the child as an undifferentiation of *our* time, of *our* space, etc. . . . ? This is to reduce the child's experience to our own, at the very moment one is trying to respect the phenomena. For it is to think it as the *negation* of *our* differentiations. It would be necessary to go all the way to thinking it *positively*, unto phenomenology.

But the same question arises with regard to every *other*, to the alter ego in particular—And *to that other than me who is the I reflected on*, for myself who reflects.

Solution: recapture the child, the alter ego, the unreflected within myself by a lateral, pre-analytic participation, which is perception, *ueberschreiten* by definition, intentional transgression. When I perceive the child, he is given precisely in a certain divergence *(écart) (originating presentation of the unpresentable)* and the same for my perceptual lived experience for myself, and the same for my alter ego, and the same for the pre-analytic thing. Here is the common tissue of which we are made. The wild Being. And the perception of this perception (the phenomenological "reflection") is the inventory of this originating departure whose documents we carry in ourselves, of this *Ineinander* that awakens to itself, it is the usage of the *immer wieder* which is the sensible, the carnal itself (for every reflection is after the model of the reflection of the hand touching by the hand touched, open generality, a prolongation of the body's reserve [*volant*]), hence reflection is not an identification with oneself (thought of seeing or of feeling) but non-difference with self = silent or blind identification. And when the reflection wishes to be done with this horizonal openness, when it wishes to apprehend itself no longer across a horizon and in virtue of an institution of nature, but directly and without anything left over, then all it can do is to sublimate itself in verbalization, give itself a body that would not be natural only, make a language germinate, a "transparent" apparatus that gives the illusion of a pure or empty presence to oneself, and which nonetheless attests only a determined void, empty of this or that . . .

The essential is to describe the vertical or wild Being as that pre-spiritual milieu without which nothing is thinkable, not even the spirit, and by which we pass into one another, and ourselves into ourselves in order to have *our own* time. It is philosophy alone that gives it—

Philosophy is the study of the *Vorhabe* of Being, a *Vorhabe* that is not *cognition*, to be sure, that is wanting with regard to cognition, to operation, but that envelops them as Being envelops the beings.

Piaget's logicism is an absolutization of our culture—so also his psychology which opens upon his logic. Incompatible with an ethnological experience. Psychology, logic, ethnology are rival dogmatisms that destroy one another; philosophy alone, precisely because it aims at the total domain of Being, renders them compatible by relativizing them. The regions of knowledge, left to themselves, are in conflict and in contradiction.

Gestalt

September, 1959

What is a *Gestalt?* A whole that does *not* reduce itself to the sum of the parts—a negative, exterior definition—A designation of the *Gestalt* by contrast with the domain of the in itself in which one is installed—the *Gestalthafte*, says Heidegger, is here left aside—

From within, then (that is: not by *interior observation*, but by approaching the *Gestalt* as much as possible, by communicating with it, which can be done by considering the others or the visible as well as by considering "states of consciousness") what is a *Gestalt*? What is a contour, what is a segregation, what is a circle or a line? Or an organization in depth, a relief?

These are *not* psychic elements (sensation), assembled psychic spatio-temporal individuals. But what then? To have the experience of a *Gestalt* is not to sense by coincidence, but what then?

It is a principle of distribution, the pivot of a system of equivalencies, it is the *Etwas* of which the fragmentary phenomena will be the manifestation—But is it then an essence, an idea? The idea would be free, intemporal, aspatial. The *Gestalt* is not a spatio-temporal individual, it is ready to integrate itself into a constellation that spans space and time—but it is not free in regard to space and time, it is not aspatial, atemporal, it only escapes the time and space conceived as a series of events in themselves, it has a certain weight that doubtless fixes it not in an objective site and in a point of objective time, but in a region, a domain, which it dominates, where it reigns, where it is everywhere present without one ever being able to say: it is here. It is transcendence. This is what one expresses again in speaking of its generality, of its *Transponierbarkeit*—It is a double ground of the lived.

And who experiences it? A mind that would grasp it as an idea or a signification? No. It is a body—In what sense? My body *is* a *Gestalt* and it is co-present in every *Gestalt*. It is a *Gestalt;* it also, and eminently, is a heavy signification, it is flesh; the system it constitutes is ordered about a central hinge or a pivot which is openness to . . . , a bound and not a free possibility—And at the same time it is a component of every *Gestalt*. The flesh of the *Gestalt* (the grain of the color, the indefinable something that animates the contour or which, in Michotte's experiments, animates the rectangle that "creeps"[10]) is what responds to its inertia, to its insertion in a "world," to its *field* biases

The *Gestalt* therefore implies the relation between a perceiving body and a sensible, i.e. transcendent i.e. horizonal i.e. vertical and not perspectival world—

It is a diacritical, oppositional, relative system whose pivot is the *Etwas*, the thing, the world, and not the idea—

The idea is the *Etwas* upon which the body is centered no longer qua *sensible* but qua *speaking*—

Every Psychology that places the *Gestalt* back into the framework of "cognition" or "consciousness" misses the meaning of the *Gestalt*—

There remains to understand precisely what the being for itself of the *Gestalt* experience is—It is being for X, not a pure agile nothingness, but an inscription in an open register, in a lake of non being, in an *Eröffnung*, in an *offene*.

Pregnancy, transcendence—

September, 1959

Show that these notions[11] represent a getting into contact with being as pure *there is*. One witnesses that event by which there is something. Something rather than nothing and this rather than something else. One therefore witnesses the advent of the positive: this rather than something *else*.

This advent is not a self-realization of a being that would be the cause of itself, identical, objective—And not even the self-realization of a preponderant possible in the sense of the logical possible (Leibniz). The ideology of the logical possible is no different from the ideology of the necessary: the necessary is simply the unique possible; the possible already contains the idea of intrinsic existence; if there is a conflict between several possibles with regard to existence, it is because, by virtue of a veritable mystery (Leibniz), the possibles are not compossible.

Hence the *gestaltung* is not being by definition, essentialization—It is [verbal) *Wesen*, the operation of *ester*, the apparition of an Etwas existing by radiation—*Warum ist etwas eine gestalt*? Why is this rather than that a "good" form, or a *strong form*, or an orientation toward a possibility? [see Egon Brunswik[12] and show that the effort of the *New Look*[13] and of information theory is to find an operational, scientific expression of what is not the being-object, the in itself]—[reproduce here my critique of Lévi-Strauss's explanation of the *gestaltung by* the pooling of "chances," by *combination*[14]—yes a combination is needed, but what is elaborated through this combination, the symbolic matrix of the West is not a *product* of causality] Show that since the *Gestalt* arises from polymorphism, this situates us entirely outside of the philosophy of the subject and the object.

September, 1959

Descartes *(Dioptrics): who* will see the image painted in the eyes or in the brain? Therefore finally a *thought* of this image is needed—Descartes already sees that we always put a little man in man, that our objectifying view of our own body always obliges us to seek *still further inside* that *seeing man* we thought we had under our eyes.

But what he does not see is that the primordial vision that one must indeed come to cannot be the *thought of seeing*—This thought, this disclosure of being which finally is *for* someone, is still the little man inside man, but this time contracted into a metaphysical point. For finally we know no vision but that by a composite substance, and it is this subtilized vision that we call thought—If being is to disclose itself, it will do so before a transcendence, and not before an intentionality, it will be the engulfed brute being that returns to itself, it will be the *sensible* that hollows itself out—

Ontology—

October, 1959

Take topological space as a model of being. The Euclidean space is the model for perspectival being, it is a space without transcendence, positive, a network of straight lines, parallel among themselves or perpendicular according to the three dimensions, which sustains all the possible situations—Underlying appropriateness of this idea of space (and of velocity, movement, time) with the classical ontology of the *Ens realissimum*, of the infinite entity. The topological space, on the contrary, a milieu in which are circumscribed relations of proximity, of envelopment, etc. is the image of a being that, like Klee's touches of color, is at the same time older than everything and "of the first day" (Hegel), that the regressive thought runs up against without being able to deduce it directly or indirectly (by "choice of the best") from Being by itself, that is a perpetual *residue*—It is encountered not only at the level of the physical world, but again it is constitutive of life, and finally it founds the *wild* principle of Logos—It is this wild or brute being that intervenes at all levels to overcome the problems of the classical ontology (mechanism, finalism, in every case: artificialism)—the *Theodicy* of Leibniz sums up the effort of Christian theology to find a route between the necessitarian conception of Being, alone possible, and the unmotivated upsurge of brute Being, which latter is finally linked up with the first by a compromise, and, to this extent, the hidden god sacrificed to the *Ens realissimum*.

Sunday, October 10, 1959

Malraux asks why, how, one painter learns from another, of whom he makes copies (Van Gogh of Millet)—to be *himself*, learn himself in the other, with and against him.

Likewise one can ask why he who knows how to handle colors knows also how to handle the pencil or sometimes to sculpture—What there is in *common*—

All this is indeed obscure as long as one thinks that to sketch or to paint is to produce something positive out of nothing. Then the act of sketching and of painting—the act of painting like oneself and that of painting like the other are isolated from one another, and one no longer sees any relation between them. But we would see a relation if we understood that to paint, to sketch, is not to produce something from nothing, that the drawing, the touch of the brush, and the visible work are but the trace of a total movement of Speech, which goes unto Being as a whole, and that this movement contains the expression with lines as well as the expression with colors, *my* expression as well as that of the other painters. We dream of systems of equivalenc*ies*, and indeed they do function. But their logic, like the logic of a phonematic system, is summed up in one sole tuft, in one sole gamut, they are all animated with one sole movement, they each and all are one sole vortex, one sole contraction of Being. What is needed is to make explicit this horizonal totality which is not a *synthesis*

Wild perception—The Immediate—Cultural perception—learning.[15]

October 22, 1959

I say that the Renaissance perspective is a cultural fact, that perception itself is polymorphic and that if it becomes Euclidean, this is because it allows itself to be oriented by the system.

Whence the question: how can one return from this perception fashioned by culture to the "brute" or "wild" perception? What does the informing consist in? By what act does one undo it (return to the phenomenal, to the "vertical" world, to lived experience)?

Whence also the question: does this informing of perception by culture, this descent of the invisible into the visible, oblige us to say, as does Egon Brunswik, for example, that the perceptual pregnancy is a *learning* [16] of the ecological milieu, that the autoconstitutional *Gestalten* of the Berlin school are derived from the "empirical *Gestalten*"?[17]

What I maintain is that:

1. there is an informing of perception by culture which enables us to say that culture is perceived —There is a dilatation of perception, a carrying over of the *Aha Erlebnis* of "natural" perception to instrumental relations for example (chimpanzees) which obliges us to put in continuity the perceptual openness to the world (λόγος ἐνδιάθετος) and the openness to a cultural world (acquisition of the use of instruments).

2. this original layer above *nature* shows that *learning*[18] is *In der Welt Sein*, and not at all that *In der Welt Sein* is *learning*,[19] in the American sense or in the cognitive sense of Brunswik.

My position in the problem of the "return to the immediate" to be defined: the perceptual in the sense of the non-projective, vertical world—is always given with sense experience *(le sentir)*, with the phenomenal, with the silent transcendence. And yet someone like Piaget ignores this absolutely, has totally converted his perception into a cultural-Euclidean perception. What right have I therefore to call immediate this original that can be forgotten to such an extent?

Describe very precisely the way perception masks itself to itself, makes itself Euclidean. Show that the pregnancy of the geometrical forms is grounded intrinsically (not culturally) in that they, better than others, allow an ontogenesis (they stabilize being. What Piaget expresses—badly—in saying that in them the "deformations" annul one another,[20] but that this intrinsic pregnancy, in order to retain all its meaning, must be maintained within the zone of transcendence, within the context of the pre-Being, of the *Offenheit* of the *Umwelt,* and not dogmatically considered self-evident—the Euclidean perception has a privilege, but it is not an absolute privilege, and it is contested as absolute by the transcendence—which demands the Euclidean world as one of its aspects—

With life, natural perception (with the savage mind) is perpetually given to us the wherewithal to set up the universe of immanence—And yet, this universe tends of itself to become autonomous, realizes of itself a repression of transcendence—*The key is in this idea that perception qua wild perception is of itself ignorance of itself, imperception,* tends of itself to see itself as an *act* and to forget itself as latent intentionality, as *being at*—

Same problem: how every philosophy is language and nonetheless consists in rediscovering silence.

Perception and language

October 27, 1959

I describe perception as a diacritical, relative, oppositional system—the primordial space as topological (that is, cut out in a total voluminosity which surrounds me, in which I am, which is behind me as well as before me . . .)

This is right. But there is all the same this difference between perception and language, that I *see* the perceived things and that the significations on the contrary are invisible. The natural being is at rest in itself, my look can stop on it. The Being whose home is language cannot be fixed, looked at, it is only from afar Hence it is necessary to account for this relative positivity of the perceived (even if it is only non-negation, even if it does not resist *observation,* even if every crystallization is illusory in some respect), especially since it is upon it that the positivity of the invisible rests. There is no intelligible world, *there is* the sensible world.

(But also what is this *there is of* the sensible world, of nature?)

The sensible is precisely that medium in which there can be *being* without it having to be posited; the sensible appearance of the sensible, the silent persuasion of the sensible is Being's unique way of manifesting itself without becoming positivity, without ceasing to be ambiguous and transcendent. The sensible world itself in which we gravitate, and which forms our bond with the other, which makes the other be for us, is not, precisely qua sensible, "given" except by allusion—The sensible is that: this possibility to be evident in silence, to be understood implicitly, and the alleged positivity of the sensible world (when one scrutinizes it unto its roots, when one goes beyond the empirical-sensible, the secondary sensible of our "representation," when one discloses the Being of Nature) precisely proves to be an *ungraspable*, the only thing finally that is seen in the full sense is the totality wherein the sensibles are cut out. Thought is only a little further still from the *visibilia*.

The chiasm

November 1, 1959

—the cleavage, in what regards the essential, is not *for Itself for the Other* (subject-ob-ject) it is more exactly that between someone who goes unto the world and who, from the exterior, seems to remain in his own "dream." *Chiasm* by which what announces itself to me as being appears in the eyes of the others to be only "states of consciousness"—But, like the chiasm of the eyes, this one is also what makes us belong to the same world—a world which is not projective, but forms its unity across incompossibilities such as that of *my* world and the world of the other—By reason of this mediation through reversal, this chiasm, there is not simply a for-Oneself for-the-Other antithesis, there is Being as containing all that, first as sensible Being and then as Being without restriction—

Chiasm, instead of the For the Other: that means that there is not only a me-other rivalry, but a co-functioning. We function as one unique body

The chiasm is not only a me other exchange (the messages he receives reach me, the messages I receive reach him), it is also an exchange between me and the world, between the phenomenal body and the "objective" body, between the perceiving and the perceived: what begins as a thing ends as consciousness of the thing, what begins as a "state of consciousness" ends as a thing.

One cannot account for this double "chiasm" by the cut of the For Itself and the cut of the In Itself. A relation to Being is needed that would form itself *within Being*—This at bottom is what Sartre was looking. for. But since for him there is no *interior* except me, and every *other is* exteriority, Being for him remains intact after this decompression that occurs in it, it remains pure positivity, object, and the For Itself participates in it only through a sort of folly—

November, 1959

. . . .

Meaning is *invisible,* but the invisible is not the contradictory of the visible: the visible itself has an invisible inner framework *(membrure),* and the in-visible is the secret counterpart of the visible, it appears only within it, it is the *Nichturpräsentierbar* which is presented to me as such within the world—one cannot see it there and every effort to *see it there* makes it disappear, but it is *in the line* of the visible, it is its virtual focus, it is inscribed within it (in filigree)—

The *comparisons* between the invisible and the visible (the *domain,* the *direction* of thought . . .) are not *comparisons* (Heidegger), they mean that the visible is pregnant with the invisible, that to comprehend fully the visible relations (house) one must go unto the relation of the visible with the invisible . . . . The other's visible is my invisible; my visible is the other's invisible; this formula (that of Sartre) is not to be retained. We have to say: Being is this strange encroachment by reason of which my visible, although it is not superposable on that of the other, nonetheless opens upon it, that both open upon the same sensible world—And it is the same encroachment, the same junction at a distance, that makes the messages from my organs (the monocular images) reassemble themselves into one sole vertical existence and into one sole world.

Hence meaning is not nihilation, nor a sacrifice of the For Itself to the In Itself—To envisage such a sacrifice, such a *creation* of the truth, is still to think according to the model of the In Itself, on the basis of the In Itself, and, since it escapes, to confide in the For Itself the heroic mission of making it be—To envisage that is still to think the *Weltlichkeit* of minds according to the model of that of Cartesian space. Lacking an In Itself of the For Itselfs, the For Itself is charged with the task of *making* it. But I do not think the *Weltlichkeit* of minds in terms of the In Itself—and it is chimerical to seek in the future what is not. The *Weltlichkeit* of minds is ensured by the roots they push forth, not in the Cartesian space, to be sure, but in the aesthetic world. The aesthetic world to be described as a space of transcendence, a space of incompossibilities, of explosion, of dehiscence, and not as objective-immanent space. And then thought, the subject, to be described as a spatial situation also, with its own "locality" And hence the spatial "metaphors" to be understood as an indivision of being and nothingness. And hence meaning is not nihilation—

This *separation (écart)* which, in first approximation, forms meaning, is not a no I affect *myself* with, a lack which I constitute as a lack by the upsurge of an *end* which I give myself—it is a *natural* negativity, a first institution, always already there—

Consider the right, the left: these are not simply contents within a relational spatiality (i.e. *positive*): they are not *parts* of space (Kant's reasoning is valid here: the whole is primary), they are total parts, cuts in an encompassing, topological space—Consider the *two*, the *pair*, this is not *two acts, two syntheses*, it is a fragmentation of being, it is a possibility for separation (two eyes, two ears: the possibility for *discrimination*, for the use of the diacritical), it is the advent of difference (on the ground of *resemblance* therefore, on the ground of the ὁμοῦ ἦν πάντα).

. . . .

The visible and the invisible

November, 1959

Must one not say that
the idea of transcendence = adjourns ad infinitum. all *that which* we think we touch or see?

No, however: the visible, which is always "further on," is *presented* as such. It is the *Urpräsentation* of the *Nichturpräsentierbar*—*To see* is precisely, in spite of the infinite analysis always possible, and although no *Etwas* ever remains *in our hands*, to have an *Etwas*.

Is this then a pure and simple contradiction? Not at all: the visible ceases to be an inaccessible if I conceive it, not according to the proximal thought, but as an encompassing, lateral investment, *flesh*.

The "senses"—dimensionality—Being

November, 1959

Each "sense" is a "world," i.e. absolutely incommunicable for the other senses, and yet constructing a *something* which, through its structure, is from the first *open* upon the world of the other senses, and with them forms one sole Being. Sensoriality: for example, a color, yellow; it surpasses itself of itself: as soon as it becomes the color of the illumination, the dominant color of the field, it ceases to be such or such a color, it has therefore of itself an ontological function, it becomes apt to represent all things (like engravings, *Dioptrics*, Discourse IV). With one sole movement it imposes itself as particular and ceases to be visible as particular. The "World" is this whole where each "part," when one takes it for itself, suddenly opens unlimited dimensions—becomes a *total part*.

Now this particularity of the color, of the yellow, and this universality are not a *contradiction*, are *together* sensoriality itself: it is by the same virtue that the color, the yellow, at the same time gives itself as a *certain* being and as a *dimension,* the expression *of every possible being*—What is proper to the sensible (as to language) is to be representative of the whole, not by a sign-signification relation, or by the immanence of the parts in one another and in the whole, but because each part is *torn up* from the whole, comes with its roots, encroaches upon the whole, transgresses the frontiers of the others. It is thus that the parts overlap (transparency), that the present does not stop at the limits of the visible (behind my back). Perception opens the world to me as the surgeon opens a body, catching sight, through the window he has contrived, of the organs in full functioning, taken *in their activity,* seen sideways. It is thus that the sensible initiates me to the world, as language to the other: by encroachment, *Ueberschreiten.* Perception is not first a perception of *things,* but a perception of *elements* (water, air . . .) of *rays of the world,* of things which are dimensions, which are worlds, I slip on these "elements" and here I am in the *world,* I slip from the "subjective" to Being.

The alleged "contradiction" between the yellow as some thing and the yellow as the title of a world: this is not a contradiction, for it is precisely within its particularity as yellow and through it that the yellow becomes a universe or an *element*—That a color can become a level, a fact become a category (exactly as in music: describe a note as particular, i.e. in the field of another *tone*—and "the same" note that has become that within whose key a music is written) = the veritable movement toward the universal. The universal is not above, it is beneath (Claudel), it is not before, but *behind* us—atonal music = the equivalent of the philosophy of Being in indivision. Like paintings without identifiable things, without the *skin* of things, but giving their *flesh*—The *Transponierbarkeit* is a particular case of a more general transposition of which atonal music is the thematization All this implies the Being in indivision—

This universality of the sensible = *Urpräsentation* of what is not *Urpräsentierbar* = the sensible hollowed out in the being without restriction, that Being which is *between* my perspective and that of the other, my past and my present.

What is proper to the perceived: to be already there, to not be *through* the act of perception, to be the reason for that act, and not the reverse. Sensoriality = transcendence, or a mirror of transcendence.

Depth

November, 1959

Depth and "back" (and "behind")—It is pre-eminently the dimension of the hidden—(every dimension is of the hidden)—

There must be depth since there is a point whence I see—since the world surrounds me—

Depth is the means the things have to remain distinct, to remain things, while not being what I look at at present. It is pre-eminently the dimension of the simultaneous. Without it, there would not be a world or Being, there would only be a mobile zone of distinctness which could not be brought here without quitting all the rest—and a "synthesis" of these "views." Whereas, by virtue of depth, they coexist in degrees of proximity, they slip into one another and integrate themselves. It is hence because of depth that the things have a flesh: that is, oppose to my inspection obstacles, a resistance which is precisely their reality, their "openness," their *totum simul.* The look does not overcome depth, it goes round it.

Depth is *urstiftet* in what I see in clear vision as the retention is in the present—without "intentionality"—

cf. Metzger saying that it arises at the moment when it was going to be impossible to have a distinct vision of 2 points at the same time. Then, the two images that are out of phase and not superposable "take" suddenly as profiles *of* the same thing in depth[21] —This is not an *act* or an intentionality (which would go to an *in itself* and would give only juxtaposed in itselfs)—It is in general, and by virtue of a field property, that this identification of two incomposible views is made, and because depth is open to me, because I have this dimension so as to move my look in it, *this openness*—

November, 1959

Say that the things are structures, frameworks, the stars of our life: not before us, laid out as perspective spectacles, but gravitating about us.

Such things do not presuppose man, who is made of their flesh. But yet their eminent being can be understood only by him who enters into perception, and with it keeps in distant-contact with them—

The essence, the *Wesen.* Underlying kinship between the essence and perception: the essence, likewise, is an inner framework, it is not above the sensible world, it is beneath, or in its depth, its thickness. It is the secret bond—the Essences are *Etwases* at the level of speech, as the things are Essences at the level of Nature. Generality of the things: why are there several samples of each thing? This is imposed by the very definition of the things as field beings: how could there be a field without *generality*?

With transcendence I show that the visible is invisible, *that vision is in principle what convinces me by an appearance already-there that there is no room to seek a proximal being*

perception, what assures me of an inapperceived (of a hidden-revealed: transparency, encroachment) This invisible of the visible is then what enables me to rediscover in productive thought all the structures of vision, and to radically distinguish thought from operation, from logic.

Blindness *(punctum caecum)* of the "consciousness"

May, 1960

What it does not see it does not see for reasons of principle, it is because it is consciousness that it does not see. *What* it does not see is what in it prepares the vision of the rest (as the retina is blind at the point where the fibers that will permit the vision spread out into it). *What* it does not see is what makes it see, is its tie to Being, is its corporeity, are the existentials by which the world becomes visible, is the flesh wherein the *ob*ject is born. It is inevitable that the consciousness be mystified, inverted, indirect, in principle it sees the things *through the other end,* in principle it disregards Being and prefers the *ob*ject to it, that is, a Being with which it has broken, and which it posits beyond this negation, by negating this negation—In it it ignores the nondissimulation of Being, the *Unverborgenheit,* the non-mediated presence which is not something positive, which is being of the far-offs (*étre des lointains*)

Flesh of the world—Flesh of the body—Being

May, 1960

Flesh of the world, described (apropos of time, space, movement) as segregation, dimensionality, continuation, latency, encroachment—Then interrogate once again these phenomena-questions: they refer us to the perceiving-perceived *Einfühlung,* for they mean that we are already *in* the being thus described, that we *are of it,* that between it and us there is *Einfühlung*

That means that my body is made of the same flesh as the world (it is a perceived), and moreover that this flesh of my body is shared by the world, the world *reflects* it, encroaches upon it and it encroaches upon the world (the felt *[senti]* at the same time the culmination of subjectivity and the culmination of materiality), they are in a relation of transgression or of overlapping—This also means: my body is not only one perceived among others, it is the measurant *(mesurant)* of all, *Nullpunkt* of all the dimensions of the world. For example, it is not one mobile or moving among the mobiles or movings, I am not conscious of its movements as *a distance taken by relation to me,* it *sich bewegt* whereas the things *are moved.* This means a sort of "reflectedness" *(sich bewegen),* it thereby constitutes itself *in itself*—In a parallel way: it touches *itself,* sees *itself.* And consequently it is capable of *touching or seeing* something, that is, of being open to the things in which

(Malebranche) it reads its own modifications (because we have no idea of the soul, because the soul is a being of which there is no idea, a being *we are* and do not see). The touching oneself, seeing oneself, a "knowing by sentiment"—

The *touching itself, seeing itself* of the body is itself to be understood in terms of what we said of the seeing and the visible, the touching and the touchable. I.e. it is not an act, it is a being at *(étre à)*. To touch *oneself,* to see *oneself,* accordingly, is not to apprehend oneself as an ob-ject, it is to be open to oneself, destined to oneself (narcissism) —Nor, therefore, is it to reach *oneself,* it is on the contrary to escape *oneself,* to be ignorant of *oneself,* the self in question is by divergence *(d'écart),* is *Unverborgenheit of the Verborgen* as such, which consequently does not cease to be hidden or latent—

The feeling that one feels, the seeing one sees, is not a thought of seeing or of feeling, but vision, feeling, mute experience of a mute meaning—

The quasi "reflective" redoubling, the reflexivity of the body, the fact that it touches itself touching, sees itself seeing, does not consist in surprising a connecting activity behind the connected, in reinstalling oneself in this constitutive activity; the self-perception (sentiment of oneself, Hegel would say) or perception of perception does not convert what it apprehends into an object and does not coincide with a constitutive source of perception: in fact I do not entirely succeed in touching myself touching, in seeing myself seeing, the experience I have of myself perceiving does not go beyond a sort of *imminence,* it terminates in the invisible, simply this invisible is *its* invisible, i.e. the reverse of *its* specular perception, of the concrete vision I have of my body in the mirror. The self-perception is still a perception, i.e. it gives me a *Nicht Urpräsentierbar* (a non-visible, myself), but this it gives me through an *Urpräsentierbar* (my tactile or visual appearance) in transparency (i.e. as a latency)—My invisibility for myself does not result from my being a *positive* mind, a *positive* "consciousness," a *positive* spirituality, an existence as consciousness (i.e. as pure *appearing to self*), it comes from the fact that I am he who: 1) has a visible world, i.e. a dimensional body, and open to participation; 2) i.e. a body visible for itself; 3) and therefore, finally, a self-presence that is an absence from self—The progress of the inquiry toward the *center* is not the movement from the conditioned unto the condition, from the founded unto the *Grund:* the so-called *Grund* is *Abgrund.* But the abyss one thus discovers is not such *by lack of ground,* it is upsurge of a *Hoheit* which supports from above *(tient par le haut)* (cf. Heidegger, *Unterwegs zur Sprache*[22]), that is, of a negativity that *comes to the world.*

The flesh of the world is not explained by the flesh of the body, nor the flesh of the body by the negativity or self that inhabits it—the 3 phenomena are *simultaneous*—

The flesh of the world is not *self-sensing (se sentir)* as is my flesh—It is sensible and not sentient—I call it flesh, nonetheless (for example, the relief, depth, "life" in Michotte's experiments[23]) in order to say that it is a *pregnancy* of possibles, *Weltmöglichkeit* (the possible worlds variants of this world, the world beneath the singular and the plural) that it is therefore absolutely not an ob-ject, that the *blosse Sache* mode of being is but a partial and second expression of it. This is not hylozoism: inversely, hylozoism is a conceptualization—A false thematization, in the order of the explicative-Entity, of our experience of carnal presence—It is by the flesh of the world that in the last analysis one can understand the lived body *(corps propre)*—The flesh of the world is of the Being-seen, i.e. is a Being that is *eminently percipi*, and it is by it that we can understand the *percipere:* this perceived that we call my body applying itself to the rest of the perceived, i.e. treating itself as a perceived by itself and hence as a perceiving, all this is finally possible and means something only because *there is* Being, not Being in itself, identical to itself, in the night, but the Being that also contains its negation, its *percipi*—cf. Bergson saying: we have already given ourselves the consciousness by positing the "images," and therefore we do not have to deduce it at the level of the "conscious" living being, which is *less* and not more than the universe of images, which is one concentration or abstraction of them—It was meaningless to thus realize the consciousness before the consciousness. And this is why we say, for our part, that what is primary is not the diffuse "consciousness" of the "images" (a diffuse consciousness which is nothing, since Bergson explains that there is consciousness only through the "camera obscura" of the centers of indetermination and the bodies[24]), it is Being

Metaphysics—Infinity
World—Offenheit

May, 1960

World and Being:

their relation is that of the visible with the invisible (latency) the invisible is not another visible ("possible" in the logical sense) a positive only *absent*

It is *Verborgenheit by* principle i.e. invisible *of the visible, Offenheit* of the *Umwelt* and not *Unendlichkeit*—*Unendlichkeit is* at bottom the *in itself*, the *ob-ject*—For me the infinity of Being that one can speak of is *operative*, militant finitude: the openness of the *Umwelt*—I am against finitude in the empirical sense, a factual existence that *has limits*, and this is why I am for metaphysics. But it lies no more in infinity than in the factual finitude

Chiasm—Reversibility

November 16, 1960

Speech does indeed have to enter the child as silence—break through to him through silence and as silence (i.e. as a thing simply perceived—difference between the word *Sinnvoll* and the word-perceived) — Silence = absence of the word due. It is this fecund negative that is instituted by the flesh, by its dehiscence —the negative, nothingness, is the doubled-up, the two leaves of my body, the inside and the outside articulated over one another—Nothingness is rather the difference between the identicals

Reversibility: the finger of the glove that is turned inside out —There is no need of a spectator who would be *on each side*. It suffices that from one side I see the wrong side of the glove that is applied to the right side, that I touch the one *through* the other (double "representation" of a point or plane of the field) the chiasm is that: the reversibility—

It is through it alone that there is passage from the "For Itself" to the For the Other—In reality there is neither me nor the other as positive, positive subjectivities. There are two caverns, two opennesses, two stages where something will take place—and which both belong to the same world, to the stage of Being

There is not the For Itself and the For the Other—They are each the other side of the other. This is why they incorporate one another: projection-introjection—There is that line, that frontier surface at some distance before me, where occurs the veering I-Other Other-I—

The axis alone given—the end of the finger of the glove is nothingness—but a nothingness one can turn over, and where then one sees *things*—The only "place" where the negative would really be is the fold, the application of the inside and the outside to one another, the turning point—

Chiasm I—the world
I—the other—

chiasm my body—the things, realized by the doubling up of my body into inside and outside—and the doubling up of the things (their inside and their outside)

It is because there are these 2 doublings-up that are possible: the insertion of the world between the two leaves of my body

the insertion of my body between the 2 leaves of each thing and of the world

This is not anthropologism: by studying the 2 leaves we ought to find the structure of being—

Start from this: there is not identity, nor non-identity, or non-coincidence, there is inside and outside turning about one another—

My "central" nothingness is like the point of the stroboscopic spiral, which is *who knows where*, which is "nobody"

The *I—my body chiasm:* I know this, that a body *[finalized?]* is *Wahrneh-*

mungsbereit, offers itself to . . . , opens upon . . . an imminent spectator, is a *charged field*—

Position, negation, negation of negation: this side, the other, the other than the other. What do I bring to the problem of the same and the other? This: that the same be the other than the other, and identity difference of difference—this 1) does not realize a surpassing, a dialectic in the Hegelian sense; 2) is realized on the spot, by encroachment, thickness, *spatiality*—

November, 1960

. . . .

Activity: passivity—Teleology

The chiasm, reversibility, is the idea that every perception is doubled with a counter-perception (Kant's real opposition), is an act with two faces, one no longer knows who speaks and who listens. Speaking-listening, seeing-being seen, perceiving-being perceived circularity (it is because of it that it seems to us that perception forms itself *in the things themselves)* —*Activity=passivity.*

This is obvious when one thinks of what nothingness is, that is, *nothing.* How would this nothing be active, efficacious? And if the subjectivity is not it, but it plus my body, how would the operation of the subjectivity not be borne by the teleology of the body?

What then is my situation with regard to *finalism?* I am not a finalist, because the interiority of the body (= the conformity of the internal leaf with the external leaf, their folding back on one another) is not something *made, fabricated,* by the assemblage of the two leaves: they have never been apart—

(I call the evolutionist perspective in question I replace it with a cosmology of the visible in the sense that, considering endotime and endospace, for me it is no longer a question of origins, nor limits, nor of a series of events going to a first cause, but one sole explosion of Being which is forever. Describe the world of the "rays of the world" beyond every serial-eternitarian or ideal alternative—Posit the existential eternity—the eternal body)

I am not a finalist because there is dehiscence, and not positive production—through the finality of the body—of a man whose teleological organization our perception and our thought would prolong

Man is not the *end* of the body, nor the organized body the *end* of the components: but rather the subordinated each time slides into the void of a new dimension opened, the lower and the higher gravitate around one another, as *the high and the low* (variants of the side-other side relation) —Fundamentally I bring the high-low distinction into the vortex where it rejoins the side-other side distinction, where the two distinctions are integrated into a *universal dimensionality* which is Being (Heidegger)

There is no other meaning than carnal, figure and ground—Meaning = their dislocation, their gravitation (what I called "leakage" *[échappement]* in *Ph.P*[25])

"The other"

November, 1960

What is interesting is not an expedient to solve the "problem of the other"—
It is a transformation of the problem

If one starts from the visible and the vision, the sensible and the sensing, one acquires a wholly new idea of the "subjectivity": there are no longer "syntheses," there is a contact with being through its modulations, or its reliefs—

The other is no longer so much a freedom seen *from without* as destiny and fatality, a rival subject for a subject, but he is caught up in a circuit that connects him to the world, as we ourselves are, and consequently also in a circuit that connects him to us—And this world is *common* to us, is intermundane space—And there is transitivism by way of generality—And even freedom has its generality, is understood as generality: activity is no longer *the contrary* of passivity

Whence carnal relations, from below, no less than from above and the fine point Entwining

Whence the essential problem = not to make common in the sense of creation *ex nihilo* of a common situation, of a common event plus engagement by reason of the past, but in the sense of uttering—language—

the other is a relief as I am, not absolute vertical existence

. . . .

Body and flesh—
Eros—
Philosophy of Freudianism

December, 1960

Superficial interpretation of Freudianism: he is a sculptor because he is anal, because the feces are already clay, molding, etc.

But the feces are not the *cause:* if they were, everybody would be sculptors

The feces give rise to a character *(Abscheu)* only if the subject lives them in such a way as to find in them a dimension of being—

It is not a question of renewing empiricism (feces imprinting a certain character on the child). It is a question of understanding that the relationship with feces is in the child a concrete ontology. Make not an existential psychoanalysis, but an *ontological* psychoanalysis

Overdetermination (= circularity, chiasm) = any entity can be *accentuated* as an emblem of Being (= character) → it is to be read as such

In other words to be anal *explains* nothing: for, to be so, it is necessary to have the ontological capacity (= capacity to take a being as representative of Being)—

Hence what Freud wants to indicate are not chains of causality; it is, on the basis of a polymorphism or amorphism, what is contact with the Being in promiscuity, in transitivism, the fixation of a "character" by investment of the openness to Being in an Entity—which, henceforth, takes place *through this Entity*

Hence the philosophy of Freud is not a philosophy of the body but of the flesh—

The Id, the unconscious—and the Ego (correlative) to be understood on the basis of the flesh

The whole architecture of the notions of the psycho-logy (perception, idea—affection, pleasure, desire, love, Eros) all that, all this bric-a-brac, is suddenly clarified when one ceases to think all these terms as *positive* (the more or less dense "spiritual") in order to think them not as negatives or negentities (for that brings back the same difficulties), but as *differentiations* of one sole and *massive* adhesion to Being which is the flesh (eventually as "lace-works") —Then problems such as those of Scheler (how to understand the relation of the intentional with the affective which it crosses transversally, a love being transversal to the oscillations of pleasure and pain → personalism) disappear: for there is no *hierarchy* of orders or layers or planes (always founded on the individual-essence distinction), there is dimensionality of every fact and facticity of every dimension—This in virtue of the "ontological difference"—

Notes

1. New York and London, 1945.—Ed.

2. The author refers to this passage: "But this duration which science eliminates, and which is so difficult to conceive and express, is what one feels and lives. Suppose we try to find out what it is? How would it appear to a consciousness which desired only to see it without measuring it, which would then grasp it without stopping it, which in short, would take itself as object, and which, spectator and actor alike, at once spontaneous and reflective, would bring ever closer together—to the point where they would coincide—the attention which is fixed, and the time which passes?" (*La Pensée et le mouvant* [Paris, 1934], p. 10.) [English translation by Mabelle L. Andison, *The Creative Mind* (New York, 1946), p. 13.]—Ed.

3. Ibid., p. 293. [Eng. trans., p. 229]—Ed.

4. Finally there is something profound in Ruyer when he says that the in itself and the for itself are the same thing. But not to be understood as: the things are souls.

5. Husserl, "Vorlesungen zur Phänomenologie der inneren Zeitbewusstseins," *Jahrbuch für Philosophie und Phänomenologische Forschung*, IX (1928), 22. See the exposition and discussion of the analysis *of* Husserl's diagram in *Phénoménologie de la perception*, pp. 477 ff. [Eng. trans., pp. 417 ff.]—Ed.

6. *La Pensée et le mouvant*, p. 294. [Eng. trans., p. 230]—Ed.

7. Lecture given by the author at the University of Manchester, May 1, 1959.—Ed.

8. Under the parenthesis, between the lines, as according to the author's habit, these words appear: *positivism, negativism*. The first manifestly refers to Freud and the second to Sartre.—Ed.

9. At the head of the note, this reference: "see Souriau. *L'Instauration philosophique* (Paris, 1939); Gueroult, 'La Voie de l'objectivité esthétique,' *Mélanges Souriau* (Paris, 1952)."—Ed.

10. *The Perception of Causality*.—Ed.

11. Pregnancy, *Gestalt*, phenomenon.

12. Cf. *Perception and the Representative Design of Psychological Experiments* (Berkeley, 1956).—Ed.

13. In English in the text.—Ed.

14. We have no knowledge of such a critique; doubtless it was formulated in a course or in a personal note. M. Lévi-Strauss, we recall, had posed in new terms the problem of the cumulative or non-cumulative history of cultures in comparing non-cumulative cultures to players trying for series in roulette. He showed that the collaboration of cultures, voluntary or involuntary, had had an effect analogous to that which would be obtained by "a coalition of gamblers betting on the same series at several different tables, with an agreement that they would pool the numbers which each of them might require to proceed with his series." Cf. *Race and History*, UNESCO (Paris, 1952), pp. 37–38.—Ed.

15. In English in the text.—Tr.

16. In English in the text.—Tr.

17. *Cf. Perception and the Representative Design of Psychological Experiments* (Berkeley, 1956). For the discussion of the *Gestalten* of the Berlin school, cf. pp. 132–34; for perception as learning, cf. pp. 122–23.—Ed.

18. In English in the text.—Tr.

19. In English in the text.—Tr.

20. Cf. in particular, *La Perception*, Symposium de l'Association psychologique scientifique de langue française (Louvain, 1953; Paris, 1955). Piaget discusses geometrical pregnancy and empirical pregnancy, and writes: "Likewise, we think that a good form is that which, within perceptual structures where everything is deformation, gives rise to maximum compensations, hence to minimum deformations" (p. 19).—Ed.

21. Wolfgang Metzger, *Gesetze des Sehens* (Frankfurt, 1936; 2d ed. expanded, 1953), p. 285.—Ed.

22. *Unterwegs zur Sprache* (Tübingen, 1959), p. 13. "Die Sprache ist: Sprache. Die Sprache spricht. Wenn wir uns in den Abgrund, den dieser Satz nennt, fallen lassen, stürzen wir nicht ins Leere weg. Wir fallen in die Höhe. Deren Hoheit öffnet eine Tiefe."—Ed.

23. Cf. above, p. 178, n. 14.—Ed.

24. Bergson says that "living beings constitute 'centers of indetermination' in the universe . . ." and further he explains: ". . . if we consider any other given place in the universe we can regard the action of all matter as passing through it without resistance and without loss, and the photograph of the whole as translucent: here there is wanting behind the plate the black screen on which the image could be shown. Our 'zones of indetermination' play in some sort the part of the screen." *Matiére et mémoire* (10th ed., Paris, 1913), pp. 24, 26–27. [English translation by N. M. Paul and W. Scott Palmer, *Matter and Memory* (London, 1912), Pp. 28, 32.]—Ed.

25. *Phénoménologie de la perception*, p. 221. [Eng. trans., p. 189.]—Ed.

PART THREE

Gilles Deleuze

Élan Vital as Movement of Differentiation

Our problem is now this: By moving from dualism to monism, from the idea of differences in kind to that of levels of expansion *(détente)* and contraction, is Bergson not reintroducing into his philosophy everything that he had condemned—the differences in degree and intensity that he so strongly criticized in *Time and Free Will?*[1] Bergson says in turn that the past and the present differ in kind and that the present is only the most contracted level or degree of the past: How can these two propositions be reconciled? The problem is no longer that of monism; we have seen how the coexisting degrees of expansion *(détente)* and contraction effectively implied a single time in which even the "fluxes" were simultaneous. The problem is that of the harmony between the dualism of differences in kind and the monism of degrees of expansion *(détente)*, between the two moments of the method or the two "beyonds" the turn in experience—recognizing that the moment of dualism has not been suppressed at all, but completely retains its sense.

The critique of intensity in *Time and Free Will* is highly ambiguous. Is it directed against the very notion of intensive quantity, or merely against the idea of an intensity of psychic states? If it is true that intensity is never given in a pure experience, is it not then intensity that *gives* all the qualities with which we make experience? Hence, *Matter and Memory* recognizes intensities, degrees or vibrations in the qualities that we live as such outside ourselves and that, as such, belong to matter. There are numbers enclosed in qualities, intensities included in duration. Here again, must we speak of a contradiction in Bergson? Or are there, rather, different moments of the method, with the emphasis sometimes on one, sometimes on another, but all coexisting in a dimension of depth?

(1) Bergson begins by criticizing any vision of the world based on differences in degree or intensity. These in fact lose sight of the essential point; that is, the articulations of the real or the qualitative differences, the differences in kind. There is a difference in kind between space and duration, matter and memory, present and past, etc. We only discover this difference by dint of decomposing the composites given in experience and going beyond the "turn." We discover the differences in kind between two actual tendencies, between two actual directions toward the pure state into which each composite divides. This is the moment of pure dualism, or of the division of composites.

(2) But we can already see that it is not enough to say that the difference in kind is *between* two tendencies, between two directions, between space and duration. . . . For one of these two directions takes all the differences in kind on itself and all the differences in degree fall away into the other direction, the other tendency. It is duration that includes all the qualitative differences, to the point where it is defined as alteration in relation to itself. It is space that only presents differences in degree, to the point where it appears as the schema of an indefinite divisibility. Similarly, Memory is essentially difference and matter essentially repetition. There is therefore no longer any difference in kind between two tendencies, but a difference *between* the differences in kind that correspond to one tendency and the differences in degree that refer back to the other tendency. This is the moment of neutralized, balanced dualism.

(3) Duration, memory or spirit is difference in kind in itself and for itself; and space or matter is difference in degree outside itself and for us. Therefore, between the two there are all the *degrees of difference* or, in other words, the whole *nature of difference*. Duration is only the most contracted degree of matter, matter the most expanded *(détendu)* degree of duration. But duration is like a naturing nature *(nature naturante)*, and matter a natured nature *(nature naturée)*. Differences in degree are the lowest degree of Difference; differences in kind *(nature)* are the highest nature of Difference. There is no longer any dualism between nature and degrees. All the degrees coexist in a single Nature that is expressed, on the one hand, in differences in kind, and on the other, in differences in degree. This is the moment of monism: All the degrees coexist in a single Time, which is nature in itself.[2] There is no contradiction between this monism and dualism, as moments of the method. For the duality was valid between actual tendencies, between actual directions leading beyond the first turn in experience. But the unity occurs at a second turn: The coexistence of all the degrees, of all the levels is virtual, only virtual. The point of unification is itself virtual. This point is not without similarity to the One-Whole of the Platonists. All the levels of expansion *(détente)* and contraction

coexist in a single Time and form a totality; but this Whole, this One, are pure virtuality. This Whole has parts, this One has a number—but only potentially.[3] This is why Bergson is not contradicting himself when he speaks of different intensities or degrees in a virtual coexistence, in a single Time, in a simple Totality.

* * *

A philosophy like this assumes that the notion of the virtual stops being vague and indeterminate. In itself, it needs to have the highest degree of precision. This condition is only fulfilled if, starting from monism, we are able to rediscover dualism and account for it on a new plane. A fourth moment must be added to the three preceding ones—that of dualism recovered, mastered and in a sense, generated.

What does Bergson mean when he talks about *élan vital?* It is always a case of a virtuality in the process of being actualized, a simplicity in the process of differentiating, a totality in the process of dividing up: Proceeding "by dissociation and division," by "dichotomy," is the essence of life.[4] In the most familiar examples, life is divided into plant and animal; the animal is divided into instinct and intelligence; an instinct in turn divides into several directions that are actualized in different species; intelligence itself has its particular modes or actualizations. It is as if Life were merged into the very movement of differentiation, in ramified series. Movement is undoubtedly explained by the insertion of duration into matter: Duration is differentiated according to the obstacles it meets in matter, according to the materiality through which it passes, according to the kind of extension that it contracts. But differentiation does not merely have an external cause. Duration is differentiated within itself through an internal explosive force; it is only affirmed and prolonged, it only advances, in branching or ramified series.[5] Duration, to be precise, is called life when it appears in this movement. Why is differentiation an "actualization"? Because it presupposes a unity, a virtual primordial totality that is dissociated according to the lines of differentiation, but that still shows its subsisting unity and totality in each line. Thus, when life is divided into plant and animal, when the animal is divided into instinct and intelligence, each side of the division, each ramification, carries the whole with it. From a certain perspective it is like an accompanying nebulosity, testifying to its undivided origin. And there is a halo of instinct in intelligence, a nebula of intelligence in instinct, a hint of the animate in plants, and of the vegetable in animals.[6] Differentiation is always the actualization of a virtuality that persists across its actual divergent lines.

We then encounter a problem that is peculiar to Bergsonism: There are two types of division that must not be confused. According to the first type, we begin with a composite, for example the space-time mixture or the perception-image and recollection-image mixture. We divide this composite into two actual divergent lines that are different in kind and that we extend beyond the turn in experience (pure matter and pure duration, or else pure present and pure past). But now we are speaking of a completely different type of division: Our starting point is a unity, a simplicity, a virtual totality. This unity is actualized according to divergent lines differing in kind; it "explains," it develops what it had kept enclosed in a virtual manner. For example, at each instant pure duration divides in two directions, one of which is the past, the other the present; or else the *élan vital* at every instant separates into two movements, one of relaxation *(détente)* that descends into matter, the other of tension that ascends into duration. It can be seen that the divergent lines produced in the two types of division coincide and are superimposed, or at least correspond closely to each other. In the second type of division we rediscover differences in kind identical or analogous to those that had been determined in the first type. In both cases a vision of the world is criticized for only taking account of differences in degree where, more profoundly, there are differences in kind.[7] In both cases a dualism is established between tendencies that differ in kind. But this is *not* the same state of dualism, and *not* the same division. In the first type, it is a reflexive dualism, which *results from the decomposition of an impure composite:* It constitutes the first moment of the method. In the second type it is a genetic dualism, *the result of the differentiation of a Simple or a Pure:* It forms the final moment of the method that ultimately rediscovers the starting point on this new plane.

One question becomes pressing: What is the nature of this one and simple Virtual? How is it that, as early as *Time and Free Will*, then in *Matter and Memory*, Bergson's philosophy should have attributed such importance to the idea of virtuality at the very moment when it was challenging the category of possibility? It is because the "virtual" can be distinguished from the "possible" from at least two points of view. From a certain point of view, in fact, the possible is the opposite of the real, it is opposed to the real; but, in quite a different opposition, the virtual is opposed to the actual. We must take this terminology seriously: The possible has no reality (although it may have an actuality); conversely, the virtual is not actual, but *as such possesses a reality*. Here again Proust's formula best defines the states of virtuality: "real without being actual, ideal without being abstract." On the other hand, or from another point of view, the possible is that which is "realized" (or is not realized). Now the process of realization is subject to two essential rules, one of resemblance and another of limitation. For the real is supposed to be in the image of the possible that it realizes. (It simply has existence or reality added to it, which is translated by saying that, from the point of view of the concept, there is no difference between the possible and the real.) And, every possible is not realized, realization involves a limitation by which some possibles are supposed to be repulsed or thwarted, while others "pass" into the real. The virtual, on the other hand, does not have to be realized, but rather actualized; and the rules of actualization are not those of resemblance and limitation, but those of difference or divergence and of creation. When certain biologists invoke a notion of organic virtuality or potentiality and nonetheless maintain that this potentiality is actualized by simple limitation of its global capacity, they clearly fall into a confusion of the virtual and the possible.[8] For, in order to be actualized, the virtual cannot proceed by elimination or limitation, but must *create* its own lines of actualization in positive acts. The reason for this is simple: While the real is in the image and likeness of the possible that it realizes, the actual, on the other hand, does *not* resemble the virtuality that it embodies. It is difference that is primary in the process of actualization—the difference between the virtual from which we begin and the actuals at which we arrive, and also the difference between the complementary lines according to which actualization takes place. In short, the characteristic of virtuality is to exist in such a way that it is actualized by being differentiated and is forced to differentiate itself, to create its lines of differentiation in order to be actualized.

Why does Bergson challenge the notion of the possible in favor of that of the virtual? It is precisely because—by virtue of these preceding characteristics—the possible is a false notion, the source of false problems. The real is supposed to resemble it. That is to say, we give ourselves a real that is ready-made, preformed, pre-existent to itself, and that will pass into existence according to an order of successive limitations. Everything is already *completely given:* all of the real in the image, in the pseudo-actuality of the possible. Then the sleight of hand becomes obvious: If the real is said to resemble the possible, is this not in fact because the real was expected to come about by its own means, to "project backward" a fictitious image of it, and to claim that it was possible at any time, before it happened? In fact, it is not the real that resembles the possible, it is the possible that resembles the real, because it has been abstracted from the real once made, arbitrarily extracted from the real like a sterile double.[9] Hence, we no longer understand anything either of the mechanism of difference or of the mechanism of creation.

Evolution takes place from the virtual to actuals. Evolution is actualization, actualization is creation. When we speak of biological or living evolution we must therefore avoid two misconceptions: that of interpreting it in terms of the "possible" that is realized, or else interpreting it in terms of pure actuals. The first misconception obviously appears in preformism. And, contrary to preformism, evolutionism will always have the merit of reminding us that life is production, creation of differences. The whole problem is that of the nature and the causes of these differences. The vital differences or variations can certainly be conceived of as purely accidental. But three objections to an interpretation of this kind arise:

(1) since they are due to chance, these variations, however small they are, would remain external, "indifferent" to each other;

(2) since they are external, they could not logically enter into anything but relations of association and addition with one another;

(3) since they are indifferent, they could not even have the means to really enter into such relations (for there would be no reason why the small successive variations should link up and add together in the same direction; nor any reason for sudden and simultaneous variations to be coordinated into a livable whole).[10]

If we invoke the action of the environment and the influence of external conditions, the three objections persist in another form: For the differences are still interpreted from the perspective of a purely external causality. In their nature they would only be passive effects, elements that could be abstractly combined or added together. In their relationships they would, however, be incapable of functioning "as a bloc," so as to control or utilize their causes.[11]

The mistake of evolutionism is, thus, to conceive of vital variations as so many actual determinations that should then combine on a single line. The three requirements of a philosophy of life are as follows:

(1) the vital difference can only be experienced and thought of as internal difference; it is only in this sense that the "tendency to change" is not accidental, and that the variations themselves find an internal cause in that tendency;

(2) these variations do not enter into relationships of association and addition, but on the contrary, they enter into relationships of dissociation or division;

(3) they therefore involve a virtuality that is actualized according to the lines of divergence; so that evolution does not move from one actual term to another actual term in a homogeneous unilinear series, but from a virtual term to the heterogeneous terms that actualize it along a ramified series.[12]

But this leads to the question of how the Simple or the One, "the original identity," has the power to be differentiated. The answer is already contained in *Matter and Memory*. And the linkage between *Creative Evolution* and *Matter and Memory* is perfectly rigorous. We know that the *virtual as virtual has a reality*; this reality, extended to the whole universe, consists in all the coexisting degrees of expansion *(détente)* and contraction. A gigantic memory, a universal cone in which everything coexists with itself, except for the differences of level. On each of these levels there are some "outstanding points," which are like remarkable points peculiar to it. All these levels or degrees and all these points are themselves virtual. They belong to a single Time; they coexist in a Unity; they are enclosed in a Simplicity; they form the potential parts of a Whole that is itself virtual. They are *the reality of this virtual*. This was the sense of the theory of virtual multiplicities that inspired Bergsonism from the start. When the virtuality is actualized, is differentiated, is "developed," when it actualizes and develops its parts, it does so according to lines that are divergent, but each of which corresponds to a particular degree in the virtual totality. There is here no longer any coexisting whole; there are merely lines of actualization, *some successive, others simultaneous,* but each representing an actualization of the whole in one direction and not combining with other lines or other directions. Nevertheless, each of these lines corresponds to one of these degrees that all coexist in the virtual; it actualizes its level, while separating it from the others; it embodies its prominent points, while being unaware of everything that happens on other levels.[13] We must think of it as follows: When duration is divided into matter and life, then life into plant and animal, different levels of contraction, which only coexist insofar as they remain virtual, are actualized. And when the animal instinct is itself divided into various instincts, or when a particular instinct is itself divided according to species, levels are again separated, or are actually cut out in the region of the animal or of the genus. And however strictly the lines of actualization correspond to the levels or the virtual degrees of expansion *(détente)* or contraction, it should not be thought that the lines of actualization confine themselves to tracing these levels or degrees, to reproducing them by simple resemblance. For what coexisted in the virtual ceases to coexist in the actual and is distributed in lines or parts that cannot be summed up, each one retaining the whole, except from a certain perspective, from a certain point of view. These lines of differentiation are therefore truly creative: They only actualize by inventing, they create in these conditions the physical, vital or psychical representative of the ontological level that they embody.

If we concentrate only on the actuals that conclude each line, we establish relationships between them—whether of gradation or opposition. Between plant and animal, for example, between animal and man, we now only see differences in degree. Or we will situate a fundamental opposition in each one of them: We will see in one the negative of the other, the inversion of the other, or the obstacle that is opposed to the other. Bergson often expresses himself in this way, in terms of contrariety: Matter is presented as the obstacle that the *élan vital* must get around, and materiality, as the inversion of the movement of life.[14] It should not, however, be thought that Bergson is going back to a conception of the negative that he had previously condemned, any more than he returns to a theory of deteriorations. For one only has to replace the actual terms in the movement that produces them to bring them back to the virtuality actualized in them, in order to see that differentiation is never a negation but a creation, and that difference is never negative but essentially positive and creative.

* * *

We always rediscover the laws common to these lines of actualization or of differentiation. There is a correlation between life and matter, between expansion *(détente)* and contraction, which shows

Summary Diagram of Differentiation (CE, Ch. 2)

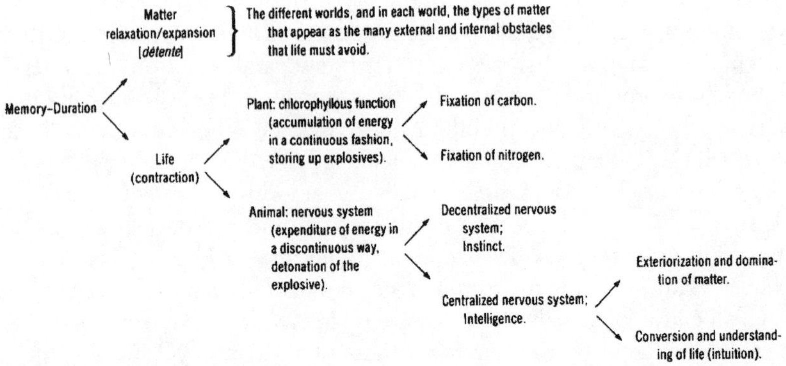

the coexistence of their respective degrees in the virtual Whole, and their essential relativity in the process of actualization. Each line of life is related to a type of matter that is not merely an external environment, but in terms of which the living being manufactures a body, a form, for itself. This is why the living being, in relation to matter, appears primarily as the stating of a problem, and the capacity to solve problems: The construction of an eye, for example, is primarily the solution to a problem posed in terms of light.[15] And each time, we will say that the solution was as good as it could have been, given the way in which the problem was stated, and the means that the living being had at its disposal to solve it. (It is in this way that, if we compare a similar instinct in various species, we ought not to say that it is more or less complete, more or less perfected, but that it is as perfect as it can be in varying degrees.)[16] It is nevertheless clear that each vital solution is not in itself a success: By dividing the animal in two, Arthropods and Vertebrates, we have not taken into account the two other directions, Echinoderms and Mollusks, which are a setback for the *élan vital.*[17] Everything takes place as though living beings themselves also stated false problems for themselves in which they risk losing their way. Moreover, if every solution is a relative success in relation to the conditions of the problem or the environment, it is still a relative setback, in relation to the movement that invents it: Life as *movement* alienates itself in the material *form* that it creates; by actualizing itself, by differentiating itself, it loses "contact with the rest of itself." Every species is thus an arrest of movement; it could be said that the living being turns on itself and *closes itself.*[18] It cannot be otherwise, since the Whole is only virtual, dividing itself by being acted out. It cannot assemble its actual parts that remain external to each other: The Whole is never "given." And, in the actual, an irreducible pluralism reigns—as many worlds as living beings, all "closed" on themselves.

But we must, in another oscillation, be delighted that the *Whole* is not given. This is the constant theme of Bergsonism from the outset: The confusion of space and time, the assimilation of time into space, make us think that the whole is given, even if only in principle, even if only in the eyes of God. And this is the mistake that is common to mechanism and to finalism. The former assumes that everything is calculable in terms of a state; the latter, that everything is determinable in terms of a program: In any event, time is only there now as a screen that hides the eternal from us, or that shows us successively what a God or a superhuman intelligence would see in a single glance.[19] Now this illusion is inevitable as soon as we spatialize time. Indeed, in space it is sufficient to have a dimension supplementary to those where a phenomenon happens for the movement in the course of happening to appear to us as a ready-made form. If we consider time as a fourth dimension of space, this fourth dimension will thus be assumed to contain all the possible forms of the universe as a whole; and movement in space, as well as flowing in time, will now only be appearances linked to the three dimensions.[20] But the fact that real space has only three dimensions, that Time is not a dimension of space, really means this: There is an efficacity, a positivity of time, that is identical to a "hesitation" of things and, in this way, to creation in the world.[21]

It is clear that there is a Whole of duration. But this whole is virtual. It is actualized according to divergent lines; but these lines *do not* form a whole on their own account, and do not resemble what they actualize. If the choice is between mechanism and finalism, finalism is preferable; *providing that it is corrected in two ways.* On the one hand, it is right to compare the living being to the whole of the universe, but it is wrong to interpret this comparison as if it expressed a kind of analogy between two closed totalities (macrocosm and microcosm). The finality of the living being exists only insofar as it is essentially open onto a totality that is itself open: "finality is external, or it is nothing at all."[22] It is thus the whole classical comparison that takes on another meaning; it is not the whole that closes like an organism, it is the organism that opens onto a whole, like this virtual whole.

On the other hand, there is a proof of finality to the extent that we discover similar actualizations, identical structures or apparatuses on divergent lines (for example, the eye in the Mollusk and in the Vertebrate). The example will be all the more significant the further apart the lines are, and the more the organ that is similar is obtained by dissimilar means.[23] We see here how, in the process of actualization, the very category of resemblance finds itself subordinated to that of divergence, difference or differentiation. While actual forms or products can resemble each other, the movements of production do not resemble each other, nor do the products resemble the virtuality that they embody. This is why actualization, differentiation, are a genuine creation. The Whole must *create* the divergent lines according to which it is actualized and the dissimilar means that it utilizes on each line. There is finality because life does not operate without directions; but there is no "goal," because these directions do not preexist ready-made, and are themselves created "along with" the act that runs through them.[24] Each line of actualization corresponds to a virtual level; but each time, it must invent the figure of this correspondence and create the means for the development of that which was only enveloped in order to distinguish that which was confused.

* * *

Duration, Life, is *in principle (en droit)* memory, in principle consciousness, in principle freedom. "In principle" means virtually. The whole question *(quid facti?) is* knowing under what conditions duration becomes *in fact* consciousness of self, how life *actually* accedes to a memory and freedom of fact.[25] Bergson's answer is that it is only on the line of Man that the *élan vital* successfully "gets through"; man in this sense *is* "the purpose of the entire process of evolution."[26] It could be said that in man, and only in man, the actual becomes adequate to the virtual. It could be said that man is capable of rediscovering all the levels, all the degrees of expansion *(détente)* and contraction that coexist in the virtual Whole. As if he were capable of all the frenzies and brought about in himself successively everything that, elsewhere, can only be embodied in different species. Even in his dreams he rediscovers or prepares matter. And durations that are inferior or superior to him are still internal to him. Man therefore creates a differentiation that is valid for the Whole, and he alone traces out an open direction that is able to express a whole that is itself open. Whereas the other directions are closed and go round in circles, whereas a distinct "plane" of nature corresponds to each one, man is capable of scrambling the planes, of going beyond his own plane as his own condition, in order finally to express naturing Nature.[27]

How does this privilege of man come about? At first sight, its origin is a humble one. Every contraction of duration still being relative to an expansion *(détente)*, and every life to a matter, the point of departure is in a certain state of cerebral matter. We recall that this latter "analyzed" the received excitation, selected the reaction, made possible an *interval* between excitation and reaction; nothing here goes beyond the physico-chemical properties of a particularly complicated type of matter. But, as we have seen, it is the whole of memory that descends into this interval, and that becomes actual. It is the whole of freedom that is actualized. On man's line of differentiation, the *élan vital* was able to use matter to create an instrument of freedom, "to make a machine which should triumph over mechanism," "to use the determinism of nature to pass through the meshes of the net which this very determinism had spread."[28] Freedom has precisely this physical sense: "to detonate" an explosive, to use it for more and more powerful movements.[29]

But where does this starting point seem to lead? To perception; and also to a utilitarian memory, since useful recollections are actualized in the cerebral interval; and to intelligence as the organ of domination and utilization of matter. We even understand that men form *societies*. It is not that society is solely or essentially intelligent. From the outset, human societies undoubtedly imply a certain intelligent comprehension of needs and a certain rational organization of activities. But they are also formed, and only subsist through irrational or even absurd factors. Take, for example, obligation: It has no rational ground. Each particular obligation is conventional and can border on the absurd; the only thing that is grounded is the obligation to have obligations, "the whole of obligation"; and it is not grounded in reason, but in a requirement of nature, in a kind of "virtual instinct," that is, on a counterpart that nature produces *in* the reasonable being in order to compensate for the partiality of his intelligence. Each line of differentiation, being exclusive, seeks to recapture, by its own means, the advantages of the other line. Thus, in their separation, instinct and intelligence are such that the one produces an ersatz of intelligence, the other, an equivalent of instinct. This is the "story-telling function": virtual instinct, creator of gods, inventor of religions, that is, of fictitious representations "which will stand up to the representation of the real and which will succeed, by the intermediary of intelligence itself, in thwarting intellectual work." And as in the case of obligation, each god is contingent, or even absurd, but what is natural, necessary and grounded is *having* gods; it is the pantheon of gods.[30] In short, sociability (in the human sense) can only exist *in* intelligent beings, but it is not grounded *on* their intelligence: Social life is immanent to intelligence, it begins with it but does not derive from it. Hence our problem appears to have become more complicated instead of being solved. For if we consider intelligence and sociability, both in their complementarity and in their difference, nothing yet justifies man's privilege. The societies that he forms are no less closed than animal species; they form part of a plan *(plan)* of nature, as much as animal species and societies; and man goes round in circles in his society just as much as the species do in theirs or ants in their domain.[31] Nothing here seems to be capable of giving man the previously mentioned exceptional opening, as the power of going beyond his "plane" (plan) and his condition.

Unless this kind of play of intelligence and of society, this small interval between the two, is itself a decisive factor. The small intracerebral interval has already made intelligence possible, and the actualization of a memory useful. Moreover, thanks to it, the body imitates the whole life of the mind, and we were able with a leap to place ourselves in the pure past. We now find ourselves before *another intercerebral interval* between intelligence itself and society: Is it not this "hesitation" of the intelligence that will be able to imitate the superior "hesitation" of things in duration, and that will allow man, with a leap, to break the circle of closed societies? At first sight, the answer is no. For, if intelligence hesitates and sometimes rebels, it is primarily in the name of an egoism that it seeks to preserve against social requirements.[32] And while society makes itself obeyed it is thanks to the story-telling function, which persuades the intelligence that it is in its interest to confirm the social obligation. We therefore seem to be constantly sent back from one term to another. But everything changes when something appears in the interval.

What is it that appears in the interval between intelligence and society (in the same way as the recollection-image appeared in the cerebral interval appropriate to intelligence)? We cannot reply: It is intuition. In fact, we must on the contrary carry out a genesis of intuition, that is, determine the way in which intelligence itself was converted or is converted into intuition. And if we recall, according to the laws of differentiation, that intelligence, in separating itself from instinct, nevertheless keeps an equivalent of instinct that would be like the nucleus of intuition. We are not saying anything of importance, for this equivalent of instinct finds itself completely mobilized in the closed society as such, through the story-telling function.[33] Bergson's real answer is completely different: What appears in the interval is *emotion*. In this answer, "We have no choice."[34] Only emotion differs in nature from both intelligence and instinct, from both intelligent individual egoism and quasi-instinctive social pressure. Obviously no one denies that egoism produces emotions; and even more so social pressure, with all the fantasies of the story-telling function. But in both these cases, emotion is always connected to a representation on which it is supposed to depend. We are then placed in a composite of emotion and of representation, without noticing that it is potential *(en puissance)*, the nature of emotion as pure element. The latter in fact precedes all representation, itself generating new ideas. It does not have, strictly speaking, an object, but merely an *essence* that spreads itself over various objects, animals, plants and the whole of nature. "Imagine a piece of music which expresses love. It is not love for a particular person. . . . The quality of love will depend upon its essence and not upon its object."[35] Although personal, it is not individual; transcendent, it is like the God in us. "When music cries, it is humanity, it is the whole of nature which cries with it. Truly speaking, it does not introduce these feelings in us; it introduces us rather into them, like the passers-by that might be nudged in a dance." In short, emotion is creative (first, because *it* expresses the whole of creation, then because *it* creates the work in which it is expressed; and finally, because it communicates a little of this creativity to spectators or hearers).

The little interval "between the pressure of society and the resistance of intelligence" defines a variability appropriate to human societies. Now, by means of this interval, something extraordinary is produced or embodied: creative emotion. This no longer has anything to do with the pressures of society, nor with the disputes of the individual. It no longer has anything to do with an individual who contests or even invents, nor with a society that constrains, that persuades or even tells stories.[36] It has only made use of their circular play in order to break the circle, just as Memory uses the circular play of excitation and reaction to embody recollections in images. And what is this creative emotion, if not precisely a cosmic Memory, that actualizes all the levels at the same time, that liberates man from the plane *(plan)* or the level that is proper to him, in order to make him a creator, adequate to the whole movement of creation?[37] This liberation, this embodiment of cosmic memory in creative emotions, undoubtedly only takes place in privileged souls. It leaps from one soul to another, "every now and then," crossing closed deserts. But to each member of a closed society, if he opens himself to it, it communicates a kind of reminiscence, an excitement that allows him to follow. And from soul to soul, it traces the design of an *open* society, a society of creators, where we pass from one genius to another, through the intermediary of disciples or spectators or hearers.

It is the genesis of intuition in intelligence. If man accedes to the open creative totality, it is therefore by acting, by creating rather than by contemplating. In philosophy itself, there is still too much alleged contemplation: Everything happens as if intelligence were already imbued with emotion, thus with intuition, but not sufficiently so for creating in conformity to this emotion.[38] Thus the great souls—to a greater extent than philosophers—are those of artists and mystics (at least those of a Christian mysticism that Bergson describes as being completely superabundant activity, action, creation).[39] At the limit, it is the mystic who plays with the whole of creation, who invents an expression of it whose adequacy increases with its dynamism. Servant of an open and finite God (such are the characteristics of the *Élan Vital)*, the mystical soul actively plays the whole of the universe, and reproduces the opening of a Whole in which there is nothing to see or to contemplate. Already motivated by emotion, the philosopher extracted the lines that divided up the composites given in experience. He prolonged the outline to beyond the "turn"'; he showed in the distance the virtual point at which they all met. Everything happens as if that which remained indeterminate in philosophical intuition gained a new kind of determination in mystical intuition—as though the properly philosophical "probability" extended itself into mystical certainty. Undoubtedly philosophy can only consider the mystical soul from the outside and from the point of view of its lines of probability.[40] But it is precisely the existence of mysticism that gives a higher probability to this final transmutation into certainty, and also gives, as it were, an envelope or a limit to all the aspects of method.

* * *

At the outset we asked: What is the relationship between the three fundamental concepts of Duration, Memory and the *Élan Vital?* What progress do they indicate in Bergson's philosophy? It seems to us that Duration essentially defines a virtual multiplicity *(what differs in nature)*. Memory then appears as the coexistence of all the *degrees of difference* in this multiplicity, in this virtuality. The *élan vital*, finally, designates the actualization of this virtual according to the *lines of differentiation* that correspond to the degrees—up to this precise line of man where the *Élan Vital* gains self-consciousness.

Notes

1. Cf. above pp. 75–76.

2. This ontological "naturalism" appears clearly in MR: On naturing Nature and natured Nature cf. 49 (1024, 56). The apparently strange notion of "nature's plan" appears in MR, 48 (1022, 54). Despite some of Bergson's expressions ("Nature intended," MR, 55 [1029, 63]), this notion should not be interpreted in too finalistic a sense: There are several *plans* and each, as we shall see, corresponds to one of the degrees or levels of contraction that all coexist in duration. Therefore, they are "planes" rather than "plans," they refer to sections, to sections of the cone rather than to a project or to an aim.

3. According to Bergson, the word "Whole" has a sense, but only on condition that it does *not* designate anything actual. He constantly recalls that: Whole is not given. This means, not that the idea of the whole is devoid of sense, but that it designates a virtuality, actual parts do not allow themselves to be totalized.

4. Cf. CE, 99 (571, 90). And MR, 282 (1225, 313): "the essence of a vital tendency is to develop fan-wise, creating, by the mere fact of its growth, divergent directions, each of which will receive a certain proportion of the impetus." On the primacy, here, of an undivided Totality, of Unity or of a Simplicity, cf. CE, 99–101 (571–572, 90–91); 130–131 (595, 119) "the original identity."

5. CE, 109 (578, 99).

6. In fact, the products of differentiation are never completely *pure* in experience. Moreover, each line "balances" that which is exclusive in it: For example, the line that ends in intelligence arouses in intelligent beings an equivalent of instinct, a "virtual instinct" represented by *story telling:* cf. MR, 100 (1068, 114).

7. Bergson's great reproach to the philosophies of nature is that they only saw differences of degree on a single line in evolution and differentiation: CE, 149 (609,136).

8. Philosophically, one might find in a system like Leibniz's a similar hesitation between the two concepts of the virtual and of the possible.

9. Cf. CM, "The Possible and the Real."

10. CE, 72–78 (549–554, 64–70).

11. CE, 80 (555, 72): How could an external physical energy, light for example, have "converted an impression left by it into a machine capable of using it"?

12. The idea of diverging lines or of ramified series was undoubtedly not unknown to classifiers from the eighteenth century. But what matters to Bergson is the fact that the divergences of directions can only be interpreted from the perspective of the actualization of the virtual. In R. Ruyer, today, we find requirements analogous to those of Bergson: the appeal to an "inventive, mnemonic and trans-spatial potential," the refusal to interpret evolution in purely actual terms (cf. his *Eléments de psycho-biologie*, Presses Universitaires de France).

13. When Bergson (CE, 184 [637, 168]) says, "It seems as if life, as soon as it has become bound up in a species, is cut off from the rest of its own work, save at one or two

points that are of vital concern to the species just arisen. Is it not plain that life goes to work here exactly like consciousness, exactly like memory?" The reader must understand that these *points* correspond to the outstanding points that became detached at each level of the cone. Each line of differentiation or actualization thus constitutes a "plane *(plan)* of nature" that takes up again in its own way a virtual section or level (cf. note 2, above).

14. On this negative vocabulary, cf. CE, Ch. 3.

15. This character of life, posing and solution of a problem, appears to Bergson to be more important than the negative determination of need.

16. CE, 188 (640, 172); MR, 116 (1082, 132) ". . . at each stopping-place a combination, perfect of its kind."

17. CE, 145 (606, 132).

18. On the opposition of life and form, CE, 141 (603ff., 129ff.): "Like eddies of dust raised by the wind as it passes, the living turn upon themselves, borne up by the great blast of life. They are therefore relatively stable and counterfeit immobility so well . . ." On the species as "stopping place" see MR, 198 (1153, 221). This is the origin of the notion of *enclosure*, which will take on such great importance in the study of human society. The point is that, from a certain point of view, Man is no less turned in on himself, closed in on himself, circular, than the other animal species: It might be said that he is "closed." Cf. MR, 29–30 (1006, 34); 245–246 (1193, 273).

19. CE, 43–46 (526–528, 37–40).

20. Cf. DS, 137 (203ff.) on the example of the "curved plane" and of the "three dimensional curve."

21. DS, 63 (84): There is "a certain hesitation or indetermination inherent in a certain part of things" that becomes merged with "creative evolution."

22. CE, 47 (529, 41).

23. CE, 62 (541 ff., 55ff.) "How do we assume that accidental causes, presenting themselves in an accidental order, have several times ended in the same result, the causes being infinitely numerous and the effect infinitely complicated?" L. Cuenot has set out all kinds of examples going in the direction of the Bergsonian theory, cf., *Invention et finalité en biologie*.

24. CE, 58 (538, 51).

25. Cf. CE, 198–199 (649, 182); ME, 8 (818ff., 5ff.).

26. MR, 200 (1154, 223).

27. On the man who tricks nature, extending beyond the "plane" *(plan)* and returning to a naturing Nature, cf. MR, 48–57 (1022–1029, 55–64). On man's going beyond his own condition, MR, passim, and CM, 229 (1425–218).

28. CE, 288 (719, 264).

29. ME, 18–20 (825–826, 14–15).

30. MR, 189–190 (1145, 211). On the story-telling function and the virtual instinct, 99 (1067ff., 113ff.) and 109–110 (1076, 124). On obligation and the virtual instinct, 20 (998, 23).

31. MR, 29–30 (1006, 34).

32. MR, 83–84 (1053, 94); 198–199 (1153, 222).

33. Bergson nevertheless suggests this explanation in certain texts, for example, MR, 200–201 (1155, 224). But it only has a provisional value.

34. MR, 31 (1008, 35). The theory of the creative emotion is all the more important as it gives affectivity a status that it lacked in the preceding works. In *Time and Free*

Will, affectivity tended to become intermingled with duration in general. In *Matter and Memory*, on the contrary, it had a much more precise role, but was impure and rather painful. On the creative emotion and its relations with intuition, the reader is referred to the study of M. Gouhier, in *L'histoire et sa philosophie* (Vrin, pp. 76ff.).

35. MR, 243 (1191–1192, 270) and 30–32 (1007–1008, 35–36).

36. It will be noted that art, according to Bergson, also has two sources. There is a *story-telling* art, sometimes collective, sometimes individual: MR, 184–186 (1141–1142, 206–207). And there is an *emotive* or *creative* art: MR, 241 (1190, 268). Perhaps all art presents these two aspects, but in variable proportions. Bergson does not disguise the fact that the story-telling aspect appears to him to be inferior in art; the novel would above all be story-telling, music on the contrary, emotion and creation.

37. Cf. MR, 243 (1192, 270): ". . . create creators."

38. MR, 55–56 (1029, 63).

39. On the three mysticisms, Greek, Oriental and Christian, cf. MR, 205–206 (1158ff., 229ff.).

40. Cf. MR, 234 (1184, 260). Let us remember that the notion of probability has the greatest importance in the Bergsonian method, and that intuition is no less a method of exteriority than of interiority.

References to Bergson's Works

TF *Time and Free Will*, translated by F. L. Pogson. London: George Allen & Unwin Ltd. New York: Macmillan & Co., 1919. (*Essai sur les données immédiates de la conscience*, 1889.)

MM *Matter and Memory*, translated by Nancy Margaret Paul and W. Scott Palmer. London: George Allen & Unwin Ltd., 1911. (*Matiére et Mémoire*, 1896.)

CE *Creative Evolution*, translated by Arthur Mitchell. New York: Henry Holt & Co., 1911. New York: Macmillan & Co., 1944. (*L'Evolution créatrice*, 1907.)

ME *Mind-Energy*, translated by H. Wildon Carr. New York: Henry Holt & Co., 1920. (*L'Energie spirituelle*, 1919.)

DS *Duration and Simultaneity*, translated by Leon Jacobson. Indianapolis: Bobbs-Merrill, 1965. (*Durée et Simultanéité*, 1922.)

MR *The Two Sources of Morality and Religion*, translated by R. Ashley Audra and Cloudesley Brereton with the assistance of W. Horsfall Carter. New York: Henry Holt & Co., 1935. (*Les deux sources de la morale et de la religion*, 1932.)

CM *The Creative Mind*, translated by Mabelle L. Andison. Westport, Connecticut: Greenwood Press, 1946. (*La Pensée et le Mouvant*, 1941.)

References to the original French are in parentheses. The DS references are to the 4th Edition. For all the other works, French references are, first, to the Centenary Edition (Presses Universitaires de France), and then to the 1939–1941 reprints.

Numerical and Real Distinction

Expression presents us with a triad. In it we must distinguish substance, attributes and essence. Substance expresses itself, attributes are expressions, and essence is expressed. The idea of expression remains unintelligible while we see only two of the terms whose relations it presents. We confuse substance and attribute, attribute and essence, essence and substance, as long as we fail to take into account the presence of a third term linking each pair. Substance and attribute are distinct, but only insofar as each attribute expresses a certain essence. Attribute and essence are distinct, but only insofar as every essence is expressed as an essence of substance, rather than of attribute. The originality of the concept of expression shows itself here: essence, insofar as it has existence, has no existence outside the attribute in which it is expressed; and yet, as essence, it relates only to substance. An essence is expressed by each attribute, but this as an essence of substance itself. Infinite essences are distinguished through the attributes in which they find expression, but are identified in the substance to which they relate. We everywhere confront the necessity of distinguishing three terms: substance which expresses itself, the attribute which expresses, and the essence which is expressed. It is through attributes that essence is distinguished from substance, but through essence that substance is itself distinguished from attributes: a triad each of whose terms serves as a middle term relating the two others, in three syllogisms.

Expression is inherent in substance, insofar as substance is absolutely infinite; in its attributes, insofar as they constitute an infinity; in essence, insofar as each essence in an attribute is infinite. Thus infinity has a nature. Merleau-

Ponty has well brought out what seems to us now the most difficult thing to understand in the philosophies of the seventeenth century: the idea of a positive infinity as the "secret of grand Rationalism"—"an innocent way of setting out in one's thinking from infinity," which finds its most perfect embodiment in Spinozism.[1] Innocence does not of course exclude the "labor of the concept " Spinoza needed all the resources of a novel conceptual frame to bring out the power and the actuality of positive infinity. If the idea of expression provided this, it did so by introducing into infinity various distinctions corresponding to the three terms, substance, attribute and essence. What is the character of distinction within infinity? What sort of distinction can one introduce into what is absolute, into the nature of God? Such is the first problem posed by the idea of expression, and it dominates Part One of the *Ethics*.

At the very beginning of the *Ethics* Spinoza asks how two things, in the most general sense of the word, can be distinguished, and then how two substances, in the precise sense of that word, must be distinguished. The first question leads into the second, and the answer to the second question seems unequivocal: if two "things" in general differ either by the attributes of their substance, or by its modes, then two substances cannot differ in mode, but only in attribute. So that there cannot be two or more substances of the same attribute.[2] There is no question that Spinoza is here setting out from a Cartesian framework, but what must be most carefully considered is just what he takes over from Descartes, what he discards and, above all, what he takes over from Descartes in order to turn it against him.

The principle that there are only substances and modes, modes being in something else, and substance in itself, may be found quite explicitly in Descartes.[3] And if modes always presuppose a substance, and are sufficient to give us knowledge of it, they do so through a primary attribute which they imply, and which constitutes the essence of the substance itself. Thus two or more substances are distinguished and distinctly known through their primary attributes.[4] From this Descartes deduces that we can conceive a real distinction between two substances, a modal distinction between a substance and a mode that presupposes it (without in turn being presupposed by it) and a distinction of reason between a substance and the attribute without which we could have no distinct knowledge of the substance.[5] Exclusion, unilateral implication and abstraction correspond to these as criteria applicable to corresponding ideas, or rather as the elementary data of representation[a] which allow us to define and recognize these varieties of distinction. The characterization and application of these kinds of distinction play a crucial part in the elaboration of the Cartesian system. Descartes no doubt drew on the earlier efforts made by Suarez to bring order into this complicated area,[6] but his own use of the three distinctions seems, in its very richness, to introduce many further ambiguities.

An initial ambiguity, admitted by Descartes, concerns the distinction of reason, modal distinction and the relation between them. The ambiguity comes out in the use of the words "mode," "attribute" and "quality" themselves. Any given attribute is a quality, in that it qualifies a substance as this or that, but also a mode, in that it diversifies it.[7] How do primary attributes appear in this light? I cannot separate a substance from such an attribute except by abstraction; but as long as I do not make it something subsisting by itself, I can also distinguish such an attribute from the substance, by considering it just as the substance's property of changing (of having, that is to say, various different shapes or different thoughts). Thus Descartes says that extension and thought may be distinctly conceived in two ways: "insofar as one constitutes the nature of body, and the other that of the soul"; and also through distinguishing each from their substance, by taking them simply as "modes" or "dependents."[8] Now, if in the first case attributes distinguish the substances that they qualify, then it surely appears, in the second case, that modes distinguish substances with the same attribute. Thus different shapes may be referred to this or that body, really distinct from any other; and different thoughts to really distinct souls. An attribute constitutes the essence of the substance it qualifies, but this doesn't prevent it from also constituting the essence of the modes which it links to substances sharing the same attribute. This dual aspect generates major difficulties in the Cartesian system.[9] Let it suffice here to note the conclusion that *there exist substances sharing the same attribute*. In other words, *there are numerical distinctions that are at the same time real or substantial.*

A second difficulty concerns real distinction considered alone. It is, no less than the other forms, a datum of representation. Two things are really distinct if one can conceive one of them clearly and distinctly while excluding everything belonging to the concept of the other. So that Descartes explains the criterion of real distinction to Arnauld as the completeness of the *idea* alone. He can quite rightly claim never to have confused things conceived as really distinct with really distinct things; and yet the passage from one to the other does appear to him to be perfectly legitimate—the question is, where to make this passage. In the progress of the *Meditations* we need only proceed as far as a divine Creator to see that he would be singularly lacking in truthfulness if he were to create things differing from the clear and distinct ideas he gives us of them. Real distinction does not contain within it the ground of things differing, but this ground is furnished by the external and transcendent divine causality that creates substances conformably to our manner of conceiving them as possible. Here again, all sorts of difficulties develop in relation to the idea of creation. The primary ambiguity attaches to the definition of substance: "A thing that can exist by itself."[10] Is there not a contradiction in presenting existing-by-itself as itself being simply a possibility? Here we may note a second conclusion: God as creator effects our passage from substances conceived as really distinct to really distinct substances. *Real distinction*, whether between substances with different attributes, or those with the same attribute, *brings with it a division of things, that is, a corresponding numerical distinction.*

The opening of the *Ethics is* organized around these two Cartesian conclusions. Where lies the error, Spinoza asks, in supposing several substances sharing the same attribute? He refutes the error in two ways, using a favorite style of argument: first through a *reductio ad absurdum,* and then through a more complex proof. If there were several substances with the same attribute, they would have to be distinguished by their modes, which is absurd, since substance is in its very nature anterior to its modes, none of which it implies (this is the short way, taken at 1.5). The positive demonstration comes further on, in a scholium to Proposition 8: two substances with the same attribute would be only *numerically* distinct—and the character of numerical distinction is such as to exclude the possibility of making of it a real or substantial distinction.

According to the Scholium, a distinction would not be numerical if the things distinguished did not have the same concept or definition; but in that case the things would not be distinct, were there not an external cause, beside the definition, which determined that they exist in such a number. So that two or more numerically distinct things presuppose something outside their concept. Thus substances could only be numerically distinct through the operation of some external causality that could produce them. But only by holding conjointly a number of confused ideas can we claim that substances are produced. We say they have a cause, but that we do not know how this cause operates; we imagine that we have a true idea of these substances, since they are conceived in themselves, but we are unsure of the truth of this idea, because we do not know, from the substances themselves, whether they exist. This amounts to a criticism of the odd Cartesian formula "what *can* exist by itself." External causality does make sense, but only in relation to the existence of finite modes: every existing mode may be referred to another, precisely because it *cannot* exist by itself. To apply such causality to substance is to make it operate outside the terms that legitimate and define it—to propose its operation in a sort of void, and quite indeterminately. In short, external causality and numerical distinction share the same fate of applying to modes, and to modes alone.

The argument of Scholium 8 has, then, the following form: (1) Numerical distinction requires an external cause to which it may be referred; (2) But a substance cannot be referred to an external cause, because of the contradiction implied in such a use of causal principles; (3) So two or more substances cannot be distinguished *in numero,* and there cannot be two substances with the same attribute. The structure of the argument here differs from that of the first eight proofs, which runs: (1) Two or more substances cannot share the same attribute, for they would then have to be distinguished by their modes, which is absurd; (2) So that a substance cannot have a cause external to it, for to be produced or limited by another substance it would have to share the same nature or the same attribute; (3) So that there cannot be numerical distinction in any substance, of whatever attribute, and "Every substance must be infinite."[11]

On the one hand, one deduces from the nature of numerical distinction that it is inapplicable to substance; on the other, one deduces from the nature of substance its infinity, and thus the impossibility of applying to it numerical distinctions. In either case, numerical distinction can never distinguish substances, but only modes that involve the same attribute. For number expresses in its own way the character of existing modes: the composite nature of their parts, their limitation by other things of the same nature, their determination from outside themselves. Number thus goes on *ad infinitum*. But the question is, can it ever reach infinity itself? Or, as Spinoza puts it: even in the case of modes, is it from the multitude of parts that we infer their infinity?[12] When we make of numerical distinction a real or substantial distinction, we carry it to infinity, if only to ensure the convertibility that then becomes necessary between the attribute as such and the infinity of finite parts which we distinguish in it. Great absurdities then follow: "If an infinite quantity is measured by parts equal to a foot, it will consist of an infinitely many such parts, as it will also, if it is measured by parts equal to an inch. And therefore, one infinite number will be twelve times greater than another."[13] The absurdity does not, as Descartes thought, lie in hypostatizing extension as an attribute, but rather in conceiving it as measurable and composed of finite parts into which one supposes it convertible. Physics here intervenes to support the principles of logic: the absence of a vacuum in nature means simply that division into parts is not real distinction. Numerical distinction is division, but division takes place only in modes, only modes are divisible.[14]

There cannot be several substances with the same attribute. From which one may infer: from the viewpoint of relation, that one substance is not produced by another; from the viewpoint of modality, that it belongs to the nature of substance to exist; and from the viewpoint of quality, that any substance is necessarily infinite.[15] But all these results are, so to speak, involved in the argument relating to numerical distinction, and it is the latter that brings us back around to our starting point: "There exists only one substance of the same attribute."[16] Then, from Proposition 9 on, Spinoza's objective seems to shift. It is no longer a question of demonstrating that there is only one substance for each attribute, but that there is only one substance for all attributes. The passage from one theme to the next seems difficult to grasp. For, in this new perspective, what implication should be assigned to the first eight propositions? The problem is clarified if we see that the passage from one theme to the other may be effected by what is called in logic the conversion of a negative universal. Numerical distinction is never real; then conversely, real distinction is never numerical. Spinoza's argument now becomes: attributes are really distinct; but real distinction is never numerical; so there is only one substance for all attributes.

Spinoza says that attributes are "conceived to be really distinct."[17] One should not see in this formulation a weakened sense of real distinction. Spinoza is neither suggesting that attributes are other than we conceive them, nor that they are just conceptions we have of substance. Nor indeed should we think that he is making a purely hypothetical or polemical use of real distinction.[18] Real distinction, in the strictest sense, is always a datum of representation. Two things are really distinct when they are so *conceived*—that is, "one without the aid of the other," in such a way that we *conceive* one while denying everything belonging to the *concept* of the other. In this respect there is no disagreement whatever with Descartes: Spinoza accepts both his criterion and his definition. The only thing at issue is whether real distinction thus understood is, or is not, attended by a real division among things. For Descartes, only the assumption of a divine creator sustained such association. According to Spinoza, one can only make division correspond to a real distinction by making of the latter at least a potential numerical distinction, that is, by confusing it with modal distinction. But real distinction cannot be numerical or modal.

When Spinoza is asked how he comes to the idea of a single substance for all attributes, he points out that he has put forward two arguments: the more reality a being has, the more attributes must be ascribed to it; and the more attributes we ascribe to a being, the more we must accord it existence.[19] But no such argument would suffice were it not supported by the analysis of real distinction. Only that analysis, in fact, shows it to be *possible* to ascribe all attributes to one being, and so to pass from the infinity of each attribute to the absoluteness of a being that possesses them all. And this passage, being possible, or implying no contradiction, is then seen to be necessary, as in the proof of God's existence. Furthermore, it is the same argument over real distinction which shows that *all* the attributes amount to an infinity. For we cannot pass through just three or four attributes without bringing back into the absolute the same numerical distinction which we have just excluded from infinity.[20]

If substance were to be divided according to its attributes, it would have to be taken as a genus, and the attributes as specific differences. Substance would be posited as a genus which would tell us nothing in particular about anything. It would differ from its attributes, as a genus from its differentia, and the attributes would be distinct from corresponding substances, as specific differences are distinct from the species themselves. Thus, by making of the real distinction between attributes a numerical distinction between substances, one carries over mere *distinctions of reason* into substantial reality. There can be no necessity of existence in a substance of the same "species" as an attribute—a specific difference determines only the possible existence of objects corresponding to it within the genus. So substance is once more reduced to the mere possibility of existence, with attributes being nothing but an *indication*, a *sign*, of such possible existence. The first critique to which Spinoza subjects the notion of sign in the Ethics appears precisely in relation to real distinction.[21] Real distinction between attributes is no more the "sign" of a diversity of substances than each attribute is the specific character of some substance that corresponds, or might correspond, to it. Substance is not a genus, nor are attributes differentia, nor are qualified substances species.[22] Spinoza condemns equally a thinking that proceeds by genus and differentia, and a thinking that proceeds by signs.

Régis, in a book in which he defends Descartes against Spinoza, invokes the existence of two sorts of attributes: "specific" ones which distinguish substances of different species, and "numerical" ones which distinguish substances of the same species.[23] But this is just what Spinoza objects to in Cartesianism: according to him, attributes are never specific or numerical. It seems we may sum up Spinoza's thesis thus: (1) In positing several substances with the same attribute we make of numerical distinction a real distinction, but this is to confuse real and modal distinctions, treating modes as substances; and (2) in positing as many substances as there are different attributes we make of real distinction a numerical distinction, confusing real distinction not only with modal distinction, but with distinctions of reason as well.

In this context *it appears difficult to consider the first eight propositions as having only a hypothetical sense.* Some proceed as though Spinoza began by arguing on the basis of a hypothesis that he didn't accept, as if setting out from a hypothesis that he intended to refute. But this misses the categorical sense of the first eight propositions. There are not several substances of the same attribute, and numerical distinction is not real: we are not here confronting a provisional hypothesis, valid up to the point where we discover absolutely infinite substance, but have before us, rather, a development that leads us inevitably to posit such a substance. And the categorical sense of the initial propositions is not merely negative. As Spinoza says, "there exists only one substance of a certain nature." The identification of an attribute as belonging to an infinitely perfect substance is, in the *Ethics* as in the *Short Treatise*, no provisional hypothesis, but should be interpreted positively from the viewpoint of *quality*. There is one substance per attribute from the viewpoint of quality, but one single substance for all attributes from the viewpoint of *quantity*. What is the sense of this purely qualitative multiplicity? The obscure formulation reflects the difficulties of a finite understanding rising to the comprehension of absolutely infinite substance, and is justified by the new status of real distinction. It means: substances as qualified are qualitatively, but not quantitatively, distinct—or to put it better, they are "formally," "quidditatively," and not "ontologically" distinct.

One of the sources of Spinoza's Anticartesianism is to be found in the theory of distinctions. In the *Metaphysical Thoughts* he sets out the Cartesian conception: "There are three kinds of distinction between things, real, modal, and of reason." And he seems to give his approval: "For the rest, we pay no attention to the hodgepodge of Peripatetic distinctions."[24] But what counts is not so much the list of accepted distinctions, but their meaning and precise application. In this respect Spinoza retains nothing Cartesian. The new status of real distinction is fundamental: as purely qualitative, quidditative or formal, real distinction excludes any division. Yet isn't this just one of those apparently discredited Peripatetic distinctions returning under a Cartesian name? That real distinction is not and cannot be numerical appears to me to be one of the principal themes of the *Ethics*. This thoroughly upsets the other distinctions. Not only is real distinction no longer referred to numerically distinguished *possible* substances, but modal distinction, in its turn, is no longer referred to accidents as *contingent* determinations. In Descartes a certain contingency of modes echoes the simple possibility of substances. It's all very well for Descartes to insist that accidents are not real, but substantial reality still has accidents. To be produced, modes require something other than the substance to which they relate—either another substance that impresses them in the first, or God who creates the first along with all that depends on it. Spinoza's view is quite different: there is no more a contingency of modes in relation to substance than a possibility of substance in relation to attributes. Everything is necessary, either from its essence or from its cause: Necessity is the only affection of Being, the only modality. And the distinction of reason is, in turn, thereby transformed. We will see that there is no Cartesian axiom (Nothing has no properties, and so on) that does not take on a new meaning, hostile to Cartesianism, on the basis of the new theory of distinctions. The theory has as its fundamental principle the qualitative status of real distinction. Detached from all numerical distinction, real distinction is carried into the absolute, and becomes capable of expressing difference within Being, so bringing about the restructuring of other distinctions.

Notes

1. Cf. Merleau-Ponty in *Les Philosophes célèbres* (Paris, 1956), p. 136.

2. E 1.5.

3. This is how Spinoza presents the Cartesian position (M II.V): "We need to recall what Descartes has taught *(Principles* 1.48,49), viz. that there is nothing in nature but substances and their modes. From this a threefold distinction of things is deduced (1.60–62), viz. *real, modal,* and *of reason*" [323].

4. Descartes, *Principles* 1.53.

5. *Principles* 1.60–62.

6. Cf. Suarez, *Metaphysicarum disputationum* d.VIII. The only distinctions recognized by Suarez were real, modal and of reason—he criticized Duns Scotus's formal distinction in terms very similar to those employed by Descartes.

7. Descartes, *Principles* 1.56.

8. *Principles* 1.63–64.

9. On these paragraphs, 63 and 64, see the discussion between F. Alquié and M. Gueroult in the proceedings of the Royaumont colloquium: *Descartes* (Paris, 1967), pp. 32–56.

10. Descartes, *Replies to the Fourth Objections*, AT IX. 175.

11. This tripartite formulation is given in Letter 2 (to Oldenburg, III.5 [166]).

12. Letter 81 (to Tschirnhaus), III.241; cf. also Letter 12 (to Meyer), III.41: number does not adequately express the nature of modes as an infinity, that is, as they depend on substance.

13. E 1.15s [422].

14. ST I.ii.19–22.

15. E 1.5–7,8e.

16. E 1.8s2 [416: with "nature" for "attribute"].[b]

17. E 1.10s [416].

18. Cf. P. Lachièze-Rey's interpretation in *Les Origines cartésiennes du Dieu de Spinoza*[2] (Paris, 1934), p. 151: "Nor does such a use of the distinction in any way imply its admissibility, according to Spinoza. It remains solely a means of demonstration, given a hypothesized plurality of substances, intended to nullify any possible consequences of such hypothetical plurality."

19. Letter 9 (to De Vries, III.32). In the *Ethics* the first argument appears almost verbatim at 1.9, the second, less directly, at 1.11s.

20. Cf. Letter 64 (to Schuller, III.206).

21. E 1.10s: "But if someone now asks by what sign we shall be able to distinguish the diversity of substances, let him read the following propositions, which show that in Nature there exists only one substance, and that it is absolutely infinite. So that sign would be sought in vain."

22. ST I.vii.9–10.

23. Cf. Régis, *Refutation de l'opinion de Spinoza touchant l'existence et la nature de Dieu* (Paris, 1704).

24. M II.v [323, 325].

Translator's Notes

Deleuze has commented on a few points raised in these notes, and his comments are sometimes quoted or alluded to below. His reply to a general query relating to his use of capitalization may be given here: "My use of capitals is often somewhat arbitrary. I usually capitalize a word for one of two reasons: (1) When an important notion appears for the first time in some passage (subsequent uses being in lower-case), or (2) when some notion has a particular importance in a specific sentence (but not in adjacent sentences)."

a. In Spinoza, the Dutch *vertoning* is both *repraesentamen and species*, "presentation" and "appearance"; the difficulty involved in translating Deleuze's *donnée de la représentation* is that both "representation" and "appearance" are more technically loaded in English than *représentation* in French, which corresponds rather to Spinoza's less technical *vertoning*.

b. "Attribute" nowhere occurs in the Scholium, although it is used as equivalent to "nature" in (the "equivalent") Proposition 5 (*. . . eiusdem naturae sive attributi*).

Difference in Itself

Indifference has two aspects: the undifferenciated abyss, the black nothingness, the indeterminate animal in which everything is dissolved—but also the white nothingness, the once more calm surface upon which float unconnected determinations like scattered members: a head without a neck, an arm without a shoulder, eyes without brows. The indeterminate is completely indifferent, but such floating determinations are no less indifferent to each other. Is difference intermediate between these two extremes? Or is it not rather the only extreme, the only moment of presence and precision? Difference is the state in which one can speak of determination *as such.* The difference 'between' two things is only empirical, and the corresponding determinations are only extrinsic. However, instead of something distinguished from something else, imagine something which distinguishes itself—and yet that from which it distinguishes itself does not distinguish itself from it. Lightning, for example, distinguishes itself from the black sky but must also trail it behind, as though it were distinguishing itself from that which does not distinguish itself from it. It is as if the ground rose to the surface, without ceasing to be ground. There is cruelty, even monstrosity, on both sides of this struggle against an elusive adversary, in which the distinguished opposes something which cannot distinguish itself from it but continues to espouse that which divorces it. Difference is this state in which determination takes the form of unilateral distinction. We must therefore say that difference is made, or makes itself, as in the expression 'make the difference'. This difference or determination *as such* is also cruelty. The Platonists used to say that the not-One distinguished itself from the One but not the converse, since the One does not flee that which flees it; and at the other pole, form distinguishes itself from matter or from the ground, but not the converse, since distinction itself is a form. In truth, all the forms are dissolved when they are reflected in this rising ground. It has ceased to be the pure indeterminate which remains below, but the forms also cease to be the coexisting or complementary determinations. The rising ground is no longer below, it acquires autonomous existence; the form reflected in this ground is no longer a form but an abstract line acting directly upon the soul. When the ground rises to the surface, the human face decomposes in this mirror in which both determinations and the indeterminate combine in a single determination which 'makes' the difference. It is a poor recipe for producing monsters to accumulate heteroclite determinations or to overdetermine the animal. It is better to raise up the ground and dissolve the form. Goya worked with aquatint and etching, the grisaille of the one and the severity of the other. Odilon Redon used *chiaroscuro* and the abstract line. The abstract line acquires all its force from giving up the model—that is to say, the plastic symbol of the form—and participates in the ground all the more violently in that it distinguishes itself from it without the ground distinguishing itself from the line.[1] At this point, in such a mirror, faces are distorted. Nor is it certain that it is only the sleep of reason which gives rise to monsters: it is also the vigil, the insomnia of thought, since thought is that moment in which determination makes itself one, by virtue of maintaining a unilateral and precise relation to the indeterminate. Thought 'makes' difference, but difference is monstrous. We should not be surprised that difference should appear accursed, that it should be error, sin or the figure of evil for which there must be expiation. There is no sin other than raising the ground and dissolving the form. Recall Artaud's idea: cruelty is nothing but determination *as such*, that precise point at which the determined maintains its essential relation with the undetermined, that rigorous abstract line fed by *chiaroscuro*.

To rescue difference from its maledictory state seems, therefore, to be the project of the philosophy of difference. Cannot difference become a harmonious organism and relate determination to other determinations within a form—that is to say, within the coherent medium of an organic representation? There are four principal aspects to 'reason' in so far as it is the medium of representation: identity, in the form of the *undetermined* concept; analogy, in the relation between ultimate *determinable* concepts; opposition, in the relation between *determinations* within concepts; resemblance, in the *determined* object of the concept itself. These forms are like the four heads or the four shackles of mediation. Difference is 'mediated' to the extent that it is subjected to the fourfold root of identity, opposition, analogy and resemblance. On the basis of a first impression (difference is evil), it is proposed to 'save' difference by representing it, and to represent it by relating it to the requirements of the concept in general. It is therefore a question of determining a propitious moment—the Greek propitious moment—at which difference is, as it were, reconciled with the concept. Difference must leave its cave and cease to be a monster; or at least only that which escapes at the propitious moment must persist as a monster, that which constitutes only a bad encounter, a bad occasion. At this point the expression 'make the difference' changes its meaning. It now refers to a selective test which must determine which differences may be inscribed within the concept in general, and how. Such a test, such a selection, seems to be effectively realised by the Large and the Small. For the Large and the Small are not naturally said of the One, but first and foremost of difference. The question arises, therefore, how far the difference can and must extend—how large? how small?—in order to remain within the limits of the concept, neither becoming lost within nor escaping beyond it. It is obviously difficult to know whether the problem is well posed in this way: is difference really an evil in itself? Must the question have been posed in these moral terms? Must difference have been 'mediated' in order to render it both livable and thinkable? Must the selection have consisted in that particular test? Must the test have been conceived in that manner and with that aim? But we can answer these questions only once we have more precisely determined the supposed nature of the propitious moment.

Aristotle says: there is a difference which is at once the greatest and the most perfect, *megistē* and *teleios*. Difference in general is distinguished from diversity or otherness. For two terms differ when they are other, not in themselves, but in something else; thus when they also agree in something else: in genus when they are differences in species, in species for differences in number, or even 'in being, according to the analogy' for differences in genus. Under these conditions, what is the greatest difference? The greatest difference is always an opposition, but of all the forms of opposition, which is the most perfect, the most complete, that which 'agrees' best? Related terms belong to one another; contradiction already belongs to a subject, but only in order to make its subsistence impossible and to qualify the change by which it begins or ceases to be; privation again expresses a determinate incapacity on behalf of an existing subject. Contrariety alone expresses the capacity of a subject to bear opposites while remaining substantially the same (in matter or in genus). Under what conditions, however, does contrariety impart its perfection to difference? So long as we consider the concrete being with respect to its matter, the contrarieties which affect it are corporeal modifications which give us only the empirical, accidental concept of a still extrinsic difference *[extra quidditatem]*. Accidents may be separable from the subject, as 'white' and 'black' are from 'man'; or inseparable, as 'male' and 'female' are from 'animal': accordingly, the difference will be called either *communis* or *propria*, but in so far as it pertains to matter, it will always be accidental. Thus, only a contrariety in the essence or in the form gives us the concept of a difference that is itself essential *[differentia essentialis aut propriissima]*. Contraries in this case are modifications which affect a subject with respect to its genus. Genera are in effect divided by differences in essence which take the form of contraries, such as 'with feet' and 'with wings'. In short, contrariety in the genus is the perfect and maximal difference, and contrariety in the genus is specific difference. Above and below that, difference tends to become simple otherness and almost to escape the identity of the concept: generic difference is too large, being established between uncombinable objects which do not enter into relations of contrariety; while individual difference is too small, being between indivisible objects which have no contrariety either.[2]

It seems indeed, on the other hand, that specific difference meets all the requirements of a harmonious concept and an organic representation. It is pure because it is formal, intrinsic because it applies to the essence. It is qualitative, and to the extent that the genus designates the essence, difference is even a very special quality 'according to the essence', a quality of the essence itself. It is synthetic, since the determination of species is composition, and the difference is actually added to the genus in which it was hitherto only virtually included. It is mediated, it is itself mediation, the middle term in person. It is productive, since genera are not divided into differences but divided by differences which give rise to corresponding species. That is why it is always a cause, the formal cause: the shortest distance is the specific difference of the straight line, compression the specific difference of the colour black, dissociation that of the colour white. That is also why it is a predicate of such a peculiar type, since it is attributed to the species but at the same time attributes the genus to it and constitutes the species to which it is attributed. Such a synthetic and constitutive predicate, attributive more than attributed, a veritable rule of production, has one final property: that of carrying with itself that which it attributes. In effect, the quality of the essence is sufficiently special to make the genus something other, and not simply of another quality.[3] It is thus in the nature of genera to remain the same in themselves while becoming other in the differences which divide them. Difference carries with itself the genus and all the intermediary differences. The determination of species links difference with difference across the successive levels of division, like a transport of difference, a *diaphora* (difference) of *diaphora*, until a final difference, that of the *infima species* (lowest species), condenses in the chosen direction the entirety of the essence and its continued quality, gathers them under an intuitive concept and grounds them along with the term to be defined, thereby becoming itself something unique and indivisible *[atomon, adiaphoron, eidos]*. In this manner, therefore, the determination of species ensures coherence and continuity in the comprehension of the concept.

Return to the expression 'the greatest difference'. It is now evident that specific difference is the greatest only in an entirely relative sense. Absolutely speaking, contradiction is greater than contrariety—and above all, generic difference is greater than specific. Already, the manner in which Aristotle distinguishes between difference and diversity or otherness points the way: only in relation to the supposed identity of a concept is specific difference called the greatest. Furthermore, it is in relation to the form of identity in the generic concept that difference goes as far as opposition, that it is pushed as far as contrariety. Specific difference, therefore, in no way represents a universal concept (that is to say, an Idea) encompassing all the singularities and turnings of difference, but rather refers to a particular moment in which difference is merely reconciled with the concept in general. Thus Aristotle's *diaphora* of the *diaphora is* only a false transport: it never shows difference changing its nature, we never discover in it a differenciator of difference which would relate, in their respective immediacy, the most universal and the most singular. Specific difference refers only to an entirely relative maximum, a point of accommodation for the Greek eye—in particular for the Greek eye which sees the mean, and has lost the sense of Dionysian transports and metamorphoses. Here we find the principle which lies behind a confusion disastrous for the entire philosophy of difference: assigning a distinctive concept of difference is confused with the inscription of difference within concepts in general—the determination of the concept of difference is confused with the inscription of difference in the identity of an undetermined concept. This is the sleight of hand involved in the propitious moment (and perhaps everything else follows: the subordination of difference to opposition, to analogy, and to resemblance, all the aspects of mediation). Difference then can be no more than a predicate in the comprehension of a concept. Aristotle constantly reminds us of this predicative character of specific difference, but he is forced to lend it strange powers such as that of attributing as much as that of being attributed, or of altering the genus as much as of modifying its quality. All of the ways in which specific difference seems to satisfy the requirements of a distinctive concept (purity, interiority, productivity, transportivity . . .) are thus shown to be illusory, even contradictory, on the basis of this fundamental confusion.

Specific difference is thus small in relation to a larger difference which concerns the genera themselves. Even in biological classification, it becomes quite small in relation to the large genera; no doubt not a material difference, but nevertheless a simple difference 'in' the material, one which works through the more and the less. The fact is that specific difference is maximal and perfect, but only on condition of the identity of an undetermined concept (genus). It is insignificant, by contrast, in comparison with the difference between genera as ultimate determinable concepts (categories), for these latter are not subject to the condition that they share an identical concept or a common genus. Remember the reason why Being itself is not a genus: it is, Aristotle says, because differences *are* (the genus must therefore be able to attribute itself to its differences in themselves: as if animal was said at one time of the human species, but at another of the difference 'rational' in constituting another species . . .).[4] It is therefore an argument borrowed from the nature of specific difference which allows him to conclude that generic differences are of *another* nature. It is as though there were two 'Logoi', differing in nature but intermingled with one another: the logos of Species, the logos of what we think and say, which rests upon the condition of the identity or univocity of concepts in general taken as genera; and the logos of Genera, the logos of what is thought and said through us, which is free of that condition and operates both in the equivocity of Being and in the diversity of the most general concepts. When we speak the univocal, is it not still the equivocal which speaks within us? Must we not recognise here a kind of fracture introduced into thought, one which will not cease to widen in another atmosphere (non-Aristotelian)? But above all, is this not already a new chance for the philosophy of difference? Will it not lead towards an absolute concept, once liberated from the condition which made difference an entirely relative maximum?

Nothing of the kind, however, occurs with Aristotle. The fact is that generic or categorial difference remains a difference in the Aristotelian sense and does not collapse into simple diversity or otherness. An identical or common concept thus still subsists, albeit in a very particular manner. This concept of Being is not collective, like a genus in relation to its species, but only distributive and hierarchical: it has no content in itself, only a content in proportion to the formally different terms of which it is predicated. These terms (categories) need not have an equal relation to being: it is enough that each has an *internal* relation to being. The two characteristics of the concept of being—having no more than a distributive common sense and having a hierarchical primary sense—show clearly that being does not have, in relation to the categories, the role of a genus in relation to univocal species. They also show that the equivocity of being is quite particular: it is a matter of analogy.[5] Now, if we ask what is the instance capable of proportioning the concept to the terms or to the subjects of which it is affirmed, it is clear that it is judgement. For judgement has precisely two essential functions, and only two: distribution, which it ensures by the *partition* of concepts; and hierarchization, which it ensures by the *measuring* of subjects. To the former corresponds the faculty of judgement known as common sense; to the latter the faculty known as good sense (or first sense). Both constitute just measure or 'justice' as a value of judgement. In this sense, every philosophy of categories takes judgement for its model—as we see in the case of Kant, and still even in the case of Hegel. With its common sense and first sense, however, the analogy of judgement allows the identity of a concept to subsist, either in implicit and confused form or in virtual form. Analogy is itself the analogue of identity within judgement. Analogy is the essence of judgement, but the analogy within judgement is the analogy of the identity of concepts. That is why we cannot expect that generic or categorial difference, any more than specific difference, will deliver us a proper concept of difference. Whereas specific difference is content to inscribe difference in the identity of the indeterminate concept in general, generic (distributive and hierarchical) difference is content in turn to inscribe difference in the quasi-identity of the most general determinable concepts; that is, in the analogy within judgement itself. The entire Aristotelian philosophy of difference is contained in this complementary double inscription, both grounded in the same postulate and together drawing the arbitrary boundaries of the propitious moment.

Generic and specific differences are tied together by their complicity in representation. Not that they in any way share the same nature: genus is determinable only by specific difference from without; and the identity of the genus in relation to the species contrasts with the impossibility for Being of forming a similar identity in relation to the genera themselves. However, it is precisely the nature of the specific differences (the fact that they *are)* which grounds that impossibility, preventing generic differences from being related to being as if to a common genus (if being were a genus, its differences would be assimilable to specific differences, but then one could no longer say that they 'are', since a genus is not in itself attributed to its differences). In this sense, the univocity of species in a common genus refers back to the equivocity of being in the various genera: the one reflects the other. We see this clearly in the requirements of the ideal of classification: at once the large units—*genē megista,* which will eventually be called branches—are determined according to relations of analogy, which suppose a choice of characters carried out by judgement in the abstract representation, and the small units, the little genera or species, are determined by a direct perception of *resemblances,* which suppose a continuity of sensible intuition in the concrete representation. Even neo-evolutionism will rediscover these two related aspects of the categories of the Large and the Small, when it distinguishes the large precocious embryological differenciations from the small, tardy, adult, species or intraspecies differenciations. Alternatively, these two aspects enter into conflict according to whether the large genera or the species are taken to be concepts of Nature, both constituting the limits of organic representation, and the *requisites* equally necessary for classification: methodological continuity in the perception of resemblances is no less indispensable than systematic distribution in the judgement of analogy. However, from one point of view as from the other, Difference appears only as a *reflexive concept.* In effect, difference allows the passage from similar neighbouring species to the identity of a genus which subsumes them—that is, the extraction or cutting out of generic identities from the flux of a continuous perceptible series. At the other pole, it allows the passage from respectively identical genera to the relations of analogy which obtain between them in the intelligible. As a concept of reflection, difference testifies to its full submission to all the requirements of representation, which becomes thereby 'organic representation'. In the concept of reflection, mediating and mediated difference is in effect fully subject to the identity of the concept, the opposition of predicates, the analogy of judgement and the resemblance of perception. Here we rediscover the necessarily quadripartite character of representation. The question is to know whether, under all these reflexive aspects, difference does not lose both its own concept and its own reality. In effect, difference ceases to be reflexive and recovers an effectively real concept only to the extent that it designates catastrophes: either breaks of continuity in the series of resemblances or impassable fissures between the analogical structures. It ceases to be reflexive only in order to become catastrophic. No doubt it cannot be the one without the other. But does not difference as catastrophe precisely bear witness to an irreducible ground which continues to act under the apparent equilibrium of organic representation?

There has only ever been one ontological proposition: Being is univocal. There has only ever been one ontology, that of Duns Scotus, which gave being a single voice. We say Duns Scotus because he was the one who elevated univocal being to the highest point of subtlety, albeit at the price of abstraction. However, from Parmenides to Heidegger it is the same voice which is taken up, in an echo which itself forms the whole deployment of the univocal. A single voice raises the clamour of being. We have no difficulty in understanding that Being, even if it is absolutely common, is nevertheless not a genus. It is enough to replace the model of judgement with that of the proposition. In the proposition understood as a complex entity we distinguish: the sense, or what is expressed in the proposition; the designated (what expresses itself in the proposition); the expressors or designators, which are numerical modes—that is to say, differential factors characterising the elements endowed with sense and designation. We can conceive that names or propositions do not have the same sense even while they designate exactly the same thing (as in the case of the celebrated examples: morning star–evening star, Israel–Jacob, *p*lan–*b*lanc). The distinction between these senses is indeed a real distinction *[distinctio realis]*, but there is nothing numerical—much less ontological—about it: it is a formal, qualitative or semiological distinction. The question whether categories are directly assimilable to such senses, or—more probably—derive from them, must be left aside for the moment. What is important is that we can conceive of several formally distinct senses which none the less refer to being as if to a single designated entity, ontologically one. It is true that such a point of view is not sufficient to prevent us from considering these senses as analogues and this unity of being as an analogy. We must add that being, this common designated, in so far as it expresses itself, is said in turn *in a single and same sense* of all the numerically distinct designators and expressors. In the ontological proposition, not only is that which is designated ontologically the same for qualitatively distinct senses, but also the sense is ontologically the same for individuating modes, for numerically distinct designators or expressors: the ontological proposition involves a circulation of this kind (expression as a whole).

In effect, the essential in univocity is not that Being is said in a single and same sense, but that it is said, in a single and same sense, *of* all its individuating differences or intrinsic modalities. Being is the same for all these modalities, but these modalities are not the same. It is 'equal' for all, but they themselves are not equal. It is said of all in a single sense, but they themselves do not have the same sense. The essence of univocal being is to include individuating differences, while these differences do not have the same essence and do not change the essence of being—just as white includes various intensities, while remaining essentially the same white. There are not two 'paths', as Parmenides' poem suggests, but a single 'voice' of Being which includes all its modes, including the most diverse, the most varied, the most differenciated. Being is said in a single and same sense of everything of which it is said, but that of which it is said differs: it is said of difference itself.

No doubt there is still hierarchy and distribution in univocal being, in relation to the individuating factors and their sense, but distribution and even hierarchy have two completely different, irreconcilable acceptations. Similarly for the expressions *logos* and *nomos*, in so far as these refer to problems of distribution. We must first of all distinguish a type of distribution which implies a dividing up of that which is distributed: it is a matter of dividing up the distributed as such. It is here that in judgement the rules of analogy are all-powerful. In so far as common sense and good sense are qualities of judgement, these are presented as principles of division which declare themselves *the best distributed*. A distribution of this type proceeds by fixed and proportional determinations which may be assimilated to 'properties' or limited territories within representation. The agrarian question may well have been very important for this organisation of judgement as the faculty which distinguishes parts ('on the one hand and on the other hand'). Even among the gods, each has his domain, his category, his attributes, and all distribute limits and lots to mortals in accordance with destiny. Then there is a completely other distribution which must be called nomadic, a nomad *nomos*, without property, enclosure or measure. Here, there is no longer a division of that which is distributed but rather a division among those who distribute *themselves* in an open space—a space which is unlimited, or at least without precise limits.[6] Nothing pertains or belongs to any person, but all persons are arrayed here and there in such a manner as to cover the largest possible space. Even when it concerns the serious business of life, it is more like a space of play, or a rule of play, by contrast with sedentary space and *nomos*. To fill a space, to be distributed within it, is very different from distributing the space. It is an errant and even 'delirious' distribution, in which things are deployed across the entire extensity of a univocal and undistributed Being. It is not a matter of being which is distributed according to the requirements of representation, but of all things being divided up within being in the univocity of simple presence (the One—All). Such a distribution is demonic rather than divine, since it is a peculiarity of demons to operate in the intervals between the gods' fields of action, as it is to leap over the barriers or the enclosures, thereby confounding the boundaries between properties.

Oedipus' chorus cries: 'Which demon has leapt further than the longest leap?' The leap here bears witness to the unsettling difficulties that nomadic distributions introduce into the sedentary structures of representation. The same goes for hierarchy. There is a hierarchy which measures beings according to their limits, and according to their degree of proximity or distance from a principle. But there is also a hierarchy which considers things and beings from the point of view of power: it is not a question of considering absolute degrees of power, but only of knowing whether a being eventually 'leaps over' or transcends its limits in going to the limit of what it can do, whatever its degree. 'To the limit', it will be argued, still presupposes a limit. Here, limit *[peras]* no longer refers to what maintains the thing under a law, nor to what delimits or separates it from other things. On the contrary, it refers to that on the basis of which it is deployed and deploys all its power; hubris ceases to be simply condemnable and *the smallest becomes equivalent to the largest* once it is not separated from what it can do. This enveloping measure is the same for all things, the same also for substance, quality, quantity, etc., since it forms a single maximum at which the developed diversity of all degrees touches the equality which envelops them. This ontological measure is closer to the immeasurable state of things than to the first kind of measure; this ontological hierarchy is closer to the hubris and anarchy of beings than to the first hierarchy. It is the monster which combines all the demons. The words 'everything is equal' may therefore resound joyfully, on condition that they are said *of* that which is not equal in this equal, univocal Being: equal being is immediately present in everything, without mediation or intermediary, even though things reside unequally in this equal being. There, however, where they are borne by hubris, all things are in absolute proximity, and whether they are large or small, inferior or superior, none of them participates more or less in being, nor receives it by analogy. Univocity of being thus also signifies equality of being. Univocal Being is at one and the same time nomadic distribution and crowned anarchy.

Nevertheless, can we not conceive a reconciliation between analogy and univocity? For if being, as being, is univocal in itself, is it not 'analogous' in relation to its intrinsic modes or individuating factors (what we called above expressors or designators)? If it is equal in relation to itself, is it not unequal in relation to the modalities which reside within it? If it designates a common entity, is this not for existents which have nothing 'really' in common? If its metaphysical state is univocal, does it not have a physical state of analogy? Finally, if analogy recognises an identical quasi-concept, does not univocity recognise a quasi-judgement of analogy, if only in order to relate being to these particular existents?[7] However, such questions risk distorting the two theses they attempt to bring together. For analogy, as we have seen, rests essentially upon a certain complicity between generic and specific differences (despite their difference in kind): being cannot be supposed a common genus without destroying the reason for which it was supposed thus; that is, the possibility of *being* for specific differences. . . . It is not, therefore, surprising that from the standpoint of analogy, everything happens in the middle regions of genus and species in terms of mediation and generality—identity of the concept in general and analogy of the most general concepts. It is henceforth inevitable that analogy falls into an unresolvable difficulty: it must essentially relate being to particular existents, but at the same time it cannot say what constitutes their individuality. For it retains in the particular only that which conforms to the general (matter and form), and seeks the principle of individuation in this or that element of the fully constituted individuals. By contrast, when we say that univocal being is related immediately and essentially to individuating factors, we certainly do not mean by the latter individuals constituted in experience, but that which acts in them as a transcendental principle: as a plastic, anarchic and nomadic principle, contemporaneous with the process of individuation, no less capable of dissolving and destroying individuals than of constituting them temporarily; intrinsic modalities of being, passing from one 'individual' to another, circulating and communicating underneath matters and forms. The individuating is not the simple individual. In these conditions, it is not enough to say that individuation differs in kind from the determination of species. It is not even enough to say this in the manner of Duns Scotus, who was nevertheless not content to analyse the elements of an individual but went as far as the conception of individuation as the 'ultimate actuality of form' We must show not only how individuating difference differs in kind from specific difference, but primarily and above all how individuation properly *precedes* matter and form, species and parts, and every other element of the constituted individual. Univocity of being, in so far as it is immediately related to difference, demands that we show how individuating difference precedes generic, specific and even individual differences within being; how a prior field of individuation within being conditions at once the determination of species of forms, the determination of parts and their individual variations. If individuation does not take place either by form or by matter, neither qualitatively nor extensionally, this is not only because it differs in kind but because it is already presupposed by the forms, matter and extensive parts.

Thus it is not at all in the same manner that in the analogy of being, generic and specific differences are in general mediated in relation to individuating differences, and that in univocity, univocal being is said immediately of individual differences or the universal is said of the most singular independently of any mediation. If it is true that analogy denies being the status of a common genus because the (specific) differences 'are', then conversely, univocal being is indeed common in so far as the (individuating) differences 'are not' and must not be. No doubt we shall see that they are not, in a very particular sense: if in univocal being they are not, it is because they depend upon a non-being without negation. With univocity, however, it is not the differences which are and must be: it is being which is Difference, in the sense that it is said of difference. Moreover, it is not we who are univocal in a Being which is not; it is we and our individuality which remains equivocal in and for a univocal Being.

There are three principal moments in the history of the philosophical elaboration of the univocity of being. The first is represented by Duns Scotus. In the greatest book of pure ontology, the *Opus Oxoniense*, being is understood as univocal, but univocal being is understood as neutral, *neuter*, indifferent to the distinction between the finite and the infinite, the singular and the universal, the created and the uncreated. Scotus therefore deserves the name 'subtle doctor' because he saw being on this side of the intersection between the universal and the singular. In order to neutralise the forces of analogy in judgement, he took the offensive and neutralised being itself in an abstract concept. That is why he only *thought* univocal being. Moreover, we can see the enemy he tried to escape in accordance with the requirements of Christianity: pantheism, into which he would have fallen if the common being were not neutral. Nevertheless, he was able to define two types of distinction which relate that indifferent, neutral being to difference. *Formal distinction* is, in effect, a real distinction, since it is grounded in being or in the object; but it is not necessarily a numerical distinction because it is established between essences or senses, between 'formal reasons' which may allow the persistence of the unity of the subject to which they are attributed. In this manner, not only is the univocity of being (in relation to God and to creatures) extended in the univocity of its 'attributes', but, given his infinity, God can possess his formally distinct univocal attributes without losing anything of his unity. The other type of distinction, *modal distinction*, is established between being or the attributes on the one hand, and the intensive variations of which these are capable on the other. These variations, like degrees of whiteness, are individuating modalities of which the finite and the infinite constitute precisely singular intensities. From the point of view of its own neutrality, univocal being therefore does not only implicate distinct attributes or qualitative forms which are themselves univocal, it also relates these and itself to intensive factors or individuating degrees which vary the mode of these attributes or forms without modifying their essence in so far as this is being. If it is true that distinction in general relates being to difference, formal distinction and modal distinction are two types under which univocal being is related, by itself, to difference in itself.

With the second moment, Spinoza marks a considerable progress. Instead of understanding univocal being as neutral or indifferent, he makes it an object of pure affirmation. Univocal being becomes identical with unique, universal and infinite substance: it is proposed as *Deus sive Natura*. Moreover, the struggle undertaken against Descartes by Spinoza is not unrelated to that which Duns Scotus led against Saint Thomas. Against the Cartesian theory of substances thoroughly imbued with analogy, and against the Cartesian conception of distinctions which runs together the ontological, the formal and the numerical (substance, quality and quantity), Spinoza organises a remarkable division into substance attributes and modes. From the opening pages of the *Ethics,* he shows that real distinctions are never numerical but only formal—that is, qualitative or essential (essential attributes of the unique substance); and conversely that numerical distinctions are never real, but only modal (intrinsic modes of the unique substance and its attributes). The attributes behave like real qualitatively different senses which relate to substance as if to a single and same designated; and substance in turn behaves like an ontologically unique sense in relation to the modes which express it, and inhabit it like individuating factors or intrinsic and intense degrees. From this follows a determination of modes as degrees of power, and a single 'obligation' for such modes: to deploy all their power or their being *within* the limit itself. Attributes are thus absolutely common to substance and the modes, even though modes and substance do not have the same essence. Being itself is said in a single unique sense of substance and the modes, even though the modes and substance do not have the same sense or do not have that being in the same manner *[in se* and *in alio].* Any hierarchy or pre-eminence is denied in so far as substance is equally designated by all the attributes in accordance with their essence, and equally expressed by all the modes in accordance with their degree of power. With Spinoza, univocal being ceases to be neutralised and becomes expressive; it becomes a truly expressive and affirmative proposition.

Nevertheless, there still remains a difference between substance and the modes: Spinoza's substance appears independent of the modes, while the modes are dependent on substance, but as though on something other than themselves. Substance must itself be said *of* the modes and only *of* the modes. Such a condition can be satisfied only at the price of a more general categorical reversal according to which being is said of becoming, identity of that which is different, the one of the multiple, etc. That identity not be first, that it exist as a principle but as a second principle, as a principle *become;* that it revolve around the Different: such would be the nature of Copernican revolution which opens up the possibility of difference having its own concept, rather than being maintained under the domination of a concept in general already understood as identical. Nietzsche meant nothing more than this by eternal return. Eternal return cannot mean the return of the Identical because it presupposes a world (that of the will to power) in which all previous identities have been abolished and dissolved. Returning is being, but only the being of becoming. The eternal return does not bring back 'the same', but returning constitutes the only Same of that which becomes. Returning is the becoming-identical of becoming itself. Returning is thus the only identity, but identity as a secondary power; the identity of difference, the identical which belongs to the different, or turns around the different. Such an identity, produced by difference, is determined as 'repetition'. Repetition in the eternal return, therefore, consists in conceiving the same on the basis of the different. However, this conception is no longer merely a theoretical representation: it carries out a practical selection among differences according to their capacity to produce—that is, to return or to pass the test of the eternal return. The selective character of eternal return appears clearly in Nietzsche's idea: it is not the Whole, the Same or the prior identity in general which returns. Nor is it the small or the large, either as parts of the whole or as elements of the same. Only the extreme forms return—those which, large or small, are deployed within the limit and extend to the limit of their power, transforming themselves and changing one into another. Only the extreme, the excessive, returns; that which passes into something else and becomes identical. That is why the eternal return is said only of the theatrical world of the metamorphoses and masks of the Will to power, of the pure intensities of that Will which are like mobile individuating factors unwilling to allow themselves to be contained within the factitious limits of this or that individual, this or that Self. Eternal return or returning expresses the common being of all these metamorphoses, the measure and the common being of all that is extreme, of all the realised degrees of power. It is the being-equal of all that is unequal and has been able to fully realise its inequality. All that is extreme and becoming the same communicates in an equal and common Being which determines its return. That is why the Overman is defined as the superior form of everything that 'is'. We must discover what Nietzsche means by noble: he borrows the language of energy physics and calls noble that energy which is capable of transforming itself. When Nietzsche says that hubris is the real problem of every Heraclitan, or that hierarchy is the problem of free spirits, he means one—and only one—thing: that it is in hubris that everyone finds the being which makes him return, along with that sort of crowned anarchy, that overturned hierarchy which, in order to ensure the selection of difference, begins by subordinating the identical to the different.[8] In all these respects, eternal return is the univocity of being, the effective realisation of that univocity. In the eternal return, univocal being is not only thought and even affirmed, but effectively realised. Being is said in a single and same sense, but this sense is that of eternal return as the return or repetition of that of which it is said. The wheel in the eternal return is at once both production of repetition on the basis of difference and selection of difference on the basis of repetition.

The test of the Small and the Large seemed to us to misconstrue selection because it renounced any concept of difference itself in favour of the requirements of the identity of the concept in general. By inscribing itself within the identical concept or within analogous concepts (minimum and maximum), it only fixed the limits within which determination became difference. That is why the selection which consists of 'making the difference' seemed to us to have another sense: to allow the extreme forms to appear and be deployed in the simple presence of a univocal Being, rather than to measure and to divide up the average forms according to the requirements of organic representation.

Even so, can it be said that we have exhausted all the resources of the Small and the Large in so far as they apply to difference? Or will we not rediscover them as an alternative characteristic of the extreme forms themselves? For it seems that the extreme can be defined by the infinite, in the small or in the large. The infinite, in this sense, even signifies the identity of the small and the large, the identity of extremes. When representation discovers the infinite within itself, it no longer appears as *organic* representation but as *orgiastic* representation: it discovers within itself the limits of the organised; tumult, restlessness and passion underneath apparent calm. It rediscovers monstrosity. Henceforth it is no longer a question of a propitious moment which marks determination's entrance into and exit from the concept in general, the relative maximum and minimum, the *punctum proximum* and the *punctum remotem*. On the contrary, a short-sighted and a long-sighted eye are required in order for the concept to take upon itself all moments: the concept is now the Whole, either in the sense that it extends its benediction to all parts or in the sense that the division between the parts and their misery are reflected back on the Whole, granting them a kind of absolution. The concept thus follows and espouses determination in all its metamorphoses, from one end to the other, and represents it as pure difference in delivering it up to a *ground* in relation to which it no longer matters whether one is before a relative minimum or maximum, a large or a small, nor before a beginning or an end, since the two coincide in this ground which is like a single and unique 'total' moment, simultaneously the moment of the evanescence and production of difference, of disappearance and appearance.

In this sense, it is noticeable how far Hegel, no less than Leibniz, attaches importance to the infinite movement of evanescence as such—that is, to the moment at which difference both vanishes and is produced. The signification of the very notion of limit changes completely: it no longer refers to the limits of finite representation, but on the contrary to the womb in which finite determination never ceases to be born and to disappear, to be enveloped and deployed within orgiastic representation. It no longer refers to the limitation of a form, but to the *convergence* towards a ground; no longer to the distinction of forms but to the correlation of the grounded and the ground; no longer to the arrestation of power but to the element in which power is effectuated, on which it is grounded. In effect, differential calculus no less than the dialectic is a matter of 'power' and of the power of the limit. If we consider the limits of finite representation to be two abstract mathematical determinations, the Small and the Large, we notice that it is a matter of complete indifference to Leibniz (as to Hegel) to know whether the determined is large or small, the largest or the smallest. By subjecting it to an architectonic element which discovers the most perfect or the best grounded in every case, consideration of the infinite renders the determined independent of that question.[9] It is in this sense that orgiastic representation must be said to *make* the difference, because it selects it by introducing this infinite which relates it to the ground (either grounding by the Good which functions as a rule of the game or principle of choice, or grounding by negativity which functions as suffering and labour). Moreover, if the limits of finite representation, the Small and the Large, are considered with regard to the character or the concrete content given to them by the genus and species, then here again the introduction of the infinite into representation renders the determined independent of the genus as determinable and the species as determination, by retaining in a middle term both the true universality which escapes the genus and the authentic singularity which escapes the species. In short, orgiastic representation has the ground as its principle and the infinite as its element, by contrast with organic representation which retains form as its principle and the finite as its element. It is the infinite which renders determination conceivable and selectable: difference thus appears as the orgiastic representation of determination and no longer as its organic representation.

Instead of animating judgements about things, orgiastic representation makes things themselves so many expressions or so many propositions: infinite analytic or synthetic propositions. Why, then, is there a choice within orgiastic representation, given that the two points, the small and the large, the maximum and the minimum, have become indifferent or identical in the infinite, while difference has become completely independent of them in the ground? It is because the infinite is not the point at which finite determination disappears (that would be to project a mistaken conception of limit on to the infinite). Orgiastic representation can discover the infinite within itself only by allowing finite determination to subsist: better, by saying the infinite *of* that finite determination itself, by representing it not as having vanished and disappeared but as vanishing and on the point of disappearing, thus as also being engendered in the infinite. This representation is such that the infinite and the finite have here the same 'restlessness', which is precisely what allows the one to be represented in the other. However, when the infinite is said of the finite itself under the conditions of representation, there are two ways in which it can be said: either as infinitely small or as infinitely large. These two ways, these two 'differences', are by no means symmetrical. Thus duality is reintroduced into orgiastic representation, no longer in the form of a complementarity or a reflection of two finite assignable moments (as was the case for specific difference and generic difference) but in the form of a choice between two infinite, unassignable processes—in the form of a choice between Leibniz and Hegel. If it is true that the small and the large become identical in the infinite, the infinitely small and the infinitely large separate once more, even more sharply in so far as the infinite is said of the finite. Leibniz and Hegel separately both escape the choice between the Large and the Small, but together they fall back into the choice between the infinitely small and the infinitely large. That is why orgiastic representation involves a duality which only increases its restlessness, or is even the real reason for it, and divides it into two kinds.

It seems that, according to Hegel, 'contradiction' poses very few problems. It serves a quite different purpose: contradiction resolves itself and, in resolving itself, resolves difference by relating it to a ground. Difference is the only problem. The criticism that Hegel addresses to his predecessors is that they stopped at a purely relative maximum without reaching the absolute maximum of difference, namely contradiction; they stopped before reaching the infinite (as infinitely large) of contradiction They dared not go all the way:

> Difference as such is already *implicitly* contradiction. . . . Only when the manifold terms have been driven to the point of contradiction do they become active and lively towards one another, receiving in contradiction the negativity which is the indwelling pulsation of self-movement an spontaneous activity. . . . More precisely, when the difference of reality is taken into account, it develops from difference into opposition, and from this into contradiction, so that in the end the sum total of all realities simply becomes absolute contradiction within itself.[10]

Like Aristotle, Hegel determines difference by the opposition of extreme or of contraries. However, opposition remains abstract so long as it does not extend to the infinite, and the infinite remains abstract every time it is posed outside of finite oppositions: the introduction of the infinite here entails the identity of contraries, or makes the contrary of the Other a contrary of the Self. It is true that contrariety represents only the movement of interiority in the infinite. This movement allows indifference to subsist since each determination, in so far as it contains the other, is independent of the other as though of a relation with the outside. Each contrary must further expel its other, therefore expel itself, and become the other it expels. Such is the movement of contradiction as it constitutes the true pulsation of the infinite, the movement of exteriority or real objectivation. This goes beyond the simple identity of contraries as the identity of the positive and negative. For it is not in the same manner that the positive and the negative are the Same: the negative is now at once both the becoming of the positive when the positive is denied, and the return of the positive when it denies or excludes itself. No doubt each of the contraries determined as positive and negative was already contradiction, 'But the Positive is only *implicitly* this contradiction, whereas the negative is the contradiction *posited*. . . .'[11] Difference finds its own concept in the posited contradiction: it is here that it becomes pure, intrinsic, essential, qualitative, synthetic and productive; here that it no longer allows indifference to subsist. To maintain or to raise contradiction is the selective test which 'makes' the difference (between the effectively real and the passing or contingent phenomenon). In this manner, difference is pushed to the limit—that is, to the ground which is no less its return or its reproduction than its annihilation.

Even though it is said of opposition or of finite determination, this Hegelian infinite remains the infinitely large of theology, of the *Ens quo nihil majus*. We should even consider that the nature of real contradiction, in so far as it distinguishes a thing from *everything that it is not*, was formulated for the first time by Kant, under the name of 'complete determination'. He made it depend upon the positing of a whole of reality as an *Ens summum*. There is therefore no reason to expect a mathematical treatment of this theological infinitely large, this sublime of the infinitely large. This is not the case with Leibniz. For in order to avoid any admixture of God and his creatures, for the modesty of those creatures, Leibniz introduces the infinite into the finite only in the form of the infinitely small. Nevertheless, we hesitate to say that he does not go as far as Hegel in this sense. He too goes beyond organic representation towards orgiastic representation, albeit by another route. If Hegel discovers in serene representation the intoxication and restlessness of the infinitely large, Leibniz discovers in the clear, finite idea the restlessness of the infinitely small, a restlessness also made up of intoxication, giddiness, evanescence and even death. It seems, therefore, that the difference between Hegel and Leibniz is a matter of two ways of going beyond the organic. Certainly, the essential and the inessential are inseparable: they are like the one and the many, the equal and the unequal, the identical and the different. However, Hegel begins with the essential as a genus, and treats the infinite as that which divides the genus and suppresses division in the species. The genus is thus itself and the species, the whole is itself and the part. Henceforth, it contains the other essentially, it contains it *in essence.*[12] Leibniz, on the other hand, begins with the inessential so far as phenomena are concerned, with movement, inequality and difference. By virtue of the infinitely small, it is the inessential which is now posed a species and genus, and terminates as such in the 'opposing quasi-species'. This implies that it does not contain the other in essence but only with respect to properties, in *cases*. It is a mistake to impose upon infinitesimal analysis the alternative of being either a language of essences or convenient fiction. For the subsumption under 'cases', or the language of properties, has its own originality. This procedure of the infinitely small which maintains the distinction between essences (to the extent that on plays the role of inessential to the other), is quite different to contradiction. We should therefore give it a special name, that of 'vice-diction'. In the infinitely large, the equal contradicts the unequal to the extent that it possesses it in essence, and contradicts itself to the extent that it denies itself in denying the unequal. In the infinitely small, however, the unequal vice-dicts the equal and vice-dicts itself to the extent that it includes in the case what it excludes in essence. The inessential includes the essential in the case, whereas the essential contains the inessential in essence.

Must we say that vice-diction does not go as far as contradiction, on the grounds that it concerns only properties? In reality, the expression 'infinitely small difference' does indeed indicate that the difference vanishes so far as intuition is concerned. Once it finds its concept, however, it is rather intuition itself which disappears in favour of the differential relation as is shown by saying that dx is minimal in relation to x, as dy is in relation to y, but that dy/dx *is* the internal qualitative relation, expressing the universal of a function independently of its particular numerical values. However, if this relation has no numerical determinations, it does have degrees of variation corresponding to diverse forms and equations. These degrees are themselves like the relations of the universal, and the differential relations, in this sense, are caught up in a process of reciprocal determination which translates the interdependence of the variable coefficients.[13] But once again, *reciprocal determination* expresses only the first aspect of a veritable principle of reason; the second aspect is *complete determination.* For each degree or relation, regarded as the universal of given function, determines the existence and distribution of distinctive points on the corresponding curve. We must take great care here not to confuse 'complete' with 'completed'. The difference is that, for the equation of a curve, for example, the differential relation refers only to straight lines determined by the nature of the curve. It is already a complete determination of the object, yet it expresses only a part of the entire object, namely the part regarded as 'derived' (the other part, which is expressed by the so-called primitive function, can be found only by integration, which is not simply the inverse of differentiation. Similarly, it is integration which defines the nature of the previously determined distinctive points). That is why an object can be completely determined—*ens omni modo determinatum*—without, for all that, possessing the integrity which alone constitutes its actual existence. Under the double aspect of reciprocal determination and complete determination, however, it appears already as if the limit coincides with the power itself. The limit is defined by convergence. The numerical values of a function find their limit in the differential relation; the differential relations find their limit in the degrees of variation; and at each degree the distinctive points are the limits of series which are analytically continued one into the other. Not only is the differential relation the pure element of potentiality, but the limit is the power of the continuous, as continuity is the power of these limits themselves. Difference thus finds its concept in a negative, but a negative of pure limitation, a *nihil respectivum* (dx is nothing in relation to x). From all these points of view, the distinction between the distinctive and the ordinary, the singular and the regular, forms the two categories of the inessential in the continuous. They inform the whole language of limits and properties, they constitute the structure of phenomena as such. We see in this sense all that philosophy must expect from a distribution of distinctive points and ordinary points for the description of experience. But already the two kinds of point prepare and determine, in the inessential, the constitution of the essences themselves. The inessential here refers not to that which lacks importance but, on the contrary, to the most profound, to the universal matter or continuum from which the essences are finally made.

In effect, Leibniz, for his part, never saw any contradiction between the law of continuity and the principle of indiscernibles. The one governs properties, affections or complete cases; the other rules essences understood as completed individual notions. We know that each one of these completed notions (monads) expresses the totality of the world: but it expresses it precisely under a certain differential relation and around certain distinctive points which correspond to this relation.[14] It is in this sense that the differential relations and distinctive points already indicate centres of envelopment within the continuum, centres of possible implication or involution which are brought about by individual essences. It suffices to show that the continuum of affections and properties in a sense precedes the constitution of these individual essences (which amounts to saying that the distinctive points are themselves pre-individual singularities; this in no way contradicts the idea that individuation precedes the actual determination of species, even though it is preceded by the whole differential continuum). This condition is fulfilled in Leibniz's philosophy in the following manner: the world, as that which is expressed in common by all monads, pre-exists its expressions. It is nevertheless true that it does not *exist* apart from that which expresses it, apart from the monads themselves; but these expressions refer to the expressed as though to the *requisite* of their constitution. It is in this sense (as Leibniz constantly reminds us in his letters to Arnauld) that the inherence of predicates in each subject supposes the compossibility of the world expressed by all these subjects: God did not create Adam as a sinner, but rather the world in which Adam sinned. It is undoubtedly continuity which defines the compossibility of each world; and if the real world is the best, this is to the extent that it presents a maximum of continuity in a maximum number of cases, in a maximum number of relations and distinctive points. That is to say: for each world a series which converges around a distinctive point is capable of being continued in all directions in other series converging around other points, while the incompossibility of worlds, by contrast, is defined by the juxtaposition of points which would make the resultant series diverge. We can see why the notion of incompossibility in no way reduces to contradiction and does not even imply real opposition: it implies only divergence, while compossibility is only an analytic continuation which translates the originality of the process of vice-diction. In the continuum of a compossible world, differential relations and distinctive points thus determine expressive centres (essences or individual substances) in which, at each moment, the entire world is contained from a certain point of view. Conversely, the action and unfolding of these centres restores the world in which they themselves play the role of simple distinctive points and of 'cases' in the expressed continuum. The law of continuity appears here as a law of properties or cases of the world, a law of development which applies to the expressed world, but also to the monads in the world themselves. The principle of indiscernibles is a principle of essences and a principle of envelopment which applies to expressions—that is, to monads and to the world within the monads. The two languages continually translate into one another. Together they relate difference, both as infinitely small difference and as finite difference, to sufficient reason as the foundation which selects or chooses the best world—in this sense, the best of all worlds does indeed imply a comparison, but it is not a comparative: since each world is finite, it is a superlative which carries difference to an absolute maximum through the very test of the infinitely small. Finite difference is determined in a monad as that part of the world clearly expressed, infinitely small difference as the confused ground which underpins that clarity. In these two ways, orgiastic representation mediates determination and makes it a concept of difference by assigning it a 'reason'.

Finite representation is that of a form which contains a matter, but a secondary matter in so far as it is defined by contraries. We have seen that it represented difference by mediating it, by subordinating it to identity as the genus, and by ensuring that subordination by means of analogy among the genera themselves, by means of the logical opposition of determinations and the resemblance of properly material contents. It is not the same with infinite representation, since this includes the Whole or ground as primary matter and the essence as subject, absolute form or Self. Infinite representation relates at once both the essence and the ground, and the difference between the two, to a foundation or sufficient reason. Mediation itself has become foundation. However, in the one case the ground is the infinite continuity of the properties of the universal which is itself contained in finite particular Selves considered as essences. In the other case, particulars are only properties or figures which are developed in the infinite universal ground, but refer to essences as the true determinations of a pure Self, or rather a 'Self' enveloped by this ground. In both cases, infinite representation is the object of a double discourse: that of properties and that of essences—that of physical points and metaphysical points or points of view in the case of Leibniz; that of figures and moments or categories in the case of Hegel. It cannot be said that Leibniz does not go as far as Hegel: there is even a greater depth in his case, more orgiastic or bacchanalian delirium, in the sense that the ground plays a greater role. In both cases, as well, it seems that infinite representation does not suffice to render the thought of difference independent of the simple analogy of essences, or the simple similarity of properties. The point is that in the last resort *infinite representation does not free itself from the principle of identity as a presupposition of representation.* That is why it remains subject to the condition of the convergence of series in the case of Leibniz and to the condition of the monocentring of circles in the case of Hegel. Infinite representation invokes a foundation. While this foundation is not the identical itself, it is nevertheless a way of taking the principle of identity particularly seriously, giving it an infinite value and rendering it coextensive with the whole, and in this manner allowing it to reign over existence itself. It matters little whether identity (as the identity of the world and the self) be considered analytic, in the form of the infinitely small, or synthetic, in the form of the infinitely large. In the former case, the foundation or sufficient reason is that which vice-dicts identity; in the latter case, it is that which contradicts it. In all cases, however, the foundation or sufficient reason employs the infinite only to lead the identical to *exist* in its very identity. Moreover, what is apparent here with Leibniz is no less so with Hegel. Hegelian contradiction does not deny identity or non-contradiction: on the contrary, it consists in inscribing the double negation of *non*-contradiction within the existent in such a way that identity, under that condition or on that basis, is sufficient to think the existent as such. Those formulae according to which 'the object denies what it is not', or 'distinguishes itself from everything that it is not', are logical monsters (the Whole of everything which is not the object) in the service of identity. It is said that difference is negativity, that it extends or must extend to the point of contradiction once it is taken to the limit. This is true only to the extent that difference is already placed on a path or along a thread laid out by identity. It is true only to the extent that it is identity that pushes it to that point. Difference is the ground, but only the ground for the demonstration of the identical. Hegel's circle is not the eternal return, only the infinite circulation of the identical by means of negativity. Hegel's innovation is the final and most powerful homage rendered to the old principle. Between Leibniz and Hegel it matters little whether the supposed negative of difference is understood as a vice-dicting limitation or a contradicting limitation, any more than it matters whether infinite identity be considered analytic or synthetic. In either case, difference remains subordinated to identity, reduced to the negative, incarcerated within similitude and analogy. That is why, in infinite representation, the delirium is only a pre-formed false delirium which poses no threat to the repose or serenity of the identical. Infinite representation, therefore, suffers from the same defect as finite representation: that of confusing the concept of difference in itself with the inscription of difference in the identity of the concept in general (even though it treats identity as a pure infinite principle instead of treating it as a genus, and extends the rights of the concept in general to the whole instead of fixing their limits).

There is a crucial experience of difference and a corresponding experiment: every time we find ourselves confronted or bound by a limitation or an opposition, we should ask what such a situation presupposes. It presupposes a swarm of differences, a pluralism of free, wild or untamed differences; a properly differential and original space and time; all of which persist alongside the simplifications of limitation and opposition. A more profound real element must be defined in order for oppositions of forces or limitations of forms to be drawn, one which is determined as an abstract and potential multiplicity. Oppositions are roughly cut from a delicate milieu of overlapping perspectives, of communicating distances, divergences and disparities, of heterogeneous potentials and intensities. Nor is it primarily a question of dissolving tensions in the identical, but rather of distributing the disparities in a multiplicity.

Limitations correspond to a simple first-order power—in a space with a single dimension and a single direction, where, as in Leibniz's example of boats borne on a current, there may be collisions, but these collisions necessarily serve to limit and to equalise, but not to neutralise or to oppose. As for opposition, it represents in turn the second-order power, where it is as though things were spread out upon a flat surface, polarised in a single plane, and the synthesis itself took place only in a false depth—that is, in a fictitious third dimension added to the others which does no more than double the plane. In any case, what is missing is the original, intensive depth which is the matrix of the entire space and the first affirmation of difference: here, that which only afterwards appears as linear limitation and flat opposition lives and simmers in the form of free differences. Everywhere, couples and polarities presuppose bundles and networks, organised oppositions presuppose radiations in all directions. Stereoscopic images form no more than an even and flat opposition, but they depend upon something quite different: an arrangement of coexistent, tiered, mobile planes, a 'disparateness' within an original depth. Everywhere, the depth of difference is primary. It is no use rediscovering depth as a third dimension unless it has already been installed at the beginning, enveloping the other two and enveloping itself as third. Space and time display oppositions (and limitations) only on the surface, but they presuppose in their real depth far more voluminous, affirmed and distributed differences which cannot be reduced to the banality of the negative. It is as though we were in Lewis Carroll's mirror where everything is contrary and inverted on the surface, but 'different' in depth. We shall see that it is the same with every space: geometrical, physical, biophysical, social and linguistic (in this respect, how unlikely Trubetzkoy's declaration of principle appears: 'the idea of difference presupposes the idea of opposition . . .'). There is a false profundity in conflict, but underneath conflict, the space of the play of differences. The negative is the image of difference, but a flattened and inverted image, like the candle in the eye of the ox—the eye of the dialectician dreaming of a futile combat?

In this sense, too, Leibniz goes further or deeper than Hegel when he distributes the distinctive points and the differential elements of a multiplicity throughout the ground, and when he discovers a play in the creation of the world. It seems, therefore, as though the first dimension, that of the limit, despite all its imperfection, remains closest to the original depth. Leibniz's only error was to have linked difference to the negative of limitation, because he maintained the dominance of the old principle, because he linked the series to a principle of convergence, without seeing that divergence itself was an object of affirmation, or that the incompossibles belonged to the same world and were affirmed as the greatest crime and the greatest virtue of the one and only world, that of the eternal return.

It is not difference which presupposes opposition but opposition which presupposes difference, and far from resolving difference by tracing it back to a foundation, opposition betrays and distorts it. Our claim is not only that difference in itself is not 'already' contradiction, but that it cannot be reduced or traced back to contradiction, since the latter is not more but less profound than difference. On what condition is difference traced or projected on to a flat space? Precisely when it has been forced into a previously established identity, when it has been placed on the slope of the identical which makes it reflect or desire identity, and necessarily takes it where identity wants it to go—namely, into the negative.[15] The imprint of the Hegelian dialectic on the beginnings of Phenomenology has often been noted: the here and the now are posited as empty identities, as abstract universalities which claim to draw difference along with them, when in fact difference does not by any means follow and remains attached in the depths of its own space, in the here-now of a differential reality always made up of singularities. It is said that there were thinkers who explained that movement was impossible, but that this did not prevent movement from occurring. With Hegel it is the other way round: he creates movement, even the movement of the infinite, but because he creates it with words and representations it is a false movement, and nothing follows. It is the same every time there is mediation or representation. The representant says: 'Everyone recognises that . . .', but there is always an unrepresented singularity who does not recognise precisely because it is not everyone or the universal. 'Everyone' recognises the universal because it is itself the universal, but the profound sensitive conscience which is nevertheless presumed to bear the cost, the singular, does not recognise it. The misfortune in speaking is not speaking, but speaking *for others* or representing something. The sensitive conscience (that is, the particular difference or *ta alla*) refuses. One can always mediate, pass over into the antithesis, combine the synthesis, but the thesis does not follow: it subsists in its immediacy, in its difference which itself constitutes the true movement. Difference is the true content of the thesis, the persistence of the thesis. The negative and negativity do not even capture the phenomenon of difference, only the phantom or the epiphenomenon. The whole of Phenomenology is an epiphenomenology.

This is what the philosophy of difference refuses: *omnis determinatio negatio. . . .* We refuse the general alternative proposed by infinite representation: the indeterminate, the indifferent, the undifferenciated or a difference already determined as negation, implying and enveloping the negative (by the same token, we also refuse the particular alternative: negative of limitation or negative of opposition). In its essence, difference is the object of affirmation or affirmation itself. In its essence, affirmation is itself difference. At this point, does the philosophy of difference not risk appearing as a new version of the beautiful soul? The beautiful soul is in effect the one who sees differences everywhere and appeals to them only as respectable, reconcilable or federative differences, while history continues to be made through bloody contradictions. The beautiful soul behaves like a justice of the peace thrown on to a field of battle, one who sees in the inexpiable struggles only simple 'differends' or perhaps misunderstandings. Conversely, however, it is not enough to harden oneself and invoke the well-known complementarities between affirmation and negation, life and death, creation and destruction (as if these were sufficient to ground a dialectic of negativity) in order to throw the taste for pure differences back at the beautiful soul, and to weld the fate of real differences to that of the negative and contradiction. For such complementarities as yet tell us nothing about the relation between one term and the other (does the determined affirmation result from an already negative and negating difference, or does the negative result from an already differential affirmation?). In very general terms, we claim that there are two ways to appeal to 'necessary destructions': that of the poet, who speaks in the name of a creative power, capable of overturning all orders and representations in order to affirm Difference in the state of permanent revolution which characterizes eternal return; and that of the politician, who is above all concerned to deny that which 'differs', so as to conserve or prolong an established historical order, or to establish a historical order which already calls forth in the world the forms of its representation. The two may coincide in particularly agitated moments, but they are never the same. No one passes less for a beautiful soul than Nietzsche. His soul is extremely beautiful, but not in the sense of the beautiful soul: no one is more endowed than he with a sense for cruelty or a taste for destruction. Moreover, throughout his work he never ceases to contrast two conceptions of the affirmation–negation relation.

In one case, it is negation which is the motor and driving force. Affirmation results from it—like an ersatz, as it were. It may well be that two negations are not too many to produce a phantom of affirmation. But how would affirmation result from negation unless it conserved that which is denied? Accordingly, Nietzsche indicates the terrifying conservatism of such a conception. Affirmation is indeed produced, but in order to say yes to all that is negative and negating, to all that *can be denied*. Thus Zarathustra's Ass says yes, but for him to affirm is to bear, to assume or to shoulder a burden. He bears everything: the burdens with which he is laden (divine values), those which he assumes himself (human values), and the weight of his tired muscles when he no longer has anything to bear (the absence of values).[16] This Ass and the dialectical ox leave a moral aftertaste. They have a terrifying taste for responsibility, as though one could affirm only by expiating, as though it were necessary to pass through the misfortunes of rift and division in order to be able to say yes. It is as though Difference were evil and already negative, so that it could produce affirmation only by expiation—that is, by assuming at once both the weight of that which is denied and negation itself. Always the same old malediction which resounds from the heights of the principle of identity: alone will be saved not that which is simply represented, but the infinite representation (the concept) which conserves all the negative finally to deliver difference up to the identical. Of all the senses of *Aufheben*, none is more important than that of 'raise up'. There is indeed a dialectical circle, but this infinite circle has everywhere only a single centre; it retains within itself all the other circles, all the other momentary centres. The reprises or repetitions of the dialectic express only the conservation of the whole, all the forms and all the moments, in a gigantic Memory. Infinite representation is a memory which conserves. In this case, repetition is no more than a conservatory, a power of memory itself. There is indeed a circular dialectical selection, but one which always works to the advantage of that which is conserved in infinite representation—that which bears and that which is borne. The selection works in reverse, and mercilessly eliminates whatever would render the circle tortuous or shatter the transparence of memory. In infinite representation, the bearer and the borne incessantly enter, leaving only to re-enter, like the shadows in the cave, and by this means they claim to have assumed themselves the properly dialectical power.

According to the other conception, difference is primary: it affirms difference and distance. Difference is light, aerial and affirmative. To affirm is not to bear but, on the contrary, to discharge and to lighten. It is no longer the negative which produces a phantom of affirmation like an ersatz, but rather a No which results from affirmation. This is also in turn a shadow, but rather in the sense of a consequence—one could say a *Nachfolge*. The negative is an epiphenomenon. Negation, like the ripples in a pond, is the effect of an affirmation which is too strong or too different. Perhaps two affirmations are necessary in order to produce the shadow of negation as a *Nachfolge*. Moreover, perhaps there are two moments at which the shadow disappears: difference as midnight and as noon. It is in this sense that Nietzsche opposes the Yes *and* the No of the Ass to the Yes *and* the No of Dionysus-Zarathustra: the point of view of the slave who draws from 'No' the phantom of an affirmation, and the point of view of the 'master' who draws from 'Yes' a consequence of negation and destruction; the point of view of the conservers of old values and that of the creators of new values.[17] Those whom Nietzsche calls masters are certainly powerful men, but not men of power, since power is in the gift of the values of the day. A slave does not cease to be a slave by taking power, and it is even the way of the world, or the law of its surface, to be led by slaves. Nor must the distinction between established values and creation be understood as implying an historical relativism, as though the established values were new in their day, while the new ones had to be established once their time had come. On the contrary, the difference is one of kind, like the difference between the conservative order of representation and a creative disorder or inspired chaos which can only ever coincide with a historical moment but never be confused with it. The most profound difference in kind is between the average forms and the extreme forms (new values): the extreme is not reached by carrying the average forms to infinity or by using their opposition in the finite to affirm their identity in the infinite. Pseudo-affirmation in infinite representation does not escape the average forms. Thus Nietzsche reproaches all those selection procedures based upon opposition or conflict with working to the advantage of the average forms and operating to the benefit of the 'large number'. Eternal return alone effects the true selection, because it eliminates the average forms and uncovers 'the superior form of everything that is'. The extreme is not the identity of opposites, but rather the univocity of the different; the superior form is not the infinite, but rather the eternal formlessness of the eternal return itself, throughout its metamorphoses and transformations. Eternal return 'makes' the difference because it creates the superior form. Eternal return employs negation like a *Nachfolge* and invents a new formula for the negation of the negation: *everything which can be denied is* and must be denied. The genius of eternal return lies not in memory but in waste, in active forgetting. All that is negative and all that denies, all those average affirmations which bear the negative, all those pale and unwelcome 'Yeses' which come from 'Nos', *everything which cannot pass the test of eternal return*—all these must be denied. If eternal return is a wheel, then it must be endowed with a violent centrifugal movement which expels everything which 'can' be denied, everything which cannot pass the test. Nietzsche announces only a light punishment for those who do not 'believe' in eternal return: they will have, and be aware of, only an ephemeral life! They will be aware of themselves and know themselves for what they are: epiphenomena. This will be their absolute Knowledge. In this manner, negation as a consequence, as the result of full affirmation, consumes all that is negative, and consumes itself at the mobile centre of eternal return. For if eternal return is a circle, then Difference is at the centre and the Same is only on the periphery: it is a constantly decentred, continually tortuous circle which revolves only around the unequal.

Negation is difference, but difference seen from its underside, seen from below. Seen the right way up, from top to bottom, difference is affirmation. This proposition, however, means many things: that difference is an object of affirmation; that affirmation itself is multiple; that it is creation but also that it must be created, as affirming difference, as being difference in itself. It is not the negative which is the motor. Rather, there are positive differential elements which determine the genesis of both the affirmation and the difference affirmed. It is precisely the fact that there is a genesis of affirmation as such which escapes us every time we leave affirmation in the undetermined, or put determination in the negative. Negation results from affirmation: this means that negation arises in the wake of affirmation or beside it, *but only as the shadow of the more profound genetic element*—of that power or 'will' which engenders the affirmation and the difference in the affirmation. Those who bear the negative know not what they do: they take the shadow for the reality, they encourage phantoms, they uncouple consequences from premisses and they give epiphenomena the value of phenomena and essences.

Representation fails to capture the affirmed world of difference. Representation has only a single centre, a unique and receding perspective, and in consequence a false depth. It mediates everything, but mobilises and moves nothing. Movement, for its part, implies a plurality of centres, a superposition of perspectives, a tangle of points of view, a coexistence of moments which essentially distort representation: paintings or sculptures are already such 'distorters', forcing us to create movement—that is, to combine a superficial and a penetrating view, or to ascend and descend within the space as we move through it. Is it enough to multiply representations in order to obtain such effects? Infinite representation includes precisely an infinity of representations—either by ensuring the convergence of all points of view on the same object or the same world, or by making all moments properties of the same Self. In either case it maintains a unique centre which gathers and represents all the others, like the unity of a series which governs or organises its terms and their relations once and for all. The fact is that infinite representation is indissociable from a law which renders it possible: the form of the concept as a form of identity which constitutes on the one hand the in-itself of the represented (A is A) and on the other the for-itself of the representant (Self = Self). The prefix RE- in the word representation signifies this conceptual form of the identical which subordinates differences. The immediate, defined as 'sub-representative', is therefore not attained by multiplying representations and points of view. On the contrary, each composing representation must be distorted, diverted and torn from its centre. Each point of view must itself be the object, or the object must belong to the point of view. The object must therefore be in no way identical, but torn asunder in a difference in which the identity of the object as seen by a seeing subject vanishes. Difference must become the element, the ultimate unity; it must therefore refer to other differences which never identify it but rather differenciate it. Each term of a series, being already a difference, must be put into a variable relation with other terms, thereby constituting other series devoid of centre and convergence. Divergence and decentring must be affirmed in the series itself. Every object, every thing, must see its own identity swallowed up in difference, each being no more than a difference between differences. Difference must be shown *differing*. We know that modern art tends to realise these conditions: in this sense it becomes a veritable *theatre* of metamorphoses and permutations. A theatre where nothing is fixed, a labyrinth without a thread (Ariadne has hung herself). The work of art leaves the domain of representation in order to become 'experience', transcendental empiricism or science of the sensible.

It is strange that aesthetics (as the science of the sensible) could be founded on what *can* be represented in the sensible. True, the inverse procedure is not much better, consisting of the attempt to withdraw the pure sensible from representation and to determine it as that which remain once representation is removed (a contradictory flux, for example, or a rhapsody of sensations). Empiricism truly becomes transcendental, and aesthetics an apodictic discipline, only when we apprehend directly in the sensible that which can only be sensed, the very being of the sensible: difference, potential difference and difference in intensity as the reason behind qualitative diversity. It is in difference that movement is produced as an 'effect', that phenomena flash their meaning like signs. The intense world of differences, in which we find the reason behind qualities and the being of the sensible, is precisely the object of a superior empiricism. This empiricism teaches us a strange 'reason', that of the multiple, chaos and difference (nomadic distributions, crowned anarchies). It is always differences which resemble one another, which are analogous, opposed or identical: difference is behind everything, but behind difference there is nothing. Each difference passes through all the others; it must 'will' itself or find itself through all the others. That is why eternal return does not appear second or come after, but is already present in every metamorphosis, contemporaneous with that which it causes to return. Eternal return relates to a world of differences implicated one in the other, to a complicated, properly chaotic world *without identity*. Joyce presented the *vicus of recirculation* as causing a *chaosmos* to turn; and Nietzsche had already said that chaos and eternal return were not two distinct things but a single and same *affirmation*. The world is neither finite nor infinite as representation would have it: it is completed and unlimited. Eternal return is the unlimited of the finished itself, the univocal being which is said of difference. With eternal return, chao-errancy is opposed to the coherence of representation; it excludes both the coherence of a subject which represents itself and that of an object represented. *Re*-petition opposes *re*-presentation: the prefix changes its meaning, since in the one case difference is said only in relation to the identical, while in the other it is the univocal which is said of the different. Repetition is the formless being of all differences, the formless power of the ground which carries every object to that extreme 'form' in which its representation comes undone. The ultimate element of repetition is the disparate *[dispars]*, which stands opposed to the identity of representation. Thus, the circle of eternal return, difference and repetition (which undoes that of the identical and the contradictory) is a tortuous circle in which Sameness is said only of that which differs. The poet Blood expresses transcendental empiricism's profession of faith as a veritable aesthetic:

> Nature is contingent, excessive and mystical essentially. . . . We have realised the highest divine thought of itself, and there is in it as much of wonder as of certainty. . . . Not unfortunately the universe is wild—game flavoured as a hawk's wing. Nature is miracle all. She knows no laws; the same returns not, save to bring the different. The slow round of the engraver's lathe gains but the breadth of a hair, but the difference is distributed back over the whole curve, never an instant true—ever not quite.[18]

It is sometimes argued that a considerable philosophical change took place between pre- and post-Kantianism—the former being defined by the negative of limitation, the latter by the negative of opposition; the one by analytic identity, the other by synthetic identity; the one from the point of view of infinite substance, the other from the point of view of the finite Self. In the grand Leibnizian analysis, it is the finite Self which is introduced into the development of the infinite, whereas in the grand Hegelian synthesis, it is the infinite which is reintroduced into the operation of the finite Self. However, the importance of such changes is open to question. For a philosophy of difference, it matters little whether the negative is understood in terms of limitation or opposition, or whether identity is taken to be analytic or synthetic, once difference is already reduced to the negative and subordinated to identity. The oneness and identity of the divine substance are in truth the only guarantee of a unique and identical Self, and God is retained so long as the Self is preserved. Finite synthetic Self or divine analytic substance: it amounts to the same thing. That is why the Man-God permutations are so disappointing, and do not advance matters one step. Nietzsche seems to have been the first to see that the death of God becomes effective only with the dissolution of the Self. What is then revealed is being, which is said of differences which are neither in substance nor in a subject: so many subterranean affirmations. If eternal return is the highest, the most intense thought, this is because its own extreme coherence, at the highest point, excludes the coherence of a thinking subject, of a world which is thought of as a guarantor God.[19] Rather than being concerned with what happens before and after Kant (which amounts to the same thing), we should be concerned with a precise moment within Kantianism, a furtive and explosive moment which is not even continued by Kant much less by post-Kantianism—except, perhaps, by Hölderlin in the experience and the idea of a 'categorical abduction'. For when Kant puts rational theology into question, *in the same stroke* he introduces a kind of disequilibrium, a fissure or crack in the pure Self of the 'I think', an alienation in principle, insurmountable in principle: the subject can henceforth represent its own spontaneity only as that of an Other, and in so doing invoke a mysterious coherence in the last instance which excludes its own—namely, that of the world and God. A Cogito for a dissolved Self: the Self of 'I think' includes in its essence a receptivity of intuition in relation to which *I* is already an other. It matters little that synthetic identity—and following that, the morality of practical reason—restore the integrity of the self, of the world and of God, thereby preparing the way for post-Kantian syntheses: for a brief moment we enter into that schizophrenia in principle which characterises the highest power of thought, and opens Being directly on to difference, despite all the mediations, all the reconciliations, of the concept.

The task of modern philosophy has been defined: to overturn Platonism. That this overturning should conserve many Platonic characteristics is not only inevitable but desirable. It is true that Platonism already represents the subordination of difference to the powers of the One, the Analogous, the Similar and even the Negative. It is like an animal in the process of being tamed, whose final resistant movements bear witness better than they would in a state of freedom to a nature soon to be lost: the Heraclitan world still growls in Platonism. With Plato, the issue is still in doubt: mediation has not yet found its ready-made movement. The Idea is not yet the concept of an object which submits the world to the requirements of representation, but rather a brute presence which can be invoked in the world only in function of that which is not 'representable' in things. The Idea has therefore not yet chosen to relate difference to the identity of a concept in general: it has not given up hope of finding a pure concept of difference in itself. The labyrinth or chaos is untangled, but without thread or the assistance of a thread. Aristotle indeed saw what is irreplaceable in Platonism, even though he made it precisely the basis of a criticism of Plato: the dialectic of difference has its own method—division—but this operates without mediation, without middle term or reason; it acts in the immediate and is inspired by the Ideas rather than by the requirements of a concept in general. It is true that division is a capricious, incoherent procedure which jumps from one singularity to another, by contrast with the supposed identity of a concept. Is this not its strength from the point of view of the Idea? Far from being one dialectical procedure among others which must be completed or relayed by others, is not division the one which replaces all the other procedures from the moment it appears, and gathers up all the dialectical power in favour of a genuine philosophy of difference? Is it not simultaneously the measure of both Platonism and the possibility of overturning Platonism?

Our mistake lies in trying to understand Platonic division on the basis of Aristotelian requirements. According to Aristotle, it is a question of dividing a genus into opposing species: but then this procedure not only lacks 'reason' by itself, it lacks a reason in terms of which we could decide whether something falls into one species rather than another. For example, we divide art into arts of production and arts of acquisition: but then why is fishing among the arts of acquisition? What is missing here is mediation—that is, the identity of a concept capable of serving as middle term. However, this objection clearly fails if Platonic division in no way proposes to determine the species of a genus—or if, rather, it proposes to do so, but superficially and even ironically, the better to hide under this mask its true secret.[20] Division is not the inverse of a 'generalisation'; it is not a determination of species. It is in no way a method of determining species, but one of selection. It is not a question of dividing a determinate genus into definite species, but of dividing a confused species into pure lines of descent, or of selecting a pure line from material which is not. We could speak of 'Platons' as opposed to 'Aristotelons', in the same manner that biologists oppose 'Jordanons' and 'Linnaeons', since Aristotelian species are large, whereas Platonic division deals with small species or lines of descent. Even the indivisible, *infima species* in Aristotle remains a large species, while Platonic division operates in a quite different domain. Its point of departure can therefore be either a genus or a species, but this genus or this large species is understood as an undifferenciated logical matter, an indifferent material, a mixture, an indefinite representing multiplicity which must be eliminated in order to bring to light the Idea which constitutes a pure line of descent. The search for gold provides the model for this process of division. Difference is not between species, between two determinations of a genus, but entirely on one side, within the chosen line of descent: there are no longer contraries within a single genus, but pure and impure, good and bad, authentic and inauthentic, in a mixture which gives rise to a large species. Pure difference, the pure concept of difference, not difference mediated within the concept in general, in the genus and the species. The meaning and the goal of the method of division is selection among rivals, the testing of claimants—not *antiphasis* but *antisbetesis* (we can see this clearly in Plato's two principal examples of division: in *The Statesman*, where the statesman is defined as the one who knows 'the pastoral care of men', but many introduce themselves by saying 'I am the true shepherd of men', including merchants, farmers, bakers, as well as athletes and the entire medical profession; and in the *Phaedrus*, where it is a question of defining the good madness and the true lover, but many claimants cry: 'I am love, I am the lover'). There is no question here of species, except ironically. There is nothing in common with the concerns of Aristotle: it is a question not of identifying but of authenticating. The one problem which recurs throughout Plato's philosophy is the problem of measuring rivals and selecting claimants. This problem of distinguishing between *things and their simulacra* within a pseudo-genus or a large species presides over his classification of the arts and sciences. It is a question of making the difference, thus of operating in the depths of the immediate, a dialectic of the immediate. It is a dangerous trial without thread and without net, for according to the ancient custom of myth and epic, false claimants must die.

Our question is not yet that of knowing whether the selective difference is indeed between the true and false claimants, as Plato says it is, but rather of knowing how Plato establishes the difference thanks to the method of division. To the reader's great surprise, he does so by introducing a 'myth'. It is as though division, once it abandons the mask of determining species and discloses its true goal, nevertheless renounces the realisation of this goal and is instead relayed by the simple 'play' of a myth. In effect, once the question of the claimants is reached, *The Statesman* invokes the image of an ancient God who ruled the world and men: strictly speaking, only this God deserves the name of shepherd–King of mankind. None of the claimants is his equal, but there is a certain 'care' of the human community which devolves to the statesman *par excellence*, since he is closest to the model of the archaic shepherd–God. The claimants find themselves in a sense measured according to an order of elective participation, and among the statesman's rivals we can distinguish (according to the ontological measure afforded by the myth) parents, servants, auxiliaries and, finally, charlatans and counterfeits.[21] The procedure in the *Phaedrus* is the same: when it becomes a question of distinguishing the different 'madnesses', Plato suddenly invokes a myth. He describes the circulation of souls before their incarnation, along with the memory which they carry of the Ideas they have been able to contemplate. It is the nature and degree of this mythic contemplation, but also the kind of occasions necessary for remembering, which determine the value and the order of different types of present madness. We can determine who is the false lover and who is the true lover. We can even determine which—lover, poet, priest, soothsayer or philosopher—is elected to participation in reminiscence and contemplation: which is the true claimant, the true participant, and in what order the others follow. (It will be objected that the third important text concerning division, the *Sophist*, presents no such myth. The point is that in this text, by a paradoxical utilisation of the method, a counter-utilisation, Plato proposes to isolate the false claimant *par excellence*, the one who lays claim to everything without any right: the 'sophist'.)

This introduction of myth appears, however, to confirm all Aristotle's objections: in the absence of any mediation, division lacks probative force; it has to be relayed by a myth which provides an imaginary equivalent of mediation. Here again, however, we betray the sense of this so-mysterious method. For if it is true that, within Platonism in general, myth and dialectic are distinct forces, this distinction no longer matters once dialectic discovers its true method in division. Division overcomes this duality and integrates myth into the dialectic; it makes myth an element of the dialectic itself. The structure of this myth in Plato is clear: it is a circle, with two dynamic functions—namely, turning and returning, distributing and allocation: the allocation of lots is carried out by the turning wheel of an eternally recurring metempsychosis. The reasons which establish that Plato is certainly not a protagonist of eternal return do not concern us here. It is nevertheless true that in the *Phaedrus*—as in *The Statesman* and elsewhere—myth establishes the model of a partial circulation in which appears a suitable ground on which to base the difference, on which to measure the roles or claims. In the *Phaedrus*, this ground appears as the Ideas, such as these are contemplated by the souls which circulate above the celestial vault. In *The Statesman*, it appears in the form of the shepherd–God who presides over the circular movement of the universe. The ground may be either the centre or the motor of the circle. It is constituted by the myth as the principle of a test or selection which imparts meaning to the method of division by fixing the degrees of an elective participation. Thus, in accordance with the oldest tradition, the circular myth is indeed the story-repetition of a foundation. Division demands such a foundation as the ground capable of making the difference. Conversely, the foundation demands division as the state of difference in that which must be grounded. Division is the true unity of dialectic and mythology, of the myth as foundation and of the logos as *logos tomeus*.

This role of the ground appears in all clarity in the Platonic conception of participation. (And no doubt it is this foundation which provides division with the mediation it seems to lack and, at the same time, relates difference to the One, but in such a peculiar manner . . .). To participate means to have part in, to have after, to have in second place. What possesses in first place is the ground itself. Justice alone is just, says Plato. As for those whom we call the just, they possess the quality of being just in second, third or fourth place . . . or in simulacral fashion. That justice alone should be just is not a simple analytic proposition. It is the designation of the Idea as the ground which possesses in first place. The function of the ground is then to allow participation, to give in second place. Thus, that which participates more or less in varying degrees is necessarily a claimant. The claimant calls for a ground; the claim must be grounded (or denounced as groundless). Laying claim is not one phenomenon among others, but the nature of every phenomenon. The ground is a test which permits claimants to participate in greater or lesser degree in the object of the claim. In this sense the ground measures and makes the difference. We must therefore distinguish between justice, which is the ground; the quality of justice, which is the object of the claim possessed by that which grounds; and the just, who are the claimants who participate unequally in the object. That is why the Neo-Platonists provide us with such a profound understanding of Platonism in setting out their sacred triad: the Imparticipable, the Participated, and the Participants. The grounding principle is imparticipable but nevertheless provides something to be participated in, which it gives to the participant, who is the possessor in second place, the claimant who has been able to pass the grounding test. One could say: the father, the daughter and the suitor. Moreover, since the triad is reproduced throughout a whole series of participations, and since the claimants participate within an order and in degrees which represent difference in action, the Neo-Platonists indeed saw the essential point: that the aim of division was not the broad distinction among species but the establishment of a serial dialectic, of series or lines of descent in depth which mark the operations of a selective foundation or an elective participation (Zeus I, Zeus II, etc.). It seems, then, that contradiction, far from signifying the founding test itself, represents instead the state of an ungrounded claim at the limit of participation. If the true claimant (the first grounded, the well grounded, the authentic) has rivals who are like parents, auxiliaries or servants, all participating in his claim in various capacities, he also has simulacra or counterfeits who would be exposed by the test. Such, according to Plato, is the 'sophist', the buffoon, centaur or satyr who lays claim to everything, and who, in laying such claims to everything, is never grounded but contradicts everything, including himself . . .

However, in what, exactly, does the grounding test consist? Myth tells us that it always involves a further task to be performed, an enigma to be resolved. The oracle is questioned, but the oracle's response is itself a problem. The dialectic is ironic, but irony is the art of problems and questions. Irony consists in treating things and beings as so many responses to hidden questions, so many cases for problems yet to be resolved. We recall that Plato defined the dialectic as proceeding by 'problems', by means of which one attains the pure grounding principle—that is, the principle which measures the problems as such and distributes the corresponding solutions. Memory is discussed in the *Meno* only in connection with a geometric problem which must be understood before it can be resolved, and must have the solution it deserves according to the manner in which the rememberer has understood it. We are not concerned at the moment with the distinction which should be drawn between the two instances of the problem and the question, but rather with the essential role which both together play in the Platonic dialectic—a role comparable to that which the negative will play later, for example in the Hegelian dialectic. However, it is precisely *not* the negative which plays this role in Plato—so much so that we must consider whether or not the celebrated thesis of the *Sophist,* despite certain ambiguities, should be understood as follows: 'non' in the expression 'non-being' expresses *something other than the negative.* On this point, the mistake of the traditional accounts is to impose upon us a dubious alternative: in seeking to dispel the negative, we declare ourselves satisfied if we show that being is full positive reality which admits no non-being; conversely, in seeking to ground negation, we are satisfied if we manage to posit, in being itself or in relation to being, some sort of non-being (it seems to us that this non-being is necessarily the being of the negative or the ground of negation). The alternative is thus the following: either there is no non-being and negation is illusory and ungrounded, or there is non-being, which puts the negative in being and grounds negation. Perhaps, however, we have reasons to say *both* that there is non-being *and* that the negative is illusory.

Neither the problem nor the question is a subjective determination marking a moment of insufficiency in knowledge. Problematic structure is part of objects themselves, allowing them to be grasped as signs, just as the questioning or problematising instance is a part of knowledge allowing its positivity and its specificity to be grasped in the act of *learning.* More profoundly still, Being (what Plato calls the Idea) 'corresponds' to the essence of the problem or the question as such. It is as though there were an 'opening', a 'gap', an ontological 'fold' which relates being and the question to one another. In this relation, being is difference itself. Being is also non-being, *but non-being is not the being of the negative;* rather, it is the being of the problematic, the being of problem and question. Difference is not the negative; on the contrary, non-being is Difference: *heteron,* not *enantion.* For this reason non-being should rather be written (non)-being or, better still, ?-being. In this sense, it turns out that the infinitive, the *esse,* designates less a proposition than the interrogation to which the proposition is supposed to respond. This (non)-being is the differential element in which affirmation, as multiple affirmation, finds the principle of its genesis.

As for negation, this is only the shadow of the highest principle, the shadow of the difference alongside the affirmation produced. Once we confuse (non)-being with the negative, contradiction is inevitably carried into being; but contradiction is only the appearance or the epiphenomenon, the illusion projected by the problem, the shadow of a question which remains open and of a being which corresponds as such to that question (before it has been given a response). Is it not already in this sense that for Plato contradiction characterises only the so-called aporetic dialogues? Beyond contradiction, difference—beyond *non*-being (non)-being; beyond the negative, problems and questions.

Note on Heidegger's Philosophy of Difference

It seems that the principal misunderstandings which Heidegger denounced as misreadings of his philosophy after *Being and Time* and 'What Is Metaphysics?' have to do with the following: the Heideggerian *Not* refers not to the negative in Being but to Being as difference; it refers not to negation but to questioning. When Sartre analysed interrogation at the beginning of *Being and Nothingness*, he made it a preliminary to the discovery of the negative and negativity. This was, in a sense, the opposite of Heidegger's procedure. None the less, it involved no misunderstanding, since Sartre did not set out to write a commentary on Heidegger. Merleau-Ponty, on the other hand, undoubtedly followed a more thoroughly Heideggerian inspiration in speaking of 'folds' and 'pleating' (by contrast with Sartrean 'holes' and 'lakes of non-being') from *The Phenomenology of Perception* onwards, and in returning to an ontology of difference and questioning in his posthumous book *The Visible and the Invisible*.

It seems that Heidegger's theses may be summarised as follows:

1. The *not* expresses not the negative but the difference between Being and being. See the preface to *The Essence of Reasons*, 3rd edn, 1949, transl. Terrence Malick, Evanston, IL: Northwestern University Press, 1969, p. 3: 'The Ontological Difference is the Not between being and Being'; and the postscript to 'What Is Metaphysics?', in *Existence and Being*, London: Vision Press, 1949, p. 384, where Heidegger asks: 'whether that which never and nowhere "is" discloses itself as that which differs from everything that "is", i.e. what we call "Being"'.
2. This difference is not 'between' in the ordinary sense of the word. It is the Fold, *Zwiefalt*. It is constitutive of Being and of the manner in which Being constitutes being, in the double movement of 'clearing' and 'veiling'. Being is truly the differenciator of difference—whence the expression 'ontological difference'. See 'Overcoming Metaphysics', transl. Joan Stambaugh, in *The End of Philosophy*, New York: Harper & Row, 1973, pp. 91 ff.

3. Ontological Difference corresponds to questioning. It is the being of questions, which become problems, marking out the determinant fields of existence. See *The Essence of Reasons*.
4. Understood in this manner, difference is not an object of representation. As the element of metaphysics, representation subordinates difference to identity, if only in relating it to a third term as the centre of a comparison *between* two supposedly different terms (Being and being). Heidegger recognises that this point of view of metaphysical representation is still present in *The Essence of Reasons* (see the French translation, p. 59, where the third term is found in the 'transcendence of being-there'). But metaphysics is unable to think difference in itself, or the importance of that which separates as much as of that which unites (the differenciator). There is no synthesis, mediation or reconciliation in difference, but rather a stubborn differenciation. This is the 'turning' beyond metaphysics: 'Being itself can open out in its truth the difference of Being and beings preserved in itself only when the difference explicitly takes place' ('Overcoming Metaphysics', p. 91). On this point, see Beda Alleman, *Hölderlin et Heidegger*, French translation, Paris: Presses Universitaires de France, pp. 157–62, 168–72; Jean Beaufret, Introduction to *Poème de Parménide*, Paris: Presses Universitaires de France, 1955, pp. 69–72, 455.
5. Difference cannot, therefore, be subordinated to the Identical or the Equal but must be thought as the Same, in the Same. See *Identity and Difference*, transl. Joan Stambaugh, New York: Harper & Row, 1969; and 'Poetically Man Dwells . . .' in *Poetry, Language, Thought*, transl. Albert Hofstadter, New York: Harper & Row, 1971, pp. 218–19:

   > The same never coincides with the equal, not even in the empty indifferent oneness of what is merely identical. The equal or identical always moves toward the absence of difference, so that everything may be reduced to a common denominator. The same, by contrast, is the belonging together of what differs, through a gathering by way of the difference. We can only say 'the same' if we think difference. . . . The same banishes all zeal always to level what is different into the equal or identical. The same gathers what is distinct into an original being-at-one. The equal, on the contrary, disperses them into the dull unity of mere uniformity.

We regard as fundamental this 'correspondence' between difference and questioning, between ontological difference and the being of the question It can nevertheless be asked whether Heidegger did not himself encourage the misunderstandings, by his conception of 'Nothing' as well as by his manner of 'striking through' Being instead of parenthesising the (non) of non-Being. Moreover, is it enough to oppose the Same and the Identical in order to think original difference and to disconnect this from all mediations? If it is true that some commentators have found Thomist echos in Husserl, Heidegger, by contrast, follows Duns Scotus and gives renewed splendour to the Univocity of Being. But does he effectuate the conversion after which univocal Being belongs only to difference and, in this sense, revolves around being? Does he conceive of *being* in such a manner that it will be truly disengaged from any subordination in relation to the identity of representation? It would seem not, given his critique of the Nietzschean eternal return.

The four figures of the Platonic dialectic are therefore: the selection of difference, the installation of a mythic circle, the establishment of a foundation, and the position of a question-problem complex. However, difference is still related to the Same or to the One through these figures. No doubt the *same* should not be confused with the identity of the concept in general: rather, it characterises the Idea as the thing itself. Nevertheless, to the extent that it plays the role of a true ground, it is difficult to see what its effect is if not to make that which is grounded 'identical', to use difference in order to make the identical exist. In reality, the distinction between the same and the identical bears fruit only if one subjects the Same to a conversion which relates it to the different, while at the same time the things and beings which are distinguished in the different suffer a corresponding radical destruction of their *identity*. Only on this condition is difference thought in itself, neither represented nor mediated. The whole of Platon- ism, by contrast, is dominated by the idea of drawing a distinction between 'the thing itself' and the simulacra. Difference is not thought in itself but related to a ground, subordinated to the same and subject to mediation in mythic form. Overturning Platonism, then, means denying the primacy of original over copy, of model over image; glorifying the reign of simulacra and reflections. Pierre Klossowski has clearly noted this point in the article referred to above: taken in its strict sense, eternal return means that each thing exists only in returning, copy of an infinity of copies which allows neither original nor origin to subsist. That is why the eternal return is called 'parodic': it qualifies as simulacrum that which it causes to be (and to return).[22] When eternal return is the power of (formless) Being, the simulacrurn is the true character or form—the 'being'—of that which is. When the identity of things dissolves, being escapes to attain univocity, and begins to revolve around the different. That which is or returns has no prior constituted identity: things are reduced to the difference which fragments them, and to all the differences which are implicated in it and through which they pass. In this sense, the simulacrum and the symbol are one; in other words, the simulacrum is the sign in so far as the sign interiorises the conditions of its own repetition. The simulacrum seizes upon a constituent *disparity* in the thing from which it strips the rank of model. If, as we have seen, eternal return serves to establish a difference in kind between the average and the superior forms, then there is also a difference in kind between the average or moderate positions of the eternal return (whether these involve partial cycles or approximate global return *in specie)* and its strict or categorical position. For eternal return, affirmed in all its power, allows no installation of a foundation–ground. On the contrary, it swallows up or destroys every ground which would function as an instance responsible for the difference between the original and the derived, between things and simulacra. It makes us party to a universal *ungrounding*. By 'ungrounding' we should understand the freedom of the non-mediated ground, the discovery of a ground behind every other ground, the relation between the groundless and the ungrounded, the immediate reflection of the formless and the superior form which constitutes the eternal return. Every thing, animal or being assumes the status of simulacrum; so that the thinker of eternal return—who indeed refuses to be drawn out of the cave, finding instead another cave beyond, always another in which to hide—can rightly say that he is himself burdened with the superior form of everything that is, like the poet 'burdened with humanity, even that of the animals'. These words themselves have their echo in the superposed caves. Moreover, that cruelty which at the outset seemed to us monstrous, demanding expiation, and could be alleviated only by representative mediation, now seems to us to constitute the pure concept or Idea of difference within overturned Platonism: the most innocent difference, the state of innocence and its echo.

Plato gave the establishment of difference as the supreme goal of dialectic. However, difference does not lie between things and simulacra, models and copies. Things are simulacra themselves, simulacra are the superior forms, and the difficulty facing everything is to become its own simulacrum, to attain the status of a sign in the coherence of eternal return. Plato opposed eternal return to chaos as though chaos were a contradictory state which must be subject to order or law from outside, as it is when the Demiurge subjugates a rebellious matter. He reduced the Sophist to contradiction, to that supposed state of chaos, the lowest power and last degree of participation. In reality the 'nth' power does not pass through two, three or four: it is immediately affirmed in order to constitute the highest power; it is affirmed of chaos itself and, as Nietzsche said, chaos and eternal return are not two different things. The sophist is not the being (or the non-being) of contradiction, but the one who raises everything to the level of simulacra and maintains them in that state. Was it not inevitable that Plato should push irony to that point—to parody? Was it not inevitable that Plato should be the first to overturn Platonism, or at least to show the direction such an overturning should take? We are reminded of the grand finale of the *Sophist:* difference is displaced, division turns back against itself and begins to function in reverse, and, as a result of being applied to simulacra themselves (dreams, shadows, reflections, paintings), shows the impossibility of distinguishing them from originals or from models. The Eleatic Stranger gives a definition of the sophist such that he can no longer be distinguished from Socrates himself: the ironic imitator who proceeds by brief arguments (questions and problems). Each moment of difference must then find its true figure: selection, repetition, ungrounding, the question–problem complex.

We have contrasted representation with a different kind of formation. The elementary concepts of representation are the categories defined as the conditions of possible experience. These, however, are too general or too large for the real. The net is so loose that the largest fish pass through. No wonder, then, that aesthetics should be divided into two irreducible domains: that of the theory of the sensible which captures only the real's conformity with possible experience; and that of the theory of the beautiful, which deals with the reality of the real in so far as it is thought. Everything changes once we determine the conditions of real experience, which are not larger than the conditioned and which differ in kind from the categories: the two senses of the aesthetic become one, to the point where the being of the sensible reveals itself in the work of art, while at the same time the work of art appears as experimentation. The fault of representation lies in not going beyond the form of identity, in relation to both the object seen and the seeing subject. Identity is no less conserved in each component representation than in the whole of infinite representation as such. Infinite representation may well multiply points of view and organise these in series; these series are no less subject to the condition of converging upon the same object, upon the same world. Infinite representation may well multiply figures and moments and organise these into circles endowed with self-movement; these circles no less turn around a single centre which is that of the great circle of consciousness. By contrast, when the modern work of art develops its permutating series and its circular structures, it indicates to philosophy a path leading to the abandonment of representation. It is not enough to multiply perspectives in order to establish perspectivism. To every perspective or point of view there must correspond an autonomous work with its own self-sufficient sense: what matters is the divergence of series, the decentring of circles, 'monstrosity'. The totality of circles and series is thus a formless *ungrounded* chaos which has no law other than its own repetition, its own reproduction in the development of that which diverges and decentres. We know how these conditions are already satisfied in such works as Mallarmé's *Book* or Joyce's *Finnegans Wake*: these are by nature problematic works.[23] The identity of the object read really dissolves into divergent series defined by esoteric words, just as the identity of the reading subject is dissolved into the decentred circles of possible multiple readings. Nothing, however, is lost; each series exists only by virtue of the return of the others. Everything has become simulacrum, for by simulacrum we should not understand a simple imitation but rather the act by which the very idea of a model or privileged position is challenged and overturned. The simulacrum is the instance which includes a difference within itself, such as (at least) two divergent series on which it plays, all resemblance abolished so that one can no longer point to the existence of an original and a copy. It is in this direction that we must look for the conditions, not of possible experience, but of real experience (selection, repetition, etc.). It is here that we find the lived reality of a sub-representative domain. If it is true that representation has identity as its element and similarity as its unit of measure, then pure presence such as it appears in the simulacrum has the 'disparate' as its unit of measure—in other words, always a difference of difference as its immediate element.

Notes

1. Odilon Redon, *A soi-même: Journal, 1867–1915*, Paris: Fleury, 1922, p. 63: 'No plastic form will be found in my works, I mean any form perceived objectively, for itself, according to the laws of light and shadow, through the conventional means of relief. . . . All of my art is confined solely to the resources of *chiaroscuro*, and also owes much to the effects of the abstract line, that agent from a profound source, acting directly on the spirit.'

2. Aristotle, *Metaphysics*, Book X, 4, 8, 9; transl. W. D. Ross, Oxford: The Clarendon Press, 1924; reprinted in *The Complete Works of Aristotle*, ed. Jonathan Barnes, vol. 2, Princeton, NJ: Princeton University Press, 1984. On the three kinds of difference, common, proper and strict, see Porphyry the Phoenician, *Isagoge*, transl. Edward W. Warren, Toronto: The Pontifical Institute of Mediaeval Studies, 1975, paras 8–9. See also The Thomist manuals: for example the chapter '*De differentia*' in the *Elementa philosophia aristotelico-thomisticae* by Joseph Gredt, Fribourg: Herder, 1909–12, vol. 1, pp. 122–25.

3. Porphyry, *Isagoge*, para. 9, pp. 42–3: 'The difference 'rational' added to animal makes another essence *[allo]*, but the difference 'moving' only makes something qualitatively different from resting, so that the one makes a difference-in-essence, the other only a difference-in-quality.'

4. Aristotle, *Metaphysics*, Book III, 3, 998b, 20–27; *Topics*, VI, 6, 144a, 35–40.

5. We know that Aristotle himself did not speak of analogy with regard to being. He determined the categories as *pros hen* and no doubt also as *ephexēs* (these are the two cases, apart from pure equivocity, where there is 'difference' without a common genus). The *pros hen* are said in relation to a unique term. This is like a *common sense*, but this common sense is not a genus, for it forms only a distributive unity (implicit and confused), not a collective, explicit and distinct unity such as we find with genera. The scholastics are therefore right to translate the *pros hen* as 'analogy of proportionality'. In effect, this analogy must not be understood in the strict mathematical sense and does not presuppose any *equality* of relation. It is defined by something completely different—by an *interiority* of relation: the relation of each category with being is interior to each category, it is on its own account that each has unity and being, by virtue of its own nature. This distributive character is clearly noted by Aristotle when he identifies categories with *diaireseis*. Moreover, despite certain recent interpretations there is indeed a division of being corresponding to the ways in which it is distributed to 'beings'. However, in the *pros hen* the unique term is not only being as common sense but already substance as *first sense*—whence the slide towards the idea that *ephexēs* imply a hierarchy. The scholastics speak here of 'analogy of proportion': there is no longer a distributive concept which is formally related to different terms but a serial concept which

is formally–eminently related to a principal term and to others in a lesser degree. Being is first, in act, analogy of proportionality; but does it not also 'virtually' present an analogy of proportion?

6. See E. Laroche, *Histoire de la racine nem—en grec ancien*, Paris: Klincksieck, 1949. Laroche shows that the idea of distribution in *nomos-nemō* does not stand in a simple relation to that of allocation *[temnō, diaō, diaireō]*. The pastoral sense of *nemo* (to pasture) only belatedly implied an allocation of the land. Homeric society had neither enclosures nor property in pastures: it was not a question of distributing the land among the beasts but, on the contrary, of distributing the beasts themselves and dividing them up here and there across an unlimited space, forest or mountainside. The *nomos* designated first of all an occupied space, but one without precise limits (for example, the expanse around a town)—whence, too, the theme of the 'nomad'.

7. Etienne Gilson raises all these questions in his book *Jean Duns Scot: Introduction à ses positions fondamentales*, Paris: Vrin, 1952, pp. 87–88, 114, 236–37, 629. He insists on the relation between analogy and judgement, especially the judgement of existence (p. 101).

8. Nietzsche: 'That dangerous word hubris is indeed the touchstone for every Heraclitan': *Philosophy in the Tragic Age of the Greeks*, transl. by M. Cowan, Chicago: Henry Regnery, 1962, S. 7, p. 61. And on the problem of order and rank, 'of which we may say it is *our* problem, we free spirits', see *Human, All Too Human*, transl. R. J. Hollingdale, Cambridge: Cambridge University Press, 1986, Preface, S. 6–7, pp. 9–10. For the Overman as 'the superior form of everything that is', see *Ecce Homo*, 'Thus Spake Zarathustra', S. 6. (*In Kaufmann's translation this phrase is rendered as 'the supreme type of all beings'.)

9. On this indifference towards the small or the large, see Leibniz, *'Tentamen Anagogicum'*, in *Philosophical Papers and Letters*, transl. and ed. Leroy E. Loemker, 2nd edn, Dordrecht, Holland: D. Reidel, 1969. Note that for Leibniz no less than for Hegel, infinite representation cannot be reduced to a mathematical structure: there is a non-mathematical or supra-mathematical architectonic element in continuity and in the differential calculus. Conversely, Hegel seems to recognise the presence of a genuine infinite in the differential calculus, the infinity of 'relation'. He criticizes calculus only for expressing this genuine infinite in the mathematical form of the 'series', which is a bad infinity: *Hegel's Science of Logic*, transl. A. V. Miller, London: George Allen & Unwin, 1969, pp. 240ff. We know that modern interpretations give an account of the differential calculus entirely in terms of finite representation: this point of view will be analysed in Chapter IV.

10. *Hegel's Science of Logic*, pp. 431, 442. See also *Hegel's Logic*, Part One of the Encyclopaedia of the Philosophical Sciences (1830), transl. William Wallace, Oxford: Clarendon Press, 1975, S. 116–22. On the passage from difference to opposition and to contradiction, see the comments by Jean Hyppolite, *Logique et Existence: Essai sur la Logique de Hegel*, Paris: Presses Universitaires de France, 1953, pp. 146–57.

11. *Hegel's Science of Logic*, p. 432.

12. On the infinite, genus and species, see Hegel's *Phenomenology of Spirit*, transl. A. V. Miller, Oxford: Clarendon Press, 1977, pp. 98–101, 107–9,175–78.

13. See Leibniz, '*Nova calculi differentialis applicatio . . .*' (1694). On the principle of reciprocal determination which Salomon Maïmon draws from Leibniz, see M. Guéroult, *La philosophie transcendentale de Salomon Maïmon*, Paris: Alcan, 1929, p. 75 ff.

(Neither Maïmon nor Leibniz distinguishes between the reciprocal determination of relations and the complete determination of the object.)

14. Leibniz, Correspondence with Arnauld, 9 October 1687: 'I have said that the soul, which naturally expresses the entire universe in a certain sense and according to the relationship which other bodies have to its own, and which as a consequence expresses more immediately the properties of the parts of its body, must therefore, by virtue of the laws of relationship which are essential to it, particularly express certain unusual motions of the parts of its body': *Philosophical Papers and Letters*, p. 339. see also the 'degrees of accidental unity' among things as a result of the degrees of relation between their component elements, in the Letter of 30 April 1687 (in Leibniz, *Discourse on Metaphysics. Correspondence with Arnauld. Monadology*, transl. George Montgomery, La Salle, IL: Open Court Publishing Company, 1979, pp. 180–99).

15. Louis Althusser denounces the all-powerful character of identity in Hegel's philosophy, in the form of the *simplicity of its internal principle*: 'The simplicity of the Hegelian contradiction is made possible *only* by the simplicity of the *internal principle* that constitutes the essence of any historical period. It is because it is possible in principle to reduce the totality, the infinite diversity of a given historical society . . . to a simple internal principle, that this very simplicity thereby accrues by right to contradiction and may be reflected in it.' This is why he criticizes the Hegelian circle for having only a single centre in which all the figures are reflected and retained. In opposition to Hegel, Althusser proposes a principle of multiple or overdetermined contradiction which he finds in the young Marx: 'This means that if the "differences" that constitute each of the instances in play . . . "*merge*" into a real unity, they are not "*dissipated*" as pure *phenomena* in the internal unity of a *simple* contradiction.' (It is still the case that for Althusser it is contradiction which is overdetermined and differential, and the totality of these differences remains legitimately grounded in a principal contradiction). See Louis Althusser, *For Marx*, transl. Ben Brewster, London: New Left Review Editions, 1977, pp. 100, 103 (*translation modified).

16. Nietzsche never ceases to denounce the assimilation of 'affirm' with 'bear'. See *Beyond Good and Evil*, S. 213, where he says of most thinkers and scholars: '"Thinking" and "taking something seriously", taking on its weight—to them these things go together, they have no other experience of it.' **Beyond Good and Evil*, transl. R. J. Hollingdale, Harmondsworth: Penguin, 1973, p. 126, has ' "taking something seriously", giving it "weighty consideration".' The point is that *to bear* implies a false activity, a false affirmation which concerns itself only with the products of nihilism. Thus Nietzsche defines Kant and Hegel as 'philosophical labourers' who amass and conserve an enormous pile of established value judgements, even if for them it is a matter of overcoming the past. In this sense, they are still enslaved to the negative (S. 211).

*Citation modified. These lines are quoted from *The Anaesthetic Revelation* (1874), by the American poet and philosopher Benjamin Paul Blood (1822–1919). Wahl cites them from the essay on Blood's pamphlet by William James, entitled 'A Pluralistic Mystic' and first published in the *Hibbert Journal*, July 1910. This essay is republished in James's *Memories and Studies*, London: Longmans Green, 1911 (see pp. 394, 409); and in vol. 15 of *The Works of William James*, Cambridge, MA: Harvard University Press, 1987.

17. *Beyond Good and Evil*, S. 211. On the 'no' of the master which is a consequence, by contrast with the 'no' of the slave which is a principle, see *On the Genealogy of Morals*, I, S. 10.

18. Cited by Jean Wahl, *Les philosophies pluralistes d'Angleterre et d'Amérique*, Paris: Alcan, 1920, p. 37. All Jean Wahl's work is a profound meditation on difference: on the possibilities within empiricism for expressing its poetic, free and wild nature; on the irreducibility of difference to the simple negative; on the *non-Hegelian* relations between affirmation and negation.

19. In two articles which renew the interpretation of Nietzsche, Pierre Klossowski uncovers this element: '*God is dead* does not mean that the divinity ceases to provide a clarification of existence, but rather that the absolute guarantee of the identity of the responsible self disappears from the horizon of Nietzsche's consciousness, which in turn becomes indistinguishable from that disappearance. . . . All that is left (to consciousness) is to declare that its very identity is a chance case arbitrarily maintained as necessary, even if this means taking itself for that universal wheel of chance, even if this means embracing if possible the totality of cases, chance itself in its necessary totality. What subsists. is thus being, and the verb "to be", which is never applied to being itself but to the fortuitous': 'Nietzsche, le polythéisme et la parodie', in *Un si funeste désir*, Paris: NRF, 1963, pp. 220–21. 'Does this mean that the thinking subject loses its identity on the basis of a coherent thought which excludes it? . . . What is my role in this circular movement in relation to which I am incoherent, in relation to that thought so perfectly coherent that it excludes me at the very moment I think it? . . . How does it threaten the reality of the self, of this self which it nevertheless exalts? By liberating the fluctuations which signify it as a self in such a fashion that it is only ever the completed which resound in its present. . . . *Circulus vitiosus deus is* only a denomination of this sign which here takes on a divine physiognomy after the manner of Dionysus': 'Oubli et anamnése dans l'expérience vécue de 1'éternel retour du Même' in *Nietzsche: Cahiers de Royaumont*, Philosophie No. vi, Paris: Editions de Minuit, 1967, pp. 233–35.

20. On Aristotle's critique of Platonic division, cf. *Prior Analytics*, 1, 31; *Posterior Analytics*, 11, 5 and 13 (In the latter text Aristotle maintains a certain role for division in the determination of species, even though the insufficiencies that he finds in Plato's conception are corrected by a principle of continuity). But we can see clearly how far the determination of species is merely an ironic appearance and not the aim of Platonic division, for example, in *The Statesman*, 266 b-d.

21. It is with regard to this aspect that the myth must be completed by another kind of model, the paradigm, which enables Plato to distinguish parents, servants, auxiliaries and counterfeits by means of analogy. In the same manner, assaying gold involves several selections: the removal of impurities, the elimination of other metals 'from the same family' (cf. *The Statesman*, 303 d-e).

22. See Note 19 above. On this notion of simulacra as it appears in Klossowski in connection with eternal return, see Michel Foucault, 'La Prose d'Actéon', *Nouvelle Revue Française*, March 1964; Maurice Blanchot, 'Le rire des dieux', *Nouvelle Revue Française*, July 1965.

23. See Umberto Eco, *The Open Work*, transl. Anna Cancogni, with an Introduction by David Robey, Cambridge, MA: Harvard University Press, 1989. Eco shows clearly that the 'classical' work of art may be seen from several perspectives and is susceptible to several interpretations, but that there is no autonomous work corresponding to each point of view or interpretation, all included in the the chaos of the work as a whole. The characteristic of the 'modern' work of art appears to be precisely the absence of any such centre or convergence (see Chapters 1 and 6).

PART FOUR

Jacques Derrida

Signs and the Blink of an Eye

The force of this demonstration presupposes the instant as a point, the identity of experience instantaneously present to itself. Self-presence must be produced in the undivided unity of a temporal present so as to have nothing to reveal to itself by the agency of signs. Such a perception or intuition of self by self in presence would not only be the case where "signification" in general could not occur, but also would assure the general possibility of a primordial perception or intuition, i.e., of *nonsignification* as the "principle of principles." Later, whenever Husserl wants to stress the sense of primordial intuition, he will recall that it is the experience of the absence and uselessness of signs.[1]

The demonstration we are now concerned with was elaborated before his lectures on *The Phenomenology of Internal Time-Consciousness;*[2] for reasons that are as much historical as systematic, the temporality of experience is not a theme of the *Logical Investigations.* At this point, however, we cannot avoid noting that a certain concept of the "now," of the present as punctuality of the instant, discretely but decisively sanctions the whole system of "essential distinctions." If the punctuality of the instant is a myth, a spatial or mechanical metaphor, an inherited metaphysical concept, or all that at once, and if the present of self-presence is not *simple,* if it is constituted in a primordial and irreducible synthesis, then the whole of Husserl's argumentation is threatened in its very principle.

We cannot here go closely into the admirable analysis of *The Phenomenology of Internal Time-Consciousness,* which Heidegger, in *Sein und Zeit,* calls the first in the history of philosophy to break with a concept of time inherited from Aristotle's *Physics,* determined according to the basic notions of the "now," the "point," the "limit," and the "circle." Let us, however, assemble some references from the lectures that are relevant for our own point of view.

1. Whether or not it is a metaphysical presupposition, the concept of *punctuality*, of the *now* as *stigmē*, still plays a major role in *The Phenomenology of Internal Time-Consciousness*. Undoubtedly, no now can be isolated as a pure instant, a pure punctuality. Not only does Husserl recognize this ("it belongs to the essence of lived experiences that they must be extended in this fashion, that a punctual phase can never be for itself" [*ITC*, § 19; ET, p. 701]), but his whole description is incomparably well adapted to the original modifications of this irreducible spreading-out. This spread is nonetheless thought and described on the basis of the self-identity of the now as point, as a "source-point." In phenomenology, the idea of primordial presence and in general of "beginning," "absolute beginning" or *principium*,[3] always refers back to this "source-point." Although the flow of time is "not severable into parts which could be by themselves nor divisible into phases, points of the continuity, which could be by themselves," the "modes of running-off of an immanent temporal Object have a beginning, that is to say, a source-point. This is the mode of running-off with which the immanent Object begins to be. In its characterized as now" (*ITC*, § 10; ET, pp. 48–49).

Despite all the complexity of its structures, temporality has a nondisplaceable center, an eye or living core, the punctuality of the real now. The "now-apprehension is, as it were, the nucleus of a comet's tail of retentions" (*ibid.*, § 11; ET, p. 52) and "a punctual phase is actually present as now at any given moment, while the others are connected as a retentional train" (*ibid.*, § 16; ET, p. 61). "The actual *now* is necessarily something punctual *(ein Punktuelles)* and remains so, *a form that persists through continuous change of matter*" (*Ideas* I, § 81; ET, p. 237, modified).

It is to this self-same identity of the actual now that Husserl refers in the "*im selben Augenblick*" we began with. Moreover, within philosophy there is no possible objection concerning this privilege of the present-now; it defines the very element of philosophical thought, it is *evidence* itself, conscious thought itself, it governs every possible concept of truth and sense. No sooner do we question this privilege than we begin to get at the core of consciousness itself from a region that lies elsewhere than philosophy, a procedure that would remove every possible *security* and *ground* from discourse. In the last analysis, what is at stake is indeed the privilege of the actual present, the now. This conflict, necessarily unlike any other, is between philosophy, which is always a philosophy of presence, and a meditation on nonpresence—which is not perforce its contrary, or necessarily a meditation on a negative absence, or a theory of nonpresence *qua* unconsciousness.

The dominance of the now not only is integral to the system of the founding contrast established by metaphysics, that between *form* (or *eidos* or idea) and *matter* as a contrast between *act* and *potency* ("the actual *now* is necessarily something punctual and remains so, *a form that persists through continuous change of matter*") (*Ideas I*, § 81; ET, p. 237); it also assures the tradition that carries over the Greek metaphysics of presence into the "modern" metaphysics of presence understood as self-consciousness, the metaphysics of the idea as representation *(Vorstellung)*. It therefore designates the locus of a problem in which phenomenology confronts every position centered on nonconsciousness that can approach what is ultimately at stake, what is at bottom decisive: the concept of time. It is no accident that *The Phenomenology of Internal Time-Consciousness* both confirms the dominance of the present and rejects the "after-event" of the becoming conscious of an "unconscious content" which is the structure of temporality implied throughout Freud's texts.[4] Husserl writes to this effect:

> It is certainly an absurdity to speak of a content of which we are "unconscious," one of which we are conscious only later *(nachträglich)*. Consciousness *(Bewusstsein)* is necessarily a being-conscious *(bewusstsein)* in each of its phases. Just as the retentional phase was conscious of the preceding one without making it an object, so also are we conscious of the primal datum—namely, in the specific form of the "now"—without its being objective; . . . retention of a content of which we are not conscious is impossible; . . . if every "content" necessarily and in itself is "unconscious" then the question of an additional dator consciousness becomes senseless (*ITC*, Appendix IX; ET, pp. 162–63, modified).

2. Despite this motif of the punctual now as "primal form" *(Urform)* of consciousness *(Ideas I)*, the body of the description in *The Phenomenology of Internal Time-Consciousness* and elsewhere prohibits our speaking of a simple self-identity of the present. In this way not only is what could be called the metaphysical assurance par excellence shaken, but, closer to our concerns, the "*im selben Augenblick*" argument in the *Investigations* is undermined.

In its critical as well as descriptive work, *The Phenomenology of Internal Time-Consciousness* demonstrates and confirms throughout the irreducibility of re-presentation *(Vergegenwärtigung, Repräsentation)* to presentative perception *(Gegenwärtigen, Präsentieren)*, secondary and reproductive memory to retention, imagination to the primordial impression, the re-produced now to the perceived or retained actual now, etc. Without being able, here, to follow the rigorous development of this text (and without its being necessary to question its demonstrative worth), we can still examine its foundation of evidence and the *context* of these distinctions, which relates the terms distinguished to one another and constitutes the very possibility of their *camparison*.

One then sees quickly that the presence of the perceived present can appear as such only inasmuch as it is *continuously compounded* with a nonpresence and nonperception, with primary memory and expectation (retention and protention). These nonperceptions are neither added to, nor do they *occasionally* accompany, the actually perceived now; they are essentially and indispensably involved in its possibility. Husserl admittedly says that retention is still a perception. But this is the absolutely unique case—Husserl never recognized any other—of a perceiving in which the perceived is not a present but a past existing as a modification of the present:

> . . . if we call perception *the act in which all "origination"* lies, which *constitutes originarily*, then *primary remembrance is perception*. For only in *primary remembrance do we see what is past*; only in it is the past constituted, i.e., *not in a representative but in a presentative way* (*ITC*, § 17, ET, p. 64).

Thus, in retention, the presentation that enables us to see gives a nonpresent, a past and unreal present. We might suspect, then, that if Husserl nonetheless calls it perception, this is because he holds to establishing a radical discontinuity between retention and reproduction, between perception and imagination, etc., and not between perception and retention. This is the *nervus demonstrandi* of his critique of Brentano. Husserl resolutely maintains that there is "no mention here of a continuous accommodation of perception to its opposite" *(ibid.)*.

And yet, did not the preceding section quite explicitly entertain this very possibility?

> If we now relate what has been said about perception to the *differences of the givenness* with which temporal Objects make their appearance, then the *antithesis of perception is primary remembrance*, which appears here, and *primary expectation* (retention and protention), whereby *perception and non-perception continually* pass over into one another (*ITC*, § 16; ET, p. 62).

Further he writes:

> In an ideal sense, then, perception (impression) would be the phase of consciousness which constitutes the pure now, and memory every other phase of the continuity. But this is just an ideal limit, something abstract which can be nothing for itself. Moreover, it is also true that even this ideal now is not something *toto caelo* different from the not-now but continually accommodates itself thereto. The continual transition from perception to primary remembrance conforms to this accommodation. (*ITC*, § 16; ET, p. 63).

As soon as we admit this continuity of the now and the not-now, perception and nonperception, in the zone of primordiality common to primordial impression and primordial retention, we admit the other into the self-identity of the *Augenblick*; nonpresence and nonevidence are admitted into the *blink of the instant*. There is a duration to the blink, and it closes the eye. This alterity is in fact the condition for presence, presentation, and thus for *Vorstellung* in general; it precedes all the dissociations that could be produced in presence, in *Vorstellung*. The difference between retention and reproduction, between primary and secondary memory, is not the radical difference Husserl wanted between perception and nonperception; it is rather a difference between two modifications of nonperception. Whatever the phenomenological difference between these two modifications may be, and despite the immense problems it poses and the necessity of taking them into account, it only serves to separate two ways of relating to the irreducible nonpresence of another now. Once again, this relation to nonpresence neither befalls, surrounds, nor conceals the presence of the primordial impression; rather it makes possible its ever renewed upsurge and virginity. However, it radically destroys any possibility of a simple self-identity. And this holds in depth for the constituting flux itself:

> If . . . we now consider the *constitutive* phenomena, we find a *flux*, and every phase of this flux is a *continuity of shading*. However, in principle, no phase of this flux is to be broadened out to a continuous succession; therefore, the flux should not be thought to be so transformed that this phase is extended in identity with itself (*ITC*, § 35; ET, p. 99; italics added).

The fact that nonpresence and otherness are internal to presence strikes at the very root of the argument for the uselessness of signs in the self-relation.

3. Doubtless Husserl would refuse to assimilate the necessity of retention and the necessity of signs, for it is only the latter which (like the image) belong to the genus of representation and symbolism. Moreover, Husserl cannot give up this rigorous distinction without bringing into question the axiomatic *principium* of phenomenology itself. The force with which he maintains that retention and protention belong to the sphere of the primordial, provided it be understood "in the broad sense," and the insistence with which he contrasts the absolute validity of primary memory with the relative validity of secondary memory,[5] clearly indicate both his intent and his uneasiness. His uneasiness stems from the fact that he is trying to retain two apparently irreconcilable possibilities. (a) The living now is constituted as the absolute perceptual source only in a state of continuity with retention taken as nonperception. Fidelity to experience and to "the things themselves" forbids that it be otherwise. (b) The source of certitude in general is the primordial character of the living now; it is necessary therefore to keep retention in the sphere of primordial certitude and to shift the frontier between the primordial and the nonprimordial. The frontier must pass not between the pure present and the nonpresent, i.e., between the actuality and inactuality of a living now, but rather between two forms of the re-turn or re-stitution of the present: re-tention and re-presentation.

Without reducing the abyss which may indeed separate retention from re-presentation, without hiding the fact that the problem of their relationship is none other than that of the history of "life" and of life's becoming conscious, we should be able to say *a priori* that their common root—the possibility of repetition in its most general form, that is, the constitution of a trace in the most universal sense—is a possibility which not only must inhabit the pure actuality of the now but must constitute it through the very movement of differance it introduces. Such a trace is—if we can employ this language without immediately contradicting it or crossing it out as we proceed—more "primordial" than what is phenomenologically primordial. For the ideality of the form *(Form)* of presence itself implies that it be infinitely re-peatable, that its re-turn, as a return of the same, is necessary *ad infinitum* and is inscribed in presence itself. It implies that the re-turn is the return of a present which will be retained in a *finite* movement or retention and that primordial truth, in the phenomenological sense of the term, is only to be found rooted in the finitude of this retention. It is furthermore implied that the relation with infinity can be instituted only in the opening of the form of presence upon ideality, as the possibility of a re-turn *ad infinitum.* How can it be explained that the possibility of reflection and re-presentation belongs by essence to every experience, without this nonself-identity of the presence called primordial? How could it be explained that this possibility belongs, like a pure and ideal freedom, to the essence of consciousness? Husserl ceaselessly emphasizes that it does, in speaking of reflection, especially in *Ideas I*,[6] and in speaking of re-presentation, already in *The Phenomenology* of *Internal Time-Consciousness.*[7] In all these directions, the presence of the present is thought of as arising from the bending-back of a return, from the movement of repetition, and not the reverse. Does not the fact that this bending-back is irreducible in presence or in self-presence, that this trace or differance is always older than presence and procures for it its openness, prevent us from speaking about a simple self-identity "*im selben Augenblick*"? Does this not compromise the usage Husserl wants to make of the concept of "solitary mental life," and consequently of the rigorous separation of indication from expression? Do indication and the several concepts on whose basis we have thus far tried to think it through (the concepts of existence, nature, mediation, the empirical, etc.) not have an ineradicable origin in the movement of transcendental temporalization? By the same token, does not everything that is announced already in this reduction to "solitary mental life" (the transcendental reduction in all its stages, and notably the reduction to the monadic sphere of "*ownness*"—*Eigenheit*—*etc.)* appear to be stricken in its very possibility by what we are calling time? But what we are calling time must be given a different name—for "time" has always designated a movement conceived in terms of the present, and can mean nothing else. Is not the concept of pure solitude—of the monad in the phenomenological sense—*undermined by* its own origin, by the very condition of its self-presence, that is, by "time," to be conceived anew on the basis now of difference within auto-affection, on the basis of identifying identity and nonidentity within the "sameness" of the *im selben Augen-*

blick? Husserl himself evoked the analogy between the relation with the *alter ego*, constituted within the absolute monad of the ego, and the relation with the other present, the past present, as constituted in the absolute actuality of the living present (*Cartesian Meditations*, § 52).

Does not this "dialectic"—in every sense of the term and before any speculative subsumption of this concept—open up living to differance, and constitute, in the pure immanence of experience, the *divergence* involved in indicative communication and even in signification in general? And we mean the divergence of indicative communication *and signification in general*, for Husserl not only intends to exclude indication from "solitary mental life"; he will consider language in general, the element of logos, in its expressive form itself, as a secondary event, superadded to a primordial and pre-expressive stratum of sense. Expressive language itself would be something supervenient upon the absolute silence of self-relationship.

Notes

1. For example, the whole of the Sixth Investigation continually points out that between intuitive acts and contents, on the one hand, and significative acts and contents, on the other, the phenomenological difference is "irreducible" (see, especially, § 26). And yet the possibility of a "mixture" is admitted there—which provokes questions. The whole of *The Phenomenology of Internal Time-Consciousness is* based upon the radical discontinuity between intuitive presentation and the symbolic representation "which not only represents the object voidly but also represents it 'by means of' signs or images" (Edmund Husserl, *Vorlesungen zur Phänomenologie des inneren Zeitbewusstseins* [Halle: Max Niemeyer, 1929]; English translation by James S. Churchill, *The Phenomenology of Internal Time-Consciousness* [Bloomington: Indiana University Press, 1964], Appendix II; ET, p. 134). [Hereafter abbreviated, in references, as *ITC*.—Translator.] In *Ideas I* we read that "between *perception* on the one hand and the *symbolic representation by means of images or signs* on the other, there exists an insurmountable eidetic difference." "We collapse into nonsense when, as is ordinarily done, we completely mix up these modes of presentation with their essentially different constructions" (*Ideas I*, § 43; ET, pp. 136–37). And what Husserl says about the perception of sensible corporeal things also holds for perception in general, namely, that, by being given in person in presence, it is a "sign for itself" (*Ideas 1*, § 52; ET, p. 161). Is being a sign of itself *(index sui)* the same as not being a sign? It is in this sense that, "in the very instant" it is perceived, experience is a sign of itself, present to itself without the indicative detour.

2. *ITC*, § 19; ET, p. 70.

3. It is perhaps opportune here to reread the definition of the "principle of principles." "But enough of such topsy-turvy theories! No theory we can conceive can mislead us in regard to the *principle of all principles:* that *every primordial dator Intuition is a source of authority (Rechtsquelle) for knowledge,* that *whatever presents itself in 'intuition' in primordial form* (as it were in its bodily reality), *is simply to be accepted as it gives itself out to be,* though *only within the limits in which it then presents itself.* Let our insight grasp this fact that the theory itself in its turn could not derive its truth

except from primordial data. Every statement which does nothing more than give expression to such data through merely unfolding their meaning and adjusting it accurately is thus really, as we have put it in the introductory words of this chapter, an *absolute beginning,* called in a genuine sense to provide foundations, a *principium*" (*Ideas* 1, § 24; ET, p. 92).

4. Cf., on this subject, our essay "Freud et la scène de l'écriture" in *L'Ecriture et la différence* (Paris: Seuil, 1967), pp. 293–340.

5. Cf., for example, among many analogous texts, Appendix III to *The Phenomenology of Internal Time-Consciousness.* "Accordingly, we have as essential modes of time-consciousness: (I) 'sensation' as actual presentation and essentially entwined *(verflochtene)* with it but also capable of autonomy, retention, and protention (originary spheres in the broader sense); (2) positing presentification (memory), co-presentification, and re-presentification (expectation); (3) phantasy-presentification as pure phantasy, in which all the same modes occur in phantasy-consciousness" (ET, p. 142). Here again, it will be observed, the core of the problem assumes the form of an interweaving *(Verflechtung)* of threads whose essences phenomenology carefully unravels.

This extension of the primordial sphere is what permits us to distinguish between the absolute certainty attached to retention and the relative certainty dependent upon secondary memory or recall *(Wiedererinnerung)* in the form of re-presentation. Speaking of perceptions as primal experiences *(Urerlebnisse),* Husserl writes in *Ideas I.* "For closer inspection reveals in their concreteness only *one,* but that always a continuously flowing *absolute primordial phase,* that of the living *now.* . . . Thus, for instance, we grasp the *absolute right* of immanent *perceiving* reflexion, i.e., of immanent perception *simpliciter,* and indeed in respect of that which it brings in its flow to real primordial givenness; likewise the *absolute right of immanent retention,* in respect of that in it of which we are conscious as 'still' living and having 'just' happened, but of course no further than the content of what is thus characterized reaches. . . . We likewise grasp the *relative* right of immanent recollection" *(Ideas I,* § 78; ET, pp. 221–22).

6. Particularly in § 77, where the problem of the difference and relations between reflection and representation is posed, for example, in secondary memory.

7. Cf., for example, § 42: "But to every present and presenting consciousness there corresponds the ideal possibility of an exactly matching presentification of this consciousness" (ET, p. 115).

The Outside ~~is~~ the Inside

The thesis of the *arbitrariness* of the sign (so grossly misnamed, and not only for the reasons Saussure himself recognizes)[1] must forbid a radical distinction between the linguistic and the graphic sign. No doubt this thesis concerns only the necessity of relationships between specific signifiers and signifieds *within* an allegedly natural relationship between the voice and sense in general, between the order of phonic signifiers and the content of the signifieds ("the only natural bond, the only true bond, the bond of sound"). Only these relationships between specific signifiers and signifieds would be regulated by arbitrariness. Within the "natural" relationship between phonic signifiers and their signifieds *in general*, the relationship between each determined signifier and its determined signified would be "arbitrary."

Now from the moment that one considers the totality of determined signs, spoken, and a fortiori written, as unmotivated institutions, one must exclude any relationship of natural subordination, any natural hierarchy among signifiers or orders of signifiers. If "writing" signifies inscription and especially the durable institution of a sign (and that is the only irreducible kernel of the concept of writing), writing in general covers the entire field of linguistic signs. In that field a certain sort of instituted signifiers may then appear, "graphic" in the narrow and derivative sense of the word, ordered by a certain relationship with other instituted—hence "written," even if they are "phonic"—signifiers. The very idea of institution—hence of the arbitrariness of the sign—is unthinkable before the possibility of writing and outside of its horizon. Quite simply, that is, outside of the horizon itself, outside the world as space of inscription, as the opening to the emission and to the spatial *distribution* of signs, to the *regulated play* of their differences, even if they are "phonic."

Let us now persist in using this opposition of nature and institution, of *physis* and *nomos* (which also means, of course, a distribution and division regulated in fact by *law*) which a meditation on writing should disturb although it functions everywhere as self-evident, particularly in the discourse of linguistics. We must then conclude that only the signs called *natural*, those that Hegel and Saussure call "symbols," escape semiology as grammatology. But they fall a fortiori outside the field of linguistics as the region of general semiology. The thesis of the arbitrariness of the sign thus indirectly but irrevocably contests Saussure's declared proposition when he chases writing to the outer darkness of language. This thesis successfully accounts for a conventional relationship between the phoneme and the grapheme (in phonetic writing, between the phoneme, signifier-signified, and the grapheme, pure signifier), but by the same token it forbids that the latter be an "image" of the former. Now it was indispensable to the exclusion of writing as "external system," that it come to impose an "image," a "representaton," or a "figuration," an exterior reflection of the reality of language.

It matters little, here at least, that there is in fact an ideographic filiation of the alphabet. This important question is much debated by historians of writing. What matters here is that in the synchronic structure and systematic principle of alphabetic writing—and phonetic writing in general—no relationship of "natural" representation, none of resemblance or participation, no "symbolic" relationship in the Hegelian-Saussurian sense, no "iconographic" relationship in the Peircian sense, be implied.

One must therefore challenge, in the very name of the arbitrariness of the sign, the Saussurian definition of writing as "image"—hence as natural symbol—of language. Not to mention the fact that the phoneme is the *unimaginable* itself, and no visibility can *resemble* it, it suffices to take into account what Saussure says about the difference between the symbol and the sign (p. 101) [pp. 68–69] in order to be completely baffled as to how he can at the same time say of writing that it is an "image" or "figuration" of language and define language and writing elsewhere as "two distinct systems of signs" (p. 45) [p. 23]. For the property of the sign is not to be an image. By a process exposed by Freud in *The Interpretation of Dreams*, Saussure thus accumulates contradictory arguments to bring about a satisfactory decision: the exclusion of writing. In fact, even within so-called phonetic writing, the "graphic" signifier refers to the phoneme through a web of many dimensions which binds it, like all signifiers, to other written and oral signifiers, within a "total" system open, let us say, to all possible investments of sense. We must begin with the possibility of that total system.

Saussure was thus never able to think that writing was truly an "image," a "figuration," a "representation" of the spoken language, a symbol. If one considers that he nonetheless needed these inadequate notions to decide upon the exteriority of writing, one must conclude that an entire stratum of his discourse, the intention of Chapter VI ("Graphic Representation of Language"), was not at all scientific. When I say this, my quarry is not primarily Ferdinand de Saussure's intention or motivation, but rather the entire uncritical tradition which he inherits. To what zone of discourse does this strange functioning of argumentation belong, this coherence of desire producing itself in a near-oneiric way—although it clarifies the dream rather than allow itself to be clarified by it—through a contradictory logic? How is this functioning articulated with the entirety of theoretical discourse, throughout the history of science? Better yet, bow does it work from within the concept of science itself? It is only when this question is elaborated—if it is some day—wben the concepts required by this functioning are defined outside of all psychology (as of all sciences of man), outside metaphysics (which can now be "Marxist" or "structuralist"); when one is able to respect all its levels of generality and articulation—it is only then that one will be able to state rigorously the problem of the articulated appurtenance of a text (theoretical or otherwise) to an entire set: I obviously treat the Saussurian text at the moment only as a telling example within a given situation, without professing to use the concepts required by the functioning of which I have just spoken. My justification would be as follows: this and some other indices (in a general way the treatment of the concept of writing) already give us the assured means of broaching the de-construction of *the greatest totality*—the concept of the *epistémè* and logocentric metaphysics-within which are produced, without ever posing the radical question of writing, all the Western methods of analysis, explication, reading, or interpretation.

Now we must think that writing is at the same time more exterior to speech, not being its "image" or its "symbol," and more interior to speech, which is already in itself a writing. Even before it is linked to incision, engraving, drawing, or the letter, to a signifier referring in general to a signifier signified by it, the concept of the *graphie* [unit of a possible graphic system] implies the framework of the *instituted trace*, as the possibility common to all systems of signification. My efforts will now be directed toward slowly detaching these two concepts from the classical discourse from which I necessarily borrow them. The effort will be laborious and we know a priori that its effectiveness will never be pure and absolute.

The instituted trace is "unmotivated" but not capricious. Like the word "arbitrary" according to Saussure, it "should not imply that the choice of the signifier is left entirely to the speaker" (p. 101) [pp. 68–69]. Simply, it has no "natural attachment" to the signified within reality. For us, the rupture of that "natural attachment" puts in question the idea of naturalness rather than that of attachment. That is why the word "institution" should not be too quickly interpreted within the classical system of oppositions.

The instituted trace cannot be thought without thinking the retention of difference within a structure of reference where difference appears *as such* and thus permits a certain liberty of variations among the full terms. The absence of *another* here-and-now, of another transcendental present, of *another* origin of the world appearing as such, presenting itself as irreducible absence within the presence of the trace, is not a metaphysical formula substituted for a scientific concept of writing. This formula, beside the fact that it is the questioning of metaphysics itself, describes the structure implied by the "arbitrariness of the sign," from the moment that one thinks of its possibility *short of* the derived opposition between nature and convention, symbol and sign, etc. These oppositions have meaning only after the possibility of the trace. The "unmotivatedness" of the sign requires a synthesis in which the completely other is announced as such—without any simplicity, any identity, any resemblance or continuity—within what is not it. *Is announced as such:* there we have all *history,* from what metaphysics has defined as "non-living" up to "consciousness," passing through all levels of animal organization. The trace, where the relationship with the other is marked, articulates its possibility in the entire field of the entity *[étant],* which metaphysics has defined as the being-present starting from the occulted movement of the trace. The trace must be thought before the entity. But the movement of the trace is necessarily occulted, it produces itself as self-occultation. When the other announces itself as such, it presents itself in the dissimulation of itself. This formulation is not theological, as one might believe somewhat hastily. The "theological" is a determined moment in the total movement of the trace. The field of the entity, before being determined as the field of presence, is structured according to the diverse possibilities—genetic and structural—of the trace. The presentation of the other as such, that is to say the dissimulation of its "as such," has always already begun and no structure of the entity escapes it.

That is why the movement of "unmotivatedness" passes from one structure to the other when the "sign" crosses the stage of the "symbol." It is in a certain sense and according to a certain determined structure of the "as such" that one is authorized to say that there is yet no immotivation in what Saussure calls "symbol" and which, according to him, does not—at least provisionally—interest semiology. The general structure of the unmotivated trace connects within the same possibility, and they cannot be separated except by abstraction, the structure of the relationship with the other, the movement of temporalization, and language as writing. Without referring back to a "nature," the immotivation of the trace has always *become.* In fact, there is no unmotivated trace: the trace is indefinitely its own becoming-unmotivated. In Saussurian language, what Saussure does not say would have to be said: there is neither symbol nor sign but a becoming-sign of the symbol.

Thus, as it goes without saying, the trace whereof I speak is not more *natural* (it is not the mark, the natural sign, or the index in the Husserlian sense) than *cultural,* not more physical than psychic, biological than spiritual. It is that starting from which a becoming-unmotivated of the sign, and with it all the ulterior oppositions between *physis* and its other, is possible.

In his project of semiotics, Peirce seems to have been more attentive than Saussure to the irreducibility of this becoming-un motivated. In his terminology, one must speak of a becoming-unmotivated of the *symbol,* the notion of the symbol playing here a role analogous to that of the sign which Saussure opposes precisely to the symbol:

> Symbols grow. They come into being by development out of other signs, particularly from icons, or from mixed signs partaking of the nature of icons and symbols. We think only in signs. These mental signs are of mixed nature; the symbol parts of them are called concepts. If a man makes a new symbol, it is by thoughts involving concepts. So it is only out of symbols that a new symbol can grow. Omne symbolum de symbolo.[2]

Peirce complies with two apparently incompatible exigencies. The mistake here would be to sacrifice one for the other. It must be recognized that the symbolic (in Peirce's sense: of "the arbitrariness of the sign") is rooted in the nonsymbolic, in an anterior and related order of signification: "Symbols grow. They come into being by development out of other signs, particularly from icons, or from mixed signs." But these roots must not compromise the structural originality of the field of symbols, the autonomy of a domain, a production, and a play: "So it is only out of symbols that a new symbol can grow. Onme symbolum de symbolo."

But in both cases, the genetic root-system refers from sign to sign. No ground of nonsignification—understood as insignificance or an intuition of a present truth—stretches out to give it foundation under the play and the coming into being of signs. Semiotics no longer depends on logic. Logic, according to Peirce, is only a semiotic: "Logic, in its general sense, is, as I believe I have shown, only another name for semiotics *(semeiotike),* the quasi-necessary, or formal, doctrine of signs." And logic in the classical sense, logic "properly speaking," nonformal logic commanded by the value of truth, occupies in that semiotics only a determined and not a fundamental level. As in Husserl (but the analogy, although it is most thought-provoking, would stop there and one must apply it carefully), the lowest level, the foundation of the possibility of logic (or semiotics) corresponds to the project of the *Grammatica speculativa* of Thomas d'Erfurt, falsely attributed to Duns Scotus. Like Husserl, Peirce expressly refers to it. It is a matter of elaborating, in both cases, a formal doctrine of conditions which a discourse must satisfy in order to have a sense, in order to "mean," even if it is false or contradictory. The general morphology of that meaning[3] *(Bedeutung, vouloir-dire)* is independent of all logic of truth.

> The science of semiotic has three branches. The first is called by Duns Scotus *grammatica speculativa*. We may term it *pure grammar*. It has for its task to ascertain what must be true of the representamen used by every scientific intelligence in order that they may embody any *meaning*. The second is logic proper. It is the science of what is quasi-necessarily true of the representamina of any scientific intelligence in order that they may hold good of any *object*, that is, may be true. Or say, logic proper is the formal science of the conditions of the truth of representations, The third, in imitation of Kant's fashion of preserving old associations of words in finding nomenclature for new conceptions, I call *pure rhetoric*. Its task is to ascertain the laws by which in every scientific intelligence one sign gives birth to another, and especially one thought brings forth another.[4]

Peirce goes very far in the direction that I have called the de-construction of the transcendental signified, which, at one time or another, would place a reassuring end to the reference from sign to sign. I have identified logocentrism and the metaphysics of presence as the exigent, powerful, systematic, and irrepressible desire for such a signified. Now Peirce considers the indefiniteness of reference as the criterion that allows us to recognize that we are indeed dealing with a system of signs. *What broaches the movement of signification is what makes its interruption impossible. The thing itself is a sign.* An unacceptable proposition for Husserl, whose phenomenology remains therefore—in its "principle of principles"—the most radical and most critical restoration of the metaphysics of presence. The difference between Husserl's and Peirce's phenomenologics is fundamental since it concerns the concept of the sign and of the manifestation of presence, the relationships between the re-presentation and the originary presentation of the thing itself (truth). On this point Peirce is undoubtedly closer to the inventor of the word *phenomenology:* Lambert proposed in fact to "reduce *the theory of things* to the *theory of signs*." According to the "phaneoroscopy" or "phenomenology" of Peirce, *manifestation* itself does not reveal a presence, it makes a sign. One may read in the *Principle of Phenomenology* that "the idea of *manifestation is* the idea of a sign."[5] There is thus no phenomenality reducing the sign or the representer so that the thing signified may be allowed to glow finally in the luminosity of its presence. The so-called "thing itself" is always already a *representamen* shielded from the simplicity of intuitive evidence. The *representamen* functions only by giving rise to an *interpretant* that itself becomes a sign and so on to infinity. The self-identity of the signified conceals itself unceasingly and is always on the move. The property of the *representamen is* to be itself and another, to be produced as a structure of reference, to be separated from itself. The property of the *representamen* is not to be *proper [propre]*, that is to say absolutely *proximate* to itself *(prope, proprius)*. The *represented* is always already a *representamen*. Definition of the sign:

> *Anything which determines something else (its interpretant) to refer to an object to which itself refers (its object) in the same way, this interpretant becoming in turn a sign, and so on ad infinitum. . . .* If the series of successive interpretants comes to an end, the sign is thereby rendered imperfect, at least.[6]

From the moment that there is meaning there are nothing but signs. We *think only in signs.* Which amounts to ruining the notion of the sign at the very moment when, as in Nietzsche, its exigency is recognized in the absoluteness of its right. One could call *play* the absence of the transcendental signified as limitlessness of play, that is to say as the destruction of ontotheology and the metaphysics of presence. It is not surprising that the shock, shaping and undermining metaphysics since its origin, lets itself *be named as such* in the period when, refusing to bind linguistics to semantics (which all European linguists, from Saussure to Hjemslev, still do), expelling the problem of *meaning* outside of their researches, certain American linguists constantly refer to the model of a game. Here one must think of writing as a game within language. (The *Phaedrus* (277e) condemned writing precisely as play—*paidia*—and opposed such childishness to the adult gravity *[spoudè]* of speech). This *play,* thought as absence of the transcendental signified, is not a play *in the* world, as it has always been defined, for the purposes of *containing* it, by the philosophical tradition and as the theoreticians of play also consider it (or those who, following and going beyond Bloomfield, refer semantics to psychology or some other local discipline). To think play radically the ontological and transcendental problematics must first be seriously *exhausted;* the question of the meaning of being, the being of the entity and of the transcendental origin of the world—of the world-ness of the world—must be patiently and rigorously worked through, the critical movement of the Husserlian and Heideggerian questions must be effectively followed to the very end, and their effectiveness and legibility must be conserved. Even if it were crossed out, without it the concepts of play and writing to which I shall have recourse will remain caught within regional limits and an empiricist, positivist, or metaphysical discourse. The counter-move that the holders of such a discourse would oppose to the precritical tradition and to metaphysical speculation would be nothing but the worldly representation of their own operation. It is therefore *the game of the world* that must be first thought; before attempting to understand all the forms of play in the world.[7]

From the very opening of the game, then, we are within the becoming-unmotivated of the symbol. With regard to this becoming, the opposition of diachronic and synchronic is also derived. It would not be able to command a grammatology pertinently. The immotivation of the trace ought now to be understood as an operation and not as a state, as an active movement, a demotivation, and not as a given structure. Science of "the arbitrariness of the sign," science of the immotivation of the trace, science of writing before speech and in speech, grammatology would thus cover a vast field within which linguistics would, by abstraction, delineate its own area, with the limits that Saussure prescribes to its internal system and which must be carefully reexamined in each speech/writing system in the world and history.

By a substitution which would be anything but verbal, one may replace *semiology* by *grammatology* in the program of the *Course in General Linguistics:*

> I shall call it [grammatology]. . . . Since the science does not yet exist, no one can say what it would be; but it has a right to existence, a place staked out in advance. Linguistics is only a part of [that] general science . . . ; the laws discovered by [grammatology] will be applicable to linguistics. (p. 33) [p. 16].

The advantage of this substitution will not only be to give to the theory of writing the scope needed to counter logocentric repression and the subordination to linguistics. It will liberate the semiological project itself from what, in spite of its greater theoretical extension, remained *governed* by linguistics, organized as if linguistics were at once its center and its telos. *Even though semiology was in fact more general and more comprehensive than linguistics, it continued to be regulated as if it were one of the areas of linguistics. The linguistic sign remained exemplary for semiology*, it dominated it as the master-sign and as the generative model: the pattern *[patron]*.

> One could therefore say that signs that are wholly arbitrary realize better than the others the ideal of the semiological process; that is why language, the most complex and universal of all svstems of expression, is also the most characteristic; in this sense linguistics can become *the master-pattern for all branches of semiology* although language is only one particular semiological system (p. 101; italics added) [p. 68].

Consequently, reconsidering the order of dependence prescribed by Saussure, apparently inverting the relationship of the part to the whole, Barthes in fact carries out the profoundest intention of the *Course:*

> From now on we must admit the possibility of reversing Saussure's proposition some day: linguistics is not a part, even if privileged, of the general science of signs, it is semiology that is a part of linguistics.[8]

This coherent reversal, submitting semiology to a "translinguistics," leads to its full explication a linguistics historically dominated by logocentric metaphysics, for which in fact there is not and there should not be "any meaning except as named" (ibid.). Dominated by the so-called "civilization of writing" that we inhabit, a civilization of so-called phonetic writing, that is to say of the logos where the sense of being is, in its telos, determined as parousia. The Barthesian reversal is fecund and indispensable for the description of the *fact and the vocation of signification* within the closure of this epoch and this civilization that is in the process of disappearing in its very globalization.

Let us now try to go beyond these formal and architectonic considerations. Let us ask in a more intrinsic and concrete way, how language is not merely a sort of writing, "comparable to a system of writing" (p. 33) [p. 16]—Saussure writes curiously—but a species *of* writing. Or rather, since writing no longer relates to language as an extension or frontier, let us ask how language is a possibility founded on the general possibility of writing. Demonstrating this, one would give at the same time an account of that alleged "usurpation" which could not be an unhappy accident. It supposes on the contrary a common root and thus excludes the resemblance of the "image," derivation, or representative reflexion. And thus one would bring back to its true meaning, to its primary possibility, the apparently innocent and didactic analogy which makes Saussure say:

> Language is [comparable to] a system of signs that express ideas, and is therefore *comparable to writing*, the alphabet of deaf-mutes, symbolic rites, polite formulas, military signals, etc. But it is the most important of all these systems (p. 33; italics added) [p. 16].

Further, it is not by chance that, a hundred and thirty pages later, at the moment of explaining *phonic difference* as the condition of linguistic *value* ("from a material viewpoint"),[9] he must again borrow all his pedagogic resources from the example of writing:

> Since an identical state of affairs is observable in writing, another system of signs, we shall use writing to draw some comparisons that will clarify the whole issue (p. 165) [p. 119].

Four demonstrative items, borrowing pattern and content from writing, follow.[10]

Once more, then, we definitely have to oppose Saussure to himself. Before being or not being "noted" "represented," "figured," in a "*graphie*," the linguistic sign implies an originary writing. Henceforth, it is not to the thesis of the arbitrariness of the sign that I shall appeal directly, but to what Saussure associates with it as an indispensable correlative and which would seem to me rather to lay the foundations for it: the thesis of *difference* as the source of linguistic value.[11]

What are, from the grammatological point of view, the consequences of this theme that is now so well-known (and upon which Plato already reflected in the *Sophist*)?

By definition, difference is never in itself a sensible plenitude. Therefore, its necessity contradicts the allegation of a naturally phonic essence of language. It contests by the same token the professed natural dependence of the graphic signifier. That is a consequence Saussure himself draws against the premises defining the internal system of language. He must now exclude the very thing which had permitted him to exclude writing: sound and its "natural bond" *[lien naturel]* with meaning. For example: "The thing that constitutes language is, as I shall show later, unrelated to the phonic character of the linguistic sign" (p. 21) [p. 7]. And in a paragraph on difference:

> It is impossible for sound alone, a material element, to belong to language. It is only a secondary thing, substance to be put to use. All our conventional values have the characteristic of not being confused with the tangible element which supports them. . . . The linguistic signifier . . . is not [in essence] phonic but incorporeal—constituted not by its material substance but the differences that separate its sound-image from all others (p. 164) [pp. 118–19]. The idea or phonic substance that a sign contains is of less importance than the other signs that surround it (p. 166) [p. 120].

Without this reduction of phonic matter, the distinction between language and speech, decisive for Saussure, would have no rigor. It would be the same for the oppositions that happened to descend from it: between code and message, pattern and usage, etc. Conclusion: "Phonology—this bears repeating—is only an auxiliary discipline [of the science of language] and belongs exclusively to speaking" (p. 56) [p. 33]. Speech thus draws from this stock of writing, noted or not, that language is, and it is here that one must meditate upon the complicity between the two "stabilities." The reduction of the *phonè* reveals this complicity. What Saussure says, for example, about the sign in general and what he "confirms" through the example of writing, applies also to language: "Signs are governed by a principle of general semiology: continuity in time is coupled to change in time; this is confirmed by orthrographic systems, the speech of deaf-mutes, etc." (p. 111) [p. 16].

The reduction of phonic substance thus does not only permit the distinction between phonetics on the one hand (and a fortiori accoustics or the physiology of the phonating organs) and phonology on the other. It also makes of phonology itself an "auxiliary discipline." Here the direction indicated by Saussure takes us beyond the phonologism of those who profess to follow him on this point: in fact, Jakobson believes indifference to the phonic substance of expression to be impossible and illegitimate. He thus criticizes the glossematics of Hjelmslev which requires and practices the neutralizing of sonorous substance. And in the text cited above, Jakobson and Halle maintain that the "theoretical requirement" of a research of invariables placing sonorous substance in parenthesis (as an empirical and contingent content) is:

1. *impracticable* since, as "Eli Fischer-Jorgensen exposes [it]," "the sonorous substance [is taken into account] at every step of the analysis."[12] But is that a

"troubling discrepancy," as Jakobson and Halle would have it? Can one not account for it as a fact serving as an example, as do the phenomenologists who always need, keeping it always within sight, an exemplary empirical content in the reading of an essence which is independent of it by right?

2. *inadmissible in principle* since one cannot consider "that in language form is opposed to substance as a constant to a variable." It is in the course of this second demonstration that the literally Saussurian formulas reappear within the question of the relationships between speech and writing; the order of writing is the order of exteriority, of the "occasional," of the "accessory," of the "auxiliary," of the "*parasitic*" (pp. 116–17; italics added) [pp. 16–17]. The argument of Jakobson and Halle appeals to the factual genesis and invokes the secondariness of writing in the colloquial sense: "Only after having mastered speech does one graduate to reading and writing." Even if this commonsensical proposition were rigorously proved—something that I do not believe (since each of its concepts harbors an immense problem)—one would still have to receive assurance of its pertinence to the argument. Even if "after" were here a facile representation, if one knew perfectly well what one thought and stated while assuring that one learns to write *after* having learned to speak, would that suffice to conclude that what thus comes "after" is parasitic? And what is a parasite? And what if writing were precisely that which makes us reconsider our logic of the parasite?

In another moment of the critique, Jakobson and Halle recall the imperfection of graphic representation; that imperfection is due to "the cardinally dissimilar patterning of letters and phonemes:"

> Letters never, or only partially, reproduce the different distinctive features on which the phonemic pattern is based and unfailingly disregard the structural relationship of these features (p. 116) [p. 17].

I have suggested it above: does not the radical dissimilarity of the two elements—graphic and phonic—exclude derivation? Does not the inadequacy of graphic representation concern only common alphabetic writing, to which glossematic formalism does not essentially refer? Finally, if one accepts all the phonologist arguments thus presented, it must still be recognized that they oppose a "scientific" concept of the spoken word to a vulgar concept of writing. What I would wish to show is that one cannot exclude writing from the general experience of "the structural relationship of these features." Which amounts, of course, to reforming the concept of writing.

In short, if the Jakobsonian analysis is faithful to Saussure in this matter, is it not especially so to the Saussure of Chapter VI? Up to what point would Saussure have maintained the inseparability of matter and form, which remains the most important argument of Jakobson and Halle (p. 117) [p. 17]? The question may be repeated in the case of the position of André Martinet who, in this debate, follows Chapter VI of the *Course* to the letter.[13] And only Chapter VI, from which Martinet *expressly* dissociates the doctrine of what, in the *Course*, effaces the privilege of phonic substance. After having explained why "a dead language with a perfect ideography," that is to say a communication effective through the system of a generalized script, "could not have any real autonomy," and why *nevertheless*, "such a system would be something so particular that one can well understand why linguists *want to exclude it* from the domain of their science" (*La linguistique syncronique*, p. 18; italics added), Martinet criticizes those who, following a certain trend in Saussure, question the essentially phonic character of the linguistic sign: "Much will be attempted to prove that Saussure is right when be announces that 'the thing that constitutes language *[l'essentiel de la langue]* is . . . unrelated to the phonic character of the linguistic sign,' and, going beyond the teaching of the master, to declare that the linguistic sign does not necessarily have that phonic character" (p. 19).

On that precise point, it is not a question of "going beyond" the master's teaching but of following and extending it. Not to do it is to cling to what in Chapter VI greatly limits formal and structural research and contradicts the least contestable findings of Saussurian doctrine. To avoid "going beyond," one risks returning to a point that falls short.

I believe that generalized writing is not just the idea of a system to be invented, an hypothetical characteristic or a future possibility. I think on the contrary that oral language already belongs to this writing. But that presupposes a modification of the concept of writing that we for the moment merely anticipate. Even supposing that one is not given that modified concept, supposing that one is considering a system of pure writing as an hypothesis for the future or a working hypothesis, faced with that hypothesis, should a linguist refuse himself the means of thinking it and of integrating its formulation within his theoretical discourse? Does the fact that most linguists do so create a theoretical right? Martinet seems to be of that opinion. After having elaborated a purely "dactylological" hypothesis of language, he writes, in effect:

> It must be recognized that the parallelism between this "dactylology" and phonology is complete as much in synchronic as in diachronic material, and that the terminology associated with the latter may be used for the former, except of course when the terms refer to the phonic substance. Clearly, if we do not *desire* to exclude from the domain of linguistics the systems of the type we have just imagined, it is most important to modify traditional terminology relative to the articulation of signifiers so as to eliminate all reference to phonic substance; as does Louis Hjelmslev when he uses "ceneme" and "cenematics" instead of "phoneme" and "phonematics." *Yet it is understandable that the majority of linguists hesitate to modify completely the traditional terminological edifice for the only theoretical advantages of being able to include in the field of their science some purely hypothetical systems. To make them agree to envisage such a revolution,*

> they must be persuaded that, in attested linguistic systems, they have no advantage in considering the phonic substance of units of expression as to be of direct interest (pp. 20–21; italics added).

Once again, we do not doubt the value of these phonological arguments, the presuppositions behind which I have attempted to expose above. Once one assumes these presuppositions, it would be absurd to reintroduce confusedly a derivative writing, in the area of oral language and within the system of this derivation. Not only would ethnocentrism not be avoided, but all the frontiers within the sphere of its legitimacy would then be confused. It is not a question of rehabilitating writing in the narrow sense, nor of reversing the order of dependence when it is evident. Phonologism does not brook any objections as long as one conserves the colloquial concepts of speech and writing which form the solid fabric of its argumentation. Colloquial and quotidian conceptions, inhabited besides—uncontradictorily enough—by an old history, limited by frontiers that are hardly visible yet all the more rigorous by that very fact.

I would wish rather to suggest that the alleged derivativeness of writing, however real and massive, was possible only on one condition: that the "original," "natural," etc. language had never existed, never been intact and untouched by writing, that it had itself always been a writing. An arche-writing whose necessity and new concept I wish to indicate and outline here; and which I continue to call writing only because it essentially communicates with the vulgar concept of writing. The latter could not have imposed itself historically except by the dissimulation of the arche-writing, by the desire for a speech displacing its other and its double and working to reduce its difference. If I persist in calling that difference writing, it is because, within the work of historical repression, writing was, by its situation, destined to signify the most formidable difference. It threatened the desire for the living speech from the closest proximity, it *breached* living speech from within and from the very beginning. And as we shall begin to see, difference cannot be thought without the *trace*.

This arche-writing, although its concept is *invoked* by the themes of "the arbitrariness of the sign" and of difference, cannot and can never be recognized as the *object of a science*. It is that very thing which cannot let itself be reduced to the form of *presence*. The latter orders all objectivity of the object and all relation of knowledge. That is why what I would be tempted to consider in the development of the *Course* as "progress," calling into question in return the uncritical positions of Chapter VI, never gives rise to a new "scientific" concept of writing.

Can one say as much of the algebraism of Hjelmslev, which undoubtedly drew the most rigorous conclusions from that progress?

The *Principes de grammaire générale* (1928) separated out within the doctrine of the *Course* the phonological principle and the principle of difference:

It isolated a concept of *form* which permitted a distinction between formal difference and phonic difference, and this even within " spoken" language (p. 117). Grammar is independent of semantics and phonology (p. 118).

That independence is the very principle of glossematics as the formal science of language. Its formality supposes that "there is no necessary connexion between sounds and language."[14] That formality is itself the condition of a purely functional analysis. The idea of a linguistic function and of a purely linguistic unit—the glosseme—excludes then not only the consideration of the substance of expression (material substance) but also that of the substance of the content (immaterial substance). "Since language is a form and not a substance (Saussure), the glossemes are by definition independent of substance, immaterial (semantic, psychological and logical) and material (phonic, graphic, etc.)."[15] The study of the functioning of language, of its *play*, presupposes that the substance of *meaning* and, among other possible substances, that of *sound*, be placed in parenthesis. The unity of sound and of sense is indeed here, as I proposed above, the reassuring closing of play. Hjelmslev situates his concept of the *scheme* or *play* of language within Saussure's heritage—of Saussure's formalism and his theory of value. Although he prefers to compare linguistic value to the "value of exchange in the economic sciences" rather than to the "purely logico-mathematical value," he assigns a limit to this analogy.

> An economic value is by definition a value with two faces: not only does it play the role of a constant vis-à-vis the concrete units of money, but it also itself plays the role of a variable vis-à-vis a fixed quantity of merchandise which serves it as a standard. In linguistics on the other hand there is nothing that corresponds to a standard. That is why the game of chess and not economic fact remains for Saussure the most faithful image of a grammar. The scheme of language is in the last analysis *a game* and nothing more.[16]

In the *Prolegomera to a Theory of Language* (1943), setting forth the opposition *expression/content*, which he substitutes for the difference *signifier/signified*, and in which each term may be considered from the point of view of *form* or *substance*, Hjelmslev criticizes the idea of a language *naturally* bound to the substance of phonic expression. It is by mistake that it has hitherto been supposed "that the substance-expression of a spoken language should consist of 'sounds'":

> Thus, as has been pointed out by the Zwirners in particular, the fact has been overlooked that speech is accompanied by, and that certain components of speech can be replaced by, gesture, and that in reality, as the Zwirners say, not only the so- called organs of speech (throat, mouth, and nose), but very nearly all the striate musculature cooperate in the exercise of "natural" language. Further,

> it is possible to replace the usual sound-and-gesture substance with any other that offers itself as appropriate under changed external circumstances. Thus the same linguistic form may also be manifested in writing, as happens with a phonetic or phonemic notation and with the so-called phonetic orthographies, as for example the Finnish. Here is a "graphic" substance which is addressed exclusively to the eye and which need not be transposed into a phonetic "substance" in order to be grasped or understood. And this graphic "substance" can, precisely from the point of view of the substance, be of quite various sorts.[17]

Refusing to presuppose a "derivation" of substances following from the substance of phonic expression, Hjelmslev places this problem outside the area of structural analysis and of linguistics.

> Moreover it is not always certain what is derived and what not; we must not forget that the discovery of alphabetic writing is hidden in prehistory [n.: Bertrand Russell quite rightly calls attention to the fact that we have no means of deciding whether writing or speech is the older form of human expression (An *Outline of Philosophy* [London, 1927], p. 47), so that the assertion that it rests on a phonetic analysis is only one of the possible diachronic hypotheses; it may also be rested on a formal analysis of linguistic structure. But in any case, as is recognized by modern linguistics, diacbronic considerations are irrelevant for synchronic descriptions (pp. 104–05).

H. J. Uldall provides a remarkable formulation of the fact that glossematic criticism operates at the same time thanks to Saussure and against him; that, as I suggested above, the proper space of a grammatology is at the same time opened and closed by *The Course in General Linguistics*. To show that Saussure did not develop "all the theoretical consequences of his discovery," he writes:

> It is even more curious when we consider that the practical consequences have been widely drawn, indeed had been drawn thousands of years before Saussure, for it is only through the concept of a difference between form and substance that we can explain the possibility of speech and writing existing at the same time as expressions of one and the same language. If either of these two substances, the stream of air or the stream of ink, were an integral part of the language itself, it would not be possible to go from one to the other without changing the language.[18]

Undoubtedly the Copenhagen School thus frees a field of research: it becomes possible to direct attention not only to the purity of a form freed from all "natural" bonds to a substance but also to everything that, in the stratification of language, depends on the substance of graphic expression. An original and rigorously delimited description of this may thus be promised. Hjelmslev recognizes that an "analysis of writing without regard to sound has not yet been undertaken" (p. 105) . While regretting also that "the substance of ink has not received the same attention on the part of linguists that they have so lavishly bestowed on the substance of air," H. J. Uldall delimits these problems and emphasizes the mutual independence of the substances of expression. He illustrates it particularly by the fact that, in orthography, no grapheme corresponds to accents of pronunciation (for Rousseau this was the misery and the menace of writing) and that, reciprocally, in pronunciation, no phoneme corresponds to the spacing between written words (pp. 13–14).

Recognizing the specificity of *writing*, glossematics did not merely give itself the means of describing the *graphic* element. It showed how to reach the *literary* element, to what in literature passes through an irreducibly graphic text, tying the *play of form* to a determined substance of expression. If there is something in literature which does not allow itself to be reduced to the voice, to epos or to poetry, one cannot recapture it except by rigorously isolating the bond that links *the play of form* to the substance of graphic expression. (It will by the same token be seen that "pure literature," thus respected in its irreducibilty, also risks limiting the play, restricting it. The desire to restrict play is, moreover, irresistible.) This interest in literature is effectively manifested in the Copenhagen School.[19] It thus removes the Rousseauist and Saussurian caution with regard to literary arts. It radicalizes the efforts of the Russian formalists, specifically of the O.PO.IAZ, who, in their attention to the being-literary of literature, perhaps favored the phonological instance and the literary models that it dominates. Notably poetry. That which, within the history of literature and in the structure of a literary text in general, escapes that framework, merits a type of description whose norms and conditions of possibility glossematics has perhaps better isolated. It has perhaps thus better prepared itself to study the purely graphic stratum within the structure of the literary text within the history of the becoming-literary of literality, notably in its "modernity."

Undoubtedly a new domain is thus opened to new and fecund researches. But I am not primarily interested in such a parallelism or such a recaptured parity of substances of expression. It is clear that if the phonic substance lost its privilege, it was not to the advantage of the graphic substance, which lends itself to the same substitutions. To the extent that it liberates and is irrefutable, glossematics still operates with a popular concept of writing. However original and irreducible it might be, the "form of expression" linked by correlation to the *graphic* "substance of expression" remains very determined. It is very dependent and very derivative with regard to the arche-writing of which I speak. This arche-writing would be at work not only in the form and substance of graphic expression but also in those of nongraphic expression. It would constitute not only the pattern uniting form to all substance, graphic or otherwise, but the movement of the *sign-function* linking a content to an expression, whether it be graphic or not. This theme could not have a place in Hjelmslev's system.

It is because arche-writing, movement of differance, irreducible arche-synthesis, opening in one and the same possibility, temporalization as well as relationship with the other and language, cannot, as the condition of all linguistic systems, form a part of the linguistic system itself and be situated as an object in its field. (Which does not mean it has a real field *elsewhere, another* assignable *site.*) Its concept could in no way enrich the scientific, positive, and "immanent" (in the Hjelmslevian sense) description of the system itself. Therefore, the founder of glossematics would no doubt have questioned its necessity, as he rejects, en bloc and legitimately, all the extralinguistic theories which do not arise from the irreducible immanence of the linguistic system .[20] He would have seen in that notion one of those appeals to experience which a theory should dispense with.[21] He would not have understood why the name writing continued to be used for that X which becomes so different from what has always been called "writing."

I have already begun to justify this word, and especially the necessity of the communication between the concept of arche-writing and the vulgar concept of writing submitted to deconstruction by it. I shall continue to do so below. As for the concept of experience, it is most unwieldy here. Like all the notions I am using here, it belongs to the history of metaphysics and we can only use it under erasure *[sous rature]*. "Experience" has always designated the relationship with a presence, whether that relationship had the form of consciousness or not. At any rate, we must, according to this sort of contortion and contention which the discourse is obliged to undergo, exhaust the resources of the concept of experience before attaining and in order to attain, by deconstruction, its ultimate foundation. It is the only way to escape "empiricism" and the "naive" critiques of experience at the same time. Thus, for example, the experience whose "theory," Hjelmslev says, "must be independent" is not the whole of experience. It always corresponds to a certain type of factual or regional experience (historical, psychological, physiological, sociological, etc.), giving rise to a science that is itself regional and, as such, rigorously outside linguistics. That is not so at all in the case of experience as arche-writing. The parenthesizing of regions of experience or of the totality of natural experience must discover a field of transcendental experience. This experience is only accessible in so far as, after having, like Hjelmslev, isolated the specificity of the linguistic system and excluded all the extrinsic sciences and metaphysical speculations, one asks the question of the transcendental origin of the system itself, as a system of the objects of a science, and, correlatively, of the theoretical system which studies it: here of the objective and "deductive" system which glossematics wishes to be. Without that, the decisive progress accomplished by a formalism respectful of the originality of its object, of "the immanent system of its objects," is plagued by a scientificist objectivism, that is to say by another unperceived or unconfessed metaphysics. This is often noticeable in the work of the Copenhagen School. It is to escape falling back into this naive objectivism that I refer here to a transcendentality that I elsewhere put into question. It is because I believe that there is a short-of and a beyond of transcendental criticism. To see to it that the beyond does not return to the within is to recognize in the contortion the necessity of a pathway *[parcours]*. That pathway must leave a track in the text. Without that track, abandoned to the simple content of its conclusions, the ultra-transcendental text will so closely resemble the precritical text as to be indistingiusbable from it. We must now form and meditate upon the law of this resemblance. What I call the erasure of concepts ought to mark the places of that future meditation. For example, the value of the transcendental arche *[archie]* must make its necessity felt before letting itself be erased. The concept of arche-trace must comply with both that necessity and that erasure. It is in fact contradictory and not acceptable within the logic of identity. The trace is not only the disappearance of origin—within the discourse that we sustain and according to the path that we follow it means that the origin did not even disappear, that it was never constituted except reciprocally by a nonorigin, the trace, which thus becomes the origin of the origin. From then on, to wrench the concept of the trace from the classical scheme, which would derive it from a presence or from an originary nontrace and which would make of it an empirical mark, one must indeed speak of an originary trace or arche-trace. Yet we know that that concept destroys its name and that, if all begins with the trace, there is above all no originary trace.[22] We must then *situate*, as a simple *moment of the discourse*, the phenomenological reduction and the Husserlian reference to a transcendental experience. To the extent that the concept of experience in general—and of transcendental experience, in Husserl in particular—remains governed by the theme of presence, it participates in the movement of the reduction of the trace. The Living Present *(lebendige Gegenwart)* is the universal and absolute form of transcendental experience to which Husserl refers us. In the descriptions of the movements of temporalization, all that does not torment the simplicity and the domination of that form seems to indicate to us how much transcendental phenomenology belongs to metaphysics. But that must come to terms with the forces of rupture. In the originary temporalization and the movement of relationship with the outside, as Husserl actually describes them, nonpresentation or depresentation is as "originary" as presentation. *That is why a thought of the trace can no more break with a transcendental phenomenology than be reduced to it.* Here as elsewhere, to pose the problem in terms of choice, to oblige or to believe oneself obliged to answer it by a *yes* or *no*, to conceive of appurtenance as an allegiance or nonappurtenance as plain speaking, is to confuse very different levels, paths, and styles. In the deconstruction of the arche, one does not make a choice.

Therefore I admit the necessity of going through the concept of the arche-trace. How does that necessity direct us from the interior of the linguistic system? How does the path that leads from Saussure to Hjelmslev forbid us to avoid the originary trace?

In that its passage through *form* is a passage through the *imprint*. And the meaning of differance in general would be more accessible to us if the unity of that double passage appeared more clearly.

In both cases, one must begin from the possibility of neutralizing the phonic substance.

On the one hand, the phonic element, the term, the plenitude that is called sensible, would not appear as such without the difference or opposition which gives them *form*. Such is the most evident significance of the appeal to difference as the reduction of phonic substance. Here the appearing and functioning of difference presupposes an originary synthesis not preceded by any absolute simplicity. Such would be the originary trace. Without a retention in the minimal unit of temporal experience, without a trace retaining the other as other in the same, no difference would do its work and no meaning would appear. It is not the question of a constituted difference here, but rather, before all determination of the content, of the *pure* movement which produces difference. *The (pure) trace is differance*. It does not depend on any sensible plentitude, audible or visible, phonic or graphic. It is, on the contrary, the condition of such a plenitude. Although it *does not exist*, although it is never a *being-present* outside of all plenitude, its possibility is by rights anterior to all that one calls sign (signified/signifier, content/expression, etc.), concept or operation, motor or sensory. This differance is therefore not more sensible than intelligible and it permits the articulation of signs among themselves within the same abstract order—a phonic or graphic text for example—or between two orders of expression. It permits the articulation of speech and writing—in the colloquial sense—as it founds the metaphysical opposition between the sensible and the intelligible, then between signifier and signified, expression and content, etc. If language were not already, in that sense, a writing, no derived "notation" would be possible; and the classical problem of relationships between speech and writing could not arise. Of course, the positive *sciences* of signification can only describe the *work* and the *fact* of differance, the determined differences and the determined presences that they make possible. There cannot be a science of differance itself in its operation, as it is impossible to have a science of the origin of presence itself, that is to say of a certain nonorigin.

Differance is therefore the formation of form. But it is *on the other hand* the being-imprinted of the imprint. It is well-known that Saussure distinguishes between the "sound-image" and the objective sound (p. 98) [p. 66]. He thus gives himself the right to "reduce," in the phenomenological sense, the sciences of accoustics and physiology at the moment that he institutes the science of language. The sound-image is the structure of the appearing of the sound *[l'apparaître du son]* which is anything but the sound appearing *[le son apparaissant]*. It is the sound-image that he calls *signifier*, reserving the name *signified* not for the thing, to be sure (it is reduced by the act and the very ideality of language), but for the "concept," undoubtedly an unhappy notion here;

let us say for the ideality of the sense. "I propose to retain the word *sign [signe]* to designate the whole and to replace *concept* and *sound-image* respectively by *signified [signifé]* and *signifier [signiflant]*." The sound-image is what is *heard*; not the *sound* heard but the being-heard of the sound. Being-heard is structurally phenomenal and belongs to an order radically dissimilar to that of the real sound in the world. One can only divide this subtle but absolutely decisive heterogeneity by a phenomenological reduction. The latter is therefore indispensable to all analyses of being-heard, whether they be inspired by linguistic, psychoanalytic, or other preoccupations.

Now the "sound-image," the structured appearing *[l'apparaitre]* of the sound, the "sensory matter" *lived* and *informed* by differance, what Husserl would name the *hylè/morphé* structure, distinct from all mundane reality, is called the "psychic image" by Saussure: "The latter [the sound-image] is not the material sound, a purely physical thing, but the psychic imprint of the sound, the impression that it makes on our senses *[la représentation que nous en donne le témoignage de nos sens]*. The sound-image is sensory, and if I happen to call it 'material,' it is only in that sense, and by way of opposing it, to the other term of the association, the concept, which is generally more abstract" (p. 98) [p. 66]. Although the word "psychic" is not perhaps convenient, except for exercising in this matter a phenomenological caution, the originality of a certain place is well marked.

Before specifying it, let us note that this is not necessarily what Jakobson and other linguists could criticize as "the mentalist point of view":

> In the oldest of these approaches, going back to Baudouin de Courtenay and still surviving, the phoneme is a sound imagined or intended, opposed to the emitted sound as a "psychophonetic" phenomenon to the "physiophonetic" fact. It is the psychic equivalent of an exteriorized sound.[23]

Although the notion of the "psychic image" thus defined (that is to say according to a prephenomenological psychology of the imagination) is indeed of this mentalist inspiration, it could be defended against Jakobson's criticism by specifying: (1) that it could be conserved without necessarily affirming that "our internal speech . . . is confined to the distinctive features to the exclusion of the configurative, or redundant features;" (2) that the qualification *psychic* is not retained if it designates exclusively *another natural reality, internal and not external.* Here the Husserlian correction is indispensable and transforms even the premises of the debate. Real *(reell* and not *real)* component of lived experience, the *hylè/morphé* structure is not a reality *(Realität)*. As to the intentional object, for example, the content of the image, it does not really *(reall)* belong either to the world or to lived experience: the nonreal component of lived experience. The psychic image of which Saussure speaks must not be an internal reality copying an external one. Husserl, who criticizes this concept of "portrait" in *Ideen* I[24] shows also in the *Krisis* (pp. 63 f.)[25] how phenomenology should overcome the naturalist opposition—whereby psychology and the other sciences of man survive—between "internal" and "external" experience. It is therefore indispensable to preserve the distinction between the appearing sound *[le son apparaissant]* and the appearing of the sound *[l'apparaître du son]* in order to escape the worst and the most prevalent of confusions; and it is in principle possible to do it without "attempt[ing] to overcome the antinomy between invariance and variability by assigning the former to the internal and the latter to the external experience" (Jakobson, op. cit., p. 112) [p. 12]. The difference between invariance and variability does not separate the two domains from each other, it divides each of them within itself. That gives enough indication that the essence of the *phonè* cannot be read directly and primarily in the text of a mundane science, of a psycho-physiophonetics.

These precautions taken, it should be recognized that it is in the specific zone of this imprint and this trace, in the temporalization of a *lived experience* which is neither in the world nor in "another world," which is not more sonorous than luminous, not more *in* time than *in* space, that differences appear among the elements or rather produce them, make them emerge as such and constitute the *texts*, the chains, and the systems of traces. These chains and systems cannot be outlined except in the fabric of this trace or imprint. The unheard difference between the appearing and the appearance *[l'apparaissant et l'apparaître]* (between the "world" and "lived experience") is the condition of all other differences, of all other traces, and it is *already a trace*. This last concept is thus absolutely and by rights "anterior" to all *physiological* problematics concerning the nature of the *engramme* [the unit of engraving], or *metaphysical* problematics concerning the meaning of absolute presence whose trace is thus opened to deciphering. *The trace is in fact the absolute origin of sense in general. Which amounts to saying once again that there is no absolute origin of sense in general. The trace is the differance* which opens appearance *[l'apparaître]* and signification. Articulating the living upon the nonliving in general, origin of all repetition, origin of ideality, the trace is not more ideal than real, not more intelligible than sensible, not more a transparent signification than an opaque energy and *no concept of metaphysics can describe it.* And as it is *a fortiori* anterior to the distinction between regions of sensibility, anterior to sound as much as to light, is there a sense in establishing a "natural" hierarchy between the sound-imprint, for example, and the visual (graphic) imprint? The graphic image is not seen; and the acoustic image is not heard. The difference between the full unities of the voice remains unheard. And, the difference in the body of the inscription is also invisible.

Notes

1. Page 101. Beyond the scruples formulated by Saussure himself, an entire system of intralinguistic criticism can be opposed to the thesis of the "arbitrariness of the sign." Cf. Jakobson, "A la rechercho de l'essence du langage," (Quest for the Essence of Language"), *Diogène*, 51, and Martinet, *La linguistique synchronique* [Paris 1965], p. 34. But these criticisms do not interfere—and, besides, do not pretend to interfere—with Saussure's profound intention directed at the discontinuity and immotivation proper to the structure if not the origin of the sign.

2. *Elements of Logic*, Bk. II [*Collected Papers*, ed. Charles Hartshorne and Paul Weiss (Cambridge, Mass., 1931–58), vol. 2], p. 169, paragraph 302.

3. I justify the translation of *bedeuten* by *vouloir-dire* [meaning, literally "wish-to-say"] in *La voix et le phénomène*.

4. *The Philosophy of Peirce: Selected Writings*, [ed. Justus Buehler (New York and London, 1940)], ch. 7, p. 99.

5. Page 93. Let us recall that Lambert opposes phenomenology to aletheiology.

6. *Elements of Logic*, Bk. I, 2, p. 302.

7. These Heideggerian themes obviously refer back to Nietzsche; cf. *La chose* [1950], tr. fr. in *Essais et conférences* [tr. André Préau (Paris, 1958)], p. 214 ["Das Ding," *Vorträge und Aufsätze* (Pfüllingen, 1954)], *Le principe de raison* (1955–56), tr. fr. André Préau (Paris, 1962) pp. 240 f. [*Der Satz vom Grund* (Pfüllingen, 1957)]. Such themes are presented also in Eugen Fink (*Le jeu comme symbole du monde* [*Spiel als Weltsymbol* (Stuttgart, 1960)]), and, in France, in Kostas Axelos, *Vers la pensée planétaire* ([Paris], 1964), and *Einführung in ein künftiges Denken* [*:über Marx und Heidegger* (Tübingen, 1966)].

8. *Communications*, 4 (1964), p. 2.

9. "The conceptual side of value is made up solely of relations and differences with respect to the other terms of language, and the same can be said of its material side. The important thing in the word is not the sound alone but the phonic differences that make it possible to distinguish this word from all others, for differences carry signification. . . . A segment of language can never in the final analysis be based on anything except its noncoincidence with the rest" (p. 163) [pp. 117–18].

10. "Since an identical state of affairs is observable in writing, another system of signs, we shall use writing to draw some comparisons that will clarify the whole issue. In fact:

"1) The signs used in writing are arbitrary; there is no connection, for example, between the letter *t* and the sound that it designates.

"2) The value of letters is purely negative and differential. The same person can write *t*, for instance, in different ways: *t* & t. The only requirement is that the sign for *t* not be confused in his script with the signs used for *l*, *d*, etc.

"3) Values in writing function only through reciprocal opposition within a fixed system that consists of a set number of letters. This third characteristic, though not identical to the second, is closely related to it, for both depend on the first. Since the graphic sign is arbitrary, its form matters little or rather matters only within the limitations imposed by the system.

"4) The means by which the sign is produced is completely unimportant, for it does not affect the system (this also follows from characteristic 1). Whether I make the letters in white or black, raised or engraved, with pen or chisel—all this is of no importance with respect to their signification" (pp. 165–66) [pp. 119–20].

11. "*Arbitrary* and *differential* are two correlative qualities" (p. 163) [p. 118].
12. Jakobson and Halle, *Fundamentals of Language*, loc. cit., p. 16.
13. This literal fidelity is expressed:

1. In the critical exposition of Hjelmslev's attempt ("Au sujet des fondements de la théorie linguistique de L. Hjelmslev," *Bulletin de la Société Linguistique de Paris*, vol. 42, p. 40): "Hjelmslev is perfectly consistent with himself when he declares that a written text has for the linguist exactly the same value as a spoken text, since the choice of the substance is not important. He refuses even to admit that the spoken substance is primitive and the written substance derived. It seems as if it would suffice to make him notice that, but for certain pathological exceptions, all human beings speak, but few know how to write, or that children know how to speak long before they learn how to write. *I shall therefore not press the point*" (italics added).

2. In the *Eléments de linguistique générale* [(Paris, 1961); *Elements of General Linguistics*, tr. Elisabeth Palmer (London, 1964)], where all the chapters on the vocal character of language pick up the words and arguments of Chapter VI of the *Course*: "[One learns to speak before learning to read:] reading comes as a reflection of spoken usage: *the reverse is never true*" (italics added. This proposition seems to me to be thoroughly debatable, even on the level of that common experience which has the force of law within this argument.) Martinet concludes: "The study of writing is a discipline distinct from linguistics proper, although practically speaking it is one of its dependencies. Thus the linguist in principle operates without regard for written forms" (p. 11) [p. 17]. We see how the concepts of *dependency* and *abstraction* function: writing and its science are alien but not independent; which does not stop them from being, conversely, immanent but not essential. Just enough "outside" not to affect the integrity of the language *itself*, in its pure original self- identity, in its property; just enough "inside" not to have the right to any practical or epistemological independence. And vice versa.

3. In "The Word" (already cited): ". . . it is from speech that one should always start in order to understand the real nature of human language" (p. 53) [p. 54].

4. And finally and above all in "La double articulation du langage," *La linguistique synchronique*, pp. 8 f. and 18 f.

14. "On the Principles of Phonematics" (1955), *Proceedings of the Second International Congress of Phonetic Sciences*, p. 51.

15. Louis Hjelmslev and H. J. Uldall, *Etudes de linguistique structurale organisées au sein du Cercle linguistique de Copenhague* (Bulletin 11, 35, pp. 13 f.).

16. "Langue et parole" (1943), *Essais linguistiques* [Copenhagen, 1959], p. 77.

17. *Omkring sprogteoriens grundlaeggelse*, Copenhagen (1943), pp. 91–93 (translated as *Prolegomena to A Theory of Language*, [by Francis J. Whitfield (2nd edition, Baltimore, 1961)], pp. 103–04.

Cf. also "La stratification du langage" (1954), *Essais linguistiques (Travaux du Cercle linguistique de Copenhague*, XII [1959]). The project and the terminology of a *graphematics*, science of the substance of graphic expression, are there presented (p. 41). The complexity of the proposed algebra aims to remedy the fact that, from the point of view of the distinction between form and substance, "Saussure's terminology can lead to confusion" (p. 48). Hjelmslev demonstrates how "one and the same form of expression can be manifested by diverse substances: phonic, graphic, flag-signals, etc." (p. 49) .

18. "Speech and Writing," 1938, *Acta Linguistica* 4 (1944): 11 f. Uldall refers also to a study by Dr. Joseph Vachek, "Zum Problem der geschriebenen Sprache" (*Travaux du*

Cercle linguistique de Prague 8, 1939) in order to indicate "the difference between the phonologic and glosseamtic points of view."

Cf. also Eli Fischer-Jorgensen, "Remarques sur les principes de l'analyse phonémique," *Recherches structurales*, 1949 (*Travaux du Cercle linguistique de Prague*, Vol. 5, pp. 231 f.); Bertha Siertsema, A *Study of Glossematics* ([The Hague] 1955), (especially ch. VI), and Hennings Spang-Hanssen, "Glossematics" *Trends in European and American Linguistics*, 1930–60 [ed. Christine Mohrmann (Utrecht, 1961)], pp. 147 f.

19. And already, in a very programmatic manner, in the *Prolegomena* (English translation, pp. 114–15). Cf. also Adolf Stender-Petersen, "Esquisse d'une théorie structurale de la littérature," and Stevan Johanson, "La notion de signe dans la glossématique et dans l'esthétique," *Travaux du Cercle linguistique de Copenhague* 5 (1949).

20. *Omkring*, p. 9 (*Prolegomena*, p. 8).

21. Page 14. Which does not prevent Hjelmslev from "venturing to call" his directing principle an "empirical principle" (p. 12, English translation, p. 11). "But," he adds, "we are willing to abandon the name if espistemological investigation shows it to be inappropriate. From our point of view this is merely a question of terminology, which does not affect the maintenance of the principle." This is only one example of the terminological conventionalism of a system, which, in borrowing all its concepts from the history of the metaphysics that it would hold at a distance (form/substance, context/expression, etc.), believes it can neutralize its entire historical burden by means of some declaration of intention, a preface or quotation marks.

22. As for this critique of the concept of origin in general (empirical and/or transcendental) we have elsewhere attempted to indicate the schema of an argument (Introduction to Husserl's *L'origine de la géométrie*, p. 60).

23. Op. cit., p. 111. Hjelmslev formulates the same reservations: "It is curious that linguistics, so long on guard against any suspicion of 'psychologism,' seems here, even if only to a certain extent and in very cautious proportions, to be on its way back to Saussure's 'accoustic image,' and equally to 'concept,' as long as that word is interpreted in strict conformity with the doctrine that I have just elaborated, in short to recognize, with however many necessary reservations, that, with the two aspects of the linguistic sign, one is in the presence of the 'purely psychological phenomenon' (*Course*, p. 28) [p. 11]. But it is rather a partial coincidence of nomenclatures than a real analogy. The terms introduced by Saussure, and the interpretations given in the *Course*, have been abandoned because they can be equivocal, and it is better not to make the same mistakes again. I too hesitate when I ask myself how much the researches advocated here may be considered as belonging to the psychological order: the reason being that psychology seems to be a discipline whose definition still leaves much to be desired" ("La stratification du langage" *Essais linguistiques* [1954], p. 56). Hjelmslev, posing the same problem, already evoked those "numerous nuances that the Genevan master could be fully aware of, but which he did not find it useful to insist upon; the motives behind this attitude naturally escapes us" (p. 76).

24. *Ideen zu einer reinen Phänomenologie und phänomenologischen Philosophie*. I. Buch, *Gesammelte Werke* (The Hague, 1950), Band 3; *Ideas: General Introduction to Pure Phenomenology*, tr. W. R. Boyce (New York, 1931).

25. *Husserliana. Gesammelte Werke*, ed. H. L. van Breda (The Hague, 1950–73), vol. 6.

The Hinge [La Brisure]

> *You have, I suppose, dreamt of finding a single word for designating difference and articulation. I have perhaps located it by chance in Robert['s Dictionary] if I play on the word, or rather indicate its double meaning. This word is* brisure *[joint, break] "—broken, cracked part. Cf. breach, crack, fracture, fault, split, fragment,* [brèche, cassure, fracture, faille, fente, fragment.]*—Hinged articulation of two parts of wood- or metal-work. The hinge, the* brisure *[folding-joint] of a shutter. Cf. joint."—Roger Laporte* (letter)

Origin of the experience of space and time, this writing of difference, this fabric of the trace, permits the difference between space and time to be articulated, to appear as such, in the unity of an experience (of a "same" lived out of a "same" body proper *[corps propre]*). This articulation therefore permits a graphic ("visual" or "tactile," "spatial") chain to be adapted, on occasion in a linear fashion, to a spoken ("phonic," "temporal") chain. It is from the primary possibility of this articulation that one must begin. Difference is articulation.

This is, indeed, what Saussure says, contradicting Chapter VI:

> The question of the vocal apparatus obviously takes a secondary place in the problem of language. One definition of *articulated* language might confirm that conclusion. In Latin, *articulus* means a member, part, or subdivision of a sequence; applied to speech *[langage]*, articulation designates either the subdivision of a spoken chain into syllables or the subdivision of the chain of meanings

> into significant units. . . . Using the second definition, we can say that *what is natural to mankind is not spoken language* but the faculty of constructing a language; i.e., a system of distinct signs corresponding to distinct ideas (p. 26; italics added) [p. 10].

The idea of the "psychic imprint" therefore relates essentially to the idea of articulation. Without the difference between the sensory appearing *[apparaissant]* and its lived appearing *[apparaître]* ("mental imprint"), the temporalizing synthesis, which permits differences to appear in a chain of significations, could not operate. That the "imprint" is irreducible means also that speech is originarily passive, but in a sense of passivity that all intramundane metaphors would only betray. This passivity is also the relationship to a past, to an always-already-there that no reactivation of the origin could fully master and awaken to presence. This impossibility of reanimating absolutely the manifest evidence of an originary presence refers us therefore to an absolute past. That is what authorized us to call *trace* that which does not let itself be summed up in the simplicity of a present. It could in fact have been objected that, in the indecomposable synthesis of temporalization, protection is as indispensable as retention. And their two dimensions are not added up but the one implies the other in a strange fashion. To be sure, what is anticipated in protention does not sever the present any less from its self-identity than does that which is retained in the trace. But if anticipation were privileged, the irreducibility of the always-already-there and the fundamental passivity that is called time would risk effacement. On the other hand, if the trace refers to an absolute past, it is because it obliges us to think a past that can no longer be understood in the form of a modified presence, as a present-past. Since past has always signified present-past, the absolute past that is retained in the trace no longer rigorously merits the name "past." Another name to erase, especially since the strange movement of the trace proclaims as much as it recalls: differance defers-differs *[diffère]*. With the same precaution and under the same erasure, it may be said that its passivity is also its relationship with the "future." The concepts of *present*, *past*, and *future*, everything in the concepts of time and history which implies evidence of them—the metaphysical concept of time in general—cannot adequately describe the structure of the trace. And deconstructing the simplicity of presence does not amount only to accounting for the horizons of potential presence, indeed of a "dialectic" of protention and retention that one would install in the heart of the present instead of surrounding it with it. It is not a matter of complicating the structure of time while conserving its homogeneity and its fundamental successivity, by demonstrating for example that the past present and the future present constitute originarily, by dividing it, the form of the living present. Such a complication, which is in effect the same that Husserl described, abides, in spite of an audacious phenomenological reduction, by the evidence and presence of a linear, objective, and mundane model. *Now*

B would be as such constituted by the retention of *Now* A and the protention of *Now* C; in spite of all the play that would follow from it, from the fact that each one of the three *Now*–s reproduces that structure in itself, this model of successivity would prohibit a *Now* X from taking the place of *Now* A, for example, and would prohibit that, by a delay that is inadmissible to consciousness, an experience be determined, in its very present, by a present which would not have preceded it immediately but would be considerably "anterior" to it. It is the problem of the deferred effect *(Nachträglichkeit) of* which Freud speaks. The temporality to which he refers cannot be that which lends itself to a phenomenology of consciousness or of presence and one may indeed wonder by what right all that is in question here should still be called time, now, anterior present, delay, etc.

In its greatest formality, this immense problem would be formulated thus: is the temporality described by a transcendental phenomenology as "dialectical" as possible, a ground which the structures, let us say the unconscious structures, of temporality would simply modify? Or is the phenomenological model itself constituted, as a warp of language, logic, evidence, fundamental security, upon a woof that is not its own? And which—such is the most difficult problem—is no longer at all mundane? For it is not by chance that the transcendental phenomenology of the internal time-*consciousness*, so careful to place cosmic time within brackets, must, as consciousness and even as internal consciousness, live a time that is an accomplice of the time of the world. Between consciousness, perception (internal or external), and the "world," the rupture, even in the subtle form of the reduction, is perhaps not possible.

It is in a certain "unheard" sense, then, that speech is in the world, rooted in that passivity which metaphysics calls sensibility in general. Since there is no nonmetaphoric language to oppose to metaphors here, one must, as Bergson wished, multiply antagonistic metaphors. "Wish sensibilized," is how Maine de Biran, with a slightly different intention, named the vocalic word. That the logos is first imprinted and that that imprint is the writing-resource of language, signifies, to be sure, that the logos is not a creative activity, the continuous full element of the divine word, etc. But it would not mean a single step outside of metaphysics if nothing more than a new motif of "return to finitude," of "God's death," etc., were the result of this move. It is that conceptuality and that problematics that must be deconstructed. They belong to the onto-theology they fight against. Differance is also something other than finitude.

According to Saussure, the passivity of speech is first its relationship with language. The relationship between passivity and difference cannot be distinguished from the relationship between the fundamental *unconsciousness* of language (as rootedness within the language) and the *spacing* (pause, blank, punctuation, interval in general, etc.) which constitutes the origin of signification. It is because "language is a form and not a substance" (p. 169) [p. 122] that, paradoxically, the activity of speech can and must always draw from it. But if it is a form, it is because "in language there are only differences" (p. 166) [p. 120]. *Spacing* (notice that this word speaks the articulation of space and time, the becoming-space of time and the becoming-time of space) is always the unperceived, the nonpresent, and the nonconscious. As *such,* if one can still use that expression in a nonphenomenological way; for here we pass the very limits of phenomenology. Arche-writing as spacing cannot occur *as such* within the phenomenological experience of a *presence.* It marks *the dead time* within the presence of the living present, within the general form of all presence. The dead time is at work. That is why, once again, in spite of all the discursive resources that the former may borrow from the latter, the concept of the trace will never be merged with a phenomenology of writing. As the phenomenology of the sign in general, a phenomenology of writing is impossible. No intuition can be realized in the place where "the 'whites' indeed take on an importance" (Preface to *Coup de dés*).[1]

Perhaps it is now easier to understand why Freud says of the dreamwork that it is comparable rather to a writing than to a language, and to a hieroglyphic rather than to a phonetic writing.[2] And to understand why Saussure says of language that it "is not a function of the speaker" (p. 30) [p. 14]. With or without the complicity of their authors, all these propositions must be understood as more than the simple *reversals* of a metaphysics of presence or of conscious subjectivity. Constituting and dislocating it at the same time, writing is other than the subject, in whatever sense the latter is understood. Writing can never be thought under the category of the subject; however it is modified, however it is endowed with consciousness or unconsciousness, it will refer, by the entire thread of its history, to the substantiality of a presence unperturbed by accidents, or to the identity of the selfsame *[le propre]* in the presence of self-relationship. And the thread of that history clearly does not run within the borders of metaphysics. To determine an X as a subject is never an operation of a pure convention, it is never an indifferent gesture in relation to writing.

Spacing as writing is the becoming-absent and the becoming-unconscious of the subject. By the movement of its drift/derivation *[dérive]* the emancipation of the sign constitutes in return the desire of presence. That becoming—or that drift/derivation—does not befall the subject which would choose it or would passively let itself be drawn along by it. As the subject's relationship with its own death, this becoming is the constitution of subjectivity. On all levels of life's organization, that is to say, of *the economy of death.* All graphemes are of a testamentary essence.[3] And the original absence of the subject of writing is also the absence of the thing or the referent.

Within the horizontality of spacing, which is in fact the precise dimension I have been speaking of so far, and which is not opposed to it as surface opposes depth, it is not even necessary to say that spacing cuts, drops, and causes to drop within the unconscious: the unconscious is nothing without this cadence and before this caesura. This signification is formed only within the hollow of differance: of discontinuity and of discreteness, of the diversion and the reserve of what does not appear. This hinge *[brisure]* of language as writing, this discontinuity, could have, at a given moment within linguistics, run up against a rather precious *continuist* prejudice. Renouncing it, phonology must indeed renounce all distinctions between writing and the spoken word, and thus renounce not itself, phonology, but rather phonologism. What Jakobson recognizes in this respect is most important for us:

> The stream of oral speech, physically continuous, originally confronted the mathematical theory of communication with a situation "considerably more involved" ([C.E.] Shannon and [W.] Weaver [*The Mathematical Theory of Communication* (Urbana, 1949), pp. 74 f., 112 f.]) than in the case of a finite set of discrete constituents, as presented by written speech. Linguistic analysis, however, came to resolve oral speech into a finite series of elementary informational units. These ultimate discrete units, the so-called "distinctive features," are aligned into simultaneous bundles termed "phonemes," which in turn are concatenated into sequences. Thus form in language has a manifestly granular structure and is subject to a quantal description.[4]

The hinge *[brisure]* marks the impossibility that a sign, the unity of a signifier and a signified, be produced within the plenitude of a present and an absolute presence. That is why there is no full speech, however much one might wish to restore it by means or without benefit of psychoanalysis. Before thinking to reduce it or to restore the meaning of the full speech which claims to be truth, one must ask the question of meaning and of its origin in difference. Such is the place of a problematic of the *trace.*

Why of the *trace?* What led us to the choice of this word? I have begun to answer this question. But this question is such, and such the nature of my answer, that the place of the one and of the other must constantly be in movement. If words and concepts receive meaning only in sequences of differences, one can justify one's language, and one's choice of terms, only within a topic [an orientation in space] and an historical strategy. The justification can therefore never be absolute and definitive. It corresponds to a condition of forces and translates an historical calculation. Thus, over and above those that I have already defined, a certain number of givens belonging to the discourse of our time have progressively imposed this choice upon me. The word *trace* must refer to itself to a certain number of contemporary discourses whose force I intend to take into account. Not that I accept them totally. But the word *trace* establishes the clearest connections with them and thus permits me to dispense with certain developments which have already demonstrated their effectiveness in those fields. Thus, I relate this concept of *trace* to what is at the center of the latest work of Emmanuel Levinas and his critique of ontology:[5] relationship to the illeity as to the alterity of a past that never was and can never be lived in the originary or modified form of presence. Reconciled here to a Heideggerian intention,—as it is not in Levinas's thought—this notion signifies, sometimes beyond Heideggerian discourse, the undermining of an ontology which, in its innermost course, has determined the meaning of being as presence and the meaning of language as the full continuity of speech. To make enigmatic what one thinks one understands by the words "proximity," "immediacy," "presence" (the proximate *[proche]*, the own *[propre]*, and the pre- of presence), is my final intention in this book. This deconstruction of presence accomplishes itself through the deconstruction of consciousness, and therefore through the irreducible notion of the trace *(Spur)*, as it appears in both Nietzschean and Freudian discourse. And finally, in all scientific fields, notably in biology, this notion seems currently to be dominant and irreducible.

If the trace, arche-phenomenon of "memory," which must be thought before the opposition of nature and culture, animality and humanity, etc., belongs to the very movement of signification, then signification is a priori written, whether inscribed or not, in one form or another, in a "sensible" and "spatial" element that is called "exterior." Arche-writing, at first the possibility of the spoken word, then of the "*graphie*" in the narrow sense, the birthplace of "usurpation," denounced from Plato to Saussure, this trace is the opening of the first exteriority in general, the enigmatic relationship of the living to its other and of an inside to an outside: spacing. The outside, "spatial" and "objective" exteriority which we believe we know as the most familiar thing in the world, as familiarity itself, would not appear without the grammè, without differance as temporalization, without the nonpresense of the other inscribed within the sense of the present, without the relationship with death as the concrete structure of the living present. Metaphor would be forbidden. The presence-absence of the trace, which one should not even call its ambiguity but rather its play (for the word "ambiguity" requires the logic of presence, even when it begins to disobey that logic), carries in itself the problems of the letter and the spirit, of body and soul, and of all the problems whose primary affinity I have recalled. All dualisms, all theories of the immortality of the soul or of the spirit, as well as all monisms, spiritualist or materialist, dialectical or vulgar, are the unique theme of a metaphysics whose entire history was compelled to strive toward the reduction of the trace. The subordination of the trace to the full presence summed up in the logos, the humbling of writing beneath a speech dreaming its plenitude, such are the gestures required by an onto-theology determining the archeological and eschatological meaning of being as presence, as parousia, as life without differance: another name for death, historical metonymy where God's name holds death in check. That is why, if this movement begins its era in the form of Platonism, it ends in infinitist metaphysics. Only infinite being can reduce the difference in presence. In that sense, the name of God, at least as it is pronounced within classical rationalism, is the name of indifference itself. Only a positive infinity can lift the trace, "sublimate" it (it has recently been proposed that the Hegelian *Aufhebung* be translated as sublimation; this translation may be of dubious worth as translation, but the juxtaposition is of interest here). We must not therefore speak of a "theological prejudice," functioning sporadically when it is a question of the plenitude of the logos; the logos as the sublimation of the trace is *theological.* Infinitist theologies are always logocentrisms, whether they are creationisms or not. Spinoza himself said of the understanding—or logos—that it was the *immediate* infinite mode of the divine substance, even calling it its eternal son in the *Short Treatise.*[6] It is also to this epoch, "reaching completion" with Hegel, with a theology of the absolute concept as logos, that all the noncritical concepts accredited by linguistics belong, at least to the extent that linguistics must confirm—and how can a *science* avoid it?—the Saussurian decree marking out "the internal system of language."

It is precisely these concepts that permitted the exclusion of writing: image or representation, sensible and intelligible, nature and culture, nature and technics, etc. They are solidary with all metaphysical conceptuality and particularly with a naturalist, objectivist, and derivative determination of the difference between outside and inside.

And above all with a "vulgar concept of time." I borrow this expression from Heidegger. It designates, at the end of *Being and Time,* a concept of time thought in terms of spatial movement or of the now, and dominating all philosophy from Aristotle's *Physics* to Hegel's *Logic.*[7] This concept, which determines all of classical ontology, was not born out of a philosopher's carelessness or from a theoretical lapse. It is intrinsic to the totality of the history of the Occident, of what unites its metaphysics and its technics. And we shall see it later associated with the linearization of writing, and with the linearist concept of speech. This linearism is undoubtedly inseparable from phonologism; it can raise its voice to the same extent that a linear writing can seem to submit to it. Saussure's entire theory of the "linearity of the signifier" could be interpreted from this point of view.

> Auditory signifiers have at their command only the dimension of time. Their elements are presented in succession; they form a chain. This feature becomes readily apparent when they are represented in writing. . . . The signifier, being auditory, is unfolded solely in time from which it gets the following characteristics: (a) it represents a span, and (b) the span is measurable in a single dimension; it is a line.[8]

It is a point on which Jakobson disagrees with Saussure decisively by substituting for the homogeneousness of the line the structure of the musical staff, "the chord in music."[9] What is here in question is not Saussure's affirmation of the temporal essence of discourse but the concept of time that guides this affirmation and analysis: time conceived as linear successivity, as "consecutivity." This model works by itself and all through the *Course*, but Saussure is seemingly less sure of it in the *Anagrams*. At any rate, its value seems problematic to him and an interesting paragraph elaborates a question left suspended:

> That the elements forming a word follow *one another* is a truth that it would be better for linguistics not to consider uninteresting because evident, but rather as the truth which gives in advance the central principle of all useful reflections on words. In a domain as infinitely special as the one I am about to enter, it is always by virtue of the fundamental law of the human word in general that a question like that of consecutiveness or nonconsecutiveness may be posed.[10]

This linearist concept of time is therefore one of the deepest adherences of the modem concept of the sign to its own history. For at the limit, it is indeed the concept of the sign itself, and the distinction, however tenuous, between the signifying and signified faces, that remain committed to the history of classical ontology. The parallelism and correspondence of the faces or the planes change nothing. That this distinction, first appearing in Stoic logic, was necessary for the coherence of a scholastic thematics dominated by infinitist theology, forbids us to treat today's debt to it as a contingency or a convenience. I suggested this at the outset, and perhaps the reasons are clearer now. The *signatum* always referred, as to its referent, to a *res*, to an entity created or at any rate first thought and spoken, thinkable and speakable, in the eternal present of the divine logos and specifically in its breath. If it came to relate to the speech of a finite being (created or not; in any case of an intracosmic entity) through the *intermediary* of a *signans*, the *signatum* had an *immediate* relationship with the divine logos which thought it within presence and for which it was not a trace. And for modem linguistics, if the signifier is a trace, the signified is a meaning thinkable in principle within the full presence of an intuitive consciousness. The signified face, to the extent that it is still originarily distinguished from the signifying face, is not considered a trace; by rights, it has no need of the signifier to be what it is. It is at the depth of this affirmation that the problem of relationships between linguistics and semantics must be posed. This reference to the meaning of a signified thinkable and possible outside of all signifiers remains dependent upon the ontotheo-teleology that I have just evoked. It is thus the idea of the sign that must be deconstructed through a meditation upon writing which would merge, as it must, with the undoing *[sollicitation]*[11] of onto-theology, faithfully repeating it in its *totality* and *making* it *insecure* in its most assured evidences.[12] One is necessarily led to this from the moment that the trace affects the totality of the sign in both its faces. That the signified is originarily and essentially (and not only for a finite and created spirit) trace, that it is *always already in the position of the signifier*, is the apparently innocent proposition within which the metaphysics of the logos, of presence and consciousness, must reflect upon writing as its death and its resource.

Notes

1. Mallarmé, tr. Anthony Hartley (Harmondsworth, 1965), p. 209.

2. I have attempted a reading of Freud from this point of view ("Freud et la scène de l'écriture," *L'écriture et la différence*). It sets forth the relationship between the concept of the trace and the structure of "a-retardation" which I mention above.

3. This theme inhabits more than one mythological system. Among many other examples, Thoth, the Egyptian god of writing evoked in *Phaedrus*, inventor of the technical ruse, the analogue of Hermes, also performed essential functions in funeral rites. When the opportunity offered, he was the conductor of the dead. He inscribed the accounts before the Last Judgment. He also occupied the function of the secretary/substitute who usurped first place; of the king, the father, the sun, of their eye. For example: "As a general rule, Horus' eye became the lunar eye. The moon, like everything that touched the astral world, intrigued the Egyptians greatly. According to one legend, the moon was created by the Sun-god to replace itself at night: it was Thoth whom Rê designated for the exercise of this high function of substitution. Another myth tried to explain the vicissitudes of the moon by a periodic battle whose protagonists were Horus and Seth. During the combat, Horus' eye was wrenched out, but Seth, finally vanquished, was obliged to return to his victorious opponent the eye that he had lifted; according to another version, the eye returned on its own, or was brought back by Thoth. Whatever the case might have been, Horus received his eye back joyfully, and put it back in its place after purifying it. The Egyptians called that eye *oudjat*, 'the healthy one.' We shall see that the *oudjat* eye played a considerable role in the funerary religion, in the Osirian legend, and in the sacrificial ceremony. This legend . . . later received a solar counterpart: it was said that the universal master, at the origin of the world, was seen, for some unknown reason, to be without an eye. He charged Shou and Tefnout to bring it back. The absence of the two messengers lasted so long that Rê was obliged to replace the unfaithful eye. The eye, when it was brought back by Shou and Tefnout, became very angry (a), seeing that its place had been taken. In appeasement, Rê transformed it into the serpent-uraeus and placed it on his forehead as the symbol of his power; furthermore, he charged it to defend him against his enemies. (a) The eye shed tears *(rémyt)* from which men were born *(rémet)*; the mythic origin of men clearly rests upon a simple wordplay" (Jacques Vandier, *La religion égyptienne*, P.U.F. [Paris, 1944], pp. 39–40). This myth of substitution can be related to the story of the eye in Rousseau (cf. below, p. 212, 148–49).

4. "Linguistique et théorie de la communication," (op. cit., pp. 87–88) [p. 245].

5. Cf. particularly "La trace de l'autre," *Tidischrift voor filosofie* (September 1963), and my essay "Violence et métaphysique: Essai sur la pensée d'Emmanuel Levinas," *L'écriture et la différence*.

6. Spinoza, *Short Treatise on God, Man and His Well Being*, tr. A. Wolf (New York, 1967).

7. I take the liberty of referring to a forthcoming essay, "Ousia et Grammè, note sur une note de *Sein und Zeit*."

8. Page 103 [p. 70]. See also everything concerning "homogeneous time," (pp. 64 f.) [pp. 38 f.].

9. Op. cit., p. 106. Cf. also the *Diogène* article already cited.

10. *Mercure de France* (February 1964): 254. Presenting this text, Starobinski evokes the musical model and concludes: "This reading is developed according to another *tempo* (and in another time); at the very limit, one leaves the time of 'consecutivity' proper to habitual language." One could of course say "proper to the habitual concept" of time and of language.

11. Derrida comments on this Latinate use of "sollicitation" in "Force et signification," *ED*, p. 13.

12. I have chosen to demonstrate the necessity of this "deconstruction" by privileging the Saussurian references, not only because Saussure still dominates contemporary linguistics and semiology; it is also because he seems to me to hold himself at the limit: at the same time within the metaphysics that must be deconstructed and beyond the concept of the sign (signifier/signified) which he still uses. But Saussure's scruples, his interminable hesitations, particularly in the matter of the difference between the two "aspects" of the sign and in the matter of "arbitrariness," are better realized through reading Robert Godel's *Les sources manuscrites du cours de linguistique générale* ([Geneva], 1957) pp. 190 f. Suffice it to say here that it is not impossible that the literality of the *Course*, to which we have indeed had to refer, should one day appear very suspect in the light of unpublished material now being prepared for publication. I am thinking particularly of the *Anagrams* [now published, see note 4]. Up to what point is Saussure responsible for the *Course* as it was edited and published after his death? It is not a new question. Need we specify that, *here at least*, we cannot consider it to be pertinent? Unless my project has been fundamentally misunderstood, it should be clear by now that, caring very little about Ferdinand de Saussure's *very* thought *itself*, *I* have interested myself in a *text* whose literality has played a well-known role since 1915, operating within a system of readings, influences, misunderstandings, borrowings, refutations, etc. What I could read—and equally what I could not read—under the title of *A Course in General Linguistics* seemed important to the point of excluding all hidden and "true" intentions of Ferdinand de Saussure. If one were to discover that this text hid another text—and there will never by anything but texts—and hid it in a determined sense, the reading that I have just proposed would not be invalidated, at least for that particular reason. Quite the contrary. Besides, at the very end of their first "Preface," the editors of the *Course* themselves foresee this situation.

Différance

I will speak, therefore, of a letter.

Of the first letter, if the alphabet, and most of the speculations which have ventured into it, are to be believed.

I will speak, therefore, of the letter *a*, this initial letter which it apparently has been necessary to insinuate, here and there, into the writing of the word *difference*; and to do so in the course of a writing on writing, and also of a writing within writing whose different trajectories thereby find themselves, at certain very determined points, intersecting with a kind of gross spelling mistake, a lapse in the discipline and law which regulate writing and keep it seemly. One can always, de facto or de jure, erase or reduce this lapse in spelling, and find it (according to situations to be analyzed each time, although amounting to the same), grave or unseemly, that is, to follow the most ingenuous hypothesis, amusing. Thus, even if one seeks to pass over such an infraction in silence, the interest that one takes in it can be recognized and situated in advance as prescribed by the mute irony, the inaudible misplacement, of this literal permutation. One can always act as if it made no difference. And I must state here and now that today's discourse will be less a justification of, and even less an apology for, this silent lapse in spelling, than a kind of insistent intensification of its play.

On the other hand, I will have to be excused if I refer, at least implicitly, to some of the texts I have ventured to publish. This is precisely because I would like to attempt, to a certain extent, and even though in principle and in the last analysis this is impossible, and impossible for essential reasons, to reassemble in a *sheaf* the different directions in which I have been able to utilize what I would call provisionally the word or concept of *différance*, or rather to let it impose itself upon me in its neographism, although as we shall see, *différance* is literally neither a word nor a concept. And I insist upon the word *sheaf* for two reasons. On the one hand, I will not be concerned, as I might have been, with describing a history and narrating its stages, text by text, context by context, demonstrating the economy that each time imposed this graphic disorder; rather, I will be concerned with the *general system of this economy*. On the other hand, the word *sheaf* seems to mark more appropriately that the assemblage to be proposed has the complex structure of a weaving, an interlacing which permits the different threads and different lines of meaning—or of force—to go off again in different directions, just as it is always ready to tie itself up with others.

Therefore, preliminarily, let me recall that this discreet graphic intervention, which neither primarily nor simply aims to shock the reader or the grammarian, came to be formulated in the course of a written investigation of a question about writing. Now it happens, I would say in effect, that this graphic difference (*a* instead of *e*), this marked difference between two apparently vocal notations, between two vowels, remains purely graphic: it is read, or it is written, but it cannot be heard. It cannot be apprehended in speech, and we will see why it also bypasses the order of apprehension in general. It is offered by a mute mark, by a tacit monument, I would even say by a pyramid, thinking not only of the form of the letter when it is printed as a capital, but also of the text in Hegel's *Encyclopedia* in which the body of the sign is compared to the Egyptian Pyramid. The *a* of *différance*, thus, is not heard; it remains silent, secret and discreet as a tomb: oikēsis. And thereby let us anticipate the delineation of a site, the familial residence and tomb of the proper[1] in which is produced, by *différance*, the *economy of death*. This stone—provided that one knows how to decipher its inscription—is not far from announcing the death of the tyrant.[2]

And it is a tomb that cannot even be made to resonate. In effect, I cannot let you know through my discourse, through the speech being addressed at this moment to the French Society of Philosophy, what difference I am talking about when I talk about it. I can speak of this graphic difference only through a very indirect discourse on writing, and on the condition that I specify, each time, whether I am referring to difference with an *e* or *différance* with an *a*. Which will not simplify things today, and will give us all, you and me, a great deal of trouble, if, at least, we wish to understand each other. In any event, the oral specifications that I will provide—when I say "with an *e*" or "with an *a*"—will refer uncircumventably to a *written text* that keeps watch over my discourse, to a text that I am holding in front of me, that I will read, and toward which I necessarily will attempt to direct your hands and your eyes. We will be able neither to do without the passage through a written text, nor to avoid the order of the disorder produced within it—and this, first of all, is what counts for me.

The pyramidal silence of the graphic difference between the *e* and the *a* can function, of course, only within the system of phonetic writing, and within the language and grammar which is as historically linked to phonetic writing as it is to the entire culture inseparable from phonetic writing. But I would say that this in itself—the silence that functions within only a so-called phonetic writing—quite opportunely conveys or reminds us that, contrary to a very widespread prejudice, there is no phonetic writing. There is no purely and rigorously phonetic writing. So-called phonetic writing, by all rights and in principle, and not only due to an empirical or technical insufficiency, can function only by admitting into its system nonphonetic "signs" (punctuation, spacing, etc.). And an examination of the structure and necessity of these nonphonetic signs quickly reveals that they can barely tolerate the concept of the sign itself. Better, the play of difference, which, as Saussure reminded us, is the condition for the possibility and functioning of every sign, is in itself a silent play. Inaudible is the difference between two phonemes which alone permits them to be and to operate as such. The inaudible opens up the apprehension of two present phonemes such as they present themselves. If there is no purely phonetic writing, it is that there is no purely phonetic *phōnē*. The difference which establishes phonemes and lets them be heard remains in and of itself inaudible, in every sense of the word.

It will be objected, for the same reasons, that graphic difference itself vanishes into the night, can never be sensed as a full term, but rather extends an invisible relationship, the mark of an inapparent relationship between two spectacles. Doubtless. But, from this point of view, that the difference marked in the "differ( )nce" between the *e* and the *a* eludes both vision and hearing perhaps happily suggests that here we must be permitted to refer to an order which no longer belongs to sensibility. But neither can it belong to intelligibility, to the ideality which is not fortuitously affiliated with the objectivity of *theōrein* or understanding.[3] Here, therefore, we must let outselves refer to an order that resists the opposition, one of the founding oppositions of philosophy, between the sensible and the intelligible. The order which resists this opposition, and resists it because it transports it, is announced in a movement of *différance* (with an *a*) between two differences or two letters, a *différance* which belongs neither to the voice nor to writing in the usual sense, and which is located, as the strange space that will keep us together here for an hour, *between* speech and writing, and beyond the tranquil familiarity which links us to one and the other, occasionally reassuring us in our illusion that they are two.

What am I to do in order to speak of the *a* of *différance*? It goes without saying that it cannot be *exposed*. One can expose only that which at a certain moment can become *present*, manifest, that which can be shown, presented as something present, a being-present[4] in its truth, in the truth of a present or the presence of the present. Now if *différance* ~~is~~ (and I also cross out the "~~is~~") what makes possible the presentation of the being-present, it is never presented as such. It is never offered to the present. Or to anyone. Reserving itself, not exposing itself, in regular fashion it exceeds the order of truth at a certain precise point, but without dissimulating itself as something, as a mysterious being, in the occult of a nonknowledge or in a hole with indeterminable borders (for example, in a topology of castration).[5] In every exposition it would be exposed to disappearing as disappearance. It would risk appearing: disappearing.

So much so that the detours, locutions, and syntax in which I will often have to take recourse will resemble those of negative theology, occasionally even to the point of being indistinguishable from negative theology. Already we have had to delineate *that différance is not*, does not exist, is not a present-being *(on)* in any form; and we will be led to delineate also everything *that* it *is not*, that is, *everything*; and consequently that it has neither existence nor essence. It derives from no category of being, whether present or absent. And yet those aspects of *différance* which are thereby delineated are not theological, not even in the order of the most negative of negative theologies, which are always concerned with disengaging a superessentiality beyond the finite categories of essence and existence, that is, of presence, and always hastening to recall that God is refused the predicate of existence, only in order to acknowledge his superior, inconceivable, and ineffable mode of being. Such a development is not in question here, and this will be confirmed progressively. *Différance* is not only irreducible to any ontological or theological—ontotheological—reappropriation, but as the very opening of the space in which ontotheology—philosophy—produces its system and its history, it includes ontotheology, inscribing it and exceeding it without return.

For the same reason there is nowhere to *begin* to trace the sheaf or the graphics of *différance*. For what is put into question is precisely the quest for a rightful beginning, an absolute point of departure, a principal responsibility. The problematic of writing is opened by putting into question the value *arkhē*.[6] What I will propose here will not be elaborated simply as a philosophical discourse, operating according to principles, postulates, axioms or definitions, and proceeding along the discursive lines of a linear order of reasons. In the delineation of *différance* everything is strategic and adventurous. Strategic because no transcendent truth present outside the field of writing can govern theologically the totality of the field. Adventurous because this strategy is not a simple strategy in the sense that strategy orients tactics according to a final goal, a *telos* or theme of domination, a mastery and ultimate reappropriation of the development of the field. Finally, a strategy without finality, what might be called blind tactics, or empirical wandering if the value of empiricism did not itself acquire its entire meaning in its opposition to philosophical responsibility. If there is a certain wandering in the tracing of *différance*, it no more follows the lines of philosophical-logical discourse than that of its symmetrical and integral inverse, empirical–logical discourse. The concept of *play* keeps itself beyond this opposition, announcing, on the eve of philosophy and beyond it, the unity of chance and necessity in calculations without end.

Also, by decision and as a rule of the game, if you will, turning these propositions back on themselves, we will be introduced to the thought of *différance* by the theme of strategy or the strategem. By means of this solely strategic justification, I wish to underline that the efficacity of the thematic of *différance* may very well, indeed must, one day be superseded, lending itself if not to its own replacement, at least to enmeshing itself in a chain that in truth it never will have governed. Whereby, once again, it is not theological.

I would say, first off, that *différance*, which is neither a word nor a concept, strategically seemed to me the most proper one to think, if not to master—thought, here, being that which is maintained in a certain necessary relationship with the structural limits of mastery—what is most irreducible about our "era." Therefore I am starting, strategically, from the place and the time in which "we" are, even though in the last analysis my opening is not justifiable, since it is only on the basis of *différance* and its "history" that we can allegedly know who and where "we" are, and what the limits of an "era" might be.

Even though *différance* is neither a word nor a concept, let us nevertheless attempt a simple and approximate semantic analysis that will take us to within sight of what is at stake.

We know that the verb *différer* (Latin verb *differre)* has two meanings which seem quite distinct;[7] for example in Littré they are the object of two separate articles. In this sense the Latin *differre* is not simply a translation of the Greek *diapherein*, and this will not be without consequences for us, linking our discourse to a particular language, and to a language that passes as less philosophical, less originally philosophical than the other. For the distribution of meaning in the Greek *diapherein* does not comport one of the two motifs of the Latin *differre,* to wit, the action of putting off until later, of taking into account, of taking account of time and of the forces of an operation that implies an economical calculation, a detour, a delay, a relay, a reserve, a representation—concepts that I would summarize here in a word I have never used but that could be inscribed in this chain: *temporization. Différer* in this sense is to temporize, to take recourse, consciously or unconsciously, in the temporal and temporizing mediation of a detour that suspends the accomplishment or fulfillment of "desire" or "will," and equally effects this suspension in a mode that annuls or tempers its own effect. And we will see, later, how this temporization is also temporalization and spacing, the becoming-time of space and the becoming-space of time, the "originary constitution" of time and space, as metaphysics or transcendental phenomenology would say, to use the language that here is criticized and displaced.

The other sense of *différer is* the more common and identifiable one: to be not identical, to be other, discernible, etc. When dealing with *differen(ts)(ds)*, a word that can be written with a final *ts* or a final *ds,* as you will, whether it is a question of dissimilar otherness or of allergic and polemical otherness, an interval, a distance, *spacing*, must be produced between the elements other, and be produced with a certain perseverence in repetition.[8]

Now the word *différence* (with an *e*) can never refer either to *différer* as temporization or to *différends* as *polemos*.[9] Thus the word *différance* (with an *a*) is to compensate—economically—this loss of meaning, for *différance* can refer simultaneously to the entire configuration of its meanings. It is immediately and irreducibly polysemic, which will not be indifferent to the economy of my discourse here. In its polysemia this word, of course, like any meaning, must defer to the discourse in which it occurs, its interpretive context; but in a way it defers itself, or at least does so more readily than any other word, the *a* immediately deriving from the present participle *(différant)*, thereby bringing us close to the very action of the verb *différer*, before it has even produced an effect constituted as something different or as *différence* (with an *e*).[10] In a conceptuality adhering to classical strictures "*différance*" would be said to designate a constitutive, productive, and originary causality, the process of scission and division which would produce or constitute different things or differences. But, because it brings us close to the infinitive and active kernel of *différer*, *différance* (with an *a*) neutralizes what the infinitive denotes as simply active, just as *mouvance* in our language does not simply mean the fact of moving, of moving oneself or of being moved. No more is resonance the act of resonating. We must consider that in the usage of our language the ending *-ance* remains undecided *between* the active and the passive. And we will see why that which lets itself be designated *différance* is neither simply active nor simply passive, announcing or rather recalling something like the middle voice, saying an operation that is not an operation, an operation that cannot be conceived either as passion or as the action of a subject on an object, or on the basis of the categories of agent or patient, neither on the basis of nor moving toward any of these *terms*. For the middle voice, a certain nontransitivity, may be what philosophy, at its outset, distributed into an active and a passive voice, thereby constituting itself by means of this repression.

Différance as temporization, *différance* as spacing. How are they to be joined?

Let us start, since we are already there, from the problematic of the sign and of writing. The sign is usually said to be put in the place of the thing itself, the present thing, "thing" here standing equally for meaning or referent. The sign represents the present in its absence. It takes the place of the present. When we cannot grasp or show the thing, state the present, the being-present, when the present cannot be presented, we signify, we go through the detour of the sign. We take or give signs. We signal. The sign, in this sense, is deferred presence. Whether we are concerned with the verbal or the written sign, with the monetary sign, or with electoral delegation and political representation, the circulation of signs defers the moment in which we can encounter the thing itself, make it ours, consume or expend it, touch it, see it, intuit its presence. What I am describing here in order to define it is the classically determined structure of the sign in all the banality of its characteristics—signification as the *différance* of temporization. And this structure presupposes that the sign, which defers presence, is conceivable only on the *basis* of the presence that it defers and *moving toward* the deferred presence that it aims to reappropriate. According to this classical semiology, the substitution of the sign for the thing itself is both *secondary* and *provisional:* secondary due to an original and lost presence from which the sign thus derives; provisional as concerns this final and missing presence toward which the sign in this sense is a movement of mediation.

In attempting to put into question these traits of the provisional secondariness of the substitute, one would come to see something like an originary *différance;* but one could no longer call it originary or final in the extent to which the values of origin, archi-, *telos, eskhaton,* etc. have always denoted presence—*ousia, parousia.*[11] To put into question the secondary and provisional characteristics of the sign, to oppose to them an "originary" *différance,* therefore would have two consequences.

1. One could no longer include *différance* in the concept of the sign, which always has meant the representation of a presence, and has been constituted in a system (thought or language) governed by and moving toward presence.

2. And thereby one puts into question the authority of presence, or of its simple symmetrical opposite, absence or lack. Thus one questions the limit which has always constrained us, which still constrains us—as inhabitants of a language and a system of thought—to formulate the meaning of Being in general as presence or absence, in the categories of being or beingness *(ousia).* Already it appears that the type of question to which we are redirected is, let us say, of the Heideggerian type, and that *différance seems* to lead back to the ontico-ontological difference. I will be permitted to hold off on this reference. I will note only that between difference as temporization-temporalization, which can no longer be conceived within the horizon of the present, and what Heidegger says in *Being and Time* about temporalization as the transcendental horizon of the question of Being, which must be liberated from its traditional, metaphysical domination by the present and the now, there is a strict communication, even though not an exhaustive and irreducibly necessary one.

But first let us remain within the semiological problematic in order to see *différance* as temporization and *différance* as spacing conjoined. Most of the semiological or linguistic researches that dominate the field of thought today, whether due to their own results or to the regulatory model that they find themselves acknowledging everywhere, refer genealogically to Saussure (correctly or incorrectly) as their common inaugurator. Now Saussure first of all is the thinker who put the *arbitrary character of the sign* and the *differential character* of the sign at the very foundation of general semiology, particularly linguistics. And, as we know, these two motifs—arbitrary and differential—are inseparable in his view. There can be arbitrariness only because the system of signs is constituted solely by the differences in terms, and not by their plenitude. The elements of signification function due not to the compact force of their nuclei but rather to the network of oppositions that distinguishes them, and then relates them one to another. "Arbitrary and differential," says Saussure, "are two correlative characteristics."

Now this principle of difference, as the condition for signification, affects the *totality* of the sign, that is the sign as both signified and signifier. The signified is the concept, the ideal meaning; and the signifier is what Saussure calls the "image," the "psychical imprint" of a material, physical—for example, acoustical—phenomenon. We do not have to go into all the problems posed by these definitions here. Let us cite Saussure only at the point which interests us: "The conceptual side of value is made up solely of relations and differences with respect to the other terms of language, and the same can be said of its material side . . . Everything that has been said up to this point boils down to this: in language there are only differences. Even more important: a difference generally implies positive terms between which the difference is set up; but in language there are only differences *without positive terms*. Whether we take the signified or the signifier, language has neither ideas nor sounds that existed before the linguistic system, but only conceptual and phonic differences that have issued from the system. The idea or phonic substance that a sign contains is of less importance than the other signs that surround it."[12]

The first consequence to be drawn from this is that the signified concept is never present in and of itself, in a sufficient presence that would refer only to itself. Essentially and lawfully, every concept is inscribed in a chain or in a system within which it refers to the other, to other concepts, by means of the systematic play of differences. Such a play, *différance*, is thus no longer simply a concept, but rather the possibility of conceptuality, of a conceptual process and system in general. For the same reason, *différance*, which is not a concept, is not simply a word, that is, what is generally represented as the calm, present, and self-referential unity of concept and phonic material. Later we will look into the word in general.

The difference of which Saussure speaks is itself, therefore, neither a concept nor a word among others. The same can be said, a fortiori, of *différance*. And we are thereby led to explicate the relation of one to the other.

In a language, in the *system* of language, there are only differences. Therefore a taxonomical operation can undertake the systematic, statistical, and classificatory inventory of a language. But, on the one hand, these differences *play*: in language, in speech too, and in the exchange between language and speech. On the other hand, these differences are themselves *effects*. They have not fallen from the sky fully formed, and are no more inscribed in a *topos noētos*, than they are prescribed in the gray matter of the brain. If the word "history" did not in and of itself convey the motif of a final repression of difference, one could say that only differences can be "historical" from the outset and in each of their aspects.

What is written as *différance,* then, will be the playing movement that "produces"—by means of something that is not simply an activity—these differences, these effects of difference. This does not mean that the *différance* that produces differences is somehow before them, in a simple and unmodified—in-different—present. *Différance* is the non-full , non- simple, structured and differentiating origin of differences. Thus, the name "origin" no longer suits it.

Since language, which Saussure says is a classification, has not fallen from the sky, its differences have been produced, are produced effects, but they are effects which do not find their cause in a subject or a substance, in a thing in general, a being that is somewhere present, thereby eluding the play of *différance.* If such a presence were implied in the concept of cause in general, in the most classical fashion, we then would have to speak of an effect without a cause, which very quickly would lead to speaking of no effect at all. I have attempted to indicate a way out of the closure of this framework via the "trace," which is no more an effect than it has a cause, but which in and of itself, outside its text, is not sufficient to operate the necessary transgression.

Since there is no presence before and outside semiological difference, what Saussure has written about language can be extended to the sign in general: "Language is necessary in order for speech to be intelligible and to produce all of its effects; but the latter is necessary in order for language to be established; historically, the fact of speech always comes first."[13]

Retaining at least the framework, if not the content, of this requirement formulated by Saussure, we will designate as *différance* the movement according to which language, or any code, any system of referral in general, is constituted "historically" as a weave of differences. "Is constituted," "is produced," "is created," "movement," "historically," etc., necessarily being understood beyond the metaphysical language in which they are retained, along with all their implications. We ought to demonstrate why concepts like *production,* constitution, and history remain in complicity with what is at issue here. But this would take me too far today—toward the theory of the representation of the "circle" in which we appear to be enclosed—and I utilize such concepts, like many others, only for their strategic convenience and in order to undertake their deconstruction at the currently most decisive point. In any event, it will be understood, by means of the circle in which we appear to be engaged, that as it is written here, *différance is* no more static than it is genetic, no more structural than historical. Or is no less so; and to object to this on the basis of the oldest of metaphysical oppositions (for example, by setting some generative point of view against a structural-taxonomical point of view, or vice versa) would be, above all, not to read what here is missing from orthographical ethics. Such oppositions have not the least pertinence to *différance,* which makes the thinking of it uneasy and uncomfortable.

Now if we consider the chain in which *différance* lends itself to a certain number of nonsynonymous substitutions, according to the necessity of the context, why have recourse to the "reserve," to "archi-writing," to the "archi-trace," to "spacing," that is, to the "supplement," or to the *pharmakon*, and soon to the hymen, to the margin-mark-march, etc.[14]

Let us go on. It is because of *différance* that the movement of signification is possible only if each so-called "present" element, each element appearing on the scene of presence, is related to something other than itself, thereby keeping within itself the mark of the past element, and already letting itself be vitiated by the mark of its relation to the future element, this trace being related no less to what is called the future than to what is called the past, and constituting what is called the present by means of this very relation to what it is not: what it absolutely is not, not even a past or a future as a modified present. An interval must separate the present from what it is not in order for the present to be itself, but this interval that constitutes it as present must, by the same token, divide the present in and of itself, thereby also dividing, along with the present, everything that is thought on the basis of the present, that is, in our metaphysical language, every being, and singularly substance or the subject. In constituting itself, in dividing itself dynamically, this interval is what might be called *spacing*, the becoming-space of time or the becoming-time of space *(temporization)*. And it is this constitution of the present, as an "originary" and irreducibly nonsimple (and therefore, *stricto sensu* nonoriginary) synthesis of marks, or traces of retentions and protentions (to reproduce analogically and provisionally a phenomenological and transcendental language that soon will reveal itself to be inadequate), that I propose to call archi-writing, archi-trace, or *différance*. Which (is) (simultaneously) spacing (and) temporization.

Could not this (active) movement of (the production of) *différance* without origin be called simply, and without neographism, *differentiation*? Such a word, among other confusions, would have left open the possibility of an organic, original, and homogeneous unity that eventually would come to be divided, to receive difference as an event. And above all, since it is formed from the verb "to differentiate," it would negate the economic signification of the detour, the temporizing delay, "deferral." Here, a remark in passing, which I owe to a recent reading of a text that Koyré (in 1934, in *Revue d'histoire et de philosophie réligieuse*, and reprinted in his *Etudes d'histoire de la pensée philosophique*) devoted to "Hegel in Jena." In this text Koyré gives long citations, in German, of the Jena *Logic*, and proposes their translation. On two occasions he encounters the expression *differente Beziehung* in Hegel's text. This word *(different)*, with its Latin root, is rare in German and, I believe, in Hegel, who prefers *verschieden* or *ungleich*, calling difference *Unterschied* and qualitative variety *Verschiedenheit*. In the Jena *Logic* he uses the word *different* precisely where he treats of time and the present. Before getting to a valuable comment of Koyré's, let us look at some sentences from Hegel, such as Koyré translates them: "The infinite, in this simplicity, is, as a moment opposed to the equal-to-itself, the negative, and in its moments, although it is (itself) presented to and in itself the totality (it is) what excludes in general, the point or limit; but in its own (action of) negating, it is related immediately to the other and negates itself by itself. The limit or moment of the present *(der Gegenwart)*, the absolute 'this' of time, or the now, is of an absolutely negative simplicity, which absolutely excludes from itself all multiplicity, and, by virtue of this, is absolutely determined; it is not whole or a *quantum* which would be extended in itself (and) which, in itself, also would have an undetermined moment, a diversity which, as indifferent *(gleichgultig)* or exterior in itself, would be related to an other *(auf ein anderes bezöge)*, but in this is a relation absolutely different from the simple *(sondern es ist absolut differente Beziehung)*." And Koyré most remarkably specifies in a note: "different Relation: *differente Beziehung*. One might say: 'differentiating relation.'" And on the next page, another text of Hegel's in which one can read this: "*Diese Beziehung ist Gegenwart, als eine differente Beziehung* (This relationship is [the] present as a different relationship)." Another note of Koyré's: "The term *different* here is taken in an active sense."[15]

Writing "*différant*"[16] or "*différance*" (with an *a)* would have had the advantage of making it possible to translate Hegel at that particular point—which is also an absolutely decisive point in his discourse—without further notes or specifications. And the translation would be, as it always must be, a transformation of one language by another. I contend, of course, that the word *différance* can also serve other purposes: first, because it marks not only the activity of "originary" difference, but also the temporizing detour of deferral; and above all because *différance* thus written, although maintaining relations of profound affinity with Hegelian discourse (such as it must be read), is also, up to a certain point, unable to break with that discourse (which has no kind of meaning or chance); but it can operate a kind of infinitesimal and radical displacement of it, whose space I attempt to delineate elsewhere but of which it would be difficult to speak briefly here.

Differences, thus, are "produced"—deferred—by *différance*. But *what* defers or *who* defers? In other words, *what is différance?* With this question we reach another level and another resource of our problematic.

What differs? Who differs? What is *différance?*

If we answered these questions before examining them as questions, before turning them back on themselves, and before suspecting their very form, including what seems most natural and necessary about them, we would immediately fall back into what we have just disengaged ourselves from. In effect, if we accepted the form of the question, in its meaning and its syntax ("what is?" "who is?" "who is it that?"), we would have to conclude that *différance* has been derived, has happened, is to be mastered and governed on the basis of the point of a present being, which itself could be some thing, a form, a state, a power in the world to which all kinds of names might be given, a *what*, or a present being as a *subject*, a *who*. And in this last case, notably, one would conclude implicitly that this present being, for example a being present to itself, as consciousness, eventually would come to defer or to differ: whether by delaying and turning away from the fulfillment of a "need" or a "desire," or by differing from itself. But in neither of these cases would such a present being be "constituted" by this *différance*.

Now if we refer, once again, to semiological difference, of what does Saussure, in particular, remind us? That "language [which only consists of differences] is not a function of the speaking subject." This implies that the subject (in its identity with itself, or eventually in its consciousness of its identity with itself, its self-consciousness) is inscribed in language, is a "function" of language, becomes a *speaking* subject only by making its speech conform—even in so-called "creation," or in so-called "transgression—to the system of the rules of language as a system of differences, or at very least by conforming to the general law of *différance*, or by adhering to the principle of language which Saussure says is "spoken language minus speech." "Language is necessary for the spoken word to be intelligible and so that it can produce all of its effects."[17]

If, by hypothesis, we maintain that the opposition of speech to language is absolutely rigorous, then *différance* would be not only the play of differences within language but also the relation of speech to language, the detour through which I must pass in order to speak, the silent promise I must make; and this is equally valid for semiology in general, governing all the relations of usage to schemata, of message to code, etc. (Elsewhere I have attempted to suggest that this *différance* in language, and in the relation of speech and language, forbids the essential dissociation of speech and language that Saussure, at another level of his discourse, traditionally wished to delineate. The practice of a language or of a code supposing a play of forms without a determined and invariable substance, and also supposing in the practice of this play a retention and protention of differences, a spacing and a temporization, a play of traces—all this must be a kind of writing before the letter, an archi-writing without a present origin, without archi-. Whence the regular erasure of the archi-, and the transformation of general semiology into grammatology, this latter executing a critical labor on everything within semiology, including the central concept of the sign, that maintained metaphysical presuppositions incompatible with the motif of *différance*.)

One might be tempted by an objection: certainly the subject becomes a *speaking* subject only in its commerce with the system of linguistic differences; or yet, the subject becomes a *signifying* (signifying in general, by means of speech or any other sign) subject only by inscribing itself in the system of differences. Certainly in this sense the speaking or signifying subject could not be present to itself, as speaking or signifying, without the play of linguistic or semiological *différance*. But can one not conceive of a presence, and of a presence to itself of the subject before speech or signs, a presence to itself of the subject in a silent and intuitive consciousness?

Such a question therefore supposes that, prior to the sign and outside it, excluding any trace and any *différance*, something like consciousness is possible. And that consciousness, before distributing its signs in space and in the world, can gather itself into its presence. But what is consciousness? What does "consciousness" mean? Most often, in the very form of meaning, in all its modifications, consciousness offers itself to thought only as self-presence, as the perception of self in presence. And what holds for consciousness holds here for so-called subjective existence in general. Just as the category of the subject cannot be, and never has been, thought without the reference to presence as *hupokeimenon* or as *ousia*, etc., so the subject as consciousness has never manifested itself except as self-presence. The privilege granted to consciousness therefore signifies the privilege granted to the present; and even if one describes the transcendental temporality of consciousness, and at the depth at which Husserl does so, one grants to the "living present" the power of synthesizing traces, and of incessantly reassembling them.

This privilege is the ether of metaphysics, the element of our thought that is caught in the language of metaphysics. One can delimit such a closure today only by soliciting[18] the value of presence that Heidegger has shown to be the ontotheological determination of Being; and in thus soliciting the value of presence, by means of an interrogation whose status must be completely exceptional, we are also examining the absolute privilege of this form or epoch of presence in general that is consciousness as meaning[19] in self-presence.

Thus one comes to posit presence—and specifically consciousness, the being beside itself of consciousness—no longer as the absolutely central form of Being but as a "determination" and as an "effect." A determination or an effect within a system which is no longer that of presence but of *différance*, a system that no longer tolerates the opposition of activity and passivity, nor that of cause and effect, or of indetermination and determination, etc., such that in designating consciousness as an effect or a determination, one continues—for strategic reasons that can be more or less lucidly deliberated and systematically calculated—to operate according to the lexicon of that which one is de-limiting.

Before being so radically and purposely the gesture of Heidegger, this gesture was also made by Nietzsche and Freud, both of whom, as is well known, and sometimes in very similar fashion, put consciousness into question in its assured certainty of itself. Now is it not remarkable that they both did so on the basis of the motif of *différance?*

Différance appears almost by name in their texts, and in those places where everything is at stake. I cannot expand upon this here; I will only recall that for Nietzsche "the great principal activity is unconscious," and that consciousness is the effect of forces whose essence, byways, and modalities are not proper to it.

Force itself is never present; it is only a play of differences and quantities. There would be no force in general without the difference between forces; and here the difference of quantity counts more than the content of the quantity, more than absolute size itself. "Quantity itself, therefore, is not separable from the difference of quantity. The difference of quantity is the essence of force, the relation of force to force. The dream of two equal forces, even if they are granted an opposition of meaning, is an approximate and crude dream, a statistical dream, plunged into by the living but dispelled by chemistry."[20] Is not all of Nietzsche's thought a critique of philosophy as an active indifference to difference, as the system of adiaphoristic reduction or repression? Which according to the same logic, according to logic itself, does not exclude that philosophy lives *in* and *on différance,* thereby blinding itself to the *same,* which is not the identical. The same, precisely, is *différance* (with an *a)* as the displaced and equivocal passage of one different thing to another, from one term of an opposition to the other. Thus one could reconsider all the pairs of opposites on which philosophy is constructed and on which our discourse lives, not in order to see opposition erase itself but to see what indicates that each of the terms must appear as the *différance* of the other, as the other different and deferred in the economy of the same (the intelligible as differing-deferring the sensible, as the sensible different and deferred; the concept as different and deferred, differing-deferring intuition; culture as nature different and deferred, differing-deferring; all the others of *physis—tekhnē, nomos, thesis,* society, freedom, history, mind, etc.—as *physis* different and deferred, or as *physis* differing and deferring. *Physis* in *différance,* And in this we may see the site of a reinterpretation of *mimēsis* in its alleged opposition to *physis).* And on the basis of this unfolding of the same as *différance,* we see announced the sameness of *différance* and repetition in the eternal return. Themes in Nietzsche's work that are linked to the symptomatology that always diagnoses the detour or ruse of an agency disguised in its *différance;* or further, to the entire thematic of active interpretation, which substitutes incessant deciphering for the unveiling of truth as the presentation of the thing itself in its presence, etc. Figures without truth, or at least a system of figures not dominated by the value of truth, which then becomes only an included, inscribed, circumscribed function.

Thus, *différance* is the name we might give to the "active," moving discord of different forces, and of differences of forces, that Nietzsche sets up against the entire system of metaphysical grammar, wherever this system governs culture, philosophy, and science.

It is historically significant that this diaphoristics, which, as an energetics or economics of forces, commits itself to putting into question the primacy of presence as consciousness, is also the major motif of Freud's thought: another diaphoristics, which in its entirety is both a theory of the figure (or of the trace) and an energetics. The putting into question of the authority of consciousness is first and always differential.

The two apparently different values of *différance* are tied together in Freudian theory: to differ as discernibility, distinction, separation, diastem, *spacing;* and to defer as detour, relay, reserve, *temporization.*

1. The concepts of trace *(Spur)*, of breaching *(Bahnung)*,[21] and of the forces of breaching, from the *Project* on, are inseparable from the concept of difference. The origin of memory, and of the psyche as (conscious or unconscious) memory in general, can be described only by taking into account the difference between breaches. Freud says so overtly. There is no breach without difference and no difference without trace.

2. All the differences in the production of unconscious traces and in the processes of inscription *(Niederschrift)* can also be interpreted as moments of *différance*, in the sense of putting into reserve. According to a schema that never ceased to guide Freud's thought, the movement of the trace is described as an effort of life to protect itself by *deferring* the dangerous investment, by constituting a reserve *(Vorrat)*. And all the oppositions that furrow Freudian thought relate each of his concepts one to another as moments of a detour in the economy of *différance.* One is but the other different and deferred, one differing and deferring the other. One is the other in *différance,* one is the *différance* of the other. This is why every apparently rigorous and irreducible *opposition* (for example the opposition of the secondary to the primary) comes to be qualified, at one moment or another, as a "theoretical fiction." Again, it is thereby, for example (but such an example governs, and communicates with, everything), that the difference between the pleasure principle and the reality principle is only *différance* as detour. In *Beyond the Pleasure Principle* Freud writes: "Under the influence of the ego's instincts of self-preservation, the pleasure principle is replaced by the reality principle. This latter principle does not abandon the intention of ultimately obtaining pleasure, but it nevertheless demands and carries into effect the postponement of satisfaction, the abandonment of a number of possibilities of gaining satisfaction and the temporary toleration of unpleasure as a step on the long indirect road *(Aufschub)* to pleasure."[22]

Here we are touching upon the point of greatest obscurity, on the very enigma of *différance,* on precisely that which divides its very concept by means of a strange cleavage. We must not hasten to decide. How are we to think *simultaneously,* on the one hand, *différance* as the economic detour which, in the element of the same, always aims at coming back to the pleasure or the presence that have been deferred by (conscious or unconscious) calculation, and, on the other hand, *différance* as the relation to an impossible presence, as expenditure without reserve, as the irreparable loss of presence, the irreversible usage of energy, that is, as the death instinct, and as the entirely other relationship that apparently interrupts every economy? It is evident—and this is the evident itself—that the economical and the noneconomical, the same and the entirely other, etc., cannot be thought *together.* If *différance is* unthinkable in this way, perhaps we should not hasten to make it evident, in the philosophical element of evidentiality which would make short work of dissipating the mirage and illogicalness of *différance* and would do so with the infallibility of calculations that we are well acquainted with, having precisely recognized their place, necessity, and function in the structure of *différance*. Elsewhere, in a reading of Bataille, I have attempted to indicate what might come of a rigorous and, in a new sense, "scientific" *relating* of the "restricted economy" that takes no part in expenditure without reserve, death, opening itself to nonmeaning, etc., to a general economy that *takes into account* the nonreserve, that keeps in reserve the nonreserve, if it can be put thus. I am speaking of a relationship between a *différance* that can make a profit on its investment and a *différance* that misses its profit, the *investiture* of a presence that is pure and without loss here being confused with absolute loss, with death. Through such a relating of a restricted and a general economy the very project of philosophy, under the privileged heading of Hegelianism, is displaced and reinscribed. The *Aufhebung—la relève*—is constrained into writing itself otherwise. Or perhaps simply into writing itself. Or, better, into taking account of its consumption of writing.[23]

For the economic character of *différance* in no way implies that the deferred presence can always be found again, that we have here only an investment that provisionally and calculatedly delays the perception of its profit or the profit of its perception. Contrary to the metaphysical, dialectical, "Hegelian" interpretation of the economic movement of *différance*, we must conceive of a play in which whoever loses wins, and in which one loses and wins on every turn. If the displaced presentation remains definitively and implacably postponed, it is not that a certain present remains absent or hidden. Rather, *différance* maintains our relationship with that which we necessarily misconstrue, and which exceeds the alternative of presence and absence. A certain alterity—to which Freud gives the metaphysical name of the unconscious—is definitively exempt from every process of presentation by means of which we would call upon it to show itself in person. In this context, and beneath this guise, the unconscious is not, as we know, a hidden, virtual, or potential self-presence. It differs from, and defers, itself; which doubtless means that it is woven of differences, and also that it sends out delegates, representatives, proxies; but without any chance that the giver of proxies might "exist," might be present, be "itself" somewhere, and with even less chance that it might become conscious. In this sense, contrary to the terms of an old debate full of the metaphysical investments that it has always assumed, the "unconscious" is no more a "thing" than it is any other thing, is no more a thing than it is a virtual or masked consciousness. This radical alterity as concerns every possible mode of presence is marked by the irreducibility of the aftereffect, the delay. In order to describe traces, in order to read the traces of "unconscious" traces (there are no "conscious" traces), the language of presence and absence, the metaphysical discourse of phenomenology, is inadequate. (Although the phenomenologist is not the only one to speak this language.)

The structure of delay *(Nachträglichkeit)* in effect forbids that one make of temporalization (temporization) a simple dialectical complication of the living present as an originary and unceasing synthesis—a synthesis constantly directed back on itself, gathered in on itself and gathering—of retentional traces and protentional openings. The alterity of the "unconscious" makes us concerned not with horizons of modified—past or future—presents, but with a "past" that has never been present, and which never will be, whose future to come will never be a *production* or a reproduction in the form of presence. Therefore the concept of trace is incompatible with the concept of retention, of the becoming-past of what has been present. One cannot think the trace—and therefore, *différance*—on the basis of the present, or of the presence of the present.

A past that has never been present: this formula is the one that Emmanuel Levinas uses, although certainly in a nonpsychoanalytic way, to qualify the trace and enigma of absolute alterity: the Other.[24] Within these limits, and from this point of view at least, the thought of *différance* implies the entire critique of classical ontology undertaken by Levinas. And the concept of the trace, like that of *différance* thereby organizes, along the lines of these different traces and differences of traces, in Nietzsche's sense, in Freud's sense, in Levinas's sense—these "names of authors" here being only indices—the network which reassembles and traverses our "era" as the delimitation of the ontology of presence.

Which is to say the ontology of beings and beingness. It is the domination of beings that *différance* everywhere comes to solicit, in the sense that *sollicitare*, in old Latin, means to shake as a whole, to make tremble in entirety. Therefore, it is the determination of Being as presence or as beingness that is interrogated by the thought of *différance*. Such a question could not emerge and be understood unless the difference between Being and beings were somewhere to be broached. First consequence: *différance* is not. It is not a present being, however excellent, unique, principal, or transcendent. It governs nothing, reigns over nothing, and nowhere exercises any authority. It is not announced by any capital letter. Not only is there no kingdom of *différance*, but *différance* instigates the subversion of every kingdom. Which makes it obviously threatening and infallibly dreaded by everything within us that desires a kingdom, the past or future presence of a kingdom. And it is always in the name of a kingdom that one may reproach *différance* with wishing to reign, believing that one sees it aggrandize itself with a capital letter.

Can *différance*, for these reasons, settle down into the division of the ontico-ontological difference, such as it is thought, such as its "epoch" in particular is thought, "through," if it may still be expressed such, Heidegger's uncircumventable meditation?

There is no simple answer to such a question.

In a certain aspect of itself, *différance* is certainly but the historical and epochal *unfolding* of Being or of the ontological difference. The *a* of *différance* marks the *movement* of this unfolding.

And yet, are not the thought of the *meaning* or *truth* of Being, the determination of *différance* as the ontico-ontological difference, difference thought within the horizon of the question of *Being*, still intrametaphysical effects of *différance?* The unfolding of *différance is* perhaps not solely the truth of Being, or of the epochality of Being. Perhaps we must attempt to think this unheard-of thought, this silent tracing: that the history of Being, whose thought engages the Greco-Western *logos* such as it is produced via the ontological difference, is but an epoch of the *diapherein.* Henceforth one could no longer even call this an "epoch," the concept of epochality belonging to what is within history as the history of Being. Since Being has never had a "meaning," has never been thought or said as such, except by dissimulating itself in beings, then *différance,* in a certain and very strange way, (is) "older" than the ontological difference or than the truth of Being. When it has this age it can be called the play of the trace. The play of a trace which no longer belongs to the horizon of Being, but whose play transports and encloses the meaning of Being: the play of the trace, or the *différance,* which has no meaning and is not. Which does not belong. There is no maintaining, and no depth to, this bottomless chessboard on which Being is put into play.

Perhaps this is why the Heraclitean play of the *hen diapheron heautōi,* of the one differing from itself, the one in difference with itself, already is lost like a trace in the determination of the *diapherein* as ontological difference.

To think the ontological difference doubtless remains a difficult task, and any statement of it has remained almost inaudible. Further, to prepare, beyond our *logos,* for a *différance so* violent that it can be interpellated neither as the epochality of Being nor as ontological difference, is not in any way to dispense with the passage through the truth of Being, or to "criticize," "contest," or misconstrue its incessant necessity. On the contrary, we must stay within the difficulty of this passage, and repeat it in the rigorous reading of metaphysics, wherever metaphysics normalizes Western discourse, and not only in the texts of the "history of philosophy." As rigorously as possible we must permit to appear/disappear the trace of what exceeds the truth of Being. The trace (of that) which can never be presented, the trace which itself can never be presented: that is, appear and manifest itself, as such, in its phenomenon. The trace beyond that which profoundly links fundamental ontology and phenomenology. Always differing and deferring, the trace is never as it is in the presentation of itself. It erases itself in presenting itself, muffles itself in resonating, like the *a* writing itself, inscribing its pyramid in *différance.*

The annunciating and reserved trace of this movement can always be disclosed in metaphysical discourse, and especially in the contemporary discourse which states, through the attempts to which we just referred (Nietzsche, Freud, Levinas), the closure of ontology. And especially through the Heideggerean text.

This text prompts us to examine the essence of the present, the presence of the present.

What is the present? What is it to think the present in its presence?

Let us consider, for example, the 1946 text entitled *Der Spruch des Anaximander* ("The Anaximander Fragment").[25] In this text Heidegger recalls that the forgetting of Being forgets the difference between Being and beings: ". . . to be the Being *of* beings is the matter of Being *(die Sache des Seins)*. The grammatical form of this enigmatic, ambiguous genitive indicates a genesis *(Genesis)*, the emergence *(Herkunft)* of what is present from presencing *(des Anwesenden aus dem Anwesen)*. Yet the essence *(Wesen)* of this emergence remains concealed *(verbogen)* along with the essence of these two words. Not only that, but even the very relation between presencing and what is present *(Anwesen und Anwesendem)* remains unthought. From early on it seems as though presencing and what is present were each something for itself. Presencing itself unnoticeably becomes something present . . . The essence of presencing *(Das Wesen des Anwesens)*, and with it the distinction between presencing and what is present, remains forgotten. *The oblivion of Being is oblivion of the distinction between Being and beings*" (p. 50).

In recalling the difference between Being and beings (the ontological difference) as the difference between presence and the present, Heidegger advances a proposition, a body of propositions, that we are not going to use as a subject for criticism. This would be foolishly precipitate; rather, what we shall try to do is to return to this proposition its power to provoke.

Let us proceed slowly. What Heidegger wants to mark is this: the difference between Being and beings, the forgotten of metaphysics, has disappeared without leaving a trace. The very trace of difference has been submerged. If we maintain that *différance* (is) (itself) other than absence and presence, if it *traces*, then when it is a matter of the forgetting of the difference (between Being and beings), we would have to speak of a disappearance of the trace of the trace. Which is indeed what the following passage from "The Anaximander Fragment" seems to imply: "Oblivion of Being belongs to the self-veiling essence of Being. It belongs so essentially to the destiny of Being that the dawn of this destiny rises as the unveiling of what is present in its presencing. This means that the history of Being begins with the oblivion of Being, since Being—together with its essence, its distinction from beings—keeps to itself. The distinction collapses. It remains forgotten. Although the two parties to the distinction, what is present and presencing *(das Anwesende und das Anwesen)*, reveal themselves, they do not do so as distinguished. Rather, even the early trace *(die frühe Spur)* of the distinction is obliterated when presencing appears as something present *(das Anwesen wie ein Anwesendes erscheint)* and finds itself in the position of being the highest being present *(in einem höchsten Anwesenden)*" (pp. 50–51).

Since the trace is not a presence but the simulacrum of a presence that dislocates itself, displaces itself, refers itself, it properly has no site—erasure belongs to its structure. And not only the erasure which must always be able to overtake it (without which it would not be a trace but an indestructible and monumental substance), but also the erasure which constitutes it from the outset as a trace, which situates it as the change of site, and makes it disappear in its appearance, makes it emerge from itself in its production. The erasure of the early trace *(die frühe Spur)* of difference is therefore the "same" as its tracing in the text of metaphysics. This latter must have maintained the mark of what it has lost, reserved, put aside. The paradox of such a structure, in the language of metaphysics, is an inversion of metaphysical concepts, which produces the following effect: the present becomes the sign of the sign, the trace of the trace. It is no longer what every reference refers to in the last analysis. It becomes a function in a structure of generalized reference. It is a trace, and a trace of the erasure of the trace.

Thereby the text of metaphysics is *comprehended*. Still legible; and to be read. It is not surrounded but rather traversed by its limit, marked in its interior by the multiple furrow of its margin. Proposing *all at once* the monument and the mirage of the trace, the trace simultaneously traced and erased, simultaneously living and dead, and, as always, living in its simulation of life's preserved inscription. A pyramid. Not a stone fence to be jumped over but itself stonelike, on a wall, to be deciphered otherwise, a text without voice.

Thus one can think without contradiction, or at least without granting any pertinence to such a contradiction, what is perceptible and imperceptible in the trace. The "early trace" of difference is lost in an invisibility without return, and yet its very loss is sheltered, retained, seen, delayed. In a text. In the form of presence. In the form of the proper. Which itself is only an effect of writing.

Having stated the erasure of the early trace, Heidegger can therefore, in a contradiction without contradiction, consign, countersign, the sealing of the trace. A bit further on: "However, the distinction between Being and beings, as something forgotten, can invade our experience only if it has already unveiled itself with the presencing of what is present *(mit dem Anwesen des Anwesenden)*; only if it has left a trace *(eine Spur geprägt hat)* which remains preserved *(gewahrt bleibt)* in the language to which Being comes" (p. 51).

Still further on, while meditating on Anaximander's *to khreon*, which he translates as *Brauch* (usage), Heidegger writes this: "Enjoining order and reck *(Fug und Ruch verfügend)*, usage delivers to each present being *(Anwesende)* the while into which it is released. But accompanying this process is the constant danger that lingering will petrify into mere persistence *(in das blosse Beharren verhärtet)*. Thus usage essentially remains at the same time the distribution *(Aushändigung*: dis- maintenance) of presencing *(des Anwesens)* into disorder *(in den Un-fug)*. Usage conjoins the dis *(Der Brauch fügt das Un-)*" (p. 54).

And it is at the moment when Heidegger recognizes *usage* as *trace* that the question must be asked: can we, and to what extent, think this trace and the *dis* of *différance* as *Wesen des Seins?* Does not the *dis* of *différance* refer us beyond the history of Being, and also beyond our language, and everything that can be named in it? In the language of Being, does it not call for a necessarily violent transformation of this language by an entirely other language?

Let us make this question more specific. And to force the "trace" out of it (and has anyone thought that we have been tracking something down, something other than tracks themselves to be tracked down?), let us read this passage: "The translation of *to khreon* as 'usage' has not resulted from a preoccupation with etymologies and dictionary meanings. The choice of the word stems from a prior crossing *over (Über-setzen;* trans-lation) of a thinking which tries to think the distinction in the essence of Being *(im Wesen des Seins)* in the fateful beginning of Being's oblivion. The word 'usage' is dictated to thinking in the experience *(Erfahrung)* of Being's oblivion. What properly remains to be thought in the word 'usage' has presumably left a trace *(Spur)* in *to khreon*. This trace quickly vanishes *(alsbald verschwindet)* in the destiny of Being which unfolds in world history as Western metaphysics" (p. 54).

How to conceive what is outside a text? That which is more or less than a text's *own, proper* margin? For example, what is other than the text of Western metaphysics? It is certain that the trace which "quickly vanishes in the destiny of Being (and) which unfolds . . . as Western metaphysics" escapes every determination, every name it might receive in the metaphysical text. It is sheltered, and therefore dissimulated, in these names. It does not appear in them as the trace "itself." But this is because it could never appear itself, *as such*. Heidegger also says that difference cannot appear as such: "Lichtung des Unterschiedes kann deshalb auch nicht bedeuten, class der Unterschied als der Unterschied erscheint." There is no essence of *différance;* it (is) that which not only could never be appropriated in the *as such* of its name or its appearing, but also that which threatens the authority of the *as such* in general, of the presence of the thing itself in its essence. That there is not a proper essence[26] of *différance* at this point, implies that there is neither a Being nor truth of the play of writing such as it engages *différance*.

For us, *différance* remains a metaphysical name, and all the names that it receives in our language are still, as names, metaphysical. And this is particularly the case when these names state the determination of *différance* as the difference between presence and the present *(Anwesen/Anwesend)*, and above all, and is already the case when they state the determination of *différance* as the difference of Being and beings.

"Older" than Being itself, such a *différance* has no name in our language. But we "already know" that if it is unnameable, it is not provisionally so, not because our language has not yet found or received this *name*, or because we would have to seek it in another language, outside the finite system of our own. It is rather because there is no *name* for it at all, not even the name of essence or of Being, not even that of "*différance*," which is not a name, which is not a pure nominal unity, and unceasingly dislocates itself in a chain of differing and deferring substitutions.

"There is no name for it": a proposition to be read in its *platitude*. This unnameable is not an ineffable Being which no name could approach: God, for example. This unnameable is the play which makes possible nominal effects, the relatively unitary and atomic structures that are called names, the chains of substitutions of names in which, for example, the nominal effect *différance* is itself *enmeshed*, carried off, reinscribed, just as a false entry or a false exit is still part of the game, a function of the system.

What we know, or what we would know if it were simply a question here of something to know, is that there has never been, never will be, a unique word, a master-name. This is why the thought of the letter *a* in *différance* is not the primary prescription or the prophetic annunciation of an imminent and as yet unheard-of nomination. There is nothing kerygmatic about this "word," provided that one perceives its decapita(liza)tion. And that one puts into question the name of the name.

There will be no unique name, even if it were the name of Being. And we must think this without *nostalgia*, that is, outside of the myth of a purely maternal or paternal language, a lost native country of thought. On the contrary, we must *affirm* this, in the sense in which Nietzsche puts affirmation into play, in a certain laughter and a certain step of the dance.

From the vantage of this laughter and this dance, from the vantage of this affirmation foreign to all dialectics, the other side of nostalgia, what I will call Heideggerian *hope*, comes into question. I am not unaware how shocking this word might seem here. Nevertheless I am venturing it, without excluding any of its implications, and I relate it to what still seems to me to be the metaphysical part of "The Anaximander Fragment": the quest for the proper word and the unique name. Speaking of the first word of Being *(das frühe Wort des Seins: to khreon)*, Heidegger writes: "The relation to what is present that rules in the essence of presencing itself is a unique one *(ist eine einzige)*, altogether incomparable to any other relation. It belongs to the uniqueness of Being itself *(Sie gehört zur Einzigkeit des Seins selbst)*. Therefore, in order to name the essential nature of Being *(das wesende Seins)*, language would have to find a single word, the unique word *(ein einziges, das einzige Wort)*. From this we can gather how daring every thoughtful word *(denkende Wort)* addressed to Being is *(das dem Sein zugesprochen wird)*. Nevertheless such daring is not impossible, since Being speaks always and everywhere throughout language" (p. 52).

Such is the question: the alliance of speech and Being in the unique word, in the finally proper name. And such is the question inscribed in the simulated affirmation of *différance*. It bears (on) each member of this sentence: "Being / speaks / always and everywhere / throughout / language."

Notes

Address given before the Société française de philosophie, 27 January 1968, published simultaneously in the *Bulletin de la société française de philosophie*, July–September 1968, and in *Théorie d'ensemble*, coll. Tel Quel (Paris: Editions du Seuil, 1968).

1. Throughout this book I will translate *le propre* as "the proper." Derrida most often intends all the senses of the word at once: that which is correct, as in *le sens propre* (proper, literal meaning), and that which is one's own, that which may be owned, that which is legally, correctly owned—all the links between proper, property, and propriety.—Tr.

2. The last three sentences refer elliptically and playfully to the following ideas. Derrida first plays on the "silence" of the *a* in *différance* as being like a silent tomb, like a pyramid, like the pyramid to which Hegel compares the body of the sign. "Tomb" in Greek is *oikēsis*, which is akin to the Greek *oikos*—house—from which the word "economy" derives *(oikos*—house and *nemein*—to manage). Thus Derrida speaks of the "economy of death" as the "familial residence and tomb of the proper." Further, and more elliptically still, Derrida speaks of the tomb, which always bears an inscription in stone, announcing the death of the tyrant. This seems to refer to Hegel's treatment of the Antigone story in the *Phenomenology*. It will be recalled that Antigone defies the tyrant Creon by burying her brother Polynices. Creon retaliates by having Antigone entombed. There she cheats the slow death that awaits her by hanging herself. The tyrant Creon has a change of heart too late, and—after the suicides of his son and wife, his *family*—kills himself. Thus family, death, inscription, tomb, law, economy. In a later work, *Glas*, Derrida analyzes Hegel's treatment of the *Antigone*.—Tr.

3. ". . . not fortuitously affiliated with the objectivity of *theōrein* or understanding." A play on words has been lost in translation here, a loss that makes this sentence difficult to understand. In the previous sentence Derrida says that the difference between the *e* and the *a* of *différence/différance* can neither be seen nor heard. It is not a sensible—that is, relating to the senses—difference. But, he goes on to explain, neither is this an intelligible difference, for the very names by which we conceive of objective intelligibility are already in complicity with sensibility. *Theōrein*—the Greek origin of "theory"—literally means "to look at," to *see*; and the word Derrida uses for "understanding" here is *entendement*, the noun form of *entendre*, to *hear*.—Tr.

4. As in the past, *être (Sein)* will be translated as Being. *Etant (Seiendes)* will be either beings or being, depending on the context. Thus, here *étant-present* is "being-present." For a justification of this translation see Derrida, *Writing and Difference*, trans. Alan Bass (Chicago: University of Chicago Press, 1978), Translator's Introduction, p. xvii.—Tr.

5. ". . . a hole with indeterminable borders (for example, in a topology of castration)." This phrase was added to "La Différance" for its publication in the French edition of this volume and refers to the polemic Derrida had already engaged (in *Positions*; elaborated further in *le Facteur de la verité*) with Jacques Lacan. For Derrida, Lacan's "topology of castration," which assigns the "hole" or lack to a place—"a hole with determinable borders"—repeats the metaphysical gesture (albeit a negative one) of making absence, the lack, the hole, a transcendental principle that can be pinned down as such, and can thereby *govern* a theoretical discourse.—Tr.

6. The Greek *arkhē* combines the values of a founding principle and of government by a controlling principle (e.g. *arche*ology, mon*archy*).—Tr.

7. In English the two distinct meanings of the Latin *differre* have become two separate words: to defer and to differ.—Tr.

8. The next few sentences will require some annotation, to be found in this note and the next two. In this sentence Derrida is pointing out that two words that sound exactly alike in French (*différents, différends*) refer to the sense of *differre* that implies spacing, otherness—difference in its usual English sense. *Les différents* are different things; *les différends* are differences of opinion, grounds for dispute—whence the references to *all*ergy (from the Greek *allos*, other) and polemics.—Tr.

9. However, to continue the last note, *différance* (in French) does not convey the sense of active putting off, of deferring (*différance* in what would be its usual sense in French, if it were a word in common usage), or the sense of active polemical difference, actively differing with someone or something. ("Active" here, though, is not really correct, for reasons that Derrida will explain below.) The point is that there is no noun-verb, no gerund for either sense in French.—Tr.

10. Such a gerund would normally be constructed from the present participle of the verb: *différant*. Curiously then, the noun *différance* suspends itself between the two senses of *différant*—deferring, differing. We might say that it defers differing, and differs from deferring, in and of itself.—Tr.

11. *Ousia* and *parousia* imply presence as both origin and end, the founding principle (*arkhē*) as that toward which one moves (*telos, eskhaton*).—Tr.

12. Ferdinand de Saussure, *Course in General Linguistics*, trans. Wade Baskin (New York: Philosophical Library, 1959), pp. 117–18, 120.—Tr.

13. Ibid., p. 18.—Tr.

14. All these terms refer to writing and inscribe *différance* within themselves, as Derrida says, according to the context. The supplement (*supplément*) is Rousseau's word to describe writing (analyzed in *Of Grammatology*, trans. Gayatri Spivak (Baltimore: Johns Hopkins University Press, 1976]). It means both the missing piece and the extra piece. The *pharmakon* is Plato's word for writing (analyzed in "Plato's Pharmacy" in *Dissemination*, trans. Barbara Johnson [Chicago: University of Chicago Press, 1981]), meaning *both* remedy and poison; the hymen (*l'hymen*) comes from Derrida's analysis of Mallarmé's writing and Mallarmé's reflections on writing ("The Double Session" in *Dissemination*) and refers *both* to virginity and to consummation; *marge-marque-marche* is the series *en différance* that Derrida applies to Sollers's *Nombres* ("Dissemination" in *Dissemination*).—Tr.

15. Alexandre Koyré, "Hegel à Iena," in *Etudes d'histoire de la pensée philosophique* (Paris: Armand Colin, 1961), pp. 153–54. In his translation of "La différance" (in *Speech and Phenomena* [Evanston: Northwestern University Press, 1973]), David Allison notes (p. 144) that the citation from Hegel comes from "Jensener Logik, Metaphysik, und Naturphilosophie" in *Sämtliche Werke* (Leipzig: F. Meiner, 1925), XVIII, 202. Allison himself translated Hegel's text, and I have modified his translation.—Tr.

16. The point here, which cannot be conveyed in English, is that Koyré's realization that Hegel is describing a "differentiating relation," or "different" in an active sense, is precisely what the formation of *différance* from the participle *différant* describes, as explained in notes 9 and 10 above. And that it is the *present* that is described as differing from and deferring itself helps clarify Derrida's argument (at the end of the essay) that

presence is to be rethought as the trace of the trace, as *différance* differed-and-deferred.—Tr.

17. Saussure, *Course in General Linguistics*, p. 37.—Tr.

18. The French *solliciter*, as the English *solicit*, derives from an Old Latin expression meaning to shake the whole, to make something tremble in its entirety. Derrida comments on this later, but is already using "to solicit" in this sense here.—Tr.

19. "Meaning" here is the weak translation of *vouloir-dire*, which has a strong sense of willing *(voluntas)* to say, putting the attempt to mean in conjunction with speech, a crucial conjunction for Derrida.—Tr.

20. Gilles Deleuze, *Nietzsche et la philosophie* (Paris: Presses Universitaires de France, 1970), p. 49.

21. Derrida is referring here to his essay "Freud and the Scene of Writing" in *Writing and Difference*. "Breaching" is the translation for *Bahnung* that I adopted there: it conveys more of the sense of breaking open (as in the German *Bahnung* and the French *frayage)* than the Standard Edition's "facilitation." The *Project* Derrida refers to here is the *Project for a Scientific Psychology* (1895), in which Freud attempted to cast his psychological thinking in a neurological framework.—Tr.

22. *The Standard Edition of the Complete Psychological Works* (London: Hogarth Press, 1950 [hereafter cited as *SE*]), vol. 18, p. 10.—Tr.

23. Derrida is referring here to the reading of Hegel he proposed in "From Restricted to General Economy: A Hegelianism Without Reserve," in *Writing and Difference*. In that essay Derrida began his consideration of Hegel as the great philosophical *speculator*; thus all the economic metaphors of the previous sentences. For Derrida the deconstruction of metaphysics implies an endless confrontation with Hegelian concepts, and the move from a restricted, "speculative" philosophical economy—in which there is nothing that cannot be made to make sense, in which there is nothing *other* than meaning—to a "general" economy—which affirms that which exceeds meaning, the excess of meaning from which there can be no speculative profit—involves a reinterpretation of the central Hegelian concept: the *Aufhebung*. *Aufhebung* literally means "lifting up"; but it also contains the double meaning of conservation and negation. For Hegel, dialectics is a process of *Aufhebung:* every concept is to be negated and lifted up to a higher sphere in which it is thereby conserved. In this way, there is nothing from which the *Aufhebung* cannot profit. However, as Derrida points out, there is always an effect of *différance* when the same word has two contradictory meanings. Indeed it is this effect of *différance*—the excess of the trace *Aufhebung* itself—that is precisely what the *Aufhebung* can never *aufheben:* lift up, conserve, and negate. This is why Derrida wishes to constrain the *Aufhebung* to write itself otherwise, or simply to write itself, to take into account its consumption of writing. Without writing, the trace, there could be no words with double, contradictory meanings.

As with *différance*, the translation of a word with a double meaning is particularly difficult, and touches upon the entire problematics of writing and *différance*. The best translators of Hegel usually cite Hegel's own delight that the most speculative of languages, German, should have provided this most speculative of words as the vehicle for his supreme speculative effort. Thus *Aufhebung is* usually best annotated and left untranslated. (Jean Hyppolite, in his French translations of Hegel, carefully annotates his rendering of *Aufheben* as both *supprimer* and *dépasser*. Baillies's rendering of *Aufhebung* as "sublation" is misleading.) Derrida, however, in his attempt to make *Aufhebung* write itself otherwise, has proposed a new translation of it that *does* take into account the effect of *différance* in its double meaning. Derrida's translation is *la relève*. The word comes from the verb *relever*, which means to lift up, as does *Aufheben*. But *relever* also means to relay, to relieve, as when one soldier on duty relieves another. Thus the conserving-and-negating lift has become *la relève*, a "lift" in which is inscribed an effect of substitution and difference, the effect of substitution and difference inscribed in the double meaning of *Aufhebung*. A. V. Miller's rendering of *Aufhebung*. as "supersession" in his recent translation of the *Phenomenology* comes close to *relever* in combining the senses of raising up and replacement, although without the elegance of Derrida's maintenance of the verb meaning "to lift" *(heben, lever)* and change of prefix *(auf-, re-)*. Thus we will leave *la relève* untranslated throughout, as with *différance*. For more on *la relève*, see below "*Ousia* and *Grammē*," note 15; "The Pit and the Pyramid," note 16; and "The Ends of Man," note 14.—Tr.

24. On Levinas, and on the translation of his term *autrui by* "Other," see "Violence and Metaphysics," note 6, in *Writing and Difference*.—Tr.

25. Martin Heidegger, *Holzwege* (Frankfurt: V. Klostermann, 1957). English translation ("The Anaximander Fragment") in *Early Greek Thinking*, trans. David Farrell Krell and Frank Capuzzi (New York: Harper and Row, 1975). All further references in the text.—Tr.

26. *Différance* is not a "species" of the genus *ontological difference*. If the "gift of presence is the property of Appropriating *(Die Gabe von Anwesen ist Eigentum des Ereignens)*" ["Time and Being," in *On Time and Being*, trans. Joan Stambaugh, New York: Harper and Row, 1972; p. 22], *différance is* not a process of propriation in any sense whatever. It is neither position (appropriation) nor negation (expropriation), but rather other. Hence it seems—but here, rather, we are marking the necessity of a future itinerary—that *différance* would be no more a species of the genus *Ereignis* than Being. Heidegger: ". . . then Being belongs into Appropriating *(Dann gehört das Sein in das Ereignen)*. Giving and its gift receive their determination from Appropriating. In that case, Being would be a species of Appropriation *(Ereignis)*, and not the other way around. To take refuge in such an inversion would be too cheap. Such thinking misses the matter at stake *(Sie denkt am Sachverhalt vorbei)*. Appropriation *(Ereignis)* is not the encompassing general concept under which Being and time could be subsumed. Logical classifications mean nothing here. For as we think Being itself and follow what is its own *(seinem Eigenen folgen)*, Being proves to be destiny's gift of presence *(gewahrte Gabe des Geschickes von Anwesenheit)*, the gift granted by the giving *(Reichen)* of time. The gift of presence is the property of Appropriating *(Die Gabe von Anwesen ist Eigentum des Ereignens)*." *(On Time and Being*, pp. 21–22.)

Without a displaced reinscription of this chain (Being, presence, propriation, etc.) the relation between general or fundamental onto-logy and whatever ontology masters or makes subordinate under the rubric of a regional or particular science will never be transformed rigorously and irreversibly. Such regional sciences include not only political economy, psychoanalysis, semiolinguistics—in all of which, and perhaps more than elsewhere, the value of the *proper* plays an irreducible role—but equally all spiritualist or materialist metaphysics. The analyses articulated in this volume aim at such a preliminary articulation. It goes without saying that such a reinscription will never be contained in theoretical or philosophical discourse, or generally in any discourse or writing, but only on the scene of what I have called elsewhere the text in general (1972).

PART FIVE

Luce Irigaray

When Our Lips Speak Together

If we keep on speaking the same language together, we're going to reproduce the same history. Begin the same old stories all over again. Don't you think so? Listen: all round us, men and women sound just the same. The same discussions, the same arguments, the same scenes. The same attractions and separations. The same difficulties, the same impossibility of making connections. The same . . . Same . . . Always the same.

If we keep on speaking sameness, if we speak to each other as men have been doing for centuries, as we have been taught to speak, we'll miss each other, fall ourselves. Again . . . Words will pass through our bodies, above our heads. They'll vanish, and we'll be lost. Far off, up high. Absent from ourselves: we'll be spoken machines, speaking machines. Enveloped in proper skins, but not our own. Withdrawn into proper names, violated by them. Not yours, not mine. We don't have any. We change names as men exchange us, as they use us, use us up. It would be frivolous of us, exchanged by them, to be so changeable.

How can I touch you if you're not there? Your blood has become their meaning. They can speak to each other, and about us. But what about us? Come out of their language. Try to go back through the names they've given you. I'll wait for you, I'm waiting for myself. Come back. It's not so hard. You stay here, and you won't be absorbed into familiar scenes, worn-out phrases, routine gestures. Into bodies already encoded within a system. Try to pay attention to yourself. To me. Without letting convention, or habit, distract you.

For example: "I love you" is addressed by convention or habit to an enigma—an other. An other body, an other sex. I love you: I don't quite know who, or what. "I love" flows away, is buried, drowned, burned, lost in a void. We'll have to wait for the return of "I love." Perhaps a long time, perhaps forever. Where has "I love" gone? What has become of me? "I love" lies in wait for the other. Has he swallowed me up? Spat me out? Taken me? Left me? Locked me up? Thrown me out? What's he like now? No longer (like) me? When he tells me "I love you," is he giving me back? Or is he giving himself in that form? His? Mine? The same? Another? But then where am I, what have I become?

When you say I love you—staying right here, close to you, close to me—you're saying I love myself. You don't need to wait for it to be given back; neither do I. We don't owe each other anything. That "I love you" is neither gift nor debt. You "give" me nothing when you touch yourself, touch me, when you touch yourself again through me. You don't give yourself. What would I do with you, with myself, wrapped up like a gift? You keep our selves to the extent that you share us. You find our selves to the extent that you trust us. Alternatives, oppositions, choices, bargains like these have no business between us. Unless we restage their commerce, and remain within their order. Where "we" has no place.

I love you: body shared, undivided. Neither you nor I severed. There is no need for blood shed, between us. No need for a wound to remind us that blood exists. It flows within us, from us. Blood is familiar, close. You are all red. And so very white. Both at once. You don't become red by losing your candid whiteness. You are white because you have remained close to blood. White and red at once, we give birth to all the colors: pinks, browns, blonds, greens, blues . . . For this whiteness is no sham. It is not dead blood, black blood. Sham is black. It absorbs everything, closed in on itself, trying to come back to life. Trying in vain . . . Whereas red's whiteness takes nothing away. Luminous, without autarchy, it gives back as much as it receives.

We are luminous. Neither one nor two. I've never known how to count. Up to you. In their calculations, we make two. Really, two? Doesn't that make you laugh? An odd sort of two. And yet not one. Especially not one. Let's leave *one* to them: their oneness, with its prerogatives, its domination, its solipsism: like the sun's. And the strange way they divide up their couples, with the other as the image of the one. Only an image. So any move toward the other means turning back to the attraction of one's own mirage. A (scarcely) living mirror, she/it is frozen, mute. More lifelike. The ebb and flow of our lives spent in the exhausting labor of copying, miming. Dedicated to reproducing—that sameness in which we have remained for centuries, as the other.

But how can I put "I love you" differently? I love you, my indifferent one? That still means yielding to their language. They've left us only lacks, deficiencies, to designate ourselves. They've left us their negative(s). We ought to be—that's already going too far-indifferent.

Indifferent one, keep still. When you stir, you disturb their order. You upset everything. You break the circle of their habits, the circularity of their exchanges, their knowledge, their desire. Their world. Indifferent one, you mustn't move, or be moved, unless they call you. If they say "come," then you may go ahead. Barely. Adapting yourself to whatever need they have, or don't have, for the presence of their own image. One step, or two. No more. No exuberance. No turbulence. Otherwise you'll smash everything. The ice, the mirror. Their earth, their mother. And what about your life? You must pretend to receive it from them. You're an indifferent, insignificant little receptacle, subject to their demands alone.

So they think we're indifferent. Doesn't that make you laugh? At least for a moment, here and now? *We* are *indifferent?* (If you keep on laughing that way, we'll never be able to talk to each other. We'll remain absorbed in their words, violated by them. So let's try to take back some part of our mouth to speak with.) Not different; that's right. Still . . . No, that would be too easy. And that "not" still keeps us separate so we can be compared. Disconnected that way, no more "us"? Are we alike? If you like. It's a little abstract. I don't quite understand "alike." Do you? Alike in whose eyes? in what terms? by what standard? with reference to what third? I'm touching you, that's quite enough to let me know that you are my body.

I love you: our two lips cannot separate to let just *one* word pass. A single word that would say "you," or "me." Or "equals"; she who loves, she who is loved. Closed and open, neither ever excluding the other, they say they both love each other. Together. To produce a single precise word, they would have to stay apart. Definitely parted. Kept at a distance, separated by *one word.*

But where would that word come from? Perfectly correct, closed up tight, wrapped around its meaning. Without any opening, any fault. "You." "Me." You may laugh . . . Closed and faultless, it is no longer you or me. Without lips, there is no more "us." The unity, the truth, the propriety of words comes from their lack of lips, their forgetting of lips. Words are mute, when they are uttered once and for all. Neatly wrapped up so that their meaning—their blood—won't escape. Like the children of men? Not ours. And besides, do we need, or want, children? What for? Here and now, we are close. Men and women have children to embody their closeness, their distance. But we?

I love you, childhood. I love you who are neither mother (forgive me, mother, I prefer a woman) nor sister. Neither daughter nor son. I love you—

and where I love you, what do I care about the lineage of our fathers, or their desire for reproductions of men? Or their genealogical institutions? What need have I for husband or wife, for family, persona, role, function? Let's leave all those to men's reproductive laws. I love you, your body, here and now. I/you touch you/me, that's quite enough for us to feel alive.

Open your lips; don't open them simply. I don't open them simply. We—you/I—are neither open nor closed. We never separate simply: *a single word* cannot be pronounced, produced, uttered by our mouths. Between our lips, yours and mine, several voices, several ways of speaking resound endlessly, back and forth. One is never separable from the other. You/I: we are always several at once. And how could one dominate the other? impose her voice, her tone, her meaning? One cannot be distinquished from the other; which does not mean that they are indistinct. You don't understand a thing? No more than they understand you.

Speak, all the same. It's our good fortune that your language isn't formed of a single thread, a single strand or pattern. It comes from everywhere at once. You touch me all over at the same time. In all senses. Why only one song, one speech, one text at at time? To seduce, to satisfy, to fill one of my "holes"? With you, I don't have any. We are not lacks, voids awaiting sustenance, plenitude, fulfillment from the other. By our lips we are women: this does not mean that we are focused on consuming, consummation, fulfillment.

Kiss me. Two lips kissing two lips: openness is ours again. Our "world." And the passage from the inside out, from the outside in, the passage between us, is limitless. Without end. No knot or loop, no mouth ever stops our exchanges. Between us the house has no wall, the clearing no enclosure, language no circularity. When you kiss me, the world grows so large that the horizon itself disappears. Are we unsatisfied? Yes, if that means we are never finished. If our pleasure consists in moving, being moved, endlessly. Always in motion: openness is never spent nor sated.

We haven't been taught, nor allowed, to express multiplicity. To do that is to speak improperly. Of course, we might—we were supposed to?—exhibit one "truth" while sensing, withholding, muffling another. Truth's other side—its complement? its remainder?—stayed hidden. Secret. Inside and outside, we were not supposed to be the same. That doesn't suit their desires. Veiling and unveiling: isn't that what interests them? What keeps them busy? Always repeating the same operation, every time. On every woman.

You/I become two, then, for their pleasure. But thus divided in two, one outside, the other inside, you no longer embrace yourself, or me. Outside, you try to conform to an alien order. Exiled from yourself, you fuse with everything you meet. You imitate whatever comes close. You become whatever touches you. In your eagerness to find yourself again, you move indefinitely far from yourself. From me. Taking one model after another, passing from master to master, changing face, form, and language with each new power that dominates you. You/ we are sundered; as you allow yourself to be abused, you become an impassive travesty. You no longer return indifferent; you return closed, impenetrable.

Speak to me. You can't? You no longer want to? You want to hold back? Remain silent? White? Virginal? Keep the inside self to yourself? But it doesn't exist without the other. Don't tear yourself apart like that with choices imposed on you. *Between us*, there's no rupture between virginal and nonvirginal. No event that makes us women. Long before your birth, you touched yourself, innocently. Your/my body doesn't acquire its sex through an operation. Through the action of some power, function, or organ. Without any intervention or special manipulation, you are a woman already. There is no need for an outside; the other already affects you. It is inseparable from you. You are altered forever, through and through. That is your crime, which you didn't commit: you disturb their love of property.

How can I tell you that there is no possible evil in your sexual pleasure—you who are a stranger to good(s). That the fault only comes about when they strip you of your openness and close you up, marking you with signs of possession; then they can break in, commit infractions and transgressions and play other games with the law. Games in which they—and you?—speculate on your whiteness. If we play along, we let ourselves be abused, destroyed. We remain indefinitely distant from ourselves to support the pursuit of their ends. That would be our flaw. If we submit to their reasoning, we are guilty. Their strategy, intentional or not, is calculated to make us guilty.

You come back, divided: "we" are no more. You are split into red and white, black and white: how can we find each other again? How can we touch each other once more? Cut up, dispatched, finished: our pleasure is trapped in their system, where a virgin is one as yet unmarked by them, for them. One who is not yet made woman by and for them. Not yet imprinted with their sex, their language. Not yet penetrated, possessed by them. Remaining in that candor that waits for them, that is nothing without them, a void without them. A virgin is the future of their exchanges, transactions, transports. A kind of reserve for their explorations, consummations, exploitations. The advent of their desire, Not of ours.

How can I say it? That we are women from the start. That we don't have to be turned into women by them, labeled by them, made holy and profaned by them. That that has always already happened, without their efforts. And that their history, their stories, constitute the locus of our displacement. It's not that we have a territory of our own; but their fatherland, family, home, discourse, imprison us in enclosed spaces where we cannot keep on moving, living, as ourselves. Their properties are our exile. Their enclosures, the death of our love. Their words, the gag upon our lips.

How can we speak so as to escape from their compartments, their schemas, their distinctions and oppositions: virginal/deflowered, pure/impure, innocent/experienced . . . How can we shake off the chain of these terms, free ourselves from their categories, rid ourselves of their names? Disengage ourselves, alive, from their concepts? Without reserve, without the immaculate whiteness that shores up their systems. You know that we are never completed, but that we only embrace ourselves whole. That one after another, parts—of the body, of space, of time—interrupt the flow of our blood. Paralyze, petrify, immobilize us. Make us paler. Almost frigid.

Wait. My blood is coming back. From their senses. It's warm inside us again. Among us. Their words are emptying out, becoming bloodless, Dead skins. While our lips are growing red again. They're stirring, moving, they want to speak. You mean . . . ? What? Nothing. Everything. Yes. Be patient. You'll say it all. Begin with what you feel, right here, right now. Our all will come.

But you can't anticipate it, foresee it, program it. Our all cannot be projected, or mastered. Our whole body is moved. No surface holds. No figure, line, or point remains. No ground subsists. But no abyss, either. Depth, for us, is not a chasm. Without a solid crust, there is no precipice. Our depth is the thickness of our body, our all touching itself. Where top and bottom, inside and outside, in front and behind, above and below are not separated, remote, out of touch. Our all intermingled. Without breaks or gaps.

If you/I hesitate to speak, isn't it because we are afraid of not speaking well? But what is "well" or "badly"? With what are we conforming if we speak "well"? What hierarchy, what subordination lurks there, waiting to break our resistance? What claim to raise ourselves up in a worthier discourse? Erection is no business of ours: we are at home on the flatlands. We have so much space to share. Our horizon will never stop expanding; we are always open. Stretching out, never ceasing to unfold ourselves, we have so many voices to invent in order to express all of us everywhere, even in our gaps, that all the time there is will not be enough. We can never complete the circuit, explore our periphery: we have so many dimensions. If you want to speak "well," you pull yourself in, you become narrower as you rise. Stretching upward, reaching higher, you pull yourself away from the limitless realm of your body. Don't make yourself erect, you'll leave us. The sky isn't up there: it's between us.

And don't worry about the "right" word. There isn't any. No truth between our lips. There is room enough for everything to exist. Everything is worth exchanging, nothing is privileged, nothing is refused. Exchange? Everything is exchanged, yet there are no transactions. Between us, there are no proprietors, no purchasers, no determinable objects, no prices. Our bodies are nourished by our mutual pleasure. Our abundance is inexhaustible: it knows neither want nor plenty. Since we give each other (our) all, with nothing held back, nothing hoarded, our exchanges are without terms, without end. How can I say it? The language we know is so limited . . .

Why speak? you'll ask me. We feel the same things at the same time. Aren't my hands, my eyes, my mouth, my lips, my body enough for you? Isn't what they are saying to you sufficient? I could answer "yes," but that would be too easy. Too much a matter of reassuring you/us.

If we don't invent a language, if we don't find our body's language, it will have too few gestures to accompany our story. We shall tire of the same ones, and leave our desires unexpressed, unrealized. Asleep again, unsatisfied, we shall fall back upon the words of men—who, for their part, have "known" for a long time. But *not our body.* Seduced, attracted, fascinated, ecstatic with our becoming, we shall remain paralyzed. Deprived of *our movements.* Rigid, whereas we are made for endless change. Without leaps or falls, and without repetition.

Keep on going, without getting out of breath. Your body is not the same today as yesterday. Your body remembers. There's no need for *you* to remember. No need to hold fast to yesterday, to store it up as capital in your head. Your memory? Your body expresses yesterday in what it wants today. If you think: yesterday I was, tomorrow I shall be, you are thinking: I have died a little. Be what you are becoming, without clinging to what you might have been, what you might yet be. Never settle. Let's leave definitiveness to the undecided; we don't need it. Our body, right here, right now, gives us a very different certainty. Truth is necessary for those who are so distanced from their body that they have forgotten it. But their "truth" immobilizes us, turns us into statues, if we can't loose its hold on us. If we can't defuse its power by trying to say, right here and now, how we are moved.

You are moving. You never stay still. You never stay. You never "are." How can I say "you," when you are always other? How can I speak to you? You remain in flux, never congealing or solidifying. What will make that current flow into words? It is multiple, devoid of causes, meanings, simple qualities. Yet it cannot be decomposed. These movements cannot be described as the passage from a beginning to an end. These rivers flow into no single, definitive sea. These streams are without fixed banks, this body without fixed boundaries. This unceasing mobility. This life—which will perhaps be called our restlessness, whims, pretenses, or lies. All this remains very strange to anyone claiming to stand on solid ground.

Speak, all the same. Between us, "hardness" isn't necessary. We know the contours of our bodies well enough to love fluidity. Our density can do without trenchancy or rigidity. We are not drawn to dead bodies.

But how can we stay alive when we are far apart? There's the danger. How can I wait for you to return if when you're far away from me you cannot also be near? If I have nothing palpable to help me recall in the here and now the touch of our bodies. Open to the infinity of our separation, wrapped up in the intangible sensation of absence, how can we continue to live as ourselves? How can we keep ourselves from becoming absorbed once again in their violating language? From being embodied as mourning. We must learn to speak to each other so that we can embrace from afar. When I touch myself, I am surely remembering you. But so much has been said, and said of us, that separates us.

Let's hurry and invent our own phrases. So that everywhere and always we can continue to embrace. We are so subtle that nothing can stand in our way, nothing can stop us from reaching each other, even fleetingly, if we can find means of communication that have our density. We shall pass imperceptibly through every barrier, unharmed, to find each other. No one will see a thing. Our strength lies in the very weakness of our resistance. For a long time now they have appreciated what our suppleness is worth for their own embraces and impressions. Why not enjoy it ourselves? Rather than letting ourselves be subjected to their branding. Rather than being fixed, stabilized, immobilized. Separated.

Don't cry. One day we'll manage to say ourselves. And what we say will be even lovelier than our tears. Wholly fluent.

Already, I carry you with me everywhere. Not like a child, a burden, a weight, however beloved and precious. You are not *in me.* I do not contain you or retain you in my stomach, my arms, my head. Nor in my memory, my mind, my language. You are there, like my skin. With you I am certain of existing beyond all appearances, all disguises, all designations. I am assured of living because you are duplicating my life. Which doesn't mean that you give me yours, or subordinate it to mine. The fact that you live lets me know I am alive, so long as you are neither my counterpart nor my copy.

How can I say it differently? We exist only as two? We live by twos beyond all mirages, images, and mirrors. Between us, one is not the "real" and the other her imitation; one is not the original and the other her copy. Although we can dissimulate perfectly within their economy, we relate to one another without simulacrum. Our resemblance does without semblances: for in our bodies, we are already the same. Touch yourself, touch me, you'll "see."

No need to fashion a mirror image to be "doubled," to repeat ourselves—a second time. Prior to any representation, we are two. Let those two—made for you by your blood, evoked for you by my body—come together alive. You will always have the touching beauty of a first time, if you aren't congealed in reproductions. You will always be moved for the first time, if you aren't immobilized in any form of repetition.

We can do without models, standards, or examples. Let's never give ourselves orders, commands, or prohibitions. Let our imperatives be only appeals to move, to be moved, together. Let's never lay down the law to each other, or moralize, or make war. Let's not claim to be right, or claim the right to criticize one another. If one of us sits in judgment, our existence comes to an end. And what I love in you, in myself, in us no longer takes place: the birth that is never accomplished, the body never created once and for all, the form never definitively completed, the face always still to be formed. The lips never opened or closed on a truth.

Light, for us, is not violent. Not deadly. For us the sun does not simply rise or set. Day and night are mingled in our gazes. Our gestures. Our bodies. Strictly speaking, we cast no shadow. There is no danger that one or the other may be a darker double. I want to remain nocturnal, and find my night softly luminous, in you. And don't by any means imagine that I love you shining like a beacon, lording it over everything around you. If we divide light from night, we give up the lightness of our mixture, solidify those heterogeneities that make us so consistently whole. We put ourselves into watertight compartments, break ourselves up into parts, cut ourselves in two, and more. Whereas we are always one and the other, at the same time. If we separate ourselves that way, we "all" stop being born. Without limits or borders, except those of our moving bodies.

And only the limiting effect of time can make us stop speaking to each other. Don't worry. I—continue. Under all these artificial constraints of time and space, I embrace you endlessly. Others may make fetishes of us to separate us: that's their business. Let's not immobilize ourselves in these borrowed notions.

And if I have so often insisted on negatives: *not, nor, without* . . . it has been to remind you, to remind us, that we only touch each other naked. And that, to find ourselves once again in that state, we have a lot to take off. So many representations, so many appearances separate us from each other. They have wrapped us for so long in their desires, we have adorned ourselves so often to please them, that we have come to forget the feel of our own skin. Removed from our skin, we remain distant. You and I, apart.

You? I? That's still saying too much. Dividing too sharply between us: all.

Notes

This text was originally published as "Quand nos lévres se parlent," in *Cahiers du Grif*, no. 12. English translation: "When Our Lips Speak Together," trans. Carolyn Burke, in *Signs*, 6:1 (Fall 1980), 69–79.

Chapter Four of *The Forgetting of Air in Martin Heidegger*

Within this economy of the copula, both of them—the male one and the female one—are deprived of their return to themselves.

He can neither grow nor set himself up apart from the wait to return within her, to return to that beginning prior to the beginning, when she gave herself entirely to him without distance or difference. Dwelling in a living house, a living body that envelops, protects, and feeds him, that supplies his existence without reciprocity. A dwelling ever in darkness, where this light alone shines: the heat and flame of life. Love's "fire"? A love, between her and him, that remains ever nocturnal.

When he turns back toward her, he has made a source for himself He has appropriated, and attributed to himself, the source. The source always hides a mourning, and hides the need for *ek-sistance* relative to that beginning when the whole gives itself always and everywhere, and nothing is withheld.

Ek-sistance?—a mourning and a triumph? The triumph of a mourning?

He no longer turns back toward her except from a point of ek-stasis. This ek-stasis deprives him of his relation to her: life at the beginning. This ek-stasis derives, first of all, from what he has taken from her, from what he has appropriated beginning with her, too little and too much, and which he now returns to her as a triumphant gift. He triumphantly gives himself back to her within him, to him within her. Thus: outside her.[1] For where he ek-sists, she is no longer. Unless she is in his memory and expectations. Touched by her in him, by him in her: and not by her, over there, by she who exists outside him, and whom he does not affect. He is touched only by the expectation, the forgetting, and the return of she who will never come back. He is touched only by memory and expectation: he neither touches her nor is touched in an immediate fashion.

The ek-stasis of the present is this, their impossible "meeting." Deprived of his return to himself by returning to her: she, at present, the absent one. He is rendered ek-static in absence.

Ek-stasis is the exit-entry out of her. But, at the same time, out of himself.

Is this how his Being as sexuate is destined? Always throwing-projecting him there? At a distance? In distancing?

In what is destined for him this way, he again confuses her with himself. He assimilates the two theres: the there where he is thrown-projected outside himself, and the there where she exists outside him. He forgets that there are two different ekstases in this there. That the there of his Being's destiny is not the there of her subsistence. He folds them up together in sameness, in the eternal return to the same. He forgets the difference between them within Being. Returning to she whom he has already assimilated in a there where she is now an other. Confusing her with this other, he begins anew from this point to assimilate her once more.

For at the point where he is thrown-projected out of himself, he will again recover himself. He will once more set himself this project as his very source. He will make of his ek-stasis the way to return to himself: the permanence of his Being. What is nearest in what is farthest away.

In order to recover himself and to restore himself to himself, ek-stasis must keep, *ek-sistance* must be maintained, and exiting himself must become the measure of his proper-proximal being: "his house."

Which is impossible without her: that female other that subsists outside. His ek-stasis must insist in her: she who remains ever outside. It is necessary that she participate in this. "There," which/who is forgotten-erased in the "there," she must continue to participate in his ek-stasis: always being available for Being's entry into presence. Gaining even the heights of the heavens, bringing the removes of ek-stasis close together there, and joining them, in the upsurgence of their lightening or unconcealment, without stitch, selvedge, or thread, preserving them, without the slightest discontinuity, in the permanence of her night. Keeping them in her repose, over which their enlightenment gleams, but remaining always at rest. Preserving them within her obscurity, transparent in the brilliance of their illuminations, though staying forever in the dark.

Wondrous home, all the more beautiful for remaining invisible to let their stars shine resplendent. Silent, imperceptibly present house of night, in which opens once again the serene and confident wait for that ek-stasis into which they are called: in her repose, she will let be this one more star. Joining it to the others already there, bringing them together without a trace of their faraway upsurgence.

Taking nothing, keeping the whole settled-arranged on or within her, lending her living body as a gathering place for the whole: she works only with proximity, unless she prefers to rest . . .

While his own kind of motion is nearly the opposite of this: waiting. Unless it be another kind of rest? The availability of a still unconstrained energy, the serenity of Being-as-action that does not know itself as such?

Doesn't that which thus maintains itself in a state of distant expectancy suspend the motion of attraction in "rest"? Doesn't it relate to the other in complete passivity?

Prior to this passivity, or in between the passivity that was at the beginning and its return in the wait, what happened that might have given rise to *ek-sistance*? *To* ek-stasis? What change occurred in the "nature" of the site that sheltered man? What operation took place between the "house" of a living body and the "house" of Being in order for the dwelling of man, his homeland, to now determine his relations to the whole and to himself, in the form of an approach that always maintains distance?

Perhaps this operation should be called the reduction to nothingness. How ought it to be understood? Whence proceeds this nothing that unfolds its essence within Being itself? This nothing that makes Being more being than any being, this nothing with which Being touches all beings, though in an imperceptible way. This nothing that has always already inserted-whispered all the "yes's" and "no's," even before what they pertain to has been set out. This nothing within Being: "which grants the unscathed its graceful rise, and furor its impulse toward ruin."[2] This nothing, which is reduced to nothingness as the mere rejection, refusal, or destruction manifesting itself among beings, but which imperceptibly abides in, and operates from, Being. Concealing, resealing, within its ek-stasis, the ever possible to-come of a birth or death.

Of love or of hatred? Love and hatred left in suspension, unaccomplished, though they are always at the same time destined within the openness of Being?

At the same time—this would mean that the "graceful rise" is always also "an impulse toward ruin." That one would never come to pass without the other. And that a certain dawning sun, in the West, would already achieve, by the very fact of its rising, a furious destruction. And not simply in virtue of its future setting but *at the same time*.

At the same time. Being—he said—is the house of man. To be and to dwell amount to the same thing.

What remains unthought is that dwelling is the fundamental trait of man's condition.[3] It still remains unsaid, hidden in language, which, nevertheless, expresses it: in silence. This fundamental character of man's relation to the spoken—man's dwelling in language, in a language as the framing for a home of and for man—is forgotten in what is habitual.

This forgetting can entail a true crisis in dwelling. Can entail, for man, crisis itself? But man does not consider it to be such. As long as he does not think through homelessness, he does not recognize that what is of principal importance for him is the Being of dwelling. Nevertheless, abiding on earth as a mortal, he always already dwells. This he forgets. He forgets the framing of this home. He forgets that for him dwelling is the fundamental trait of Being. How is he to be reminded of this *trait*[4] that is erased in the habitual?

This trait marks out a boundary.

A boundary can be drawn around something: it encloses a field or a vine for the purpose of cultivation, for example. In this sense, to build is simply to watch over the growth that, of itself, ripens its fruit. At this point, there isn't yet any fabrication on the part of man, any works produced by him: with the exception of this boundary, by means of which he will tend the flourishing of nature's works.

And tend himself as one of these? Needing, first, an abode that allows him to remain in peace, kept from harm and threat, his existence husbanded and spared. But requiring even more that he be surrounded by protection that, from the start, leaves him within his Being, that returns him to it and sets him at peace therein: enclosed within what is akin to him. Free, therefore.

Free, therefore? How could that which lends itself to surrounding someone or something in accordance with the Being of each one be free? To ensure this peaceful dwelling for another, hasn't it—or she—had to appropriate itself, or herself, to that other? Thus, to empropriate itself? To expatriate itself?

Yet the fundamental trait of dwelling is supposed to be this sparing which would pervade dwelling throughout its whole range. Throughout its whole range, dwelling must be appropriated to man. Following this trait, man would be first of all a dweller on earth: his first house would be granted him by earth, and it is on this basis that he would be able to build-rebuild a dwelling of his own.

Dweller on earth, once he is situated—sets himself up "on the earth" ("on her"),[5] man is already "under the sky." Both of these also mean "remaining before the divinities' " and imply "belonging to the community of men." The four: earth and sky, divinities and mortals, form a whole on the basis of an originary oneness.

Why four? Is it because, given the three-dimensional nature of this dwelling place, it is important to leave room for the unexpected? For the ever possible return of the gods? Or is it, on the contrary, because the fourfold constitutes a more stable dwelling? Both at the same time.

Mortals dwell as they await the divinities. This waiting preserves the pliancy of dwelling, turning the square into a circle while keeping the envelope closed. With what is nearest being left outside? With all points where proximity comes about remaining forever tangents that meet but do not by intersection penetrate the proper "house."

Of what [is] this dwelling? Of what is this "simpleness" on the basis of which these four form–re-form a whole? What power gathers them together after having divided them into four? Keeping them, in the present, within the inconspicuousness of an everlasting sameness?

Wouldn't this simpleness that keeps the secret of all permanence and magnitude be the capacity for death as death? That which is proper to man? Which is projected onto the whole that is thereby transformed into a dwelling of a world. A dwelling in the world outside of which world is nothing, but which is already kept safe from and in death, in virtue of its delineated boundary.

Would dwelling—man's—be revealed, then, as the safekeeping of death? As enclosure by a boundary within which death is—is not to be found? The dwelling that is the "world" would be the preservation of the being of the fourfold: which is maintained on the basis of the simplicity of the four. Of the relation of the four in simpleness.

"Earth and sky, divinities and mortals, are at one with each other in virtue of each other on the basis of the simplicity of the united fourfold. Each of the four reflects in its own way the Being of the others, and in this way reflects itself in its own Being, returning to this Being at the heart of the simplicity of the four."[6]

How do they all reflect each other unless in a certain capacity of man's that is projected-placed upon them? What do they reflect, if not this capacity? Isn't man, by thus animating the four—earth and sky, divinities and mortals—with the project of making this single dwelling of a world in which he is presently situated, engaged in a repetition—ascribing his desire to the four—of his first "house": his dwelling within a living body?

But this shelter of a "world" is rebuilt on the model of a proximity that always maintains distance. In each of the four can now be found the capacity to send each back to its proper Being, and thus to be reflected in its own Being, through the simpleness that unites the four. Each of them always being "near" the other three, remaining all the while at a distance.

Isn't what reflects the proper in this way that which comes nearest while staying far away? In a relation of mutual belonging *[transproprié]* to being, it restores each one to its own Being, but in distance. Receiving in distancing its own Being as well, for having taken and given back what is proper in the other. Having incorporated into itself the reflection, and the source of the being, it never gives itself to the other in an approach where a mixture of the two is always a possibility. What it gives—gives back to the other is always already transfixed by that nothing that separates all beings: their belonging to a proper Being. In this nothing, which henceforth is situated within the whole, all the parts come together, each giving and receiving within each its Being: its death.

It is no longer love that thus unites them but death. Or rather: love of, and in, death. Which, reducing all beings to nothingness in the contingent singularity of their living bodies, binds them together through this mutual belonging in death. In nothing, then, unless in that bond of a boundary-envelope around and between them that appropriates them and lets them be, joined together within one same and other distancing.

They no longer give each other back to each other except within this boundary, where they can begin to be: nothing. However, for the nothing of each to turn back into the Nothing of the whole, each must at least once give back to each one its Being: it must give back death at least once, so that death enters its Being. At least once, each one gives back to and takes back from each its relation to death—its own Being—so that death might be in simpleness: the Being of Being. Thus stripped of whatever it could still keep within it that proceeds from particular beings, and from their lives' becoming, death withdraws into death. The proper—all things proper still tainted with particular properties—returns to the proper: the very Being of Being. Death—no longer this death or that death, the death of this one or that one—death to which every being must surrender as to its *own* truth, returns to death: the sole truth, the sole transcendence, the single source of all. Ark of nothing, sole shelter of the Being of Being.

If life has been given at least twice in an unthinkable assimilation of her to him, so also must death be given back at least twice so as to keep the proper safe.

The reflection that each gives off and receives is the passage by way of a primary relation to death: in virtue of the individuation and specialness that death can still impart to each. Liberated by what is thrown back to it with this reflection, each is given back over to what is most proper, and can thus be bound to the others in the Being of their Being: the simpleness of death.

This expropriative appropriating *[transpropriation expropriante]* of all things proper that are still individual is the mirror-play of the fourfold without which the world is not. This cannot be explained, as it is without cause or foundation. The simpleness of the simplicity of the play of the world does not permit such penetration by human understanding. It is. Posed, positionless. Staying up, holding up, in air?

The Being of the fourfold is the play of the world: the two do not let themselves be separated, not even like an envelope that would be added—to boot—to what it contains, maintains, retains. The Being of the envelope is the mirror-play, the round dance of making each appear within the whole, which gathers together the world as world. The encircling loop of the ring that rolls up into itself and in which all are intertwined with their Being: one Being nevertheless proper to each. This intertwining renders them flexible for, and compliant to, the mirrorplay, brought back to what is most pliant in their Being.

The Being of the world, the copula of the world, is this mirror-play. In it, each compliantly relies on each, and leaves behind its own pliancy in the encircling loop of the pliant.

The squaring of a circle: that would take place within the transparency of each in each, let-be within the whole. Ultimately, the mirror reflects nothing: the Being of Being. Empty so as to reflect the whole back to that which binds it in Being: the reduction to nothingness.

Nevertheless, the play of mirrors gathers the whole together within its encircling loop. Imposing itself, still without a thinkable origin, it is the cincture/precinct: the "world." Cincture/precinct of mirrors/ice that, in the end, reflects nothing back. Rejoining the no-longer to the not-yet in the constancy of a furling that brings each one back to the enigma of its Being—that nothing whence it comes and to which it returns, endlessly.

Of what is this nothing such that it is perceived not as a terrifying abyss but as the "round dance of the world"? What bears it, what does it provide, such that it should be expected—recalled in this way, not merely as the appeal of a void in which all memory would be engulfed, but as the return of what is most originary and what is most ultimate?

This nothing? Wouldn't it be found in open air: that being that is already there before birth, and still there after death, rejoining the not-yet and the no-longer within a lasting expanse? Within which all come to "be" and gather in a single space, sharing a sameness that does not as such appear, but that grants the whole its permanence. One sameness, transparent, in which each one can come into presence and receive-give to each the reflection of its Being. Bound by what bestows appearance upon them, but to which they return—as to their own, most simple, element—after having received and given off that proper reflection.

Air—still silent space of speech. Where the voice of things can be heard by he who is born in the air that surrounds them. Conveying the call from the highest heaven, feeding, as well, what the earth bears. Bringing into proximity the mountain top and the country road, the hometown and today's home, children's games and a mother's gaze, the flight of birds and the work of the woodcutter, the din of machines or the breath of the gods. But joining also, in a single harmony, the rotation of the seasons: winter's storm and harvest day, the quickening turbulence of spring and the quiet decline of autumn, the playful temper of youth and the wisdom of age. Each taking place there, all crossing paths and meeting each other there, passing from one into the other within the expanse of a serene abiding. Within a space and time in which everything comes into existence and returns to death, leaving air still and already there, in a horizonless vastness and a continuity where all can come to pass without any given event stopping a kind of motion that, perpetually, abides.

Air could be this nothing of Being: the Being of Being. It could be this secret that Being keeps, could be that in which earth and sky, mortals and divinities, belong together.

But he has forgotten this simple constituent of *physis*. He no longer hears it except through the voices of the *logos*: the paths he has already laid out within and on *physis*. It is from the path—which would not be had he not opened it—that what has always already given him air now comes back to him. The elementality of *physis*—air, water, earth, fire—is always already reduced to nothingness in and by his own element: his language. An ecstasis relative to his natural environment that keeps him exiled from his first homeland.

A homeland he so often recalls because he has lost it? Because he and it always remain at a distance from one another now? At a distant proximity? Which leaves him at peace, but with a kind of serenity that considers itself above suffering, that is always marked by irony, by a kind of cheery melancholy. A wisdom divulged only in veiled expressions, already opening onto eternity. A renunciation that leads to sameness: taking nothing, but giving, rather, the inexhaustible energy of the simple. Of the nothing? Of death? Within which a native land is given back to him.

It is not for nothing that he makes the renunciation. He renounces so as to receive an inexhaustible energy. Couldn't this energy, which is given—given back to and through him with no taking on his part, proceed from the power of hatred? The hatred of nature? From his rejection, his distancing, his desire to want nature *[elle]* no more, his expectation that nature recall him. That she might not have already totally succumbed to his hatred, that she might not yet be reduced to hatred, that she might not hate him: that she might nullify the power of hatred.

For what would become of his language were nature not, and not at his disposal? So, must nature be reduced to nothingness, yet remain nevertheless, if only as an open space within which to recall oneself? To enter into presence? To sojourn? To come together? Like a dwelling that, with its very emptiness, is still destined to welcome. Were it even small, a little thing, its sheltering space must always stay open.

For hatred can be recalled but not remembered. It remains, insists, consists: in oblivion. Void, spacing, gap, border, boundary, it orders representation, it shelters, frames, and aids it without itself being expressed or presented in representation. The dwelling of man is not built without hatred of nature; that is why it must ensure the safekeeping of nature, and of man.

Empedocles told of the power of hatred.

He never recalls this, though he read and re-read it by way of the works of Aristotle and Hölderlin, on which basis he undertakes at more than one point to convey Empedocles' thinking.

From where does this silence proceed if not from hatred, whose destructive power he relays only in relation to the thrownness/forsakenness of the poets?

To this Greek thinker at the beginning of the Greek world, hatred is equal in power to the four elements: air, fire, earth, water. It is equal, still, to love. Equal does not mean: same.

Hatred and love order-disorder the relation to sameness within the whole. Cultivating therein a perpetual and double motion.

Love draws things together into the mixture that brings about birth: *physis*. Birth comes from the meeting and union of the things that are, death from their separation by hatred and from their return to their initial simplicity. Death itself is born of the separation of fire from the other elements.

Each thing has its proper *physis;* moreover, each can be the *genesis* of another thing. Mixture is not the blurring of distinctions. At the place where others see Tatary, the kingdom of death, the ether presses downward to earth itself and, going all the way to its center, binds the outermost points to the core, uniting earth and sky. Penetrating into the heart of things, love joins them without con-fusing them. Love can alter the forms they take, and can switch their places, without for all that destroying their elemental Being.

Love reunites what is dissimilar: the dry loves and attracts the wet. Hatred brings about the attraction of like to like: the dry returns to the dry. Love of the other and love of self order the world. This double attraction is apparent when the terms are crossed with each other: the love of the other for those that are the same, and of the same for others. The whole is produced by means of reciprocal proportions and of a blending that comprises alternating inversions, without the whole being dissolved.

What gathers the whole together? The attraction of the elements—which are maintained by the hot, the soft, and the wet—for each other. They are always the same elements, but they pass through each other one by one, dominating in turn within the mixture.

What unites the whole? The power of hatred. Hatred divides, separates, disperses, maintains and retains within the purity of sameness, and bounds and delimits the whole, like a solid envelope. The envelope of the world proceeds from the first element that was separated by hatred: air that surrounded the world in a circle and was transformed into ice through the action on it of fire. Air, condensed and congealed, in this manner became the crystalline vault of the universe where man is born into the world.

Within the order of hatred, man's first birthplace would be where air and fire are found to be unjoined from the first. He begins to breathe upon leaving the warmth of his first dwelling. He reaches air as if attaining the forsakenness/thrownness of an irreparable loss of love.

This mourning, the measure of which he never takes and which he does not think through, leaves him with the concern to build a place, and places, over and over again. Shelters that they fashion around a void, using earth, water, fire.

With these houses, these works, isn't he reproducing something of a useless separation? An irreparable forsakenness/thrownness from which he keeps himself safe through the economy of hatred? This is something he never expresses, never thinks through. Unless he does so in treating the forsakenness/ thrownness of the poets? Seeking a flash of illumination in the works of those who still sight that distress that is the destiny of all—earthly exile. The pain of a separation at birth that would maintain each one in his death. A life where love would never again transgress the boundary of the proper.

Notes

1. *Hors d'elle* (outside herself, out of her) and *hors de lui* (outside himself, out of him) also mean 'beside herself' and 'beside himself,' that is, 'in a state of great excitement, agitation, exaltation.'—Tr.

2. See Martin Heidegger, "Letter on Humanism," in *Basic Writings*, 261: "To healing Being first grants ascent into grace; to raging its compulsion to malignancy."—Tr.

3. See Martin Heidegger, "Building, Dwelling, Thinking:" in *Basic Writings*, 350. This and the next seven sections draw heavily on this essay.—Tr.

4. *Le trait* here means 'character' or 'feature.' But it is also the standard French translation of Heidegger's *der Riss*, 'the stroke' or 'rending-stroke', as well as 'crack,' 'fissure,' 'outline,' 'tracing,' 'rift.' The French word also has many nontechnical senses, including line, mark, lineament, arrow, bolt, dash, gulp, burst, touch, deed, and act, among others.—Tr.

5. *La terre* (earth) is a noun marked feminine; *le ciel* (sky) is a noun marked masculine.—Tr.

6. Martin Heidegger, "The Thing," in *Poetry, Language, Thought*, 179; "La chose," in *Essais et conférences*, 213. [Translation adapted. Much in this and following sections is drawn from this essay.—Tr.]

Chapter Five
of *The Forgetting of Air in Martin Heidegger*

The differing and deferring nature of the relation-between produces the place of Being—its house in language *[langage]*. In the waiting, leaving open that toward which it tends, not setting out its object before itself—which would no longer be waiting—the entire expanse of desire unencloses and reencloses of its own. That which was held out to the other is turned back toward oneself, is sent back to oneself

The farther away the other stays, the greater the wait, and the vaster the open expanse, the region of speech. Where nothing any longer happens besides dwelling in and returning to oneself Re-enveloping oneself, winding oneself up in the endless unfurling of the wait. And thus seeing the faraway come back into proximity: to think.

To think. To turn the openness of the wait over into an impalpable, invisible, imperceptible, forgotten circle of gathering meditation *[recueillement]*. . . : Being. Into a place in which to dwell in peace. Separated from all others, except through the commemorative of a noble remembrance.

To be: this mourning veil, this veiling of absence that unfurls and furls its openness within a vastness that is continuously assimilating to the thinker's serenity.

Wait and lasting openness of the absence within which and from which entry into presence—and the entry into presence of all things—will rise up.

Which things are indefinitely near, and faraway. And are so in relation to each other, as well. They are things, and are things in relation to each other, only when re-settled, in good order, within the open expanse. At the remove of a distance that, enveloping them in a sepulture of air, allows them, now, *to last.*

They last and hold together amongst themselves through a translucent medium that makes them touch only in appearance. They reach each other only by way of their capacity to appear-through. Their manner of meeting always takes the form of superficial contact. The appearance lacks depth, unless it be the depth of a mourning. And the more they near each other in their presence, the more they distance themselves within the confinement of their airs.

Is this true? It's hard to say. This operation is already of a different order once I have named it in this manner. It is less lofty, less great, and can take place only in that place that is infinitely more vast and that cannot itself be named. On pain of its essence being destroyed? But then what about any case of naming? And, further still, what about the nameless?

Being is nothing but the possibility of predication. Of the dimension of predication.

If Being can make itself into a circle, it does so within the suspension of predication. The subject-object axis has not yet been put forth there. The horizon line of understanding has yet to be drawn at that point. If its path already has been marked out, it is in the form of the encirclement, or the rolling-up into a spiral, of a mystery: the mystery of the beginning of Being's taking place. Of its springing forth from nothingness.

Whence does Being proceed? And whence proceeds its strange power? How, and in what, can it unify? What is the secret of the constitution of sameness? And of the permanence of its site? Why does the line of the spoken word revolve around this crypt? Returning to it and shutting it up with one and the same move? What sort of forgetting of the other within (it) makes the unthinkability of sameness' origin the exclusive place of thinking? What fundamental assimilation ensures the unfolding of Being as the region of sameness? And what kind of magic provides for the participation of the whole in the subsistence of this singular site?

Mustn't Being give back what it has taken from the other? Having assimilated the other so as to begin to be, and to unfold on this basis the singular power of sameness, Being gives participation back to the other.

Appropriation is founded in this double operation: an *assimilation* and a *participation.* These do not take place on the same slope of Being's constitution, but they are to be found, joined together inseparably, under its dominion. Man and world are reunited in the sorcery of this circle.

When he does not remember himself and is unable to think that nature—

vanishing within him so that he might be—nourished him first, he repays nature with this oblivion: it is only through him that she is.

Between the two of them, an operation of inversion and repayment is forgotten with the difference it neutralizes. A projection has taken place, upheld by the power of love and hatred: love of the same, which indefinitely seeks the dimension for its appropriated being, and hatred, which divides, separates, and marks out boundaries, differences.

Love of the same is the first love of the other: she who gave herself, first, for assimilation to him. But when this love is repeated with no difference it brings about the elimination of the other. Always wanting to have the same from her, he abolishes her in the singularity of his fate: compelling her to remain the one and only.

Wouldn't to ask the question of Being be to undo one of these slopes so as to confront him not with what supports him in the safety and serenity of a re-adhesion of the whole within sameness, through the other's participation in his assimilation, but with that which—repeating from the side of sameness the operation that originally constitutes him—re-opens the question of his relation to the other?

The being is given first, and irrecoverably, in the form of fluids. This gift is non-apparent: without demonstration. It takes place with no distinction between giver and receiver. The being passes from one to the other, from the other to one, before the gift as such is constituted. One or the other gives itself, without any things or objects of giving. Subject and predicate are still assimilable to each other, passing from one into the other. Subject and copula are, still, the same *[le méme]*.

Or the same *[la méme]*:[1] the being being the being. There is no activity, transitivity, or tool, yet. No subject, no world, no mediation between. There is only body, between-two-bodies, body that passes from one to the other. Her being having become his being, prior to all propositions. The proposition holds when that assimilation of her being to him is forgotten in Being. The copula marks and erases a passage by way of the difference between the being and Being and, first of all, between the being and the being.

Between the being that gives itself prior to all demonstration and the one expressed in the present being, the traces of a boundary are forgotten. She has passed into him: he has assimilated her and reassimilates her ceaselessly, without at present positing any difference between her and him, and without a trace of her left: unless it's that he exists . . .

Which is something he forgets. Thinking is not thought of as a living being. Nevertheless, it is one—at first. It passes, imperceptibly, from one life to the other. And, since there is no other, it passes from life to death: within the indifference of Being.

Being exists on the basis of indifference: this he has said. Which does not mean that the thinker can stay at rest there once and for all, with no activity or motion. In order to maintain this indifference within Being, he ceaselessly keeps assimilating the being to the being. But, in addition, so that this operation is forgotten, he likewise keeps positing the being as being.

The fact that the proposition does not convey *phuein* in its fluid medium leaves a mode of subsistence beyond, and this side of, Being-in-the-world—a mode of subsistence that is unthinkable within his categorial order. There was a kind of subsistence already, prior to the constitution of Being-in-the-world. A kind of subsistence that is not divisible into a subject and things separable from that subject, and separable from each other. A kind of subsistence more originary than that named by *logos, noein,* and "soul." The subsistence of a living body that draws its life from fluid matter. With this assimilating relation to fluids, which is necessary for his constitution and perdurance, man is no longer in that world of existences that are contiguous at best. He is in continuity. The *partes extra partes* functioning of Cartesian space, which for being-there still seems to rule the world, no longer takes place here. The subject and "things," as well as "things" among themselves, are in a relation of interpenetration: no longer one and another, a subject and a thing, a thing and a thing, no longer near each other in the sense of being "in contact," or "close to," or "gathered together within". . . but near each other in the mode of a kind of permeability of their envelopes which requires thinking out an other relation to space-time. "Things" are no longer these particular things here, in relation to a locatable and always unique section of spacetime. Their mode of being "here"—if the term still retains a meaning in this case—matches the sort of space-time they share. According to space-time as it is philosophically thinkable, they are inseparable, though this is not to say that they are fused into indistinction. Passage between them, but also, in a different way, between them and the living subject, occurs through immediate and instant penetration: without a bridge.

If interpenetration is a mode of being-there, then there is an exchange that is prior to the bridge. The bridge undoes this sharing, this relation of indivisible proximity: it distances rather than brings near. It breaks, prevents, and prohibits the relation-between.

No gap, breach, spacing, or distancing is possible between the living organism and the blood that has always already nourished it, including with oxygen. Nor is there any more of a gap between it and the ambient air it continuously breathes once born. Nor between it and milk, water, or wine, when it drinks these. No interval, no interstice, between it and that from which it derives its most originary form of subsistence. Were there in these circumstances any such distance, any void, the living organism would die.

Being-there, being spatial, and being of a space-time made by and for man, for any assimilation with an aim to the advent of a kind of lasting growth, to establishing flawless constructions, and to the fabrication of "things" that subsist ready-to-hand and in the service of his mood (which mood is serene to the extent that "things" stay within the possibility that belongs to distance), is removed, ahead of time, from what is most original in the saying as such.

She who, far from coming in place of another—as linguists would want all pronouns to do? and likewise men all women?—comes first, but without ever being able to be reached, at least within this place of monstration. Falling short of the making-seen—or of the offering-to-sight-what-occurs—which always retreats, or effaces itself to make room for all phenomena, for all names and their relations. She who does not appear but who, remaining this invisible one, with no name possible in the space of monstration, stays ever night and transparency from which all phenomena spring forth and are revealed.

That one, she there, would be for phenomenology—which sought to be the contemplation *[recueillement]* of what secretly was already living—a forgotten reserve (store) of air. But because she is not situated there, or not only there, this there will never be anything but another image of her destiny: the destiny of a transparent fluid matter that supports the coming to presence of the whole, and within which everything takes place. With the exception of her.

Moreover, even if she is recalled in the manifestation and naming of each phenomenon, she still remains without a name: beyond. Without an appeal.

How is this possible? The back-and-forth motion within her, between her and her, among them, constitutes a kind of base without fissure or closure, where everything can take place without abyssal loss. This modest back-and-forth motion, which takes place prior to all phenomena and all designation, would be the groundless ground of the relation-between. This state of touching herself within herself and of each [female] other touching each other amongst themselves, with no hindering borders, would provide the groundless ground on the basis of which the phenomenon of distance, indeed, the phenomenon in general, becomes possible. When her role as this condition of possibility is forgotten, she, or she there, is encircled in a there that always remains distanced in a beyond. In a [female] beyond. Even should one wish to bring her near, so that the now unbreachable fault that keeps her apart could be recalled.

However, it is not clear that man either could or would want to attain her sort of proximity, one without boundaries and without assimilation of the other to the one, whether a male or female one. Even if this proximity does constitute the unthought ground of his thinking. For if he gained it his thinking would no longer have the right to be: not as the same, not as such, not even as being-there.

How was the horizon, and especially the *Region*, formed then? How did things come to this (there)? To what sort of *genesis*, foreign to their own, have they been subjected to be arranged in this fashion? According to what *archē* is the whole now constructed of entry into presence, and with no memory of that more archaic beginning that caused things to stir in accordance with their "nature"?

Technē is now the *archē* of the whole: the framing of the world *is technē*, and it forgets the origin that is nature.

Physis is always already subjected to technology and science: that is, to the technology and science of the *logos*. In these, something of the manner in which physical beings grow is lost. Things, cut from their natural enrootedness, float about, wandering the propositional landscape. The *phuein* of physical beings is forgotten in the *physis* of the *logos*. The physical constitution of beings is forgotten in the metaphysics of Being. Nature is re-created by the *logos*. In oblivion of the fact that what is done over in this way keeps its physical qualities as well. Of the fact that the economy of the physical being is always recalled in every one of man's fabrications. That the living body as *Gestell* always leaves traces in these fabrications. Forgotten traces, they persist as the unthought and unthinkable aspects of the world that man has fabricated for himself.

Isn't to resubmit to language in fact to resubmit oneself—and to resubmit *physis*—to *technē*? Doesn't Heidegger's move amount to making *physis* out of *technē?* To making *phuein* from the *logos*? In a ceaseless inversion of that *archē* where the whole is lost in the density of a still-virgin "corporeal" site. Where the chance for a remainder still left to come is pre-apprehended, without yet being able to be expressed.

With this move, Heidegger indeed revisits the whole of metaphysics, heading for that which, at the start, was lost—and kept—within it. But he remains within its architectonics: the *logos*. Seeking the cause of the loss in the forgetting of this architectronics: though it is the architectonics itself that accounts for the loss. Though the loss and its oblivion proceed from an *architechnē:* from the meta-physical *logos*.

It is thus that Heidegger's hostility to, or suspicion of, science and technology can be understood. The *architechnē* must remain the site of fundamental ontology's expression of the whole. The Being of man can dwell, be preserved, and become manifest only within a single language, even if, within this "uniqueness," it can be expressed in various ways.

Don't today's sciences and technologies claim to affirm—to reveal—that the Being of man is but a part of the being? That the being, physical beings, exceed the Being of man and elude his language? That, for man, the being has thus become an indecipherable mystery?

Which it has always been. This can even be found in the Greeks: in those that Heidegger forgets, or in what he forgets to hear in their works. Which they themselves forget to restate, even if they do say it at least once: that *physis* has a "proper" *archē*, a proper space-time of unfolding, and that to submit it *[elle]* to man's *architechnē*, his language, amounts to bowing its destiny to an inappropriate form of unfolding, to suspending this destiny within a factitious blossoming, and to leaving *physis* out, a remainder still. A resource that resists technocratic power and that can only unfold according to its proper motion. When man returns to draw on it, he exhausts it as factitiously as he makes it blossom artificially. He cuts off both himself and it from its reserve store, tearing it away from the motion of unfolding that follows its *archē*.

Its *archē*: a second time. To begin to hear/understand, it always takes him at least two times, but to him this second time means the possibility of a return to the same.

So, now: its *archē*. One other than this second one that is attributed to *physis so* that he can begin to think it through. An other one, at which he cannot be thought, since this *archē is* not in language. Which will be interpreted as: it is not. Thus closing up the circle of oblivion. Until the next time. And without end, perhaps. For, to continue to be, it is necessary to persist in forgetting, endlessly.

Heidegger's question would amount to this: "How can that which ensures the foundation and conditions of possibility of a space of de-monstration—the copula—be made to enter that space while ceaselessly evading it?" This question relies upon the unfolding of the *ob-jecting* and *op-posing* aspects of the *open expanse* without which it could neither take place initially nor be taken up thereafter.

When it reaches the point at which the question of its essence as such is posed, the copula, *hypokeimenon* of all that he sets out to interpret, is left to a space of neutralization—*il y a*.[2] Left serenely suspended in a renunciation of all effectuation. In a mourning that gives rise to contemplation.

But the thinker is the one who—now wanting it, now not wanting it—"decides on" the mourning, and expects from it the opening of the space for his thinking. On this condition, however: that the other assimilate his serenity while remaining both close to and ever distant from him—in his presence.

That pleasure in her takes place, and her pleasure, her own pleasure, which he could never assimilate but in which he could only participate—here is the mourning that the thinker would be unable to carry out, unless he were to renounce thinking as proper to himself and give up the proprietary relation to thought. Offering himself, then, himself likewise, as being a kind of being in which she could discover a space for the unfolding of what she would have to say.

While waiting for this opening, what else could she do but herself try to ensure—in herself, among herself and other "hers"—this unfolding that he keeps stealing away to make his propositions.

It is man's *ek-sistance* so as to watch over truth that separates him from himself and from "things" as living. What does this erection outside his "body" and the body of the world—for the purpose of the care of Being—imply about that which has, too little or too much, been arranged within these bodies? What false boundary determines this exit from the boundaries of the universe? What will man pursue in this ek-stasis? What part of the lost relation to himself and to "things" will he keep there? Do this loss and preservation have any other possible to-come than an ek-static one?

Is the copula necessarily destined to take the form of an ekstasis? Which ek-stasis? Which instance of the copula does this ek-stasis keep in reserve? What part of the unfolding of the being, of the relation between beings, has he always reserved for himself within Being, and within the forgetting of Being?

Or, further: why is the copula suspended in an essence that radiates its effects only in the form of keeping the proper safe? Why is it maintained in this way, by being withheld? And for such a long time? A *metabolē* with such a long carry . . . A stirring that spans the history of the West without having already come to term. Opening up, on occasion, but always forgetting that which in this unconcealment is still held back. That which is kept safe in this production of Being. In the historicality of Being.

And since Being is within the technocratic *epokē*, with regard to its sexual destiny as well, the question could be rendered as: does ek-stasis proceed from erection or from ejaculation? Is it as destined for erection that man is in being-there, in a nearing that always maintains distance in the relation to him and to the whole, or is it rather as destined for emitting-producing his seed outside himself that he is thrown-projected there? Both of these? How are they linked? By the suspense between them? Would being-there take place—be held back between the two? So the erection would surge up with the entry into presence, and would produce the being that is present, remaining all the while also within the shelter of its reserve and of its own occultation. With being-there bringing both erection and ejaculation back to the present, within sameness, thanks to its dwelling within the language *[le langage]*? How have one and the other, erection and ejaculation, both within the same, determined the space-time on the basis of which language *[la langue]* unfolds? What is lost-forgotten in the way of an other kind of motion of the living, in this space-time?

Which could be examined in this way as well: wouldn't the being as presence be man's ideal production? His pro-duction in idea? Being would be erected and opened up in ek-stasis, giving rise to the present being. However, for this production to take place, a being already has lent its "matter," a being that subsists beneath presence and assists it, always staying covered over and forgotten by it.

Isn't this the sexual destiny that man has recalled-forgotten in his language *[langue]*? And out of which he has made truth? Unfolding this destiny as that which envelops and surrounds his ek-stasis with a house: the house of Being. The essence of language *[langage]* should thus be understood as a shelter for man's essence. As a shelter for man. This language *[Le langage]* would be that in which man lives, as if in the safekeeping of his sexual destiny. Or, at least, as if in what would be destined for him as his sexual destiny, until the present time. This language *[Le langage]* would always already have been fabricated to conceal and assist this destiny: making it manifest itself *[se pro-duire]* but keeping it still in a state of reserve, in a wrapped/warped condition. This language *[Le langage]* would be the technology—the architechnology, the architectonics—for man's fashioning the living according to his sexual project.

To make this sexual destiny prevail as the truth of the whole, as the advent of the whole in sameness, man has taken life from nature, and in return has given—given back death to nature. After having assimilated her to himself in that *Gestell* that is his living body, he further appropriated her to himself so as to make of her the dwelling for his Being. Thereby eternally distancing her from himself. She is like a still-living tissue connected to the production of his language *[sa langue]*—to his tongue's issue—and feeding this language, but herself being used in line with a project that is his own, and, by passing through his technology, losing the movement and breath of life. Joined to his shelter, as its still-material/matrical support, henceforth indistinguishable from this house of language *[langage]* in which he dwells, nature is indefinitely separated from herself and from him, through this assimilation of her to him in language *[la langue]*.

She, nature, thus remains in oblivion. In a double oblivion: oblivion of she who has always already given him life and has become his living body, and oblivion of she who gives life back to him by helping him with the destiny of his Being. But this oblivion of her, and of a female them, is covered over by the oblivion of his own destiny as Being *[en tant qu'être]*. By the oblivion of the sexed character of Being?

As long as he dwells in this oblivion, in the shelter of this oblivion, he cannot remember her or a female them. She, and this female they, cannot be separated from his truth. Truth whose unveiling is a frightenting thing. Beyond the fact that man can discover in it the sheltering of his sexual destiny, it further can reveal to him that his truth is the non-truth of the other: the maintenance of the other within the absence of a dreadful oblivion.

Being is this dwelling of invisible aspect that sets aside and keeps beings from the movement of life.

But within that horizon that still suspends the sense of its predication, that is to say, Being, none can know which of these is most consigned or subjugated to death: man, the "world," or "things."

Being maintains itself in-between, like an ek-stasis that separates, that prevents conjoining. Except for the conjoining, already, in death's safekeeping. Being: copula already in and for death.

This sense of the copula—that which stays suspended in-between—is a production of man's and of man. It is the historical[3] production of man as man: what Heidegger calls the historical destiny of Being.

He makes every being participate in this production—by assimilation to him and by assisting his entry into presence—imposing the sense of his ek-stasis on each. He bows the whole to his sexed destiny, including in its relation to death. He takes up the whole within his death. He envelops the whole in his project, thereby depriving it of its "proper" motion.

Language *[la langue]* becomes that which gives, that which is given, though no object of giving is constituted. It is, at present, the place where there is giving, from which *there is* [*il y a*] that which gives.

The dative structure becomes transitive at this point: lacking protagonists, the gift gives itself. With no distinction yet between subject and predicate except for the actualizing of a present that at the same time is withheld. Giving itself, the gift abides. The verb does not exhaust the subject, the present does not exhaust the past: it actualizes while maintaining the reserve (store). Giving-itself—while abiding, staying the same—obliterates the passage from the one who gives to the one who receives, the exhaustion of the (female) one when the other is formed therefrom. Obliterates the debt that could follow from this. The war that could follow. The death that could follow?

The gift gives itself. Doesn't this reduced—and, therefore, spent/given back, permanent, reproducible—dative structure represent the circle of Being? Doesn't it express this: that Being is the re-turn of she who will never come back in a superabundance of uncountable space and time, as well as the return to her? Spelling itself out in the entry into presence without ever bringing about there that reserve store on the basis of which all production takes place. She who gives herself, first, become that which gives itself, become this there on the basis of which there is giving.

The gift gives itself—the infinity of a sensible *hypokeimenon*, without boundary or distinctive trait, with no "proper" being, no singular body, no physical *physis*. A passage that abolishes the break between the physical and the metaphysical by constituting a "ground," earth, and mother other than she or they—still physical and alive—who can assimilate: eat, drink, dwell, call, name, and, thus—perhaps?—make vanish. The gift gives itself without breaking into the reserve store, if she who will never come back has become, at present, a sensible transcendental always already and nevermore there.

Does the re-turn of and to *physis* as the dwelling place of Being amount to a scaling up within oblivion or not? A sealing up of she who first gives herself? The *there is* of the gift now has its place within language. But when language holds,[4] as the shelter of Being, something of the taking-place of the gift of the being is already swallowed up. In a consumption, an assimilation, an appropriation. A gift of a physical, sensible being—fluid, non-apparent, imperceptible . . . "Proper" for constituting the transcendental.

This passage from one to the other, from a female one to a male one, can only be forgotten. Without forgetting, Being would not be. It is forgetting, repeated again and again, and kept up, that brings about passage to this new ground. And if it be too closely approached, it fades away, for it is not. Except as an effect of forgetting.

Notes

1. In French, "subject" is marked masculine and "copula" is marked feminine. According to French grammatical rules, then, "the same" or *le même* must be masculine, because masculine nouns always trump feminine ones. In the opening line of this paragraph, however, the author writes "the same—qualifying both "subject" and "copula"—as *la même,* using the feminine definite article and thus breaking, and breaking with, that rule and the sort of sameness it entails. If the subject (m) and the copula (f) are the same, what is to prevent them from being referred to with a noun marked feminine?—Tr.

2. The standard English translation of *il y a,* which is the French rendering of Heidegger's *es gibt,* is 'there is.' However, *il y a* has an existential sense without using the French verb equivalent of 'to be'; it instead uses the French equivalent of the verb 'to have.' Since 'is' is a form of the copula in English, to translate *il y a* as 'there is' in the context of this discussion of the copula would risk obscuring points of the passage, namely, the copula's inability to form predications about itself and the replacement of the copula and its silence about itself with the noncopulative locution *il y a.* For this reason, *il y a* is left untranslated here.—Tr.

3. 'Historical' is the standard English rendering of Heidegger's *geschichtlich* and the French *historial.* Heidegger distinguishes this term from *historisch,* rendered as 'historiographic' and *historique.*—Tr.

4. *Quand la langue se tient* can also mean 'when the tongue is held,' 'when language is held,' and even when language holds itself.'—Tr.

Sexual Difference

Sexual difference is one of the major philosophical issues, if not the issue, of our age. According to Heidegger, each age has one issue to think through, and one only. Sexual difference is probably the issue in our time which could be our "salvation" if we thought it through.

But, whether I turn to philosophy, to science, or to religion, I find this underlying issue still cries out in vain for our attention. Think of it as an approach that would allow us to check the many forms that destruction takes in our world, to counteract a nihilism that merely affirms the reversal or the repetitive proliferation of status quo values—whether you call them the consumer society, the circularity of discourse, the more or less cancerous diseases of our age, the unreliability of words, the end of philosophy, religious despair or regression to religiosity, scientistic or technical imperialism that fails to consider the living subject.

Sexual difference would constitute the horizon of worlds more fecund than any known to date—at least in the West—and without reducing fecundity to the reproduction of bodies and flesh. For loving partners this would be a fecundity of birth and regeneration, but also the production of a new age of thought, art, poetry, and language: the creation of a new *poetics*.

Both in theory and in practice, everything resists the discovery and affirmation of such an advent or event. In theory, philosophy wants to be literature or rhetoric, wishing either to break with ontology or to regress to the ontological. Using the same ground and the same framework as "first philosophy," working toward its disintegration but without proposing any other goals that might assure new foundations and new works.

In politics, some overtures have been made to the world of women. But these overtures remain partial and local: some concessions have been made by those in power, but no new values have been established. Rarely have these measures been thought through and affirmed by women themselves, who consequently remain at the level of critical demands. Has a worldwide erosion of the gains won in women's struggles occurred because of the failure to lay foundations different from those on which the world of men is constructed? Psychoanalytic theory and therapy, the scenes of sexuality as such, are a long way from having effected their revolution. And with a few exceptions, sexual practice today is often divided between two parallel worlds: the world of men and the world of women. A nontraditional, fecund encounter between the sexes barely exists. It does not voice its demands publicly, except through certain kinds of silence and polemics.

A revolution in thought and ethics is needed if the work of sexual difference is to take place. We need to reinterpret everything concerning the relations between the subject and discourse, the subject and the world, the subject and the cosmic, the microcosmic and the macrocosmic. Everything, beginning with the way in which the subject has always been written in the masculine form, as *man*, even when it claimed to be universal or neutral. Despite the fact that *man*—at least in French—rather than being neutral, is sexed.

Man has been the subject of discourse, whether in theory, morality, or politics. And the gender of God, the guardian of every subject and every discourse, is always *masculine and paternal*, in the West. To women are left the so-called minor arts: cooking, knitting, embroidery, and sewing; and, in exceptional cases, poetry, painting, and music. Whatever their importance, these arts do not currently make the rules, at least not overtly.

Of course, we are witnessing a certain reversal of values: manual labor and art are being revalued. But the relation of these arts to sexual difference is never really thought through and properly apportioned. At best, it is related to the class struggle.

In order to make it possible to think through, and live, this difference, we must reconsider the whole problematic of *space* and *time*.

In the beginning there was space and the creation of space, as is said in all theogonies. The gods, God, first create *space*. And time is there, more or less in the service of space. On the first day, the first days, the gods, God, make a world by separating the elements. This world is then peopled, and a rhythm is established among its inhabitants. God would be time itself, lavishing or exteriorizing itself in its action in space, in places.

Philosophy then confirms the genealogy of the task of the gods or God. Time becomes the *interiority* of the subject itself, and space, its *exteriority* (this problematic is developed by Kant in the *Critique of Pure Reason*). The subject, the master of time, becomes the axis of the world's ordering, with its something beyond the moment and eternity: God. He effects the passage between time and space.

Which would be inverted in sexual difference? Where the feminine is experienced as space, but often with connotations of the abyss and night (God being space and light?), while the masculine is experienced as time.

The transition to a new age requires a change in our perception and conception of *space-time*, the *inhabiting of places*, and of *containers*, or *envelopes of identity*. It assumes and entails an evolution or a transformation of forms, of the relations of *matter* and *form* and of the interval *between:* the trilogy of the constitution of place. Each age inscribes a limit to this trinitary configuration: *matter, form, interval*, or *power* [*puissance*], *act, intermediary-interval*.

Desire occupies or designates the place of the *interval*. Giving it a permanent definition would amount to suppressing it as desire. Desire demands a sense of attraction: a change in the interval, the displacement of the subject or of the object in their relations of nearness or distance.

The transition to a new age comes at the same time as a change in the economy of desire. A new age signifies a different relation between:

—man and god(s),
—man and man,
—man and world,
—man and woman.

Our age, which is often thought to be one in which the problematic of desire has been brought forward, frequently theorizes this desire on the basis of observations of a moment of tension, or a moment in history, whereas desire ought to be thought of as a changing dynamic whose outlines can be described in the past, sometimes in the present, but never definitively predicted. Our age will have failed to realize the full dynamic reserve signified by desire if it is referred back to the economy of the *interval*, if it is situated in the attractions, tensions, and actions occurring between *form* and *matter*, but also in the *remainder* that subsists after each creation or work, *between* what has already been identified and what has still to be identified, and so on.

In order to imagine such an economy of desire, one must reinterpret what Freud implies by *sublimation* and observe that he does not speak of the sublimation of genitality (except in reproduction? But, if this were a successful form of sublimation, Freud would not be so pessimistic about parental child-rearing practices) or of the sublimation of the *partial drives in relation to the feminine* but rather of their repression (little girls speak earlier and more skillfully than little boys; they have a better relationship to the social; and so on—qualities or aptitudes that disappear without leaving any creative achievements that capitalize on their energy, except for the task of becoming a woman: an object of attraction?)[1]

In this possible nonsublimation of herself, and by herself, woman always tends *toward* without any return to herself as the place where something positive can be elaborated. In terms of contemporary physics, it could be said that she remains on the side of the electron, with all that this implies for her, for man, for their encounter. If there is no double desire, the positive and negative poles divide themselves between the two sexes instead of establishing a chiasmus or a double loop in which each can go toward the other and come back to itself.

If these positive and negative poles are not found in both, the same one always attracts, while the other remains in motion but lacks a "proper" place. What is missing is the double pole of attraction and support, which excludes disintegration or rejection, attraction and decomposition, but which instead ensures the separation that articulates every encounter and makes possible speech, promises, alliances.

In order to distance oneself, must one be able to take? To speak? Which in a certain way comes to the same thing. Perhaps in order to take, one needs a fixed container or place? A soul? Or a spirit? Mourning nothing is the most difficult. Mourning the self in the other is almost impossible. I search for myself, as if I had been assimilated into maleness. I ought to reconstitute myself on the basis of a disassimilation. . . . [2] Rise again from the traces of a culture, of works already produced by the other. Searching through what is in them—for what is not there. What allowed them to be, for what is not there. Their conditions of possibility, for what is not there.

Woman ought to be able to find herself, among other things, through the images of herself already deposited in history and the conditions of production of the work of man, and not on the basis of his work, his genealogy.

If traditionally, and as a mother, woman represents *place* for man, such a limit means that she becomes *a thing*, with some possibility of change from one historical period to another. She finds herself delineated as a thing. Moreover, the maternal-feminine also serves as an *envelope, a container*, the starting point from which man limits his things. The *relationship between envelope and things* constitutes one of the aporias, or the aporia, of Aristotelianism and of the philosophical systems derived from it.

In our terminologies, which derive from this economy of thought but are impregnated with a psychologism unaware of its sources, it is said, for example, that the woman-mother is *castrating*. Which means that, since her status as envelope and as thing(s) has not been interpreted, she remains inseparable from the work or act of man, notably insofar as he defines her and creates *his* identity with her as his starting point or, correlatively, with this determination of her being. If after all this, she is still alive, she continuously undoes his work—distinguishing herself from both the envelope and the thing, ceaselessly creating there some interval, play, something in motion and un-limited which disturbs his perspective, his world, and his/its limits. But, because he fails to leave her a subjective life, and to be on occasion her place and her thing in an intersubjective dynamic, man remains within a master-slave dialectic. The slave, ultimately, of a God on whom he bestows the characteristics of an absolute master. Secretly or obscurely, a slave to the power of the maternal-feminine which he diminishes or destroys.

The maternal-feminine remains the *place separated from "its" own place*, deprived of "its" place. She is or ceaselessly becomes the place of the other who cannot separate himself from it. Without her knowing or willing it, she is then threatening because of what she lacks: a "proper" place. She would have to re-envelop herself with herself, and do so at least twice: as a woman and as a mother. Which would presuppose a change in the whole economy of space-time.

In the meantime, this ethical question comes into play in matters of *nudity* and *perversity*. Woman must be nude because she is not situated, does not situate herself in her place. Her clothes, her makeup, and her jewels are the things with which she tries to create her container(s), her envelope(s). She cannot make use of the envelope that she is, and must create artificial ones.

Freud's statement that woman is identified with orality is meaningful, but it still exiles her from her most archaic and constituent site. No doubt orality is an especially significant measure for her: morphologically, she has two mouths and two pairs of lips. But she can act on this morphology or make something of it only if she preserves her relation to *spatiality* and to the *fetal*. Although she needs these dimensions to create a space for herself (as well as to maintain a receptive place for the other), they are traditionally taken from her to constitute man's nostalgia and everything that he constructs in memory of this first and ultimate dwelling place. An obscure commemoration. . . . Centuries will perhaps have been needed for man to interpret the meaning of his work(s): the endless construction of a number of substitutes for his prenatal home. From the depths of the earth to the highest skies? Again and again, taking from the feminine the tissue or texture of spatiality. In exchange—but it isn't a real one—he buys her a house, even shuts her up in it, places limits on her that are the opposite of the unlimited site in which he unwittingly situates her. He contains or envelops her with walls while enveloping himself and his things with her flesh. The nature of these envelopes is not the same: on the one hand, invisibly alive, but with barely perceivable limits; on the other, visibly limiting or sheltering, but at the risk of being prison-like or murderous if the threshold is not left open.

We must, therefore, reconsider the whole question of our conception of place, both in order to move on to another age of difference (each age of thought corresponds to a particular time of meditation on difference), and in order to construct an ethics of the passions. We need to change the relations between form, matter, interval, and limit, an issue that has never been considered in a way that allows for a relationship between two loving subjects of different sexes.

Once there was the enveloping body and the enveloped body, the latter being the more mobile through what Aristotle termed *locomotion* (since maternity does not look much like "motion"). The one who offers or allows desire moves and envelops, engulfing the other. It is moreover a danger if no third term exists. Not only to serve as a limitation. This third term can occur within the one who contains as a relation of the latter to his or her own limit(s): relation to the divine, to death, to the social, to the cosmic. If a third term does not exist within and for the container, he or she becomes *all-powerful*.

Therefore, to deprive one pole of sexual difference, women, of a third term also amounts to putting them in the position of omnipotence: this is a danger for men, especially in that it suppresses an interval that is both entrance and space between.[3] A place for both to enter and exit the envelope (and on the same side, so as not to perforate the envelope or assimilate it into the digestive process); for both, a possibility of unhindered movement, of peaceful immobility without the risk of imprisonment.

***

To arrive at the constitution of an ethics of sexual difference, we must at least return to what is for Descartes the first passion: *wonder*. This passion has no opposite or contradiction and exists always as though for the first time. Thus man and woman, woman and man are always meeting as though for the first time because they cannot be substituted one for the other. I will never be in a man's place, never will a man be in mine. Whatever identifications are possible, one will never exactly occupy the place of the other—they are irreducible one to the other.

> When the first encounter with some object surprises us, and we judge it to be new, or very different from what we formerly knew, or from what we supposed that it ought to be, that causes us to wonder and be surprised; and because that may happen before we in any way know whether this object is agreeable to us or is not so, it appears to me that wonder is the first of all the passions; and it has no opposite, because if the object which presents itself has nothing in it that surprises us, we are in nowise moved regarding it, and we consider it without passion. (René Descartes, *The Passions of the Soul*, article 53).[4]

Who or what the other is, I never know. But the other who is forever unknowable is the one who differs from me sexually. This feeling of surprise, astonishment, and wonder in the face of the unknowable ought to be returned to its locus: that of sexual difference. The passions have either been repressed, stifled, or reduced, or reserved for God. Sometimes a space for wonder is left to works of art. But it is never found to reside in this locus: *between man and woman*. Into this place came attraction, greed, possession, consummation, disgust, and so on. But not that wonder which beholds what it sees always as if for the first time, never taking hold of the other as its object. It does not try to seize, possess, or reduce this object, but leaves it subjective, still free.

This has never existed between the sexes since wonder maintains their autonomy within their statutory difference, keeping a space of freedom and attraction between them, a possibility of separation and alliance.

This might take place at the time of the first meeting, even prior to the betrothal, and remain as a permanent proof of difference. The *interval* would never be *crossed*. Consummation would never take place, the idea itself being a delusion. One sex is not entirely consumable by the other. There is always a *remainder*.

Up until now this remainder has been entrusted to or reserved for *God*. Sometimes a portion was incarnated in the *child*. Or was thought of as being *neuter*. This neuter (in a different way, like the child or God?) suggests the possibility of an encounter but puts it off, deferring it until later, even when it is a question of a secondary revision *[aprés-coup]*. It always stays at an insurmountable distance, a respectful or deadly sort of no-man's-land:[5] no alliance is forged; nothing is celebrated. The immediacy of the encounter is annihilated or deferred to a future that never comes.

Of course, the neuter might signify an alchemical site of the sublimation of "genitality," and the possibility of generation, of the creation of and between different genders and genres. But it would still have to be receptive to the advent of difference, and be understood as an anticipation from this side and not as a beyond, especially an ethical one. Generally the phrase *there is* upholds the present but defers celebration. There is not, there will not be the moment of wonder of the *wedding*, an ecstasy that remains *in-stant*.[6] The *there is* remains a present that may be subject to pressure by the god, but it does not form a foundation for the triumph of sexual fecundity. Only certain oriental traditions speak of the energizing, aesthetic, and religious fecundity of the sexual act: the two sexes give each other the seed of life and eternity, the growing generation of and between them both.

We must reexamine our own history thoroughly to understand why this sexual difference has not had its chance to develop, either empirically or transcendentally. Why it has failed to have its own ethics, aesthetic, logic, religion, or the micro- and macrocosmic realization of its coming into being or its destiny.

It is surely a question of the dissociation of body and soul, of sexuality and spirituality, of the lack of a passage for the spirit, for the god, between the inside and the outside, the outside and the inside, and of their distribution between the sexes in the sexual act. Everything is constructed in such a way that these realities remain separate, even opposed to one another. So that they neither mix, marry, nor form an alliance. Their wedding is always being put off to a beyond, a future life, or else devalued, felt and thought to be less worthy in comparison to the marriage between the mind and God in a transcendental realm where all ties to the world of sensation have been severed.

The consequences of the nonfulfillment of the sexual act remain, and there are many. To take up only the most beautiful, as yet to be made manifest in the realm of time and space, there are *angels*. These messengers who never remain enclosed in a place, who are also never immobile. Between God, as the perfectly immobile act, man, who is surrounded and enclosed by the world of his work, and woman, whose task would be to take care of nature and procreation, *angels* would circulate as mediators of that which has not yet happened, of what is still going to happen, of what is on the horizon. Endlessly reopening the enclosure of the universe, of universes, identities, the unfolding of actions, of history.

The angel is that which unceasingly *passes through the envelope(s)* or *container(s)*, goes from one side to the other, reworking every deadline, changing every decision, thwarting all repetition. Angels destroy the monstrous, that which hampers the possibility of a new age; they come to herald the arrival of a new birth, a new morning.

They are not unrelated to sex. There is of course Gabriel, the angel of the annunciation. But other angels announce the consummation of marriage, notably all the angels in the Apocalypse and many in the Old Testament. As if the angel were a representation of a sexuality that has never been incarnated. A light, divine gesture (or tale) of flesh that has not yet acted or flourished. Always fallen or still awaiting parousia. The fate of a love still torn between here and elsewhere. The work of a love that is the original sinner, since the first garden, the lost earthly paradise? The fate of all flesh which is, moreover, attributable to God![7]

These swift angelic messengers, who transgress all enclosures in their speed, tell of the passage between the envelope of God and that of the world as micro- or macrocosm. They proclaim that such a journey can be made by the body of man, and above all the body of woman. They represent and tell of another incarnation, another parousia of the body. Irreducible to philosophy, theology, morality, angels appear as the messengers of ethics evoked by art—sculpture, painting, or music—without its being possible to say anything more than the gesture that represents them.

They speak like messengers, but gesture seems to be their "nature." Movement, posture, the coming-and-going between the two. They move—or stir up?—the paralysis or *apatheia* of the body, or the soul, or the world. They set trances or convulsions to music, or give them harmony.

Their touch—when they touch—resembles that of gods. They are imperious in their grace even as they remain imperceptible.

One of the questions which arises about them is whether they can be found together in the same place. The traditional answer is no. This question, which is similar to and different from that of the co-location of bodies, comes back to the question of sexual ethics. The mucous should no doubt be pictured as related to the angel, whereas the inertia of the body deprived of its relation to the mucous and its gesture is linked to the fallen body or the corpse.

A sexual or carnal ethics would require that both angel and body be found together. This is a world that must be constructed or reconstructed. A genesis of love between the sexes has yet to come about in all dimensions, from the smallest to the greatest, from the most intimate to the most political. A world that must be created or re-created so that man and woman may once again or at last live together, meet, and sometimes inhabit the same place.

***

The link uniting or reuniting masculine and feminine must be horizontal and vertical, terrestrial and heavenly. As Heidegger, among others, has written, it must forge an alliance between the divine and the mortal, such that the sexual encounter would be a festive celebration and not a disguised or polemical form of the master-slave relationship. Nor a meeting in the shadow or orbit of a Father-God who alone lays down the law, who is the immutable spokesman of a single sex.

Of course, the most extreme progression and regression goes under the name of God. I can only strive toward the absolute or regress to infinity under the guarantee of God's existence. This is what tradition has taught us, and its imperatives have not yet been overcome, since their destruction brings about terrible abandonments and pathological states, unless one has exceptional love partners. And even then . . . Unhappiness is sometimes all the more inescapable when it lacks the horizon of the divine, of the gods, of an opening onto a beyond, but also a *limit* that the other may or may not penetrate.

How can we mark this limit of a place, of place in general, if not through sexual difference? But, in order for an ethics of sexual difference to come into being, we must constitute a possible place for each sex, body, and flesh to inhabit. Which presupposes a memory of the past, a hope for the future, memory bridging the present and disconcerting the mirror symmetry that annihilates the difference of identity.

To do this requires time, both space and time. Perhaps we are passing through an era when *time must redeploy space*? A new morning of and for the world? A remaking of immanence and transcendence, notably through this *threshold* which has never been examined as such: the female sex. The threshold that gives access to the *mucous*. Beyond classical oppositions of love and hate, liquid and ice—a threshold that is always *half-open*. The threshold of the *lips*, which are strangers to dichotomy and oppositions. Gathered one against the other but without any possible suture, at least of a real kind. They do not absorb the world into or through themselves, provided they are not misused and reduced to a means of consumption or consummation. They offer a shape of welcome but do not assimilate, reduce, or swallow up. A sort of doorway to voluptuousness? They are not useful, except as that which designates a *place*, the very place of uselessness, at least as it is habitually understood. Strictly speaking, they serve neither conception nor jouissance. Is this the mystery of feminine identity? Of its self-contemplation, of this very strange word of silence? Both the threshold and reception of exchange, the sealed-up secret of wisdom, belief, and faith in all truths?

(Two sets of lips that, moreover, cross over each other like the arms of the cross, the prototype of the crossroads *between*. The mouth lips and the genital lips do not point in the same direction. In some way they point in the direction opposite from the one you would expect, with the "lower" ones forming the vertical.)

In this approach, where the borders of the body are wed in an embrace that transcends all limits—without, however, risking engulfment, thanks to the fecundity of the porous—in the most extreme experience of sensation, which is also always in the future, each one discovers the self in that experience which is inexpressible yet forms the supple grounding of life and language.

For this, "God" is necessary, or a love so attentive that it is divine. Which has never taken place? Love always postpones its transcendence beyond the here and now, except in certain experiences of God. And desire fails to act sufficiently on the porous nature of the body, omitting the communion that takes place through the most intimate mucous membranes. In this exchange, what is communicated is so subtle that one needs great perseverance to keep it from falling into oblivion, intermittency, deterioration, illness, or death.

This communion is often left to the child, as the symbol of the union. But there are other signs of union which precede the child—the space where the lovers give each other life or death? Regeneration or degeneration: both are possible. The intensity of desire and the filiation of both lovers are engaged.

And if the divine is present as the mystery that animates the copula, the *is* and the *being* in sexual difference, can the force of desire overcome the avatars of genealogical destiny? How does it manage this? With what power [*puissance*] does it reckon, while remaining nevertheless incarnate? Between the idealistic fluidity of an unborn body that is untrue to its birth and genetic determinism, how do we take the measure of a love that changes our condition from mortal to immortal? Certain figures of gods become men, of God become man, and of twice-born beings indicate the path of love.

Has something of the achievement of sexual difference still not been said or transmitted? Has something been held in reserve within the silence of a history in the feminine: an energy, a morphology, a growth and flourishing still to come from the female realm? An overture to a future that is still and always open? Given that the world has remained aporetic about this strange advent.

Notes

1. Cf. Luce Irigaray, *Speculum, de l'autre femme* (Paris: Minuit, 1984), pp. 9–162; trans. Gillian C. Gill, under the title *Speculum of the Other Woman* (Ithaca: Cornell University Press, 1985), pp. 11–129.

2. All ellipses occur in the original French text and do not indicate omissions in the translation.—Tr.

3. Irigaray plays on the double sense of *entre,* meaning both "enter" and "between."—Tr.

4. *The Philosophical Works of Descartes,* trans. E. S. Haldane and G. R. T. Ross (Cambridge: Cambridge University Press, 1931; reprinted Dover, 1955), 1: 358.

5. In English in the original text.—Tr.

6. *Instance* is rendered here as "in-stant" to underscore Irigaray's emphasis on the term's root meaning, standing within the self, as opposed to "ecstasy," standing outside the self.—Tr.

7. See Luce Irigaray, "Epistle to the Last Christians," in *Marine Lover of Friedrich Nietzsche,* trans. Gillian C. Gill (New York: Columbia University Press, 1991).

Bibliography

The following bibliography contains the major works in English translation by the authors included in this volume. Reference to bibliographies that are more comprehensive follow each section.

Martin Heidegger

Aristotle's "Metaphysics" Theta 1–3: On the Essence and Actuality of Force. Trans. Walter Brogan and Peter Warnek. Bloomington: Indiana University Press, 1995.

Basic Concepts. Trans. Gary E. Aylesworth. Bloomington: Indiana University Press, 1993.

The Basic Problems of Phenomenology. Trans. Albert Hofstadter. Bloomington: Indiana University Press, 1982.

Basic Questions of Philosophy: Selected "Problems" of "Logic." Trans. Richard Rojcewicz and Andre Schuwer. Bloomington: Indiana University Press, 1994.

Basic Writings: From Being and Time (1927) to The Task of Thinking (1964). Ed. David Farrell Krell. San Francisco: HarperCollins, 1993.

Being and Time. Trans. John Macquarrie and Edward Robinson. New York: Harper and Row, 1962.

Being and Time: A Translation of Sein and Zeit. Trans. Joan Stambaugh. Albany: State University of New York Press, 1996.

The Concept of Time. Trans. William McNeill. Oxford: Blackwell, 1992.

Contributions to Philosophy: From Enowning. Trans. Parvis Emad and Kenneth Maly. Bloomington: Indiana University Press, 1999.

Discourse on Thinking: A Translation of Gelassenheit. Trans. John M. Anderson and E. Hans Freund. New York: Harper and Row, 1966.

Early Greek Thinking: The Dawn of Western Philosophy. Trans. David Farrell Krell and Frank Capuzzi. New York: Harper and Row, 1984.

Elucidations of Holderlin's Poetry. Trans. Keith Hoeller. Amherst, N.Y.: Prometheus Books, 1999.

The End of Philosophy. Trans. Joan Stambaugh. New York: Harper and Row, 1973.

Essays in Metaphysics: Identity and Difference. Trans. Kurt F. Leidecker. New York: Philosophical Library, Inc., 1960.

The Essence of Reasons. Trans. Terrence Malick. Evanston, Ill.: Northwestern University Press, 1969.

Essence of Truth—The Nature of Death (The Collected Works of Martin Heidegger, Vol. 34). Trans. Ted Sadler. London: Athlone Press, 1999.

Existence and Being. Ed. Werner Brock. Washington, D.C.: Regnery Gateway Company, 1949.

The Fundamental Concepts of Metaphysics: World, Finitude, Solitude. Trans. William McNeill and Nicholas Walker. Bloomington: Indiana University Press, 1995.

Hegel's Concept of Experience. Trans. J. Glenn Gray. New York: Harper and Row, 1970.

Hegel's Phenomenology of Spirit. Trans. Parvis Emad and Kenneth Maly. Bloomington: Indiana University Press, 1988. [with Eugene Fink]. *Heraclitus Seminar*. Trans. Charles H. Seibert. Evanston, Ill.: Northwestern University Press, 1993.

History of the Concept of Time. Trans. Theodore Kisiel. Bloomington: Indiana University Press, 1985.

Holderlin's Hymn "The Ister." Trans. William McNeill and Julia Davis. Bloomington: Indiana University Press, 1996.

The Idea of Philosophy: Towards a Definition of Philosophy (The Collected Works of Martin Heidegger, Vol. 56/57). Trans. Ted Sadler. London: Athlone Press, 1999.

Identity and Difference. Trans. Joan Stambaugh. New York: Harper and Row, 1969.

An Introduction to Metaphysics. Trans. Ralph Manheim. New Haven, Conn.: Yale University Press, 1959.

Kant and the Problem of Metaphysics. Trans. Richard Taft. Bloomington: Indiana University Press, 1997.

Martin Heidegger and National Socialism: Questions and Answers. Ed. Gunther Neske and Emil Kettering. Intro. Karsten Harries. Trans. Lisa Harries. New York: Paragon House, 1990. (Contains "The Self-Assertion of the German University" [The Rectorial Address]; "The Rectorate 1933/34: Facts and Thoughts"; "The Spiegel Interview" ["Only a God Can Save Us"]; and "Martin Heidegger in Conversation" with Richard Wisser.)

The Metaphysical Foundations of Logic. Trans. Michael Heim. Bloomington: Indiana University Press, 1984.

Nietzsche: Volume I: The Will to Power as Art. Trans. David Farrell Krell. New York: Harper and Row, 1979.

Nietzsche: Volume II: The Eternal Recurrence of the Same. Trans. David Farrell Krell. New York: Harper and Row, 1984.

Nietzsche: Volume III. The Will to Power as Knowledge and as Metaphysics. Ed. David Farrell Krell. Trans. Joan Stambaugh. New York: Harper and Row, 1987.

Nietzsche: Volume IV: Nihilism. Ed. David Farrell Krell. Trans. Frank A. Capuzzi. New York: Harper and Row, 1982.

On the Way to Language. Trans. Peter D. Hertz. New York: Harper and Row, 1971.

On Time and Being. Trans. Joan Stambaugh. New York: Harper and Row, 1972.

Ontology: The Hermeneutics of Facticity. Trans. John van Buren. Bloomington: Indiana University Press, 1999.

Parmenides. Trans. Andre Schuwer and Richard Rojcewicz. Bloomington: Indiana University Press, 1992.

Pathmarks. Ed. William McNeill. Cambridge: Cambridge University Press, 1998.

Phenomenological Interpretation of Kant's Critique of Pure Reason. Trans. Parvis Emad and Kenneth Maly. Bloomington: Indiana University Press, 1997.

The Piety of Thinking: Essays. Trans. James G. Hart and John C. Maraldo. Bloomington: Indiana University Press, 1976.

Plato's Sophist. Trans. Richard Rojcewicz and Andre Schuwer. Bloomington: Indiana University Press, 1997.

Poetry, Language, Thought. Trans. Albert Hofstadter. New York: Harper and Row, 1971.
The Principle of Reason. Trans. Reginald Lilly. Bloomington: Indiana University Press, 1992.
The Question Concerning Technology and Other Essays. Trans. William Lovitt. New York: Harper and Row, 1977.
The Question of Being. Trans. William Kluback and Jean T. Wilde. New Haven, Conn.: College and University Press, 1958.
Schelling's Treatise on Human Freedom. Trans. Joan Stambaugh. Athens: Ohio University Press, 1985.
What Is a Thing? Trans. W. B. Barton Jr. and Vera Deutsch. Chicago: H. Regnery Co., 1968.
What Is Called Thinking? Trans. Fred D. Wieck and J. Glenn Gray. New York: Harper and Row, 1968.
What Is Philosophy? Trans. William Kluback and Jean T. Wilde. New Haven: College and University Press, 1958.
Zollikon Seminars: Protocol–Conversations–Letters. Trans. Franz K. Mayr and Richard R. Askay. Evanston, Ill.: Northwestern University Press, 2000.

Nordquist, Joan. *Martin Heidegger (II): A Bibliography*. Santa Cruz, Calif.: Reference and Research Services, 1996.
Sass, Hans-Martin. *Martin Heidegger, Bibliography and Glossary*. Bowling Green, Ohio: Philosophy Documentation Center, Bowling Green State University, 1982.

Maurice Merleau-Ponty

Adventures of the Dialectic. Trans. Joseph Bien. Evanston, Ill.: Northwestern University Press, 1973.
Consciousness and the Acquisition of Language. Trans. Hugh J. Silverman. Evanston, Ill.: Northwestern University Press, 1973.
Humanism and Terror. Trans. John O'Neill. Boston: Becon Press, 1969.
The Merleau-Ponty Aesthetics Reader: Philosophy and Painting. Ed. Galen A. Johnson. Evanston, Ill.: Northwestern University Press, 1993. (Contains "Cézanne's Doubt"; "Indirect Language and the Voices of Silence"; and "Eye and Mind.")
In Praise of Philosophy and Other Essays. Trans. J. Wild and J. M. Edie. Evanston, Ill.: Northwestern University Press, 1963.
Phenomenology, Language and Sociology: Selected Essays of Maurice Merleau-Ponty. Ed. John O'Neill. London: Heinemann Educational, 1974.
Phenomenology of Perception. Trans. Colin Smith. London: Routledge, 1962.
The Primacy of Perception. Ed. J. M. Edie. Evanston, Ill.: Northwestern University Press, 1964.
The Prose of the World. Trans. John O'Neill. Evanston, Ill.: Northwestern University Press, 1973.
Sense and Non-Sense. Trans. Hubert L. Dreyfus and Patricia Allen Dreyfus. Evanston, Ill.: Northwestern University Press, 1964.
Signs. Trans. Richard C. McClearly. Evanston, Ill.: Northwestern University Press, 1964.
The Structure of Behavior. Trans. A. L. Fisher. London: Methuen, 1965.
Texts and Dialogues: On Philosophy, Politics, and Culture. Ed. Hugh J. Silverman and James Barry. Trans. Michael B. Smith. Atlantic Highlands, N.J.: Humanities Press, 1992.

Themes from the Lectures at the College de France 1952–1960. Trans. John O'Neill. Evanston, Ill.: Northwestern University Press, 1970.

The Visible and the Invisible. Trans. Alphonso Lingis. Evanston, Ill.: Northwestern University Press, 1968.

Lapointe, François and Lapointe, Claire. *Maurice Merleau-Ponty and His Critics: An International Bibliography, 1942–1976: Preceded by a Bibliography of Merleau-Ponty's Writings*. New York: Garland Publishing, 1976.

Priest, Stephen. *Merleau-Ponty*. London: Routledge, 1998.

Whiteside, Kerry. "The Merleau-Ponty Bibliography: Additions and Corrections." *Journal of the History of Philosophy* 21, no. 2 (1983): 195–201.

Gilles Deleuze

[with Felix Guattari]. *A Thousand Plateaus: Capitalism and Schizophrenia*. Trans. Brian Massumi. Minneapolis: University of Minnesota Press, 1987.

[with Felix Guattari]. *Anti-Oedipus: Capitalism and Schizophrenia*. Trans. Robert Hurley, Mark Seem, and Helen R. Lane. Minneapolis: University of Minnesota Press, 1985.

Bergsonism. Trans. Hugh Tomlinson and Barbara Habberjam. New York: Zone Books, 1988.

"Bergson's Conception of Difference" Trans. Melissa McMahon. In *The New Bergson*. Ed. John Mullarkey. Manchester: Manchester University Press, 1999.

Cinema I: The Movement-Image. Trans. Hugh Tomlinson and Barbara Habberjam. Minneapolis: University of Minnesota Press, 1986.

Cinema II: The Time-Image. Trans. Hugh Tomlinson and Robert Galeta. Minneapolis: University of Minnesota Press, 1989.

The Deleuze Reader. Ed. Constantin Boundas. New York: Columbia University Press, 1993.

[with Claire Parnet]. *Dialogues*. Trans. Hugh Tomlinson and Barbara Habberjam. New York: Columbia University Press, 1987.

Difference and Repetition. Trans. Paul Patton. New York: Columbia University Press, 1994.

Empiricism and Subjectivity: An Essay on Hume's Theory of Human Nature. Trans. Constantin Boundas. New York: Columbia University Press, 1991.

Essays: Critical and Clinical. Trans. Daniel Smith and Michael Greco. Minneapolis: University of Minnesota Press, 1997.

Expressionism in Philosophy: Spinoza. Trans. Martin Joughin. New York: Zone Books, 1990.

Francis Bacon: The Logic of Sensation. Trans. Daniel W. Smith. London: Verso Books, 1998.

The Fold: Leibniz and the Baroque. Trans. Tom Conley. Minneapolis: University of Minnesota Press, 1993.

Foucault. Trans. Sean Hand. Minneapolis: University of Minnesota Press, 1988.

[with Felix Guattari]. *Kafka: Toward a Minor Literature*. Trans. Dana Polan. Minnesota: University of Minnesota Press, 1986.

Kant's Critical Philosophy: The Doctrine of the Faculties. Trans. Hugh Tomlinson and Barbara Habberjam. Minneapolis: University of Minnesota Press, 1984.

The Logic of Sense. Ed. Constantin Boundas. Trans. Mark Lester and Charles Stivale. New York: Columbia University Press, 1990.

[with Leopold von Sacher-Masoch]. *Masochism: An Interpretation of Coldness and Cruelty*. Trans. Jean McNeil. New York: G. Braziller, 1971.
Negotiations: 1972–1990. Trans. Martin Joughin. New York: Columbia University Press, 1995.
Nietzsche and Philosophy. Trans. Hugh Tomlinson. New York: Columbia University Press, 1983.
[with Felix Guattari]. *Nomadology: The War Machine*. Trans. Brian Massumi. New York: Autonomedia/Semiotext(e), 1986.
[with Felix Guattari]. *On the Line*. Trans. Paul Patton. New York: Autonomedia/Semiotext(e), 1983.
Proust and Signs. Trans. Richard Howard. New York: G. Braziller, 1972.
[with Michel Foucault]. *Revisions Number 2: Photogenic Painting—Gerard Fromanger*. Ed. Sarah Wilson. Black Dog Publishing, 2000.
Spinoza: Practical Philosophy. Trans. Robert Hurley. San Francisco: City Lights Books, 1988.
[with Felix Guattari]. *What Is Philosophy?* Trans. Hugh Tomlinson and Graham Burchell. New York: Columbia University Press, 1994.

Nordquist, Joan. *Felix Guattari and Gilles Deleuze: A Bibliography*. Santa Cruz, Calif.: Reference and Research Services, 1992.
Patton, Paul, ed. *Deleuze: A Critical Reader*. Oxford: Blackwell, 1996.

Jacques Derrida

Acts of Literature. Ed. Derek Attridge. New York: Routledge, 1991.
Adieu to Emmanuel Levinas. Trans. Pascale-Anne Brault and Michael Naas. Stanford, Calif.: Stanford University Press, 1999.
Aporias: Dying-Awaiting (One Another at) the "Limits of Truth." Trans. Thomas Dutoit. Stanford, Calif.: Stanford University Press, 1993.
The Archeology of the Frivolous: Reading Condillac. Trans. John P. Leavey. Pittsburgh: Duquesne University Press, 1980.
Archive Fever: A Freudian Impression. Trans. Eric Prenowitz. Chicago: The University of Chicago Press, 1996.
[with Peter Eisenman]. *Chora L. Works*. Ed. Jeffrey Kipnis and Thomas Leeser. New York: Monacelli Press, 1997.
Cinders. Trans. Ned Lukacher. Lincoln: University of Nebraska Press, 1987.
Deconstruction in a Nutshell: A Conversation with Jacques Derrida. Ed. John D. Caputo. New York: Fordham University Press, 1997.
A Derrida Reader: Between the Blinds. Ed. Peggy Kamuf. New York: Columbia, 1991.
The Derrida Reader: Writing Performances. Ed. Julian Wolfreys. Lincoln: University of Nebraska Press, 1998.
Dissemination. Trans. Barbara Johnson. Chicago: The University of Chicago Press, 1981.
The Ear of the Other: Otobiography, Transference, Translation: Texts and Discussions with Jacques Derrida. Ed. Christie V. McDonald. Trans. Peggy Kamuf. New York: Schocken Books, 1985.
Edmund Husserl's Origin of Geometry: An Introduction. Trans. John P. Leavey. Stony Brook, N.Y.: Nicolas Hays, 1978; Brighton: Harvester Press, 1978.
[ed., with Mustapha Tlili]. *For Nelson Mandela*. New York: Seaver Books, 1987.
The Gift of Death. Trans. David Wills. Chicago: The University of Chicago Press, 1995.
Given Time: I. Counterfeit Money. Trans. Peggy Kamuf. Chicago: The University of Chicago Press, 1991.

Glas. Trans. John P. Leavey and Richard Rand. Lincoln: University of Nebraska Press, 1986.

[with Maurice Blanchot]. *The Instant of My Death: Demeure: Fiction and Testimony*. Stanford, Calif.: Stanford University Press, 2000.

[with Geoffrey Bennington]. *Jacques Derrida*. Trans. Geoffrey Bennington. Chicago: The University of Chicago Press, 1993.

Limited Inc. Trans. Samuel Weber and Jeffrey Mehlman. Baltimore: Johns Hopkins University Press, 1977.

Margins of Philosophy. Trans. Alan Bass. Chicago: The University of Chicago Press, 1982.

Memoirs of the Blind: The Self-Portrait and Other Ruins. Trans. Pascale-Anne Brault and Michael Naas. Chicago: The University of Chicago Press, 1993.

Memoires: For Paul de Man. Trans. Cecile Lindsay, Jonathan Caller, and Eduardo Cadava. New York: Columbia University Press, 1986.

Monolingualism of the Other: Or, The Prosthesis of Origin. Trans. Patrick Mensah. Stanford, Calif.: Stanford University Press, 1998.

Of Grammatology. Trans. Gayatri Chakravorty Spivak. Baltimore: Johns Hopkins University Press, 1976.

On the Name. Ed. Thomas Dutoit. Trans. David Wood, John P. Leavey, and Ian McLeod. Stanford Calif.: Stanford University Press, 1995.

Of Spirit: Heidegger and the Question. Trans. Geoffrey Bennington and Rachel Bowlby. Chicago: The University of Chicago Press, 1989.

The Other Heading: Reflections on Today's Europe. Trans. Pascale-Anne Brault and Michael B. Naas. Bloomington: Indiana University Press, 1992.

Points: Interviews, 1974–1994. Ed. Elizabeth Weber. Trans. Peggy Kamuf. Stanford, Calif.: Stanford University Press, 1995.

The Politics of Friendship. Trans. George Collins. London: Verso Books, 1997.

Positions. Trans. Alan Bass. Chicago: The University of Chicago Press, 1982.

The Post Card: From Socrates to Freud and Beyond. Trans. Alan Bass. Chicago: The University of Chicago Press, 1987.

Raising the Tone of Philosophy: Late Essays by Emmanuel Kant, Transformative Critique by Jacques Derrida. Ed. Peter Fenves. Baltimore: Johns Hopkins University Press, 1993.

[ed., with Gianni Vattimo]. *Religion: Cultural Memory in the Present*. Trans. David Webb. Stanford, Calif.: Stanford University Press, 1998.

Resistances of Psychoanalysis. Trans. Peggy Kamuf, Pascale Anne Brault, and Michael Naas. Stanford, Calif.: Stanford University Press, 1998.

Right of Inspection. Trans. David Wills. Photographer Marie-Francoise Plissart. New York: The Monacelli Press, 1998.

[with Paule Thevenin]. *The Secret Art of Antonin Artaud*. Trans. Mary Ann Caws. Cambridge, Mass.: MIT Press, 1998.

Specters of Marx: The State of the Debt, the Work of Mourning, and the New International. Trans. Peggy Kamuf London: Routledge, 1994.

Signeponge / Signsponge. Trans. Richard Rand. New York: Columbia University Press, 1984.

Speech and Phenomena: And Other Essays on Husserl's Theory of Signs. Trans. David B. Allison. Evanston, Ill.: Northwestern University Press, 1973.

Spurs: Nietzsche's Styles / Eperons: Les styles de Nietzche. Trans. Barbara Harlow. Chicago: The University of Chicago Press, 1979.

The Truth in Painting. Trans. Geoff Bennington and Ian McLeod. Chicago: The University of Chicago Press, 1987.

Writing and Difference. Trans. Alan Bass. Chicago: The University of Chicago Press, 1978.

Nordquist, Joan. *Jacques Derrida (III): A Bibliography*. Santa Cruz, Calif.: Reference and Research Services, 1995.

Schultz, William and Lewis Fried. *Jacques Derrida: An Annotated Primary and Secondary Bibliography*. New York: Garland, 1992.

Luce Irigaray

Elemental Passions. Trans. Joanne Collie and Judith Still. New York: Routledge, 1992.

An Ethics of Sexual Difference. Trans. Carolyn Burke and Gillian C. Gill. Ithaca, N.Y.: Cornell University Press, 1993.

The Forgetting of Air in Martin Heidegger. Trans. Mary Beth Mader. Austin, Tex.: University of Texas Press, 1999.

I Love to You: Sketch of a Possible Felicity in History. Trans. Alison Martin. New York: Routledge, 1996.

The Irigaray Reader. Ed. Margaret Whitford. Cambridge, Mass.: Blackwell, 1991.

Je, Tu, Nous: Toward a Culture of Difference. Trans. Alison Martin. New York: Routledge, 1992.

Marine Lover of Friedrich Nietzsche. Trans. Gillian C. Gill. New York. Columbia Uni versity Press, 1991.

Sexes and Genealogies. Trans. Gillian C. Gill. New York: Columbia University Press, 1993

Sexes and Genres Through Languages: Elements of Sexual Communication. New York: Routledge, forthcoming.

This Sex Which Is Not One. Trans. Catherine Porter and Carolyn Burke. Ithaca, N.Y.: Cornell University Press, 1985.

Speculum of the Other Woman. Trans. Gillian C. Gill. Ithaca, N.Y.: Cornell University Press, 1974.

Thinking the Difference: For a Peaceful Revolution. Trans. Karin Montin. New York: Routledge, 1994.

To Be Two. Trans. Monique M. Rhodes and Marco Concito-Monoc. New York: Routledge, 2001.

To Speak Is Never Neutral. Trans. Gail Schwab. New York: Routledge, 2001.

Why Different? Ed. Sylvere Lotringer. Trans. Camille Collins. New York: Autonomedia/Semiotext(e), 2000.

Nordquist, Joan. *French Feminist Theory (III): Luce Irigaray and Helene Cixous: A Bibliography*. Sant Cruz, Calif: Reference and Research Services, 1996.

Whitford, Margaret. *Luce Irigaray: Philosopy in the Feminine*. London: Routledge, 1991.

Index